Contents

P9-CQK-571

Acknowledgements

I would like to thank my good friend Dick Way of Bonrich Data Services Ltd. in Calgary for providing me with the math tables contained in this book. Great care has been taken in the preparation of these tables, although there is no warranty of their complete accuracy.

A special thank you to my two favourite women, my wife Shana and my editor Ingrid Philipp Cook, both of whom provided many hours of painstaking work and technical assistance and whose encouragement is always appreciated.

HBZ

This book is dedicated to everyone who needs just that little bit of extra motivation to save money and invest wisely.

For a ship that has no port, no wind is the right one.
Seneca

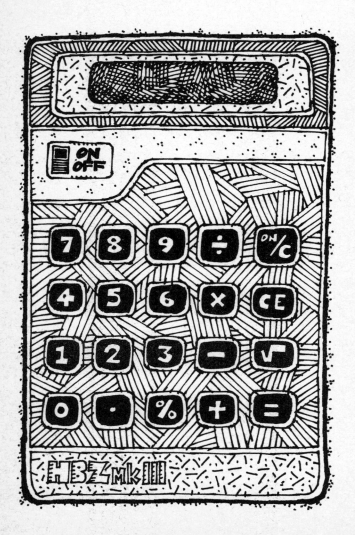

CHAPTER ONE

You Don't Have to Be a Mathematical Genius

I failed algebra in my first term in grade eight. So, why, you might ask, am I writing this book? Well, eventually I caught on and did reasonably well in my high school math courses. In fact, when I finally realized (at the age of sixteen) that I would never be a professional baseball player, I even decided to become a chartered accountant. A chartered accountant uses the initials "C.A.". In my case, C.A. stands for "Can't Add" and if I can't add, I can't do much better when it comes to subtraction, multiplication or division. Of course, that's without the benefit of a pocket calculator. In 1964, when I started in the accounting program as a junior audit clerk, my boss forced me to add columns of figures in my head for the first year to sharpen my skills.

In the last twenty years, the advances in mathematical technology have been nothing less than astounding, although the computer age has left me somewhat behind. The picture on the opposite page is a humorous but accurate drawing of the *only calculator* that I have used in the last six years. It adds, subtracts, multiplies and divides quite accurately. It has square root and percentage keys, but I have never used them. The error correction key I use often.

The book you are now starting to read will never be obsolete—even when practically every home in North America has a home computer and the software necessary to do all kinds of practical math calculations. When that day comes, what you will learn from this book will be even more relevant. Some day, you will be able to call up a program which will allow you to verify the daily interest on your savings account at the touch of a button. For the time being, however, *a simple calculator and this book are all that you will need to painlessly do virtually any mathematical calculations that you require in business and investment decision-making*. Once you learn how to use the tables at the end of this book, the rest is easy. All you really have to do is be careful to use the *right* table at the *right* time.

There are actually many books of math tables available at your local bookstore. These books, however (at least the ones that I've seen), are downright intimidating since they provide calculations to ten decimal places. This is perfectly acceptable if you are doing complex scientific calculations requiring accuracy to the nth degree. However, in order to make an intelligent business or investment decision, tables to three or four places are more than adequate. For example, they will enable you to check, within a few pennies, whether or not a lending institution is charging you the correct monthly payments on your mortgage, or calculate, within a few dollars, how much you will have at the end of ten years if you save $100 a month.

Moreover, the table headings in the other books tend to confuse as well. The authors, generally being mathematicians, use terminology with which the average business person or investor is unfamiliar, such as "sinking fund factors payable at the end of each period" or "annuity whose accumulation at compound interest is $1". What often happens is that people are afraid to use these tables because they don't always know *which table to use and when to use it*.

Take a moment and flip through the thirteen tables which make up the last hundred pages of this book. You will see that each one is accompanied by a summary page that tells you immediately what its uses are and which chapters in this book explain or use each particular table. For example, Table 1 shows you how much you will have at the end of one to fifty years if you invest $1 now at various interest rates and simply leave your money to grow. If you are presently sitting with $640 in your bank account, you need only multiply the factor in the table for $1 by 640 and there's your answer. What could be simpler?

Most of the other books that I have looked at also contain not more than ten to twenty pages of explanation. These explanations deal with money but they don't give you a practical situation to which you can relate. With a little bit of effort, almost anyone can understand the concept of compound interest which is explained in Chapter Two. Also, it is not that hard to understand annuities, which are just income flows. For example, in Chapter Three you will find out how to calculate what you will have at the end of, say, ten years if you are capable of saving $100 each month and can earn 12% on your money. This, however, is only the beginning. **Practical business and investment mathematics has many much broader applications; and this is really what this book is all about.**

In the chapters which follow, you will learn how to use tables in deciding whether you can afford to borrow money and how much. If you are thinking about buying a house, the tables will help you make up your mind whether you should own or rent. How do you evaluate a home as an investment? Sure, if you buy, you expect to sell at a profit at some *future* time. But what is that profit worth in *today's* dollars?

If you are considering real estate as an investment, you will be shown technical approaches used by "sophisticated" investors and traders. You will see how to compare the potential returns on this kind of an investment to the benefits of leaving your money in a term deposit or savings bond.

Chapter Sixteen is called "Understanding Life Insurance Policies". You will see that pure life insurance is not an investment. Life insurance has a *cost*. How can you determine this cost? It is simply a matter of figuring out what you can be expected to pay over a period of time (perhaps the rest of your life) and comparing the cost of these payments to the value of what your estate will get at the end. When you finish reading this chapter, you will be able to compare different types of policies issued by different companies and you will be able to calculate your cost in each case.

Chapter Seventeen deals with the option of either leasing property or buying it. Whether you are considering an automobile, an airplane or a personal computer, the rules are the same. You will learn how to determine the interest cost built into a lease and, at the same time, be introduced to various non-financial considerations.

But why am *I* writing this book? I've already told you that I'm not a mathematician, don't own a personal computer, and in fact, haven't the foggiest idea how to operate one, let alone program it. Those of you who have read any of my previous books know that my field of expertise, as it were, lies in taxation and related matters—not in mathematics.

This book is, however, a very natural extension of everything that I have previously written. This is because it is impossible to make any "real life" business or investment decisions without a basic knowledge of the income tax rules *and* a bit of mathematical analysis. Earlier, I told you that one of the simple things the tables in this book will help you do is calculate how much you will have at the end of ten years if you can save $100 a month and earn 12% interest on your money. But can you really earn 12%? If your employment income puts you in a 50% tax bracket, the government will then take half of your annual investment income. Thus, your real rate of return may be as little as 6%, not 12%. If you use the tables for 12% in order to get your answer, you will be hopelessly misled.

On the other hand, Chapter Fifteen deals with registered retirement savings plans. You are probably already aware that income earned in such plans is *not* taxable until you take it out. Thus, if you deposit $100 a month for 10 years and earn, on average, 12%, it is quite appropriate to use the table for a 12% yield in order to determine what you will have at the end.

Previously, I suggested using this book to help you evaluate home ownership as an investment. Anyone who buys a home expects to sell it at a profit at some point in the future. But what is that profit *after tax*? As you probably know, if the home is a "principal residence" the before-tax and after-tax return are both the same. But, what if the property is a vacation cottage or a "second" home? Under such circumstances, your profit must be reduced by the related capital gains tax. There is no sense in trying to determine the present value of this future profit unless you take income taxes into account.

I don't mean to scare you, however. It is not necessary for you to be a tax expert. Nor is it necessary for you to buy all of my other books—although I hope that you have or eventually will. This book will contain enough basic income tax information so that you can make proper business and investment decisions.

For example, Chapter Thirteen deals with stock market investments. You will become adept at making valid after-tax comparisons of dividends from Canadian stocks to interest from savings accounts, bonds and term deposits. You will also find it easier to answer questions such as this: If I borrow for stock market investments, what rate of capital growth do I need to break even, taking into account a dividend yield?

The topic of borrowing money is dealt with in Chapter Six. You must realize from the outset that you cannot possibly calculate your true cost without knowing whether your interest expense is tax-deductible. If I borrow at 14% in order to acquire real estate or invest in the stock market, my actual cost is only 7% if I am in a 50% bracket. On the other hand, if I borrow for personal purposes, such as to buy a home, all my calculations must take the full 14% rate into account.

A Few Words About the Tables

In concluding these introductory thoughts, it would be appropriate to examine some of the specifications I have adopted for the tables in this book. Tables 1 to 5 and 8 to 12 are all based on calculations for one year to fifty years. All of them deal with whole number percentages between

5% and 20%, except Tables 5 and 11, which are designed to show you how much you have to pay periodically in order to pay off a loan over various periods of time. These tables provide calculations ranging from 7% to 22%.

I have chosen to deal with whole numbers only since my major objective is to present a practical *approach*. If you are interested in precision and pinpoint accuracy, you can always buy the more detailed and sophisticated tables. Alternatively, a friend with a home computer and the necessary programs can provide you with any printout that you need—as long as you know what to ask for. Assuming, however, that you are only seeking reasonable accuracy in order to make intelligent decisions, the ranges provided in this book should suffice. For example, what if you are dealing with an interest factor of $14^{1}/_{2}$%? You might consider making calculations at both 14% and 15% and simply averaging your results. Granted, the larger your numbers, or the longer the period over which your calculations are being made, the more significant the variance. Nevertheless, in percentage terms these differences should be quite negligible. This is explained further in Chapter Two.

In two cases, I have compiled figures which provide you with greater accuracy. Table 6 provides monthly payments required to repay a mortgage loan of $1000 over various periods of time. The conventional Canadian mortgage requires payments to be made monthly, although interest is calculated semi-annually. This is in contrast to normal loans made by lending institutions where payments are ordinarily made on a monthly basis with interest *also* calculated on the monthly balance outstanding from time to time. Table 6, the Canadian Mortgage Amortization Table, deals with a range from 10% to $21^{7}/_{8}$%, increasing by one-eighth of one per cent each time. The payback periods range from one to forty years. Most mortgages today are calculated on the basis of twenty-five or thirty-year payouts (although they are usually renewed at current prevailing rates every few years). From a practical standpoint, therefore, the range of one to forty years should provide you with enough information.

Table 7 contains calculations based on interest rates from 10% to $23^{3}/_{4}$%, increasing by one-quarter of one per cent each time. This table shows the principal balance outstanding on a twenty-five-year mortgage loan of $1000 at the end of each year from year one to the end of year twenty-five. Of all the tables in this book, Table 7 is the only one with an extremely narrow application. It is designed simply as an aid to the material contained in Chapter Eleven, which deals with borrowing money to buy a home. This table will also reinforce one of my major suggestions—a home mortgage should be paid off as soon as possible, especially in Canada where your interest is non-deductible.

Finally, Table 13 deals with life expectancy for both males and females ages ten to eighty-five. This table will be of use to you in understanding life insurance policies and annuity yields (Chapters Fifteen and Sixteen). The range corresponds to the ages of the people to whom this book is addressed!

So, here it is. Go slowly. You do not have to read every chapter, although you should at least skim the next nine chapters. If real estate investing is not for you, skip Chapter Twelve. Similarly, if you find the stock market has no appeal to you, don't bother with Chapter Thirteen. In other words, this is not a novel. I hope, however, that you will quickly agree that it really isn't all that difficult to take the mystery out of ordinary business and investment mathematics.

CHAPTER TWO

Compound Interest Calculations

What Will $1 Today Be Worth at Some Time in the Future?

If you have ever dealt with a bank, trust company or any other financial institution, you are certainly familiar with the concept of compound interest. You know that if you deposit money into a savings account, the amount will increase, or compound, as time goes on. In order to determine exactly what you will have at some future time you basically need to know three things:

1. The amount of money originally deposited. This is called the "present value";
2. The number of periods (or term) that your money will be left in the account; and
3. The interest rates per period.

Once these three variables are determined, Table 1 (pages 149–57) will tell you how to calculate the future value.

From the very beginning, it is important that you understand the concept of *an interest rate per period*—the third variable mentioned above. The length of a "period" can be a day, month, or year, or, in fact, any amount of time, but whatever the period's length, we always assume that the compounding of interest takes place only *once during each period*.

Years ago, banks generally calculated interest on your savings account twice a year. Eventually, they began to make quarterly calculations, and now, with computers available to do the work, some institutions give credit for interest daily. In the tables at the back of this book, all calculations are presented assuming interest is calculated monthly, quarterly, semi-annually or annually. Again, as I indicated in the introduction, the purpose of this book is to teach you the proper techniques for making business and investment decisions by using mathematical analysis and tables. If you are ever faced with the need to prepare calculations where interest is compounded daily, you can probably obtain access to a computer program which will do the work for you.

Any time you make calculations, the *number of periods* and the *interest rate per period* must be consistent. This means that if interest periods are designated quarterly, the interest rate must be a quarterly rate as well.

For example, suppose you deposit $1000 into a bank account that pays 12% interest per year compounded quarterly and you decide to leave the money in your account for three years. You would like to know what you will have in your account at the end of this period. Because the bank calculates interest quarterly, picture the whole problem in terms of quarters. Since there are twelve quarters in three years, a time diagram of this example would have twelve divisions, as Figure 1 illustrates.

Figure 1
Time diagram for a $1000 bank deposit which earns 12% interest compounded quarterly for three years

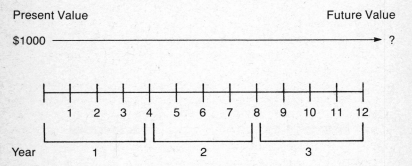

To find the interest rate per quarter, divide the annual interest (12%) by four and you get the quarterly interest rate of 3%. You now have sufficient information to calculate what your money will be worth at the end of three years if you want to make your calculations "longhand". This is illustrated in Figure 2. The first line of numbers shows that you have deposited $1000 at the beginning of the first quarter. Interest of $30 is earned during that first quarter and $1030 (your original $1000 plus $30 interest) is in your account at the end of this quarter. The amount on deposit at the end of the first quarter becomes the amount on deposit at the beginning of the second quarter, and line 2 of the table is computed in the same way as line 1.

Figure 2
Value of $1000 after three years
with interest at 12% compounded quarterly

Quarters	Amount on Deposit Beginning of Quarter	Interest for the Quarter	Amount on Deposit End of Quarter
1	$1,000.00	$ 30.00	$1,030.00
2	1,030.00	30.90	1,060.90
3	1,060.90	31.83	1,092.73
4	1,092.73	32.78	1,125.51
5	1,125.51	33.76	1,159.27
6	1,159.27	34.78	1,194.05
7	1,194.05	35.82	1,229.87
8	1,229.87	36.90	1,266.77
9	1,266.77	38.00	1,304.77
10	1,304.77	39.14	1,343.91
11	1,343.91	40.32	1,384.23
12	1,384.23	41.53	1,425.76
	Total Interest	$425.76	

You'll notice that the interest in the second quarter is greater than the interest in the first and the interest each quarter continues to increase as long as your money stays in the account. This is because the bank will pay interest not only on your original deposit of $1000 but also on the accumulated interest from previous quarters. This method of computing interest is called "compound interest" and it certainly is to your advantage. The other type of interest that you may run into from time to time is "simple interest". Under simple interest calculations, interest is paid on your *deposit only*. If you were to earn 12% simple interest only on $1000 for three years, you would have $1360 at the end instead of $1425.76.

Obviously, calculations such as the ones in Figure 2 can be quite tedious, especially over extended periods of time. Also, the more numbers you play with, the greater the chance of error. And here we come to the first application of the tables in this book. Table 1 gives you the compound value of $1 after 1 to 50 years at interest rates ranging from 5% to 20%. *This table takes into account the possibilities of interest being calculated monthly, quarterly, semi-annually or annually.* In fact, if you use this table, you don't even have to calculate an interest rate per period. The table does this for you. All you need is the *annual* rate.

Turn to Figure 3, which provides you with the calculations for interest at 11% and 12%. At the end of three years, a $1 initial deposit

Figure 3
The compound amount of $1 after three years

| End of Year | 11% Interest Compounded | | | 12% Interest Compounded | | | | |
	Monthly	Semi-Quarterly	Annually	Annually	Monthly	Semi-Quarterly	Annually	Annually
3	1.389	1.385	1.379	1.368	1.431	1.426	1.419	1.405

will amount to $1.426 if interest is calculated at 12% compounded quarterly.

Common sense and, if necessary, a small hand-held calculator will now tell you that if $1 will amount to $1.426 after three years with interest calculated at 12% compounded quarterly, then $1000 will amount to $1426. Actually, this is not quite correct since the actual accumulation is $1425.76. In other words, there is a 24¢ discrepancy. This is because the tables in this book are only accurate to three or four decimal places. If, for some reason, you need greater accuracy, tables to ten places are, as I have indicated, available. However, out of total interest of $425.76, how significant is 24¢?

Take a few moments and study the extract from Table 1 which appears in Figure 3. Try to get familiar with the various ways of compounding interest. For example, how much difference does it make if interest is compounded annually instead of quarterly? After three years, your $1000 deposit would amount to $1405 instead of $1426. In other words, you would lose $21 over this three-year period. How significant is this? It may not be all that important if you have $1000 to invest, but what if your initial investment capital was $10,000, $100,000 or even $1,000,000?

Would it really matter if you earn, say, 1% less? What if the bank were only paying you 11% interest compounded quarterly? At the end of three years, you would have $1385 instead of $1426. The difference here is $41.

Clearly, the higher the rate, the more you will have at the end of any given number of periods. Also, the more often interest is calculated, the

Figure 4
The compound amount of $1 after thirty years

| End of Year | 11% Interest Compounded | | | 12% Interest Compounded | | | | |
	Monthly	Semi-Quarterly	Annually	Annually	Monthly	Semi-Quarterly	Annually	Annually
30	26.708	25.931	24.840	22.892	35.950	34.711	32.988	29.960

better off you are. What becomes astounding, however, is the effect of compound interest on an original investment after *many* years have elapsed. Figure 4 is another extract from Table 1, using the same interest rates, but in this case the original deposit of $1 was left to compound for *thirty* years instead of three years.

After thirty years, $1 invested at 12%, with interest calculated quarterly, comes to $34.71. Thus, $1000 left to earn interest at this same rate will amount to $34,711. Mind-boggling, isn't it? Now ask yourself if it matters whether interest is calculated quarterly or annually. On a $1000 initial deposit the difference is $4751 ($34,711 minus $29,960).

Does it really matter whether you earn 11% or 12% compounded quarterly over that same thirty-year period? Yes, it does. On $1000, the difference is $8780 ($34,711 minus $25,931)! This simple exercise shows you that *it always pays to shop around for the best available interest rates*.

The GIGO Principle

The advent of the age of computers has created a brand new terminology. However, anyone who learns to use a computer quickly discovers that the output is only as good as the input. In other words, if the wrong information is fed into a computer, the answer to any question which is then asked will be incorrect as well. In computer shorthand, this concept is known as the "GIGO principle"—garbage in, garbage out.

The same principle applies equally to the use of the math tables in this or any other book. If you use the *wrong* tables, your answer will be meaningless at best, or, at worst, harmfully misleading.

Making Reasonable Estimates

What if you want to know, from Table 1, how much you would have if you deposit $1000 to earn 12% compounded quarterly and you left your money for, say, fifteen-and-a-half years? Obviously, this table will not give you an accurate answer. However, you *can* make reasonable *approximate* calculations. After fifteen years, $1 left to compound interest quarterly at 12% will amount to $5.892. After sixteen years, this same $1 will amount to $6.631. Therefore, after fifteen-and-a-half years, you might expect to have the following:

$$\frac{6.631 + 5.892}{2} = 6.262$$

Thus, $1000 will amount to approximately $6262. The real answer is $6250.40. From a practical standpoint, the discrepancy is not particularly significant. However, what if your original deposit was $1,000,000? Clearly, in some cases, greater accuracy is warranted and you should use the more sophisticated tables, which are readily available. From these, you can make calculations for periods ranging from months to years and fractions of years. Often these tables are constructed to give you results from one to a hundred periods or even more. *If you use such a table, you must make sure that the number of periods and the interest rate per period are consistent;* that is, you have divided the annual rate by the number of periods. Figure 5 is an extract from such a table with calculations at 3% for fifty-nine to sixty-three *periods*.

Figure 5
The compound amount of $1

	Interest Rate
Periods	3%
59	5.720
60	5.892
61	6.068
62	6.250
63	6.438

The table in Figure 5 can tell you many things. For example:

- $1 invested for sixty years at 3% compounded annually will amount to $5.892
- $1 invested for thirty years at 6% compounded semi-annually (3% twice a year) will also amount to $5.892, and
- $1 invested for fifteen years at 12% compounded quarterly (3% per quarter) will also amount to $5.892 at the end.

The last two points can be verified using Table 1 in this book:

- $1 @ 6% compounded semi-annually after thirty years = $5.892 (page 150)
- $1 @ 12% compounded quarterly after fifteen years = $5.892 (page 153)

For purposes of this book, I have traded some degree of accuracy and precision (such as the opportunity to calculate results for periods of time other than whole years) for the major advantage of simplicity. It will *not* be necessary for you to make any conversions in using this book. In other words, if you are told that interest is calculated at 12% compounded quarterly for fifteen years, you do not have to look for a 3% table with sixty periods. Instead, simply use the table for 12% and the column which gives the results assuming interest is computed quarterly. Thus, the figures on page 153 for interest at 12% are equivalent to 1% calculated monthly, 3% per quarter, 6% semi-annually or 12% annually. When it comes to part-year calculations, use the method described on page 11, and you will have a good approximation of the actual answer.

Realities—Taxes and Inflation

No business or investment decision should be made in a vacuum. It is well and good to assume that $1000 left to earn interest at 12% compounded quarterly will amount to $5892 at the end of fifteen years. However, two important questions arise. Is it realistic to assume a yield of 12% for an extended period? Look at how the rates have changed over just the last few years. Furthermore, even if, by some miracle, interest rates stabilized for a fifteen-year period, a second major consideration is the impact of taxes on investment yields. The table in Figure 6 summarizes the approximate Canadian personal tax brackets in force for 1984. Of course, the figures will vary from province to province but, in general, the difference isn't more than a few percentage points.

Figure 6
1984 Canadian personal tax brackets (approximate)

Taxable Income	Tax Bracket
From $22,000 to $34,500	40%
34,500 to 59,000	45%
59,000 and up	50%

This book will tread very lightly on the subject of taxation. For the most part, I will assume taxes at a 50% rate on investment income, partly because of the ease this gives me in presenting examples. Similarly, if you borrow to make investments, and the interest is tax-deductible, I will make the same assumption that your cost of borrowing is reduced to half the rate specified. Of course, you should make the required calculations using the rates applicable to your own situation. For example, if you are in a 50% tax bracket and you are earning interest at 12%, your after-tax yield is 6%. On the other hand, if your tax bracket is 40%, your actual yield is just over 7%.

In some circumstances, such as if you invest in a registered retirement savings plan (see Chapter Fifteen), your before-tax and your after-tax return are the same. In other cases, the return on an investment may be subject to capital gains taxes only and these are much lower than taxes on ordinary income.

My point is, however, that *to be of any real use, interest tables must deal with a very broad range of potential rates.* While today it may be unrealistic to assume only a 5% *before-tax* rate of return (for which the compound interest figures are provided on page 150), nevertheless, this is the actual after-tax yield for someone in a 50% bracket who earns interest at a rate of 10%. This is because one-half of the before-tax earnings will have to be removed from investment capital each year and paid over to the government. Only the remaining half can be left to compound as savings.

Additional Applications for Table 1

So far, we have only used Table 1 in a very narrow context. Table 1 has many other applications as well. For example you can answer the following question: If you lend your brother-in-law $1000 for five years and you charge him 13% annual interest compounded monthly, how much will he have to pay you as a lump sum at the end of that five-year period? In this case, *you* are the banker. The amount that you lend your brother-in-law today is the present value and the amount you will be repaid is the future value. If you look at the table on page 154 under the figures for 13% compounded monthly, the answer is $1000 × 1.909 or $1909. Of that amount, $909 will represent interest and the balance is your principal.

Here is another interesting application. You have inherited $10,000 and you are thinking of investing in the shares of Goldfinger Mining Limited which trade on the Vancouver Stock Exchange. The company owns several producing gold mines but does not pay a dividend. The stock is trading at $1 a share. Suppose this investment would only be attractive to you if you could earn an 18% return (before considering taxes on capital gains) compounded annually over the next four years. At what price would you have to sell your stock in order to realize your objective?

From the table on page 156, you can see that $1 left to compound at 18% annually for four years will amount to $1.939 at the end of this time. Therefore, for you to earn 18% on this stock market investment, your Goldfinger shares would have to be worth $19,390. This works out to just under $2 a share. In other words, before you make your investment, you must ask yourself what the chances are of this stock doubling within the next four years. This is essentially what must happen if you wish to realize your required rate of return. (In Chapter Thirteen, we will make more sophisticated calculations taking capital gains taxes as well as dividend yields into account.)

Compound Interest and Inflation

Inflation is always at work, eroding your investment yields. So, in setting goals and objectives for returns on investment, you must always take it into account. We can start our analysis of how inflation works right here in this chapter by simply using Table 1.

Let's assume, for example, that in 1954, the price of a cup of coffee was 10¢. If at that time, someone had guessed that inflation would average 7% a year, what would the price of a cup of coffee be thirty years later in 1984?

By looking at Table 1, on page 151, in the column for 7% compounded annually, we can see that $1 invested for thirty years would amount to $7.612 at the end of that time. Similarly, if something cost $1 thirty years ago, and the price went up by 7% compounded annually, that same purchase would cost $7.61 today.

If we consider a 10¢ cup of coffee in 1954, today's price would be $0.10 × 7.612, or about 76¢. And it is! In many restaurants across the country that is just about what you would have to pay (although many establishments don't charge for refills). In other words, we can conclude that, on average, over the last thirty years the price of a cup of coffee has increased by 7% a year.

Now let's look to the future. If the price of a cup of coffee today is, say, 75¢, what will the price be in thirty years? Well, if we continue to assume a 7% average annual increase, the price in thirty years will be .75 × 7.612, roughly $5.71! Hard to believe, but what would your reaction have been in 1954 if someone had told you then that the price of coffee would be more than seven times as much thirty years later?

Inflation and Wages

Here is another example of a practical application to the theory behind compound interest. Assume that you are forty-five years of age and are earning $30,000 a year from your employment. Also assume your employer can be relied on to give you an 8% raise compounded semi-annually (that is, 4% twice a year). You expect to retire at age fifty-seven with a pension equal to 60% of your final year's earnings. How much can you assume your pension will be in the first year after retirement?

If you are now earning $30,000 and expect to average an 8% increase each year (calculated semi-annually) your pay after eleven years (before age fifty-seven) can be calculated from Table 1, page 151. Your final pay will be $30,000 × 2.370, or $71,100. This is the future value of $30,000 today compounded semi-annually at 8% for eleven years. If your pension starting in year twelve is 60% of your final earnings figure, you can count on receiving 60% of $71,100, or $42,660 in that first year.

Can you then consider yourself wealthy? Well, the key question here is what has happened to your cost of living over that same period? Clearly, if your cost of living has compounded by the equivalent of 8% calculated semi-annually, it would take an income of $71,100 to purchase what $30,000 does today. This, of course, assumes that the impact of taxes on an income of $71,100 twelve years from now is no heavier a burden than the taxes on $30,000 today.

If the inflation rate exceeds your annual rate of salary increases, then you will lose. Take another look at page 151. If money is invested at 8% compounded annually, $1 invested today will amount to $2 ($1.999) at the end of only nine years. By that same token, if an expenditure costs $1 today and the price increases by 8% a year, that same item will cost $2 in nine years.

The Rule of Seventy-Two

There is a very interesting rule of thumb which will allow you to determine approximately how long it will take your money to double at various interest rates. This is called the rule of seventy-two. You simply divide the number 72 by the interest rate as shown in Figure 7.

Figure 7
The rule of seventy-two

Interest Rate Compounded Annually	Length of Time for Money to Double	Future Value of $1 Compounded From Table 1
6%	72 ÷ 6 = 12 years	12 years 2.012
8%	72 ÷ 8 = 9 years	9 years 1.999
12%	72 ÷ 12 = 6 years	6 years 1.974
18%	72 ÷ 18 = 4 years	4 years 1.939

As you can see from the last column in the illustration, this rule of thumb really works!

Summary

Take the time to go through Table 1 carefully. Get a feel for the numbers at various interest rates. You can see that the longer the period, the more important it is to try to earn a higher rate. Similarly, it starts to make larger differences whether your interest is calculated monthly, quarterly, semi-annually or annually.

In your own life, there will be other considerations, such as income taxes, to be taken into account in determining actual yields. As you continue through this book, you will see, however, that nothing is really all that complicated. Money simply has a value that changes during the time over which it is used to make more money. To be realistic in your investments and business transactions, you have to know what these values are and how they're computed. In the next chapter, you will be introduced to the concept of an annuity—what happens to you if you save money *all along* and invest it over a period of time.

CHAPTER THREE

The Future Value of a Series of Deposits

How Much Will $1 Invested at the End of Each Period Amount to at Some Point in the Future?

Many business and investment situations require the computation of the future value of not just a single amount, but a *series of amounts*. This is often referred to as an "ordinary annuity". Most people have only seen the term "annuity" used in the context of life insurance. Actually, the concept is much broader. To show you an annuity problem in its simplest form, you may want to answer the following question: If I put aside $100 a month for ten years and earn 12% interest calculated monthly, what will I have at the end?

In order to make such a calculation, your must make sure that:
• All the amounts are equal,
• The deposits occur at regular intervals whether they are monthly, quarterly, semi-annually or annually, and
• The deposits are made at the *end* of each period.

The amount you will have once you have made your last deposit is called the "future value of your annuity".

Table 2 is all you need to make these kinds of calculations. But, remember GIGO—our warning from the computer experts—"garbage in, garbage out". If you don't use the numbers from the *proper columns*, your answer will be totally worthless and confusing. To illustrate how Table 2 works, let's just take an extract from the figures on page 162

Figure 1
The future value of $1 invested at the end of each period after ten years

Deposits are made and Interest at 12% compounded

End of Year	Monthly	Quarterly	Semi-Annually	Annually
10	230.039	75.401	36.786	17.549

which reflects an interest yield of 12%. If deposits of $1 are made to earn interest at 12%, Figure 1 shows the result at the end of ten years.

In this case, the final amount varies drastically under all four alternatives. This is *not* simply because in the first column, the interest is calculated monthly, while in the column on the right, the interest is calculated once a year only. Rather, the difference is primarily because, in the first case, *the deposits are made monthly* (and the interest is calculated monthly) while in the fourth case *only one deposit a year is made* (with interest calculated annually, as well). In other words, Column 1 represents twelve monthly deposits of $1 each, Column 2, four quarterly deposits of $1 each, Column 3, two deposits a year, and Column 4 only one deposit. Column 1 therefore reflects twelve times the number of deposits as Column 4. Again, review the annuity rules on the previous page. Note that Table 2 is very different from Table 1. When we looked at Table 1, the key point was how often interest would be calculated on a single amount. In using Table 2, the major consideration is the frequency of your deposits.

Now it's time for a practical example. Suppose you deposit $100 a month into a savings account at the *end of each month* for the next ten years. The account pays 12% interest calculated monthly (1% per month). How much will you have at the end of the ten years? A time diagram would look like Figure 2.

Figure 2
Time diagram illustrating twelve monthly deposits of $100 at the end of each month over a ten-year period

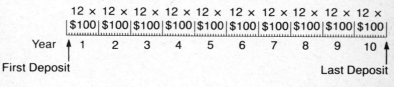

Note that the deposits are made at the end of each month. Also, in this instance, interest is calculated monthly as well. To find the future value, simply refer to the extract from Table 2 given in Figure 1. The answer is:

$100 × 230.039 = $23,003.90

Over this ten-year period, you will have deposited $12,000 in principal payments. The fact that you will have just over $23,000 at the end means that the total interest is in excess of $9000.

What would happen if, instead of depositing $100 a month at the end of each month for ten years, you deposited $1200 once a year for ten years at 12% interest compounded annually. What would you have at the end? Again, refer to Figure 1. The answer is:

$1200 × 17.549 = $21,058.80

Note that your total is $1945.10 less ($23,003.90 minus $21,058.80) than the results of $100 monthly deposits. There are two reasons for this. First, the more frequent the deposits, the more you benefit from the compounding of interest. This was illustrated in Chapter Two. Secondly, in the first illustration not only are the deposits made monthly, but interest is presumed to be calculated monthly as well. In example two, the total reflects not only annual deposits but an annual compound interest calculation, as well.

You may want to check the accuracy of Table 2 for yourself. If you want, you can develop a calculation table, period by period. It should look like the calculations in Figure 3. A new deposit is added to the amount on deposit at the start of each period to obtain the amount on deposit at the start of the *following* period. As you can see, after ten years of making $1200 annual deposits, the amount in the account, *including* the final $1200 deposit is $21,058.50, which is almost the same as the answer obtained from Table 2. The difference of 30¢ is, of course, due to rounding.

Figure 3
Verifying the future value of a series of annual deposits

	Amount on Deposit Beginning of Year	Interest for Year at 12%	Amount on Deposit End of Year	New Deposit
1	$ 0.00	$ 0.00	$ 0.00	$1,200.00
2	1,200.00	144.00	1,344.00	1,200.00
3	2,544.00	305.29	2,849.29	1,200.00
4	4,049.29	485.91	4,535.20	1,200.00
5	5,735.20	688.22	6,423.42	1,200.00
6	7,623.42	914.81	8,538.23	1,200.00
7	9,738.23	1,168.59	10,906.82	1,200.00
8	12,106.82	1,452.82	13,559.64	1,200.00
9	14,759.64	1,771.16	16,530.80	1,200.00
10	17,730.80	2,127.70	19,858.50	1,200.00
	$21,058.50			

Income Tax Considerations

Take some time to familiarize yourself with Table 2 by scanning pages 158–66. You will see that this table contains calculations at interest rates ranging from 5% to 20%. As described in Chapter Two, if you find it necessary to make calculations at an interest rate of say, 11 1/2%, from a practical standpoint, you can get a good estimate by making calculations at 11% and 12% and then simply averaging.

For example, monthly deposits of $1 at 11% for ten years will amount to $217. At 12%, the amount is $230.04. Thus, presumably, if the interest rate is 11 1/2%, you might expect the total to be *around* $223. Obviously, the longer the period, the greater your error, but the approximation is still worthwhile.

In case you have forgotten why this book deals with such a wide range of interest rates, I will remind you that you cannot project any true interest rates unless you are aware of the income tax consequences.

In Canada, interest received is generally taxable although there are two significant exceptions. One is investments in a registered retirement savings plan, which is discussed in detail in Chapter Fifteen. The other stems from the fact that any Canadian resident can earn up to $1000 a year of investment income from "arm's-length" sources (this does not include amounts received from corporations which are controlled by a taxpayer and members of his family) without paying tax. For purposes of this book, the special exemption for the first $1000 will generally be ignored.

A person in a 50% income tax bracket (taxable income over $59,000 in 1984) cannot really earn, say, 12% interest even if a lending institution is offering this rate. Anyone in that bracket will have to withdraw half of the investment yield on an annual basis just to cover taxes. If you are fortunate enough to be in this bracket, you would be better off making your calculations using an after-tax yield of 6% only. Otherwise, your results will be tremendously misleading.

Take a moment to examine the Table 2 figures on page 159 for an interest rate of 6%, and assume your deposits will be made annually for ten years. Each dollar of annual deposits would amount to $13.18 at the end. This is a far cry from an accumulation of $17.55 if the interest rate were 12%. Figure 4 compares the results for annual deposits of $1200 given the two rates.

The difference of $5241.60 is partially the result of the required income tax outlays themselves and partially because your tax payments

Figure 4
$1200 deposited at the end of each year for ten years
At 12% interest: $1,200 × 17.549 = $21,058.80
At   6% interest: $1,200 × 13.181 =   15,817.20
                                        Difference $ 5,241.60

reduce your ability to earn compound income on an ongoing basis.

Again, study the tables carefully. Most investment counsellors will advise you to save for a rainy day. But it's hard to do so—especially if you don't have the proper motivation. Table 2 can help you find the motivation necessary to become a "saver".

Assume that you can earn only 6% on your money after taxes. If you deposit $1 a month for thirty years you will have $1004.52 at the end. Thus, putting aside $100 a month at the same interest rate for thirty years would give you over $100,000! Of course, what that $100,000 will be worth in thirty-years in terms of buying power is another story. But whatever the inflation rate, I would rather have $100,000 than not have it!

Another question you could ask yourself is whether it pays to shop seriously for the "best" rate available—even if it means moving money frequently from one financial institution to another. Assume that over a thirty-year period, you are able to squeeze out an extra *half a percentage point* after tax on your savings. Let's see how important this is.

We'll assume that, without much effort, you can earn 6% interest calculated semi-annually. If you invest $1 *twice a year* at 6%, this means that you will have $163.05 at the end. This sum consists of $60 of your own money ($2 a year for thirty years) and $103.05 of after-tax interest. At 7%, you would have $196.52. Therefore, at 6½%, you could expect to have somewhere between $163.05 and $196.52.

Figure 5
One dollar deposited semi-annually for thirty years
At 6% interest $163.05
At 7% interest $196.52
At 6½% interest $\dfrac{\$196.52 + \$163.05}{2} =$ $179.78
  approximately
Accumulated difference for each $1 invested
  ($179.78 − $163.05) $16.73

Summary

From the calculations shown in Figure 5, you can see how a rate difference of only one-half a per cent means a difference of approximately $16.73 for each $1 invested. What if your semi-annual savings were $500 instead of only $1? At the end of a thirty-year period, your difference would be 500 × $16.73, or $8365. Yes, it does pay to shop! Your own total capital of $500 deposited semi-annually for thirty years is $30,000. An $8365 net return on a total capital investment of $30,000 is quite a significant amount. A one-half per cent difference, more or less, doesn't seem very much when you look at it in isolation, but if you take the time to understand your tables, you will begin to understand the importance of getting the best rates available. Remember, it's your money.

What is a Dollar Due Sometime in the Future Worth Today?

In this chapter, I will explain how to determine the value *today* (that is, the present value) of a *single* amount due sometime in the future. A typical example of the problem which you will be able to solve after reading this chapter is: How much must I deposit in a savings account *today* in order to have $1000 after five years if the account pays 12% interest, compounded quarterly? The answers can all be calculated by using Table 3 on pages 167–75.

But, before you make the calculations of the amount needed today to attain your $1000 goal at the end of five years, it's again useful to prepare a time diagram similar to Figure 1 so that you can understand what you are trying to do.

Notice the direction of the time arrow. In Chapters Two and Three, we were moving from the present to the future. Here, we are moving from the future to the present. Now let's take a look at Table 3. With interest compounded quarterly at 12%, you would have to invest $0.5537 today in order to have $1 at the end of five years. Thus, to accumulate $1000 at the end of this same period, you would need a present investment of $553.70. In other words, a single deposit of $553.70 invested today and left alone for five years to earn 12%

Figure 1
The present value of $1,000 due sometime in the future

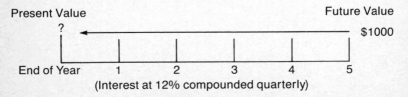

Present Value   Future Value

?   ←———————————————————— $1000

End of Year   1   2   3   4   5

(Interest at 12% compounded quarterly)

compounded quarterly, will amount to $1000 at the end of five years.

Of course, this answer can be verified. If we wanted to, we could make the calculations longhand and produce a schedule similar to the one on page 9 in Chapter Two. However, if we are compounding quarterly, this would entail twenty calculations, and really, all this work isn't necessary. To check our answer, all we need to do is refer to Table 1. This table tells us what $1 today is worth at some point in the future. Turn to page 153. Assuming interest at 12% compounded quarterly, $1 invested today would amount to $1.806 at the end of five years. Therefore, $553.70 invested today would amount to: $553.70 × 1.806 or $999.98. Of course, the 2¢ is a rounding difference only.

From these calculations, you can see that Table 1 and Table 3 are "reciprocals" or mirror images. Table 1 gives us the *future* value of a single *present* amount while Table 3 gives us the *present* value of a single *future* amount.

Now take a few minutes and flip through pages 167 to 175. You will see that Table 3 deals with interest rates ranging from 5% to 20%. Why bother starting with such a low rate? Well, remember our old enemy, income taxes. In the previous example, we looked at earning interest at 12% compounded quarterly. However, what if you are in a 50% tax bracket? If you have to draw out half your earnings each year to pay taxes to the government, your interest isn't really going to compound at 12%. Let's see what would happen if we make the assumption that you can only earn 6% on your money after tax. What would you then need to deposit in a savings account today if you want to have $1000 after five years, assuming interest is compounded quarterly? From page 168, we can determine that you would need $0.7425 today to have $1 at the end of five years. Therefore, you would need $742.50 if you wanted to attain your $1000 goal, considerably more than the $553.67 that would be required if taxes were not a factor.

Take a few minutes to carefully examine the structure of Table 3. The extract in Figure 2 gives us the present value of $1 due at the end of ten years with interest calculated at 8%.

You will notice that the numbers are quite close to each other. Of

Figure 2
The present value of $1 due at the end of ten years
at 8% interest compounded

End of Year	Monthly	Quarterly	Semi-Annually	Annually
10	0.4505	0.4529	0.4564	0.4632

course, if you can earn interest compounded monthly, you can deposit a smaller amount today to get $1 by the end of any given number of years. If your money is earning interest less frequently, an additional initial deposit is required. For example, if you can earn 8% after tax and you wish to have $1000 at the end of ten years, you need only deposit $450.50 today if interest is calculated monthly, while you must deposit $463.20 if the interest calculation will only be made once a year.

Let's take a look at a few more practical examples to show you where you may have occasion to refer to Table 3.

Assume you that you will be retiring in ten years and you would like to take a nice long vacation, which you figure will cost $7000. Suppose, as well, that you have some savings and can earn 7% on your money compounded semi-annually after taxes. How much would you need in savings today so that you could draw out the necessary funds in time to pay for your trip?

Turn to page 169. If interest is calculated semi-annually, an investment of $0.5026 today will total $1 at the end of ten years. Therefore, if you want $7000 in ten years, you would need to have savings of 0.5026 × $7000 or $3518.20. If you have these savings, your vacation goal objective is readily attainable.

What if you are short? In the next chapter, you will find out how to calculate the amount of *periodic deposits* that you would have to make from time to time to accumulate your desired level of savings. (This is called a "sinking fund".)

Here's another example of a present value calculation. You are a minority shareholder in your family's business, which has just been sold. You have been told that you will receive a lump-sum amount of $50,000 at the end of three years on which you estimate you will then have to pay $10,000 in capital gains taxes. How much can you borrow *today* at an annual rate of 14% compounded monthly so that you can pay off your debt, principal plus interest, at the end of that three-year period? Again, Table 3 will provide the answer.

What you really want to know is what single amount invested today will accumulate to $40,000 ($50,000 minus your taxes) at the end of three years, with interest at 14% compounded monthly. Your answer can be calculated from page 172. It is $40,000 × .6586 or $26,344. In other words, if you borrow $26,344 today, and allow interest to accumulate for three years, you would owe $40,000 at the end, which you could then pay off with your share of the money received from the sale of the business.

Understanding Inflation

Perhaps one of the most practical uses of Table 3 is as another aid to understanding inflation. Simply put, it was no doubt clear to you before you even began reading this book that $1 which you will either receive or pay out at some time in the future is worth considerably less than $1 today. From the last example, you can see that if the annual inflation rate were 14% (with interest compounded monthly), $40,000 three years from now would be worth only as much as $26,344 is worth today. This is why you might be willing to borrow $26,344 today even if it means paying back $40,000 three years later.

Let's assume that inflation compounds at 8% annually. Figure 3 is an extract from Table 3 which shows you what $1 due sometime in the future is worth today at an assumed interest rate of 8% compounded annually.

Figure 3
The present value of $1 due at the end of various time periods at 8% interest compounded annually

End of Year		End of Year	
1	0.9259	16	0.2919
2	0.8573	17	0.2703
3	0.7938	18	0.2502
4	0.7350	19	0.2317
5	0.6806	20	0.2145
6	0.6302	21	0.1987
7	0.5835	22	0.1839
8	0.5403	23	0.1703
9	0.5002	24	0.1577
10	0.4632	25	0.1460
11	0.4289	26	0.1352
12	0.3971	27	0.1252
13	0.3677	28	0.1159
14	0.3405	29	0.1073
15	0.3152	30	0.0994

Basically, what this illustration shows us is that, given an 8% inflation rate, $1 due at the end of next year is worth only approximately 93¢ today. Similarly, $1 due in nine years is worth 50¢ today while $1 due at the end of thirty years is worth only about 10¢ today.

Some simple examples will further reinforce your understanding of present value. Assume that you are age forty-three and you buy a life insurance policy which will pay your estate $100,000 at the time of your death. You are presently earning $30,000 a year. According to statistics, you probably won't die for another thirty years and your family will have to wait until that time to collect on this $100,000 policy. If inflation averages 8% a year over that period, the equivalent present value of $100,000 due then is $100,000 × .0994, or $9940. Compare that to your present income level. Instead of providing a benefit of more than three times your annual income, the "real" benefit is only about one-third of one year's salary.

However, before you conclude that life insurance is a rip-off, please wait until you read Chapter Sixteen. Remember, the assumption that you will live for thirty more years is a *statistical* one. What happens if you get run over by a truck tomorrow? Then, the $100,000 death benefit is really worth $100,000!

Here's another example. You and your family are looking to buy a new house. Your agent shows you a property that he is confident you can get for $100,000. "At the rate property values are going", says the agent, "this house should double in value over the next ten years." You immediately start to see the dollar signs. A $100,000 property worth $200,000 after "only" a ten-year period. And yet, what if inflation averages at 8% a year? The present value of $200,000 due at the end of ten years, assuming an 8% compound interest factor, is $200,000 × .4632, or $92,640. In other words, if inflation averages 8% and your property *only* doubles over that ten-year period, you will have actually lost $7360 in purchasing power.

One last example. Try this one on your own. Assume you have $10,000 to invest in the stock market. You feel that a reasonable rate of return before tax is 15% a year, taking into account the risk of making almost any stock market investment. Your broker tells you about a mining stock presently trading at $5 a share which he thinks will be a $10 stock within the next four years. If you invest your $10,000 and the stock does double in that four-year period, will you attain your objective of a 15% return?

If you look at Table 3 on page 173, you will see that at 15% interest, $1 due at the end of four years has a present value of 57.18¢. Therefore, $20,000 due at the end of four years has a present value of $11,436. In this case, if you only have to invest $10,000 and the broker's prediction holds true, you will attain more than your 15% required rate of return. This kind of problem is discussed in more detail in Chapter Ten, which deals with discounted cash-flow techniques—the key behind the more sophisticated investment analyses contained in the later chapters of this book.

Summary

Of all the tables, Table 3 is certainly one of the most interesting. It will help you to understand not only rates of return on investment, but also the workings of inflation. Take one last look at page 175. At 20% compounded annually, the present value of $1 due at the end of 25 years is .0105. In other words, if inflation ever reaches 20% a year, our dollar will lose 99% of its value over a twenty-five-year period. Comforting if you are trying to plan for retirement, isn't it?

CHAPTER FIVE

Saving Money to Meet Your Goals and Objectives

The last chapter addressed the question of how much you must invest today in order to accumulate a desired amount of money by the end of some future period.

What happens, however, if instead you want to save towards a definite goal by means of *regular* deposits. How much should you deposit at a time? For example, suppose you want to have $10,000 in your savings account after four years and you plan to make deposits at the end of each month. If the account pays 11% interest that is also compounded monthly, how large must each of your deposits be?

To solve this problem, we turn to Table 4, pages 176 to 184. Table 4 provides the necessary information to calculate how much must be invested at the end of various time periods to accumulate $1 by some future date. Like most of the tables in this book, Table 4 deals with interest rates ranging from 5% to 20%. The wide range is again because interest yields are in themselves meaningless unless you take income tax implications into account. The 11% yield referred to in the first example in this chapter is for illustration only. It may not be a particularly realistic after-tax rate of return.

Table 4 is structured to solve investment savings problems whether your deposits are made monthly, quarterly, semi-annually or annually. The extract from the table shown in Figure 1 gives the figures for an interest rate of 11% over four years.

Figure 1
How much must be invested at the end of each period to accumulate $1 after four years

	At 11% Interest compounded and Deposits made			
End of Year	Monthly	Quarterly	Semi-Annually	Annually
4	0.0167	0.0506	0.1029	0.2123

What this tells you, is that deposits of $0.0167 or roughly 1²/₃¢ *per month* would amount to $1 by the end of four years if interest is compounded *monthly* at an annualized rate of 11%. Similarly, *quarterly* deposits of just over 5¢ will also amount to $1 after four years, with interest at 11% calculated *quarterly*. If your deposits are made *semi-annually*, just over 10¢ would have to be deposited every half-year for four years to amount to $1 if interest at 11% is compounded *semi-annually*. Finally, it would take a little more than 21¢ deposited at the end of each *year* with interest at 11% compounded *annually* to reach a $1 objective by the end of the required four-year period.

Returning then to the example at the beginning of this chapter, anyone who wants to have $10,000 in savings after four years must make monthly deposits of $167 if interest at 11% will be calculated monthly. The time diagram in Figure 2 illustrates this point.

Figure 2
Time diagram illustrating twelve monthly deposits of $167 at the end of each month over a four-year period

| 12 × $167 | 12 × $167 | 12 × $167 | 12 × $167 |

Year   0   1   2   3   4

Interest = 11% compounded monthly   Future Value = $10,000

Can we verify our results? Certainly. All we have to do is turn back to Table 2. Table 2 gave us the future value of $1 invested at the end of each period. If you look at page 162, under the column for monthly deposits at 11%, you can calculate that $167 deposited monthly for four years will amount to $167 X 59.956 or $10,012.65. Again, because this book only contains tables to three or four decimal places, there is a rounding difference. In this case the rounding difference is $12.65. Tables 2 and 4 are "reciprocals" or reverse images. You can use either of these tables to check the other.

Here's another example. If you invest $1000 a year and earn 6% after-tax compounded annually, Table 2 (page 159) tells you that, at the end of ten years, you will have $13,181 ($1000 × 13.181). Conversely, if you want to have $13,181 at the end of ten years, and you wish to make annual deposits with interest at 6%, Table 4 tells you that you must make deposits of $13,181 × .0759, which equals $1000.44. Again, Table 2 will enable you to verify Table 4 and vice versa.

Let's look at a few more practical examples of how Table 4 can assist you in your business or investment planning. Assume that you are the proud parent of a newborn child. Eighteen years from now, you would like to have $15,000 saved up for your child's college education. You would like to make quarterly savings deposits beginning three months from now. You figure that, on average, you can earn 9% after-tax compounded quarterly. How large will each deposit need to be to achieve your $15,000 goal at the end of eighteen years? Turn to page 179. The answer is simply $15,000 × .0057 or $85.50. (Note that in using the tables presented in this book, you don't have to concern yourself with the fact that there are seventy-two quarters in eighteen years.)

Shall we verify? Turn to Table 2, page 161. If deposits of $1 are made quarterly with interest at 9% over eighteen years, you will have $176.14 at the end. Therefore, if your quarterly deposits are $85.50, your total will be $85.50 X 176.14 or $15,059.97. Again, the small difference of just under $60 is simply due to rounding.

How much better off would you be if you make your deposits monthly instead of quarterly? On an annual basis, four quarterly payments of $85.50 amount to $342 a year. To attain your $15,000 objective after eighteen years (assuming a 9% interest factor) would require monthly payments of $15,000 X .0019 or $28.50. This produces the same $342 in a year than if you made quarterly deposits. Actually, if you used sophisticated tables calculated to eight or ten decimal places, you would find that the year's total of your monthly payments would be slightly less than the annualized amount of your quarterly payments. The difference is not, however, too significant.

Here is another example just to show you how Table 4 can be used to help set investment goals and objectives. Many people dream of retiring by age sixty-five as millionaires. Assume that you are age forty and would like to retire in twenty-five years with $1,000,000 in savings. Assume that you can earn after-tax interest at 7% calculated monthly. What monthly deposits would you need to accomplish your objective?

If you turn to page 178, you will see that monthly deposits of .0012 for twenty-five years will amount to $1 at 7%. Therefore, if your objective is $1,000,000, simply multiply $1,000,000 by .0012 and you will see that the answer is $1200 a month. Anyone who can save $1200 a month and earn interest at 7% can become a millionaire in twenty-five years! See how simple it is?

Finally, it's time for our first "complicated" exercise in which we will use two tables together in order to solve one investment problem. To do this, we can modify the facts of the last example, where we made calculations for someone who wants to be a millionaire at age 65 but who starts with *no savings* at age forty.

What if, however, our ambitious investor started out at age 40 with $50,000 in accumulated savings. What would he then need to set aside monthly to attain his $1,000,000 objective twenty-five years hence, again assuming the same 7% rate of interest compounded monthly?

To solve this problem, we must use both Table 1 and 4. From Table 1 on page 151, we can see that $1 left alone to earn interest at 7% compounded monthly will amount to $5.725 at the end of twenty-five years. Therefore, $50,000 will become $50,000 × 5.725 or $286,250 by the time our hypothetical investor reaches age 65. Thus, our ambitious friend need only make monthly deposits which would accumulate to $1,000,000 *minus* $286,250 over the next twenty-five years. In other words, he need only save *an additional* $713,750 over that twenty-five-year period to attain his goal. The other $286,250 will be provided out of his initial savings of $50,000 at age 40. Again, we return to Table 4, page 178. To save $713,750 over the next twenty-five years with interest at 7% compounded monthly would require deposits of $713,750 × .0012 or $856.50. This is only about 70% of the $1200 monthly deposits which would otherwise be required if our investor had no funds to start with.

Summary

You will find that Table 4 is useful in helping you to set realistic goals and objectives for yourself. If you want to save towards a vacation, for a child's education, or to secure a comfortable retirement, you should be able to calculate what is necessary for you to attain your objectives. Once you have defined your goals, it is so much easier to go after them than to leave the build-up of your savings to haphazard and chancy investment methods.

CHAPTER SIX

To Borrow or Not to Borrow?

Before we examine Tables 5, 6, 7 and 8, which all deal with borrowing money, it would be worthwhile to take a fast look at some of the Canadian income tax rules with which you must be familiar before you can figure out the true cost of a loan and decide whether it's worth the risk. You must always compare the after-tax cost of investing to the capital growth needed to at least break even. Bear in mind that if a profit on the sale of property is treated as a capital gain, only one-half becomes taxable. Thus, if you are in a 50% personal tax bracket, the maximum tax on a capital gain is 25%. The key point is, however, the deductibility of your interest expense. If your interest is non-deductible, you would require a much greater pre-tax return on investment in order to break even. This is illustrated in Figure 1.

The results are somewhat shocking. If interest expense is non-deductible, while capital growth is taxable, you require *twice* the return before taxes just to break even. In other words, *non-deductible interest is expensive*. A good example of an investment where the cost of borrowing is non-deductible is a summer house (or vacation home).

Figure 1
An individual in a 50% tax bracket borrows money at 14% to invest in a "growth" investment

	If Interest Expense is Deductible	If Interest Expense is Non-Deductible
Cost of borrowing (gross)	14%	14%
Less: Tax savings (50%)	7%	—
Cost of borrowing (net)	7%	14%
Annual capital growth required to break even (gross)	9.33%	18.66%
Less: 25% tax on growth	2.33%	4.66%
Annual capital growth required to break even (net)	7.00%	14.00%

Most Canadians are aware that it is now no longer possible for a married couple to enjoy capital gains exemptions on two principal residences. Thus, borrowing money for a vacation home is an expensive proposition. We'll return to this subject in Chapter Eleven. For now, just realize that as much as you might like to have a second house, if you borrow at 14%, it would have to appreciate by 19% annually for you to just break even.

Interest Deductibility

When, then, is interest tax-deductible? In general, interest on money borrowed to acquire an interest in or finance the operations of a business is tax-deductible. There are, however, some important restrictions on the deductibility of interest on money borrowed for other purposes. First, interest on money borrowed to buy property for personal use is just not deductible. So, if you borrow to buy your own home or a vacation property, you will be paying off the loan with whatever money you take home after-tax. Similarly, interest on money borrowed to put into registered retirement savings plans is not deductible. This will be dealt with more fully in Chapter Fifteen which deals with RRSPs.

On the other hand, if you borrow to buy a house or property that you'll rent out or take a loan so you can play the stock market, your interest will be tax-deductible. As you will see in later chapters in this book, you can carry significantly more debt if you are receiving a government subsidy in the form of tax deductions.

There are, however, two special investments for which different rules apply. First, unless you are a real estate developer, Canadian tax law states that interest on money borrowed to acquire raw land is not tax-deductible. You are permitted to use your interest expense to offset any miscellaneous income which you derive from your land holdings, but you cannot create a loss.

Another area where caution is indicated involves transactions in investments such as gold and silver. Generally, profits from the disposition of gold and silver are subject to capital gains treatment. In the case of investments in bullion or coins, this is a result of administrative discretion on the part of Revenue Canada. Since bullion cannot pay interest or dividends and is held strictly as a speculation, whether short- or long-term, any gains should theoretically be treated as 100% taxable income. However, it has historically been the policy of Revenue Canada to accept capital gains treatment on these transactions. Nevertheless, you must realize that if you want capital gains treatment on your transactions in gold and silver, interest on money borrowed to make these investments is *not* deductible. If you decide, on the other hand, to deduct interest expense, you must be prepared to pay taxes on your full profits.

As you are no doubt well aware, the tax rules keep changing. Before borrowing money, always seek professional advice as to the tax consequences. This is the only way that you can determine the real cost of carrying your investments. When you read Chapters Ten through Seventeen, you will get a better feel for calculating after-tax costs and returns.

Introduction to Table 5

A very common financial situation involves finding the payment required to repay a loan over a period of time. Suppose you want to borrow $25,000 for five years. The lender wants to earn 14% interest compounded monthly. You are prepared to repay the loan in monthly instalments beginning one month after you receive the $25,000. What is the amount of each of your monthly payments? Again, it might be useful to start with a time diagram.

Table 5 will tell you how to calculate the periodic payments needed to pay off or "amortize" a loan of $1 over a certain length of time. Turn to page 189. If the loan payments are to be made monthly, with interest at 14% also calculated monthly, twelve payments of .0233 will be required each year to repay a $1 loan over five years. Therefore, to repay $25,000, payments of $25,000 × .0233, or $582.50, are needed. After five years, you will have made payments totalling $34,950 (sixty months × $582.50). Of this amount, $25,000 would be the full principal you would have paid back and $9950 would represent interest.

Is there any way to verify that a $25,000 loan at 14% with interest calculated monthly can be amortized by sixty payments of $582.50? Of

Figure 2
Time diagram illustrating the monthly payments required to amortize a loan of $25,000 over five years

| 12 × $? | 12 × $? | 12 × $? | 12 × $? | 12 × $? |

| 0 | 1 | 2 | 3 | 4 | 5 |

Present Loan   Ending Loan
$25,000   Nil

course there is. Any lender who is willing to accept sixty payments of $582.50 in exchange for $25,000 must, in his own mind, *consider both alternatives as having equal value* over a five-year period. In other words, the future value of $25,000 earning interest at 14% calculated monthly for five years must have the same value as sixty payments of $582.50 also at a 14% interest rate. Let's examine Figure 3 to see if the two are, in fact, identical.

Figure 3
Sixty monthly payments of $582.50 are equivalent to $25,000 if money can be invested at 14% compounded monthly

5 Years With Interest at 14% Compounded Monthly

Present Value		Future Value
$25,000	$25,000 × 2.006 (Table 1, page 154)	$50,150
or		
Sixty monthly payments of $582.50	$582.50 × 86.195 (Table 2, page 163)	50,209
	Rounding difference	$ 59

The future value of $25,000 left to earn interest at 14% compounded monthly for five years is $50,150. Similarly, the future value of sixty monthly payments of $582.50 is $50,209, also assuming interest at 14% compounded monthly. Ignoring a small rounding difference, the values of both are identical.

You will find Table 5 useful any time you face the prospect of borrowing money and would like to know the required monthly, quarterly, semi-annual or annual payments to discharge your debt.

Again, take the trouble to review pages 185 to 193. In using Table 5, always *be careful to make sure* that you are looking under the right column. Otherwise, you will become a victim of the "garbage in, garbage out" principle.

Note that in the first column of Table 5, monthly payments are assumed. It is also assumed that interest is compounded monthly as well. Similarly, in the third column, which details the required semi-annual payments, it is also assumed that interest is calculated semi-annually. Technically, it is conceivable that you could borrow money under an arrangement whereby your payments are made monthly although interest is calculated only semi-annually. In these circumstances, the figures in the first column will give you a close approximation of the required monthly payments although they won't be exact.

Actually, most Canadian mortgage loans call for monthly payments, even though interest *is* compounded semi-annually. This is why I have included Table 6, which is discussed in the next chapter.

Here is another application of Table 5. Let's assume that you can borrow money at 16%. You are looking for a $10,000 loan and want to have a nine-year repayment program. How much would you need to pay? Figure 4 contains an extract from that table.

Figure 4
Periodic payments required to amortize a loan of $10,000 at 16% over nine years

| | Payments are made | | | |
	Monthly	Quarterly	Semi-Annually	Annually
9 Years/$1	0.0175	0.0529	0.1067	0.2171
Periodic payments to amortize a loan of $10,000	$ 175	$ 529	$1,067	$2,171
	× 12	× 4	× 2	× 1
Annual Payments	$2,100	$2,116	$2,134	$2,171

You can see that it really doesn't make a tremendous amount of difference whether your payments are made monthly or annually. Of course, the more frequently your payments are made, the cheaper it is for you to discharge your debt. Over a nine-year period, though, the

Figure 5
Monthly payments required to amortize a loan of $1 at 16% interest calculated monthly over one to thirty years

1	0.0907	16	0.0145
2	0.0490	17	0.0143
3	0.0352	18	0.0141
4	0.0283	19	0.0140
5	0.0243	20	0.0139
6	0.0217	21	0.0138
7	0.0199	22	0.0137
8	0.0185	23	0.0137
9	0.0175	24	0.0136
10	0.0168	25	0.0136
11	0.0161	26	0.0136
12	0.0157	27	0.0135
13	0.0153	28	0.0135
14	0.0149	29	0.0135
15	0.0147	30	0.0134

difference between paying monthly and annually is only $71 × 9, or $639 on a $10,000 loan.

However, let's assume that your payments will be made on a monthly basis since this is usually what most lenders require. Figure 5 is another extract from Table 5 showing the monthly payments required to discharge a loan of $1 with interest at 16% over one to thirty years.

If you look at these numbers carefully, I think you will learn something very interesting. Obviously, if you want to get rid of a debt over one, two or even three years, the payments are quite high relative to the original debt. However, look what happens if the debt is extended over a long period of time. *Your payments are virtually the same whether you choose to repay over fifteen years or thirty years. In other words, there is little point in extending any debt any longer than you absolutely require.* For example, let's assume that the principal amount that you borrow is $10,000. If you are willing to pay for the privilege of borrowing $10,000 at 16% over a thirty-year period, your monthly payments will be $10,000 × .0134, or $134 per month. However, if you want to, you can shorten the payout period to, say, fifteen years. Your payments then become $10,000 × .0147, or $147 per month. Thus, if you are willing to pay out an extra $13 a month, you can save a total cash outflow of $21,780. This is illustrated in Figure 6. Astounding, isn't it?

Figure 6
Paying off a debt of $10,000 over fifteen years vs. thirty years

$10,000 × 0.0134 = $134 /Month $10,000 over thirty years
$10,000 × 0.0147 = $147 /Month $10,000 over fifteen years
Monthly difference $ 13

Thirty years × 12 monthly payments × $134/month =	$48,240
Fifteen years × 12 monthly payments × $147/month =	26,460
Total difference	$21,780

Summary

In real life, any time you are negotiating for a loan which you will repay with blended payments of principal and interest, you should always take a close look at Table 5. First, you can see how much you can afford to borrow depending on your ability to repay. Then, you will find that if you force yourself to make just slightly higher payments than the bare minimum you could afford to get away with under the lender's conditions, you will be far ahead of the game.

CHAPTER SEVEN

Canadian Mortgage Loans

In the last chapter, we dealt with Table 5, which gives the periodic payments required to amortize a loan over various time periods. For each interest factor, the first column of Table 5 shows the loan payments which must be made monthly, assuming interest is *also* calculated on a monthly basis. Although Table 5 is useful in dealing with most conventional loans from lending institutions, it is not suitable for handling problems involving Canadian mortgage loans. This is because, under Canadian law, interest is compounded *semi-annually*, although most mortgage loan payments are made *monthly*. So, the payments required to discharge a Canadian mortgage loan are slightly smaller than they would be if interest were calculated monthly.

Figure 1 compares the monthly payment required to discharge a "conventional" loan of $1000 at 10% compounded monthly to the monthly payment required to amortize a Canadian mortgage loan at the same interest rate but with interest calculated semi-annually. Granted, the difference is only a few pennies for each $1000 of debt, but it doesn't hurt to be reasonably accurate—especially since most mortgages are only repaid over fifteen to twenty-five years.

Table 6 provides you with all the information you will need to construct Canadian mortgage amortization schedules. The interest rates

Figure 1

Years	Monthly payment required to amortize a loan of $1000 at 10% interest compounded monthly over various periods of time (from Table 5)	Monthly payment required to amortize a mortgage loan of $1000 at 10% interest compounded semi-annually over various periods of time (from Table 6)
5	$21.20	$21.15
10	13.20	13.10
15	10.70	10.62
20	9.70	9.52
25	9.10	8.95

for this table range from 10% to 21.875%, increasing by one-eighth of 1% each time. In this case, since fractional percentages are built into the table, it is not necessary for you to make any approximations. You may use this table to deal with amortizations from one to forty years. One word of caution, however. It almost goes without saying that in dealing with all mathematics tables, you must be sure not to make errors in your decimal places. Most of the tables in this book deal with present value and future value calculations for $1 amounts. The only exceptions are Tables 6 and 7 which refer to mortgage loans of $1000. For example, if you are trying to calculate the payments required to amortize a $50,000 mortgage loan at 12.375% over twenty years, your required payments would be 50 (not 50,000) X 11.058. (See page 197.) The payments in this case are $552.90.

Most mortgage loans are made on the basis of a twenty-five-year amortization. Of course, they have to be renewed at the prevailing interest rate every year or so. Table 7 provides you with the balance outstanding at the end of each year on a twenty-five-year mortgage loan of $1000 at various rates of interest, with interest compounded semi-annually. Figure 2 is an extract from this table showing the progression of a $100,000 mortgage loan at 12%. As time goes on, the principal balance outstanding on the mortgage continues to decrease.

By using Tables 6 and 7 together, you should be able to calculate with a reasonable degree of accuracy which portion of any given year's mortgage payments will be applied against principal or interest.

For example, at 12% interest compounded semi-annually, a mortgage loan of $100,000 can be discharged over twenty-five years with

Figure 2
Balance outstanding on a twenty-five year
mortgage loan of $100,000 at 12% interest
(Monthly Payment $1031.90; Rounded to Nearest $100)

End of Year		End of Year		End of Year	
1	$99,300	9	$89,400	17	$64,100
2	98,500	10	87,300	18	59,000
3	97,600	11	85,100	19	53,200
4	96,600	12	82,500	20	46,700
5	95,500	13	79,600	21	39,400
6	94,200	14	76,400	22	31,200
7	92,800	15	72,800	23	22,000
8	91,200	16	68,700	24	11,600
				25	0

monthly payments of $1031.90. Yearly, the payments are $1031.90 × 12, or $12,382.80. Over the course of the first year, the mortgage principal declines from $100,000 to $99,300. This means that $700 out of payments totalling $12,383 applies towards principal in the first year. The balance of $11,683 therefore represents interest. Similarly, in year fifteen, the balance outstanding on principal declines from $76,400 to $72,800, a difference of $3600. Again, if the total payments are $12,383, the interest portion would have to be $8783. This is illustrated in Figure 3.

Figure 3
Amortizing a $100,000 mortgage at 12% over twenty-five years

Monthly payments: $\dfrac{\$100,000}{1,000} \times 10.319 = \$\ 1,031.90$

Annual payments: $1,031.90 × 12   = $12,382.80

Year	Payments Made	Principal			Interest
1	$12,383	$100,000 −	$99,300 =	$ 700	$11,683
5	12,383	96,600 −	95,500 =	1,100	11,283
10	12,383	89,400 −	87,300 =	2,100	10,283
15	12,383	76,400 −	72,800 =	3,600	8,783
20	12,383	53,200 −	46,700 =	6,500	5,883
25	12,383	11,600 −	0 =	11,600	783

Income Tax Considerations

Since Canadians cannot deduct interest on money borrowed to buy a house for their own use, home ownership is an extremely expensive proposition. If your mortgage is payable at 12% and you are in a 50% tax bracket, you must earn double the amount you have to pay off. For this reason, you must try to discharge a home mortgage as quickly as possible.

Many mortgages will allow the borrower to prepay up to 10% on the anniversary date each year. If you make ordinary payments on a monthly basis coupled with seven or eight instalments of 10% of the original balance, your mortgage can then be eliminated within seven or eight years. Take another look at Figure 2, which shows the balance outstanding on a twenty-five-year mortgage loan of $100,000 at 12%. At the end of the first year, the principal balance outstanding is $99,300 while at the end of year nine it is $89,400. Therefore, if you were to repay $9900 on the first anniversary of your mortgage, you would then be eliminating the next eight annual payments. In other words, if your monthly payments stay the same (which they would) and you make no further special payments against principal, your debt would be completely extinguished only sixteen years later. Given a special payment of $9900 at the end of the first year, you would then owe only $89,400 at the end of year two, $87,300 after year three, and so forth. Of course, if additional principal payments were made at the end of the second year (and subsequently) your debt would be extinguished that much more quickly. Certainly, most people are not in a position to pay down as much as 10% of their mortgage each year on the anniversary date — especially since you must use after-tax dollars to do this. However, whatever you can pay down will be quite helpful.

The Mortgage Term

Be careful never to confuse the *amortization* of a loan with its *term*. If you are told that a mortgage is to be amortized over twenty-five years, you must never assume that it has a twenty-five-year term. The term of a mortgage is the period of time given to the borrower before the lender can demand the principal balance owing on the loan. Until perhaps ten years ago, lenders did in fact make loans for long periods, such as twenty-five years, at fixed rates of interest. Today, however, mortgage terms never exceed five years and very often must be renewed each year. Thus, although an amortization schedule may reflect the payments necessary to discharge a debt over twenty-five years, the borrower, in most cases, must still repay the principal balance at the end of only one, two, or at most, four or five years. Of course, the lender will usually renew the mortgage at current prevailing rates.

Again, examine the schedule on page 41. If payments of $1031.90 are made monthly over twenty-five years, a loan of $100,000 at 12% would be extinguished. However, here is the problem posed by the fact that your mortgage will probably have, say, a three-year term. At the end of three years, the lender will want his money and, on a twenty-five-year loan, you would still owe him $97,600. To repay that loan, you would probably have to commit yourself to another mortgage and borrow the $97,600. Assume the new mortgage is for a further three years at the same rate and also with payments calculated over a twenty-five-year period. Figure 4 shows what your outstanding balance will be over the next three years in round figures.

Figure 4
Balance outstanding on a loan of $97,600 at 12%
(twenty-five year amortization)

End of Year		Balance
1	$97,600 × .993 =	$96,917
2	97,600 × .985 =	96,136
3	97,600 × .976 =	95,258

At the end of the second three-year period when you have to repay the loan, you may repeat the process. Each new three-year term will result in smaller monthly payments because the principal amount at the start of each succeeding term will be less. However, instead of amortizing the loan down to zero after twenty-five years, it may take over *one hundred years* to discharge the loan completely. *There is only one way a twenty-five-year mortgage can be paid off in full over twenty-five years. Each time a mortgage is renewed, you must arrange to have the remaining principal amortized for a period which is not longer than the remaining number of years in the **original** amortization.*

In other words, continuing with the preceding example, the $97,600 balance outstanding at the end of the first three-year period should be renewed with payments based on a *twenty-two-year* amortization. Then, the balance outstanding at the end of six years should be renewed for a further term based on an amortization period of only nineteen years and so on.

Especially in times of high interest rates, the tendency is to try to reduce your monthly payments by lengthening the term over which a

Figure 5
Amortization of $100,000 at 12% over various time periods

$100,000 at 12%	15 Years	20 Years	25 Years	35 Years
Monthly payment	$ 1,181.60	$ 1,081.00	$ 1,031.90	$ 992.70
Annual cost	14,179.20	12,972.00	12,382.80	11,912.40
Total cost	212,688.00	259,440.00	309.570.00	416,934.00
Total interest paid	112,688.00	159,440.00	209,570.00	316,934.00

Monthly payment over 15 years	$1,181.60
Monthly payment over 25 years	1,031.90
Difference	$ 149.70

Total interest over 25 years	$209,570.00
Total interest over 15 years	112,688.00
Difference	$96,882.00

loan is amortized. As you will shortly see, however, this can be an extremely costly mistake. The table in Figure 5 shows the payments necessary to amortize a $100,000 mortgage loan at 12% over various time periods.

Clearly, the longer the period, the smaller the monthly payments. However, the longer the term, the greater the total cost. The analysis in Figure 5 compares the difference between a fifteen-year amortization and a twenty-five-year repayment. For each $100,000, the monthly difference is less than $150. However, extending the payment period an extra ten years costs $96,882 in the long run.

Points

Many real estate loans involve special charges called "points". One point is one per cent of the loan principal. Lenders charge points in order to increase the real yield on the loan, without increasing the stated rate.

For example, if you're negotiating with a lender for a $50,000 twenty-five-year loan at 14% annual interest, the monthly payment on such a loan would be $586.95 ($11.739 × 50).

If the lender also charges three points as a service fee, 3% of $50,000 is $1500. This amount is deducted from the $50,000, to give a net loan principal of $48,500. Now, what is the true interest rate? The monthly payment on the loan will be the same as calculated above, but the loan principal is only $48,500.

Using Table 6, you can calculate that $50,000 at 14% for twenty-five years requires monthly payments of:

$50,000 ÷ $1000 = 50
11.739 × 50 = $586.95

If the loan amount is reduced to $48,500 but the payments of $586.95 remain the same, then the interest rate must increase. Tracing the twenty-five-year amortization line further to the right, you can try various factors from Table 6 for the best fit:

$48,500 ÷ $1000 = 48.5
11.829 × 48.5 = 573.71 (14 1/8%)
11.919 × 48.5 = 578.07 (14 1/4%)
12.009 × 48.5 = 582.44 (14 3/8%)
12.099 × 48.5 = 586.80 (14 1/2%)

From this trial and error process, you can see that the factor of 12.099 gives the closest approximation to a payment of $586.95 per month. This factor is for a 14.5% interest rate. In other words, the three points charged against the mortgage will cost you an extra ¹/₂% interest over the twenty-five-year life of the loan.

Summary

This chapter has explained the fundamentals concerning mortgages. In Chapter Eleven, we will return to the topic of home ownership and deal with the question of how to evaluate a home as an investment. Then, Chapter Twelve covers investing in real estate other than a home. After reading these two chapters, you should be in a better position to decide whether it is worthwhile to discharge a debt quickly or if it makes sense to extend the term over which your financing obligations will be repaid. As you will see, one of the key factors is the deductibility or non-deductibility of your interest expense.

CHAPTER EIGHT

How Much Can I Afford to Borrow?

Suppose you are looking for a loan and your income level will allow you to make up to $600 in monthly payments beginning one month from now. There is a lender who is willing to give you a five-year loan with annual interest of 14% compounded monthly. How much will you be able to borrow?

Before we examine Table 8, which will give us the answer, it might again be appropriate to sketch a simple time diagram, as in Figure 1.

If you are faced with this type of problem, you will notice that each payment occurs at the *end* of each period. In fact, most loans generally *do* require payments at the end of each period.

Now we can turn to Table 8, which gives us the present value of $1 per period payable at the end of each period. In simple terms, this table will tell you how much you can borrow today at various interest rates for each $1 you are able to pay back at the end of each period for a given number of periods. The figures for an interest rate of 14% appear on page 220.

If payments of $600 will be made monthly for five years, the amount that you can borrow today is $600 × 42.977 or $25,786.20. In other words, if you are prepared to pay back $600 each month, you could borrow $25,786.20 and extinguish your debt over a sixty-month period. Your payments would provide both principal and interest to the lender. Once you know this amount, it is then easy to determine your principal-

Figure 1
How much can you borrow if you can afford to make monthly payments of $600 over five years with interest at 14%?

	$600 × 12	$600 × 12	$600 × 12	$600 × 12	$600 × 12
Year 0	1	2	3	4	5

Original Loan ?   Ending Balance—$0

interest breakdown. In total, your payments will be sixty months ×
$600, or $36,000. Therefore, the total interest you would pay during the
life of the loan is $36,000 minus $25,786.20, or $10,213.80.

Can Your Results Be Verified?

In previous chapters, you saw that you can generally prove whether your
answers are correct. In this case, the solution can also be verified
although it takes two steps to do so. The process is, however, important
because it illustrates the meaning of "the present value of an annuity".

Let's take a look at the situation from the lender's standpoint. If our
answer is correct, a lender who is willing to earn 14% on his money
would be just as well off trading $25,786.20 for the right to receive $600
a month for the next five years. In other words, at 14% interest, his total
accumulation would be the same. We can use Tables 1 and 2 to see
whether this is, in fact, the case.

Figure 2
Future value of $25,786.20 after five years
with interest compounded at 14%, calculated monthly

$25,786.20 × 2.006 (Table 1, page 154) = $51,727.12

Figure 3
Future value of sixty monthly payments of $600
with interest compounded at 14%, calculated monthly

$600 × 86.195 (Table 2, page 163) = $51,717.00

Except for a $10.12 rounding difference, the calculations shown in
Figures 2 and 3 prove that the future value is equivalent; thus our initial
answer was correct.

Perhaps, there is one area of confusion. In the problem with which
we have been dealing, the lender would be receiving sixty monthly
payments of $600, or a total of $36,000. How does this amount reconcile
with the calculations just made which shows that the future value of these
payments is $51,717? The answer is that the verification using future
value equivalents assumes that the lender could *reinvest each payment of
$600* as it is received at 14%, so that, over a period of five years, he
could earn *an additional $15,717* in interest.

The concept of equivalents of future values is one of the most important and fundamental ideas behind all financing arrangements. It shows why a lender would be willing to give up cash in exchange for future monthly payments.

Take the time to examine Table 8 in some detail. Notice that for each percentage factor, the numbers are completely different in all four columns. This is because the first column deals with a monthly payback, while the second column deals with four quarterly payments, and column three reflects two semi-annual payments, while column four assumes one annual payment only. As is the case in Table 5, if monthly payments are to be made, it is assumed that interest is also compounded monthly. Similarly, if annual payments are required, interest is assumed to compound annually.

The practical application of Table 8 is, as already explained, its usefulness in helping you determine how much you can afford to borrow for investment based on your anticipated cash flow (that is, ability to pay back). In the example described in the first few pages of this chapter, the assumption was made that a borrower could afford to repay $600 a month over a five-year period. This gave him the opportunity to borrow $25,786 today.

Often, when it comes to investing, you don't need a substantial amount of start-up capital. *All you need is the power to carry debt.* As you will learn in later chapters, an initial borrowing which can be covered by cash flow from your job, business or profession can then be leveraged into *further* borrowings, provided the *additional* debt can be serviced out of cash flows generated from the investments themselves. In other words, if excess earnings of $600 a month from your job allows you to borrow, say, $26,000, and you invest in a stock that pays a 6% dividend, you will find that you can actually borrow substantially more than $26,000. This is because the dividend yield from the investment itself will help you pay down the additional debt commitment. The deductibility of investment interest for tax purposes can also enhance greatly your ability to carry a debt load.

Common sense should tell you two very important things about borrowing money: (1) The lower the interest rate, the more you can afford to borrow. (2) However, extending the term of a loan beyond, say, six or seven years, does not significantly increase the amount that you can borrow. This is because your interest costs are so high in proportion to your total payments that it becomes more and more difficult to amortize the principal balance.

Figure 4 illustrates how Table 8 proves these common sense points. It shows the amount of money you can borrow at various interest rates if you are prepared to pay $600 a month for five years. As you can see, the difference between borrowing at 10% and 20% is significant ($28,239 − $22,647 = $5592).

Figure 4
Principal amount of debt that can be amortized by monthly payments of $600 over five years at various rates of interest

Interest Rate	Factor from Table 8	Initial Debt to be Repaid over 5 Years
10%	$600 × 47.065	$28,239
12%	600 × 44.955	26,973
14%	600 × 42.977	25,786
16%	600 × 41.122	24,673
18%	600 × 39.380	23,628
20%	600 × 37.745	22,647

On the other hand, Figure 5 shows you that at any given interest rate, the amount which you can borrow does not vary dramatically whether you commit yourself to make payments over fifteen years or over as long as twenty years. For purposes of illustration, I will assume an interest rate of 14%.

The difference between a twenty-year and a fifteen-year repayment period represents the opportunity to borrow only an extra $3196 ($48,250 − $45,054). In exchange for that small amount, you would have to make sixty *additional* payments of $600 each or $36,000.

Figure 5
Principal amount of debt that can be amortized by monthly payments of $600 at 14% interest over various time periods

Time Period Years	Factor from Table 8	Initial Debt to be Repaid
15	$600 × 75.090	$45,054
16	600 × 76.470	45,882
17	600 × 77.671	46,603
18	600 × 78.716	47,230
19	600 × 79.626	47,776
20	600 × 80.417	48,250

Summary

Before you even think about borrowing money, your first question should be: If I borrow, how much can I afford to repay on a periodic basis (monthly, quarterly, etc.)? Of course, your answer depends on whether the property you buy with borrowed money will provide you with a cash inflow to subsidize your debt. Whenever you do borrow, you should generally try to extinguish your debts as soon as possible, even if it requires slightly higher cash outlays to do so. Over the long run, the savings in cash flow can be quite significant.

CHAPTER NINE

The Future and Present Value of Payments Made at the *Beginning* of Each Period

In our previous discussions of annuities, we always assumed that the periodic payments would be made at the *end* of each time period. In Chapter Three, for example, we calculated how much you could accumulate if you were to put aside a certain amount of money monthly, quarterly, semi-annually or annually at the *end* of each period. Similarly, in the last chapter, we calculated how much money you could afford to *borrow* if you were prepared to make *payments* at the *end* of various time periods. Savings are typically deposited at the end of various time intervals and loans are typically repaid on an ordinary annuity basis. Thus, the financial tables which we have already examined in this book are directly applicable to most saving and loan situations.

Leasing, however, is also an extremely important financial activity. The problem with leases is that they will usually call for periodic payments at the *beginning* of each time period. We are all familiar with the concept of paying rent in advance on the first of each month. *An annuity calling for payments at the beginning of each time period is called "an annuity due".*

Table 2 cannot be used directly to calculate the future value of an annuity due. It can be modified using high-school algebra, but instead I have chosen to include a separate table in this book to determine the future value of $1 invested at the beginning of each period (Table 9).

How Do You Calculate the Future Value of an Annuity Due?

Suppose you deposit $100 each month in a savings account that pays 12% interest compounded monthly—just like in the first example in Chapter Three when we dealt with ordinary annuities. This time, however, you make your deposits at the *start* of each period rather than at the end. Deposits are made for ten years. Before doing the calculations,

Figure 1
Time diagram illustrating twelve monthly deposits of $100 at the beginning of each month over a ten-year period

12 × 12 × 12 × 12 × 12 × 12 × 12 × 12 × 12 × 12 ×
|$100|$100|$100|$100|$100|$100|$100|$100|$100|$100|

Year | 1 2 3 4 5 6 7 8 9 10

First Deposit   Last Deposit

Future Value?

it would be, again, useful to construct a time diagram and then compare it to the one on page 19.

- Like the diagram in Chapter Three, this one also calls for one hundred and twenty monthly payments. However, they are all moved *one period closer to the present*. Instead of waiting one month before making the first deposit, you do so immediately. The last deposit is made at the *start* of the 120th month. The future value of the sixty payments at 12% compounded monthly is 232.339 X $100 or $23,233.90. In the ordinary annuity problem (deposits made at the *end* of each month), the future value turned out to be $23,003.90. You'll notice that the future value of the "annuity due" is higher because deposits into the account are made *sooner* and therefore *earn more interest*. The difference over a ten-year period is $230.

How Much Do I Have to Save to Meet My Goals and Objectives—If I Start NOW?

In Chapter Five, we saw that, in order to accumulate $10,000 in a savings account after four years with interest at 11% compounded monthly, you had to make monthly deposits of $167 on an ordinary annuity basis. But, what would have happened if, instead of making your deposits at the end of each month, you had made your first deposit right away? How much would each deposit have to be?

To solve this problem, you may use Table 10. The only difference between Table 10 and Table 4 is that Table 10 deals with payments made at the *beginning* of each period. From page 237, the monthly payment factor at 11% is 0.0165. In other words, you need only make monthly payments of $165 at the beginning of each month, if you wish to accumulate $10,000 after four years. The difference is $2 a month.

How Do You Determine the Present Value of an Annuity Due?

The present value of an annuity due is an important quantity to consider when you analyse a lease or an insurance policy. Both of these will be discussed later in this book, but here's a simple example just to illustrate the concept.

Suppose you purchase a computer with the intention of leasing it out for five years. You figure that the property will have no value at the end of this time because it will have been rendered obsolete by changes in technology. You want lease payments large enough to allow you to recover the cost of the computer as well as an 18% annual rate of return on your investment (compounded monthly). If you pay $30,000 for the computer, how much do you have to charge as a monthly lease payment in order to realize your objectives? Again, we should refer to a time diagram.

Figure 2
Time diagram illustrating the required monthly lease payments to recover $30,000 over five years with interest at 18%

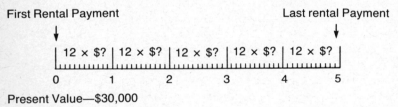

Present Value—$30,000

As you can see in Figure 2, this is an annuity due situation with the lease payments occurring at the start of each of the sixty consecutive monthly periods. If you look at Table 11, and the figures on page 248, you will see that the answer is $30,000 × .0250, or $750 a month. If you can find a lessee who agrees to those terms, you would receive 60 × $750 or $45,000 over the five-year period. This would cover your $30,000 cost and give you an 18% return on your investment with interest calculated monthly.

In this lease example, your only return on the computer is the annuity of sixty monthly payments. Again, please note the assumption made earlier that the computer itself would have no value after the five-year period. In Chapter Seventeen, we will deal with more realistic examples, which make the assumption that the property does have some value at the end of the lease. You will see that the present value of the final sale price must be taken into account in determining a fair market value leasing rate.

As the final example in this chapter, suppose you understand from your cousin, who is a real estate broker, that duplexes in your city are renting for $600 a month ($300 each). You have just inherited a sizeable amount of money and would like to buy a duplex property as long as you can earn a 16% return on your investment compounded monthly over the next twenty-five years. What is the most you should spend for the property?

In this case, you would expect a return on investment of $600 a month for the next twenty-five years, starting immediately. The present value of an annuity due is given in Table 12. Table 12 is very similar to Table 6 except that Table 6 deals with the present value of payments made at the *end* of each period while Table 12 deals with payments made at the *beginning*.

At 16% interest, the present value of twenty-five years of $600 monthly payments can be determined from the figures on page 257. The answer is 74.571 multiplied by the $600 monthly rent, or $44,742.60. This amount represents the purchase price that would give you your 16% return over the next twenty-five years. If you can buy the house for less and still rent it out at $600 a month, your return will be greater than 16%. Of course, this example is not realistic since you would expect rents to increase annually instead of being held constant over twenty-five years. Also, the example assumes that the property would be worthless at the end of twenty-five years. Actually, you would be able to sell the house at the end of that time.

Suppose the sales price is $150,000. The present value of $150,000 to be received thirty years from now can be found by using Table 3. Assuming a 16% interest factor, compounded monthly, the present value is $150,000 × .0188, or $2820. You can add this $2820 to the $44,742 present value of the lease payments to arrive at a total of approximately $47,500 that you could pay for the house and attain your objectives (ignoring potential rent increases). Note that the final sales proceeds do not make much of a difference in the calculations because the sale is projected to take place so far in the future. As you will see in subsequent chapters, given shorter holding periods, the final sales price has a much more important effect on your investment decisions.

Also, please take note that these last few examples have not taken taxes into account. In a true situation you would have to compute your net income from rental payments and the net sales proceeds after taxes, including those levied on capital gains, and *then* use the tables. But, for the time being, the more simplified computations will serve just to introduce the workings of the various tables.

Summary

To this stage, we have covered the applications of Tables 1 through 12 inclusive. The only table not yet discussed is Table 13, which deals with mortality rates. This will be covered in Chapter Sixteen when we examine the subject of life insurance and annuities.

With what we have covered so far as background, we are almost ready to examine how the various tables can be used to assist you to make specific investment decisions. But, before we do this, we must examine the concept of "discounted cash flow", which is the subject of the next chapter.

CHAPTER TEN

Discounted Cash-Flow Analysis

Most investments require an initial outlay of cash. Then, some investments will provide a cash return during the period of ownership, while others will require you to subsidize their costs through additional outflows of money. Finally, when an investment is sold, there is usually one final net cash inflow.

In making any financial analysis, the key point to remember is that a dollar which you will either receive or pay out sometime in the future is worth less than a dollar today. How much less, depends on the interest rate which you choose for your calculations. This interest rate can be the presumed rate of inflation or it can be your own desired rate of return for an investment.

Often, in dealing with the concept of future dollars being worth less than dollars today, financial analysts refer to the process of "discounting". Future dollars are discounted at the selected interest rate to translate them into a more meaningful framework—today's dollars.

In this chapter and in the remainder of this book, we will refer often to Table 3, which gives you the present value of $1 due at the end of various time periods. You will need this to perform present value analysis, or discounting.

Figure 1
**The present value of $1 due at the end of various time
periods at 10% interest compounded annually**
End of Year

1	0.9091
2	0.8264
3	0.7513
4	0.6830
5	0.6209

The excerpt from Table 3 in this section provides figures for an assumed annual interest rate of 10%. These figures can be read in one of two ways. First, if you invest 62 cents today at 10% interest and leave your money alone for five years, you will have $1 at the end. Or, we can take the opposite approach. If you are to receive $1 at the end of five years, this right is only worth an equivalent of .62 cents today, if a 10% annual interest (or inflation) rate is assumed.

Discounted Cash-Flow Techniques

Professional investment analysts use discounted cash-flow techniques to evaluate all kinds of property—including real estate, stock market transactions and other investments such as gold and silver. The actual technique used may vary from analyst to analyst but most have several common factors:

1. Income taxes are considered and calculations are made using after-tax values only.
2. The techniques consider the time value of money.
3. The emphasis is on cash flow and not net income since cash flow is regarded as the best test of investment performance.
4. A percentage rate of return is used to measure the value of the investment. This is something that is easily understood and interpreted. For example, if an investment yields a return of 14.73%, this result can be compared to other alternatives.
5. Discounted cash-flow techniques all take into account the actual amount you as an investor commit to an investment.

As long as you are willing to devote a bit of time and effort, these techniques are quite easy to apply. The most widely used discounted cash-flow techniques are called the *net present value method* and the *internal rate of return method*. Wherever possible, these should be used together when analysing a potential investment.

The Net Present Value Method

To determine the net present value of an investment, you must go through several steps.

1. First, you must choose a minimum satisfactory after-tax rate of return for your investment. This is often referred to as the discount rate. How you select a satisfactory discount rate is discussed in the next section of this chapter.

2. Then, you must detail all of the after-tax cash flows from an investment on a year-by-year basis.
3. Next, you calculate the present value of each year's net after-tax cash flow using the discount rate established in Step 1. Add them together and the total is your net present value.
4. Finally, you analyse and interpret the result.

If the net present value is a positive number, then your investment is earning more than your required rate of return. A net present value less than zero means your investment is earning less than you wanted and should perhaps be discarded. The closer the net present value is to exactly zero, the closer the investment will perform according to your exact specifications.

How to Select the Required Rate of Return

To set your own required rate of return, you'll need two reference points: the rate of return offered at a particular time on other investments, and the degree of risk associated with the particular investment compared to the risk of alternatives.

For example, your simplest investment is a bank term deposit which might yield 12% before tax and would carry very little risk. However, if you are in a 50% marginal tax bracket, a yield of 12% translates to only 6% (12% × 50%) after taxes. Now, if you feel that a particular investment is just as safe as a term deposit, you could set the after-tax required rate of return at only 6%. On the other hand, if you feel that a prospective investment is riskier, you should increase that percentage. How much you add is purely a matter of your own judgement. If you feel that a potential investment is quite risky, add a 10% "risk premium" to the 6% to arrive at your required after-tax rate of return.

Clearly, the greater you set your required after-tax rate of return, the higher the investment performance has to be before the net present value will be positive. In other words, an investment that may have a positive net present value at a 10% required rate of return could have a negative net present value if your required return is 20%. In the following chapters, we will often use a 12% to 20% factor for the required after-tax rate of return. Remember that a 20% return would be calculated *after taxes*, and is equivalent to as much as a 40% rate of return before tax, depending on your marginal tax bracket. However, in your own calculations, you are certainly free to choose whatever rates you desire.

Determining After-Tax Cash Flows

Of course, tax laws and tax rates are always changing. So, I will try to keep my examples relatively simple. I will assume that an investor is in a 50% income tax bracket. Most of the ground rules for tax assumptions have already been covered in Chapter Two, pages 13 and 14.

Simplifying Your Investment Analysis

Wherever possible, you should keep your analysis as simple as you can. In the next chapter, we will analyse a possible investment in a house. This will be followed with another example involving a vacation home. Both analyses are made with yearly projections, rather than monthly. By making a few such simplifications, the time required to prepare a financial analysis can be reduced to only a few minutes with no major loss of accuracy for purposes of decision making. Always remember that most financial analysis relies on estimates. Future incomes are not certain nor are projections of future expenses, nor for that matter, tax rates.

Take a moment to examine the blank Investment Analysis Form on pages 62–63. The first column represents the purchase of the investment. In this column, you would show your personal cash outlay to acquire whatever you are buying. Notice that the first column includes not only your downpayment but any other initial costs associated with an investment. If you are buying a home these could include legal fees or appraisal costs. In the case of a stock market investment, brokerage commissions would be a "front end" cost as well. Clearly, no matter what discount rate you are using, *the present value factor here is always 1.000*. This is because the initial outlay is made in *today's dollars*. Then, Columns 1 through 5 represent future years, starting with the first year after the date the initial investment is made.

The form in Figure 2 is geared to an investment in real estate. It can be adopted quite nicely, as you will see in Chapters Thirteen and Fourteen, to deal with other investments as well, such as the stock market or gold. The various descriptions on the form are, for the most part, self-explanatory. In any example dealing with the purchase of a home, depreciation and income tax considerations are not applicable. In other cases, you may have to calculate these amounts on an annual basis and also compute the tax on any eventual capital gain at the time of sale.

An investment analysis form provides for the calculation of taxable income arising from the particular investment so that you can determine any income taxes payable (over and above your other taxes). Then, items not affecting cash flow or income tax matters are accounted for separately. *Remember that it is cash flow that really determines whether an investment is desirable and cash flow is quite different from net income.* In a given year, you could have a high net income but no cash flow. A good example would be if you use whatever revenue an investment provides to pay off debt owing against that investment. Remember that you cannot reinvest your net income—you can only reinvest your cash. Again, this is why the net present value method is called a *discounted cash flow* technique.

One small formality. I suggest you use a simple accounting trick to help you in your calculations. When a number represents a cash *outflow*, record it in parentheses. This is the same as a minus sign but is harder to miss.

The rate of return you require will determine the present value factor which you must insert at the bottom of each column. For these purposes, you will use Table 3. For example, if you require a 10% after-tax rate of return, a cash inflow or outflow at the end of one year has a present value of 0.9091 (see page 170), while an amount due at the end of two years has a present value of 0.8264. To translate after-tax cash flows into present dollars, simply multiply these cash flows by the present value factor.

Interpreting the Net Present Value

Once you have calculated your after-tax cash flows and have translated them into present dollars, you are ready to interpret your results. If your net present value is positive, this means you could have made an even larger initial investment and you still would have realized your desired rate of return. If the net present value is negative, then you are earning less than your target.

Reinvestment Assumption in the Net Present Value Method

You should be careful, however, when you use the concept of net present value analysis in real life. *The net present value that you derive will only be true if you can reinvest all positive cash flows* during *the life of the investment at the required after-tax rate of return.* This is a reasonable assumption in many cases unless you have established a required rate so high that the reinvestment of the "intermediate proceeds" at that rate is not possible or likely.

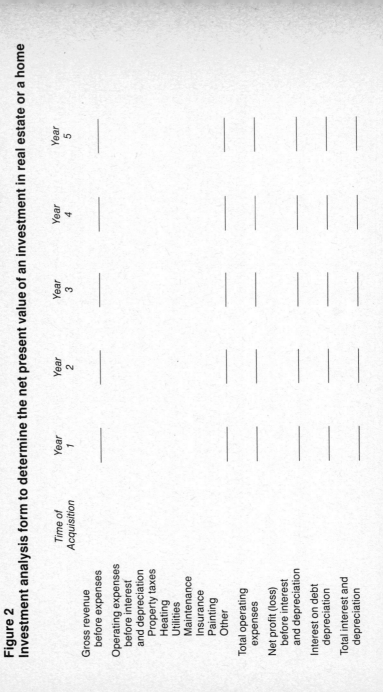

Figure 2
Investment analysis form to determine the net present value of an investment in real estate or a home

	Time of Acquisition	Year 1	Year 2	Year 3	Year 4	Year 5
Gross revenue before expenses		—	—	—	—	—
Operating expenses before interest and depreciation						
Property taxes						
Heating						
Utilities						
Maintenance						
Insurance						
Painting						
Other						
Total operating expenses		—	—	—	—	—
Net profit (loss) before interest and depreciation		—	—	—	—	—
Interest on debt depreciation		—	—	—	—	—
Total interest and depreciation		—	—	—	—	—

Taxable income (loss)	___	___	___	___	___
Estimated income taxes	___	___	___	___	___
Net after-tax income (loss)					
Add: Depreciation					
Rent savings due to ownership					
Less: Capital outlays					
Cost of investment					
Expenses of acquisition					
Add: Sales proceeds net of expenses of sale					
Less: Debt repayment —principal					
Tax on gain	___ ___	___ ___	___ ___	___ ___	___ ___
After-tax cash flow	___ ___	___ ___	___ ___	___ ___	___ ___
Required rate of return	___	___	___	___	___
Present value factor (Table 3)	___ ___	___ ___	___ ___	___ ___	___ ___
Net present value	___ ___	___ ___	___ ___	___ ___	___ ___

In the next chapter, we will not run into this potential problem because, if you buy a house, there are usually no positive cash flows until the house is eventually sold. The issue only arises when there are positive after-tax cash flows *before* the final year of the investment.

In Chapter Twelve, we will look at investments in land and rental property. While no depreciation may be claimed with respect to land, depreciation may be taken on most rental property, although there are restrictions against creating losses for tax purposes. However, because depreciation is tax-deductible and can shelter cash flow, it is a major factor in the financial success of many real estate investments.

Also, don't over-estimate the validity of your conclusions just because you have used a rather sophisticated procedure in order to evaluate a potential investment. Similarly, don't assume that you can compute your answers using tables to seven, eight, or even ten decimal places and achieve a great degree of precision and accuracy. The final result of any analytical technique is only as good as the *data* you put in. Remember that most of your input is estimates. In every real estate example, operating expenses and final sales proceeds are only estimates. *If a property actually appreciates by half of what you project, the entire analysis could show quite different results.*

On the other hand, I do not mean to imply that it is a waste of time to make such an analysis. This is because this process forces you to look at certain details of an investment that you might otherwise pass over. A more cautious approach would be to prepare *three* analyses using the same data, estimating the appreciation of an investment at low, medium and high ranges with resulting differences in the ultimate sales price. Your results would then provide a reasonable mid-range estimate along with a forecast of the investment's maximum up-side and down-side potential.

The Internal Rate of Return

What if an investment yields either a positive or negative net present value at your selected rate of return? Can the actual return be calculated with any degree of precision? Of course, such a computation is possible, and, again, you will find Table 3 useful.

By definition, the internal rate of return on an investment is the required rate of return or discount rate that results in a net present value of exactly zero. You can find the internal rate of return by using the present value factors from Table 3 and through trial and error.

For example, assume that at a 10% desired rate of return, the net present value of an investment is +$5000. If you use a higher rate of return, the net present value will be reduced and it will eventually become zero. Try applying a 14% discount rate to your cash flows and recalculate your net present value. Perhaps it is now −$1750. From this you can conclude that your internal rate of return is between 10% and 14%. Repeat the procedure using a 13% discount rate and your final result might now be +$123. For most purposes, this is close enough and you can conclude that your internal rate of return is "just over 13%". Once you become familiar with this approach, you will be able to zero in on accurate numbers without too much difficulty.

Where Do I Go From Here?

Discounted cash-flow techniques can provide an essential tool for investment analysis. I hope that this chapter has convinced you of their usefulness by introducing the basic mechanics involved in filling out a sample form. (Feel free to use it as your own worksheet.)

The following chapters will illustrate the application of these techniques. Chapter Eleven deals with home ownership. Even if you don't want to buy a home or are not interested in analysing the home you presently own, I recommend that you read this chapter carefully. This is for two reasons. First, the examples are easy to relate to and do not require any in-depth knowledge of tax concepts. Second, once you understand these examples, you can go on to apply discounted cash-flow to other investments which may be more suitable to your preferences, such as real estate (other than a home), the stock market, gold or certain life insurance policies.

CHAPTER ELEVEN

How to Evaluate an Investment in a Home or Vacation Property

Possibly the most important investment that any of us can make is to buy our own home. Historically, high inflation has created a tremendous increase in residential values in many parts of the country. Of course, events of the last two or three years have shown us that the real estate market is cyclical and if you can acquire property in a downturn phase, you can certainly get a better deal than during a boom period.

The reason that home ownership is so important is that all of us need a place to live. From a Canadian perspective, mortgage interest on your own home is not deductible—but, then again, neither are rental costs. When faced with a choice between non-deductible mortgage payments and non-deductible rent, you are still better off in the long run, at least in theory, as an owner so that you can gain from the appreciation.

In this chapter, we will examine how to use the tables and techniques introduced in previous chapters to assess home ownership as an *investment*. Of course, there are many subjective factors such as the size of your family and your lifestyle. However, it is only after you have made a comprehensive analysis that you can really answer the question intelligently: Should I own or rent?

Then, after going through a typical example of a home purchase, we will examine the subject of a *second* home or vacation cottage since there is one major difference between a principal residence and a second home. The capital gain on the eventual sale of a primary residence is tax-free; capital growth (after 1981) on a second home is subject to capital gains tax at the time of sale. You will see that this tax can reduce your investment potential significantly.

Buying a Home

Let's assume that you have always lived in a rented apartment. You are now considering buying your first home and, based on your current

Figure 1
Projected operating expenses of a proposed investment in a home

	Year of Acquisition	Estimated Annual Increase
Property taxes	$1,600	10%
Heating	1,200	12%
Utilities	1,200	12%
Maintenance	600	5%
Insurance	400	7%
Painting		$1,500 in Year 4

income level, you feel that you can afford to buy a house for $90,000. You have $22,000 in savings and you can get a $68,000 mortgage at a variable interest rate you think will average 13% over the next five years. At the end of five years, your goal is to sell the house and perhaps move into something a bit more luxurious. You figure that property values will probably appreciate 10% a year, although your selling costs will be about 3% of the final sales price.

You have estimated that the operating expenses on this property in the first year will be as described in Figure 1, and you have projected reasonable annual increases as well.

Rent Savings Due to Ownership

If you buy and occupy this house, you will no longer be paying rent. Your annual rent is $7800 and you figure that it would rise, on average, 8% a year. The concept of rent savings due to ownership is one of the most important and yet most often overlooked factors when deciding about a home as an investment. *Many home buyers fail to consider that the rent savings is a real, positive cash flow.* This is why a separate line for this item has been provided for in the analysis sheets.

Making Your Analysis

Your first step is to prepare a mortgage amortization schedule to determine the total principal and interest year-by-year. You can do this quite easily using Tables 6 and 7. As mentioned in Chapter Seven, most mortgage payments are calculated over a twenty-five-year period. Assuming a 13% rate, the monthly payment required for a $68,000 mortgage at 13% would be $749.63 (68 × 11.024). Of course, if you can arrange to obtain financing with a twenty-year amortization you could pay back your debt that much more quickly. However, the monthly payments then become 68 × 11.475 or $780.30. Unfortunately, since your previous rent was $650 a month, a twenty-five-year amortization already means an outlay of an additional $100 each month. You therefore decide to stick with a twenty-five-year period. Using Table 7, we can prepare the amortization schedule shown in Figure 2.

Figure 2
Mortgage amortization schedule: $68,000 at 13%
(first five years)

25-year amortization 68 × 11.024 = $749.63/Month
Loan balance   = $8995.56/Year

End of Year	Outstanding Principal Balance		Annual Payment	Principal	Interest
0		$68,000	$8996		
1	.994 × $68,000 =	$67,592	$8,996	$408	$8,588
2	.987 × 68,000 =	67,116	8,996	476	8,520
3	.979 × 68,000 =	66,572	8,996	544	8,452
4	.971 × 68,000 =	66,028	8,996	544	8,452
5	.961 × 68,000 =	65,348	8,996	680	8,316

Now we are almost ready to prepare a complete investment analysis form. At the time of acquisition the outlays are $22,000, representing the initial cash downpayment, plus the expenses of acquisition (including moving), which we will estimate to be $1000 in total. Since this is an immediate outlay, no matter what we assume for a required rate of return on investment, the present value is always 1.000. This is because the initial outlay is made in today's dollars.

What About the Required Rate of Return?

Normally, as I explained in the last chapter, you might require a 15% to 16% after-tax rate on any investment that involves even a modest risk factor. On the other hand, when we consider a house and take into account the fact that you need shelter for yourself and your family in any event, it might be appropriate to use a 10% required rate of return. Again, what you do is up to you, although the investment analysis form has been completed on the basis of an annual return of 10%. The present value factors are taken from Table 3.

The only other table computation that you need to make refers back to the anticipated appreciation. You will recall that this hypothetical investment is assumed to appreciate by 10% over each of the next five years. So, the 10% will be compounded annually. Selling costs are then projected to be 3% of the final sales price. The selling price at the end of year five is calculated from Table 1. The future value of $90,000 at 10% interest compounded annually after five years is $90,000 × 1.611, or $144,990. If expenses to sell are 3%, the net anticipated selling price is therefore 97% of $144,990, or $140,640. Out of those funds, the debt owing at the end of five years ($65,348) must be repaid.

Since this investment involves a principal residence, we do not have to concern ourselves with tax calculations. Take a few moments and review the investment analysis form in Figure 3. You will notice that the operating cost figures in Year 1 come from the assumptions which were made in Figure 1. The operating expenses are then estimated to increase annually as illustrated, while the rent savings is computed at $7800 in the first year, increasing by 8% a year. Interest on debt is calculated using the schedule in Figure 2. No depreciation is permitted since this is a principal residence and, because the investment is not a rental property, there is no gross revenue.

The conclusion that we can draw is that the owner of this property investment would get an after-tax rate of return slightly in excess of 10%, as well as providing shelter for the entire family.

Interpretation of the Net Present Value

What does the $27 net present value figure on the investment analysis form signify? Since the figure is positive, it means that the present value of the after-tax cash inflows (of which there is only one in the example) exceeds the present value of the after-tax outflows (of which there are five) by $27. This means that the initial outlay of $23,000 could have been $27 higher and the investment would still have yielded the required 10% after-tax rate of return. Remember the financial decision rule described in Chapter Ten—any investment with a positive net present value is acceptable while investments with (large) negative net present values should be rejected. Another way to look at this situation is that your $23,000 investment would be earning the required 10% rate of return plus an extra $27. If it earned exactly the required rate of return, the net present value would be zero. If the rate of return were less than you desired, the net present value would be negative.

Figure 3
Investment analysis form to determine the net present value of an investment in a home

	Time of Acquisition	Year 1	Year 2	Year 3	Year 4	Year 5
Gross revenue before expenses		—	—	—	—	—
Operating expenses before interest and depreciation						
Property taxes		(1,600)	(1,760)	(1,936)	(2,130)	(2,343)
Heating		(1,200)	(1,344)	(1,505)	(1,685)	(1,887)
Utilities		(1,200)	(1,344)	(1,505)	(1,685)	(1,887)
Maintenance		(600)	(630)	(662)	(695)	(730)
Insurance		(400)	(428)	(458)	(490)	(524)
Painting		—	—	—	(1,500)	—
Other		—	—	—	—	—
Total operating expenses		(5,000)	(5,506)	(6,066)	(8,185)	(7,371)
Net profit (loss) before interest and depreciation		(5,000)	(5,506)	(6,066)	(8,185)	(7,371)
Interest on debt		(8,588)	(8,520)	(8,452)	(8,452)	(8,316)
Depreciation		—	—	—	—	—
Total interest and depreciation		(8,588)	(8,520)	(8,452)	(8,452)	(8,316)
Taxable income (loss)		(13,588)	(14,026)	(14,518)	(16,637)	(15,687)

Estimated income taxes		—	—	—	—	—
Net after-tax income (loss)		(13,588)	(14,026)	(14,518)	(16,637)	(15,687)
Add: Depreciation		—	—	—	—	—
Rent savings due to ownership		7,800	8,424	9,098	9,825	10,611
Less: Capital outlays						
Cost of investment	(22,000)	—	—	—	—	—
Expenses of acquisition	(1,000)					
Add: Sales proceeds net of expenses of sale						140,640
Less: Debt repayment —principal		(408)	(476)	(544)	(544)	(680)
Tax on gain						(65,348)
After-tax cash flow	(23,000)	(6,196)	(6,078)	(5,964)	(7,356)	69,536
Required rate of return	10%					
Present value factor (Table 3)	1.000	.909	.826	.751	.683	.621
Net present value $27	(23,000)	(5,632)	(5,020)	(4,479)	(5,024)	43,182

The Internal Rate of Return

But what is the actual rate of return? All you know to this point is that it is more than 10%. To find the approximate rate of return on your $23,000 investment, you should calculate the internal rate of return. We'll continue the example with which we've been working.

As I explained in Chapter Ten, *the internal rate of return is the required rate of return or discount rate that results in a net present value of exactly zero.* You can find the internal rate of return by using the present value factors in Table 3 and through trial and error. You know that when 10% is used, the net present value comes out to $27. If you use a higher rate of return, the net present value will be reduced and, eventually, the net present value will become zero. Again, the required rate that produces a net present value of exactly zero is the internal rate of return. Let's assume that instead of a 10% discount rate, we use a rate of, say, 11%. Figure 4 shows the computation of net present value using 11% as the discount rate.

Figure 4
Calculating the internal rate of return on an investment in a home

Year	Present Value Factor at 11%	Cash Flow	Present Value of Cash Flow
0	1.000	($23,000)	($23,000)
1	.901	(6,196)	(5,582)
2	.812	(6,078)	(4,935)
3	.731	(5,964)	(4,360)
4	.659	(7,356)	(4,848)
5	.594	69,536	41,304
			($1,421)

In this case, at 11%, the net present value is already negative. Therefore the internal rate of return really is almost exactly 10%! Again, you shouldn't be concerned about being more than one or two percentage points away from the true internal rate of return, because your initial assumptions are likely to contain several errors. In other words, if your required rate of return on a particular investment was 15% and the internal rate of return comes out at 14%, this doesn't necessarily mean the investment should be rejected.

The 10% internal rate of return computed in the example which we've just looked at is an after-tax rate. Remember that to keep 10%

after paying taxes on ordinary income, you would need to earn approximately 20% before taxes. To earn 10% on an investment where capital gains tax applies, your investment would have to pay you a 13.3% return before tax. So, to get an idea of relative performance, compare the after-tax return on an investment in your home to other alternatives such as savings accounts, stock market investments, other real estate projects, or investments in gold and silver.

Summary of Home Evaluation

Any potential investment in a home can be analysed by using the approach shown in this chapter. Remember, if you buy a home, you will save the rent you are otherwise going to pay.

In the example, I assumed that the buyer has $23,000 to invest and I calculated an after-tax rate of return of 10%. What if the rate of return were, say, only 2%? Under those circumstances, our conclusions might be that the family is better off renting and investing its savings elsewhere.

Even if you already own your home, you can still make similar calculations to see whether you are getting a reasonable return on investment. Just substitute your present net equity in your home for the $23,000 original investment in the example. To determine your net equity take today's selling price and deduct your costs to sell plus all amounts owing against the property.

Go on, try it. . . .

A Summer Cottage

In the second part of this chapter, we will examine a possible investment in a summer cottage. You will see that we can prepare the same kind of analysis as we did for a principal residence, subject to two changes. First, there will be no rent savings due to ownership as there was with a principal residence. On the other hand, *you may use the line on the investment analysis form for rent savings to record the vacation savings that your family would realize as a result of vacation property ownership.* In this respect, therefore, there is a similarity between your home and a vacation property.

The major difference, however, is with respect to capital gains. In the example of a home purchase, we assumed the property could be sold for $140,640 tax-free. By way of contrast, a profit on the sale of a second residence is taxed as a capital gain. For purposes of the illustration which follows, we will assume that the effective tax cost will be 25% of the gain.

Financial Analysis of a Second Residence

Now let's take a specific example. Assume that you and your family already own a principal residence and that you would like to buy a country house. You have found a nice property in a good area which will cost you $60,000. Because it is somewhat harder to borrow against country property than it is to borrow against a city house, you would need a $25,000 downpayment and there would be about $1000 in closing costs. The $35,000 balance could be bank-financed over a five-year term at 14%. Since this is a regular bank loan instead of a mortgage loan, the interest will be compounded monthly. You estimate that expenses on the property will be as shown in Figure 5.

Figure 5
Projected operating expenses of a proposed investment in a vacation property

	Year of Acquisition	Estimated Annual Increase
Property taxes	$600	10%
Heating	800	12%
Utilities	500	12%
Maintenance	300	7%
Insurance	200	10%

By using the country house, you estimate that you will save approximately $4000 a year in vacation costs in today's dollars. You think that these costs would go up by 10% a year. However, you realize that you must immediately lay out approximately $5000 for furnishings which, for all practical purposes, will be worthless after a five-year period.

You don't really expect to sell the house in the near future, although you do expect the value of the property to increase about 10% a year. If you were to sell, you are confident that you could do so privately and avoid incurring any substantial selling costs.

What you are really interested in doing is assessing the merits of this country house as an investment over the next five years, because you recognize that your initial downpayment plus furnishings and closing costs represent an investment of $31,000. You would be satisfied with a 10% after-tax rate of return on your investment capital since a vacation home does not appear to be a very risky investment.

Before you can prepare an investment analysis form similar to the one in Figure 7, you must first prepare a loan amortization schedule. In this case, we turn to Table 5, which gives us the monthly payments required to pay off a five-year loan at 14% with interest calculated monthly. As illustrated in Figure 6, the payments are $35,000 × .0233, or $815.50 a month. Over the five-year period, your total payments will be 60 × $815.50, or $48,930. Note that for this problem, we would not use the regular mortgage amortization schedules, which call for monthly payments with interest compounded semi-annually.

Figure 6
Loan amortization schedule: $35,000 at 14% compounded monthly over five years

Payments: From Table 5
$35,000 × .0233 = $815.50

Total Payments: 60 × $815.50 = $48,930
Payment Each Year: 1/5 × $48,930 = $9,786

$48,930	Total Payments
35,000	Principal
$13,930	Interest

Allocation Between Principal and Interest

Clearly, if your total payments over five years are $48,930 and your principal amortization is $35,000, the difference of $13,930 represents interest. If we were working with a problem involving a revenue property, it would be important to have separate figures for principal and interest in order to determine taxable income and taxes payable. In this case, however, we needn't bother. This is because *none* of the expenses are tax-deductible—in spite of the fact that the capital gain at the time of sale is subject to income tax! Remember, what we are concerned with is cash flow and, in this case, the cash outflow against the loan is $9786 a year for five years. As you will see, the investment analysis form for a vacation property treats interest and principal together.

In order to assess the value of the property five years down the road, we turn to Table 1, which gives us the future value of an investment made today. Page 152 contains the factors for a compound interest rate of 10%. If our projections are correct, a vacation property worth $60,000 today would be worth $60,000 × 1.611, or $96,660 in five years. The capital gains tax is computed in Figure 8.

Figure 7
Investment analysis form to determine the net present value of an investment in a vacation property

	Time of Acquisition	Year 1	Year 2	Year 3	Year 4	Year 5
Gross revenue before expenses		—	—	—	—	—
Operating expenses before interest and depreciation						
Property taxes		(600)	(660)	(726)	(799)	(878)
Heating		(800)	(896)	(1,003)	(1,123)	(1,258)
Utilities		(500)	(560)	(627)	(702)	(787)
Maintenance		(300)	(321)	(343)	(367)	(393)
Insurance		(200)	(220)	(242)	(266)	(293)
Other						
Total operating expenses		(2,400)	(2,657)	(2,941)	(3,257)	(3,609)
Net profit (loss) before interest and depreciation		(2,400)	(2,657)	(2,941)	(3,257)	(3,609)
Interest and principal on debt		(9,786)	(9,786)	(9,786)	(9,786)	(9,786)
Depreciation		—	—	—	—	—
Total interest and depreciation		(9,786)	(9,786)	(9,786)	(9,786)	(9,786)
Income (loss)		(12,186)	(12,443)	(12,727)	(13,043)	(13,395)

Estimated income taxes		—	—	—	—	—
Net income (loss)		(12,186)	(12,443)	(12,727)	(13,043)	(13,395)
Add: Depreciation		4,000	4,400	4,840	5,324	5,856
Vacation cost savings due to ownership						
Less: Capital outlays						
Cost of investment	(25,000)					
Expenses of acquisition	(1,000)					
Furnishings	(5,000)					
Add: Sales proceeds net of expenses of sale						96,660
Less: Debt repayment				Included above		Already repaid (7,665)
Tax on gain						
After-tax cash flow	(31,000)	(8,186)	(8,043)	(7,887)	(7,719)	81,456
Required rate of return	10%					
Present value factor (Table 3)	1.000	.909	.826	.751	.683	.621
Net present value $(5,695)	(31,000)	(7,441)	(6,643)	(5,923)	(5,272)	50,584

Figure 8
Computation of capital gain and taxes payable
on the sale of a vacation property

Value of Second Home After Five Years
Assuming a 10% Annual Growth in Value
$60,000 × 1.611 = $96,660

Anticipated selling price		$96,660
Cost of property: Original cost	$60,000	
Expenses of acquisition	1,000	
Furnishings	5,000	66,000
Capital gain		$30,660
Taxable capital gain (1/2)		$15,330
Income tax at an assumed tax rate of 50%		$ 7,665

Now, examine the completed investment analysis form in Figure 7. In this case, the investment fails to provide a 10% rate of return. *The rate would be almost 10% if there were no tax on the capital gain.*

Let's try to determine what the rate of return really is. The calculations in Figure 9 use present value factors at 5% from Table 3. In this case, assuming a 5% net after-tax return on investment were acceptable, this investment would be more than adequate. Therefore, the real rate of return is somewhere *between* 5% and 10%.

Figure 9
Calculating the internal rate of return on an investment
in vacation property

Year	Present Value Factor at 5%	Cash Flow	Present Value of Cash Flow
0	1.000	($31,000)	($31,000)
1	.952	(8,186)	(7,793)
2	.907	(8,043)	(7,295)
3	.864	(7,887)	(6,814)
4	.823	(7,719)	(6,352)
5	.784	81,456	63,861
			$ 4,607

Finally, let's make calculations assuming a 7% return is acceptable. As we can see from Figure 10, in this case, the internal rate of return is almost exactly 7%.

Figure 10
Calculating the internal rate of return on an investment in vacation property

Year	Present Value Factor at 7%	Cash Flow	Present Value of Cash Flow
0	1.000	($31,000)	($31,000)
1	.935	(8,186)	(7,654)
2	.873	(8,043)	(7,021)
3	.816	(7,887)	(6,436)
4	.763	(7,719)	(5,889)
5	.713	81,456	58,078
			$78

Summary—Is a Country House Really a Good Investment?

Can we come to any general conclusions from this example? Again, note that your final results are strictly a function of the input provided in the first place. If your annual vacation cost is well in excess of $4000 (the assumption made in this investment), clearly the opportunity to save more dollars would increase your rate of return.

On the other hand, what if the property does not appreciate by 10% a year? In this instance, it appears that carrying the property over the first four years is really quite expensive, since the net outflows are about $8000 a year. Remember, however, that over the first four-year period, approximately $28,000 out of $35,000 of debt principal is being discharged. *In other words, even before considering capital growth, the investor's equity in the property is increasing.*

My major point is that this example is only hypothetical. However, try to apply the concepts to your own circumstances. If you own a house or a vacation property or are planning to buy either one, you won't be sorry that you took the time to make this kind of analysis.

CHAPTER TWELVE

Real Estate Investment for Fun and Profit

Just as basic mathematical techniques can help to evaluate the purchase of real estate for personal use, so can they be used in the assessment of investment properties acquired primarily for future growth. There are really only a few differences, primarily with respect to tax-related matters. If you concentrate on a few basic rules which will be highlighted in this chapter, you shouldn't get confused. If, from time to time, you have some tax questions, a few minutes spent with your own advisers can give you the answers you need to complete your analysis. So let's get started.

Investing in Raw Land

Suppose you have found a nice parcel of farm land priced at $100,000. The vendor will take back a $60,000 mortgage against the property with interest at 14% compounded annually for five years. He does, however, require that you make annual principal payments of $2000 at the end of each year. The only expenses which you would have to consider besides interest are property and school taxes, which are presently $500 a year but are anticipated to increase by 10% annually. There is a farmer who lives three miles away who is prepared to pay you $300 a year for the right to cut hay on the property. Because this amount is so small, you do not think it is worthwhile to negotiate an annual escalation clause.

The big attraction is that you expect to be able to sell the land for $200,000 after a five-year holding period because the neighbouring municipality is expanding rapidly. Of course, you would have a sizeable commitment of funds—$40,000 down and the obligation to pay $2000 a year in principal payments, plus interest on your financing. Also, an investment in raw land is a little tricky. What if the municipality starts to expand in the other direction? Because of the risk factor, you decide that if the investment doesn't have the potential to yield a net 18% return, you're going to pass. After all, if this opportunity isn't good enough, there are always others. Being in a 50% tax bracket, you figure that 25% of your ultimate gain would be confiscated by the government in any event.

So, how do you proceed?

The first step is to phone your tax adviser and confirm the current tax implications of such an investment. You learn that, in Canada, rental losses on raw or vacant land are generally not tax-deductible. However, to the extent that they arise as a result of mortgage interest and property taxes, they are added to the cost of the land and therefore decrease the capital gain for tax purposes in the year of sale. In other words, for the first four years in which you hold this investment, there will be neither any tax benefits nor any costs.

Your next step is to prepare a mortgage amortization schedule so that you can calculate cash flows. In this case, none of the tables in this book will help you because the financial arrangement calls for interest at 14% compounded annually, subject to annual principal payments of $2000 a year. There really is no shortcut to a longhand computation unless you have access to a computer. Fortunately, however, the calculations are not difficult, as illustrated by Figure 1.

Figure 1
Amortization of a $60,000 loan at 14% compounded annually with $2000 principal payments at the end of each year

Year	Principal Owing Beginning of Year	Interest at 14%	Principal Payment	Principal Owing End of Year
1	$60,000	$8,400	$ 2,000	$58,000
2	58,000	8,120	2,000	56,000
3	56,000	7,840	2,000	54,000
4	54,000	7,560	2,000	52,000
5	52,000	7,280	52,000	0

In this case, we will assume that the entire balance owing is paid off at the end of five years, at the same time that the property is sold.

Now we are ready to start preparing the investment analysis form on pages 82–83. Because losses arising from undeveloped land are added to the tax cost of the land itself, we cannot calculate the anticipated capital gain and related income taxes until we are partway through the analysis. We can, however, prepare the figures for the first four years and then complete the capital gains schedule (Figure 3) after.

Figure 2
Investment analysis form to determine the net present value of an investment in raw land

	Time of Acquisition	Year 1	Year 2	Year 3	Year 4	Year 5
Gross revenue before expenses		300	300	300	300	300
Operating expenses before interest and depreciation						
Property taxes		(500)	(550)	(605)	(665)	(732)
Heating						
Utilities						
Maintenance						
Insurance						
Other						
Total operating expenses		(500)	(550)	(605)	(665)	(732)
Net profit (loss) before interest and depreciation		(200)	(250)	(305)	(365)	(432)
Interest on debt		(8,400)	(8,120)	(7,840)	(7,560)	(7,280)
Depreciation		—	—	—	—	—
Total interest and depreciation		(8,400)	(8,120)	(7,840)	(7,560)	(7,280)

Taxable income (loss)		(8,600)	(8,370)	(8,145)	(7,925)	(7,712)
Estimated income taxes		—	—	—	—	—
Net after-tax income (loss)		(8,600)	(8,370)	(8,145)	(7,925)	(7,712)
Add: Depreciation						
Less: Capital outlays						
Cost of investment	(40,000)					
Expenses of acquisition						
Add: Sales proceeds net of expenses of sale						200,000
Tax on gain						(52,000)
Less: Debt repayment		(2,000)	(2,000)	(2,000)	(2,000)	(14,812)
After-tax cash flow	(40,000)	(10,600)	(10,370)	(10,145)	(9,925)	125,476
Required rate of return	18%					
Present value factor (Table 3)	1.000	.847	.718	.609	.516	.437
Net present value $(12,890)	(40,000)	(8,978)	(7,446)	(6,178)	(5,121)	54,833

Figure 3
Calculation of capital gains tax on sale of land

Anticipated sales price			$200,000
Original cost		$100,000	
Property taxes and interest in excess of rental revenue	$8,600		
	8,370		
	8,145		
	7,925		
	7,712	40,752	140,752
Capital gain			$ 59,248
Taxable capital gain (1/2)			$ 29,624
Tax payable by investor in a 50% tax bracket			$ 14,812

If you examine the investment analysis form in Figure 2, you can see that this particular investment will not come close to providing an 18% annual return based on the assumptions made. As illustrated in Figure 4, the actual internal rate of return is approximately 12%. This example illustrates one of the fundamental concepts in this book—*a dollar due sometime in the future isn't worth anything close to a dollar today*. On the surface, a property which doubles in value over five years appears to be an attractive investment, and yet when you take into account carrying costs, the return can be considerably below your expectations.

(Of course, this deal involved raw land only, on which the gross revenue was projected to be negligible. In the next example, we will take a look at a rental property where most of the carrying costs are defrayed by rental income. You will see how this changes the picture.)

Figure 4
Calculating the internal rate of return on an investment in raw land

Year	Present Value Factor at 12% (From Table 3)	Cash Flow	Present Value of Cash Flow
0	1.000	($40,000)	($40,000)
1	.893	(10,600)	(9,466)
2	.797	(10,370)	(8,265)
3	.712	(10,145)	(7,223)
4	.636	(9,925)	(6,312)
5	.567	125,476	71,145
			($121)

Before leaving this particular land investment, we might ask ourselves what the selling price would have to be at the end of five years to achieve our desired 18% rate of return. If we use a little common sense, we can figure this out. As it stands, the investment is short by $12,890 in providing the required rate of return. Since all the positive cash flow is deferred until year five, what is needed is a selling price sufficient to provide enough cash so that the present value is an additional $12,890.

The additional cash flow required would be $12,890 ÷ .437, or $29,497. In other words, if the after-tax cash flow in year five were $29,497 higher than the anticipated after-tax cash flow of $125,476, the present value of this extra $29,497 would be .437 × $29,497, or $12,890. This would make the net present value zero and would therefore result in an internal rate of return of 18%.

However, given an income tax rate of 25% on the gross capital gain, the $29,497 additional after-tax cash flow would have to represent *three-quarters* of the *additional selling price*. If the total selling price were $239,329 instead of $200,000, the capital gain would be $39,329 higher. Of that amount, the investor would retain 75%, or $29,497 and, again, the present value of this would be $12,890.

In round numbers, therefore, the property would have to command a selling price of $240,000 in order to provide the required 18% rate of return on investment over the five-year holding period.

A Condominium Investment

Our next real estate example will show a financial analysis on a condominium investment acquired for rental income and capital growth potential. Here, for the first time in this book, you will see how income tax considerations—beyond just capital gains—interact with the other financial aspects that we looked at before.

Specifically, the major tax consideration is that rental losses may be deducted from income which is otherwise taxable and the tax refund then provides a positive cash flow. Of course, if a property yields a positive rental income after all expenses, taxes payable during the ownership period reduce your cash flow.

In all cases, taxable income may be affected by depreciation (a percentage write-off which is also known as capital cost allowance). Depreciation may be used to reduce taxable income from a rental property down to zero as long as you do not exceed the maximum allowable percentage for that type of property. However, in general, capital cost allowance cannot be used to create or increase a rental loss.

In working out an example such as this one, tax depreciation must be calculated year-by-year. Since depreciation reduces the net income for tax purposes, but not the actual cash flow, the tax write-off is added back in the lower part of the investment analysis form. Now, let's now look at a specific example.

Assume that your neighbour is a real estate broker and he tells you about a "super" condominium investment that has come on the market. The present owner has just died and the estate is very anxious to sell in order to gain some liquidity.

The condominium has a purchase price of $95,000. Of this amount, $5000 can reasonably be allocated to land, $85,000 to the building itself, and $5000 for furniture and fixtures (stove, dishwasher, refrigerator, etc.). The agent tells you that you can get a brand new $70,000 mortgage at 14% with a twenty-five-year amortization. "At the rate real estate values are going," he says, "you should be able to sell the condominium for $135,000 after five years." He presents you with the analysis of projected incomes and expenses shown here as Figure 5.

Figure 5
Condominium investment—projected income and expenses

	First Year	Annual % Increase
Rental income	$12,600	8%
Property taxes	1,200	12%
Maintenance	900	10%
Insurance	400	10%
Utilities	Paid by Tenant	–

Your accountant tells you that tax depreciation (capital cost allowance) may be claimed at $2\frac{1}{2}\%$ of the cost of a building in the year of acquisition and at 5% of the undepreciated cost (cost minus accumulated depreciation, or the declining balance) every year thereafter. You are also told that the depreciation on the furniture and fixtures is 10% in the year of acquisition and 20% (declining balance) in subsequent years. However, he cautions you to be aware that capital cost allowance may not be used to create or increase a rental loss. Assume that you are in a 50% tax bracket because of your other income.

As you can see, this property would require a commitment of $25,000 of your own funds if you do not wish to obtain a second mortgage. You find the idea of owning real estate intriguing but only if you can earn a 15% rate of return on your investment capital over the five-year projected term of this investment.

Before you can complete an analysis form similar to the one in Figure 9, you will first have to prepare a mortgage amortization schedule using Tables 6 and 7 and a schedule of projected capital cost allowances. The capital cost allowances should be calculated *year-by-year*, keeping in mind the prohibition against creating rental losses. See Figures 6 and 7 for these schedules.

Figure 6
Condominium investment mortgage amortization schedule
$70,000 mortgage @ 14%—twenty-five-year amortization

Monthly Payments: From Table 7

$$\frac{\$70,000}{1,000} \times 11.739 = \$821.73$$

Annual Payments: 12 × $821.73 = $9,860.76

Year	Opening Balance	Principal Payments	Interest Payments	Balance End of Year From Table 7
1	$70,000	$350	$9,511	.995 × $70,000 = $69,650
2	69,650	420	9,441	.989 × 70,000 = 69,230
3	69,230	490	9,371	.982 × 70,000 = 68,740
4	68,740	490	9,371	.975 × 70,000 = 68,250
5	68,250	630	9,231	.966 × 70,000 = 67,620

Figure 7
Condominium investment capital cost allowance schedule

	Building	Furniture & Fixtures
Capital Cost Allowance (CCA)		
—first year	2¹⁄₂%	10%
—thereafter	5%	20%
Cost	$85,000	$5,000
Year 1 (maximum)	589	–
	84,411	5,000
Year 2 (maximum)	1,393	–
	83,018	5,000
Year 3 (maximum)	2,248	–
	80,770	5,000
Year 4 (maximum)	3,085	–
	$77,685	$5,000

Notes:
1. No capital cost allowance is claimed on the furniture and fixtures since the capital cost allowance on the building is enough to reduce the net rental income to zero in years one through four.
2. No capital cost allowance is claimed in year five since it is anticipated that a sale will take place at the end of that year. Any depreciation taken would automatically be recaptured in any event.

You will not be able to finalize your figures for year five until you calculate the tax on your projected capital gain (see Figure 8). In this case, there is not only a capital gain on sale but "recaptured depreciation" as well. Recaptured depreciation comes about in the year of sale if capital cost allowance has been claimed but the property has *not* really depreciated. In this case, since the selling price is well in excess of the original cost, we can assume that all the depreciation will be recaptured. But keep in mind that the difference between the selling price of $135,000 and the original cost of $95,000 will be taxed as a capital gain, half your normal rate.

Figure 8
Condominium investment calculation of taxes on projected gain

		Tax Payable
Anticipated selling price	$135,000	
Cost	95,000	
Capital gain	$40,000	
Taxable capital gain (1/2)	$20,000	
Tax at 50% assumed tax rate		$10,000
Recaptured depreciation: $85,000–$77,685	$ 7,315	
Tax at 50% assumed tax rate		3,658
		$13,658

Why Claim Depreciation?

Why bother claiming depreciation on a property if there will be a recapture in the year of sale? The answer, of course, ties into the fact that a dollar today is worth more than a dollar in the future. *In other words, the tax savings from depreciation in years one through four are worth more than the offsetting tax on recapture in year five.* This is, of course, provided that your tax bracket doesn't start out low and then increase substantially in the year of sale. In this case, we have assumed that you would be in a 50% bracket throughout the period.

If you examine the depreciation schedule in this case study (Figure 7) carefully, you will see that the net rental income after operating expenses (including interest) is never large enough to permit a full capital cost allowance claim. Again, this is because of the general rule that depreciation cannot be used to create a rental loss.

For Canadian tax purposes, the one major exception to this rule pertains to construction projects built under the multiple unit residential building (MURB) program. This program expired for construction starts initiated after 1981. If, however, you have occasion to examine a property which qualifies as a MURB, you may project the full benefits from depreciation and a tax saving from the taxable loss. In this particular case, the return on investment would be larger if the property qualified as a MURB. This is because the tax saving from a taxable loss would increase the after-tax cash flow year-by-year, even though there would be a larger recaptured depreciation at the end.

The results of the investment analysis form in Figure 9 indicate clearly that the projected return on investment is well in excess of the required rate of 15%. In fact, the internal rate of return is really about 20%. Of course, bear in mind that all the calculations are based on projections only.

Summary

Financial analysis procedures are essential if you want to make a proper evaluation of the desirability of any particular investment opportunity. Most mistakes are made by investors who make commitments without sufficient careful thought and planning.

An investment analysis also represents a *plan* for the future—a sort of road map to get you to your destination of making profits. It can tell you whether the destination is worth reaching (if the net present value is greater than zero at your selected required after-tax rate of return). If you decide that an investment looks good and you proceed with the project, the year-by-year figures in the analysis will serve as a guide to let you know whether your plan is being realized as scheduled. If you find that you are falling behind because cash out-flows are greater than planned, or inflows are smaller, you can try to improve your situation. On the other hand, if you have no plan or no guideline analysis, you have no standard against which to measure your investment performance. You won't know when corrective action becomes necessary and you won't know how well you could or should have done with your investment.

Figure 9
Investment analysis form to determine the net present value of an investment in a condominium

	Time of Acquisition	Year 1	Year 2	Year 3	Year 4	Year 5
Gross revenue before expenses		12,600	13,608	14,697	15,872	17,142
Operating expenses before interest and depreciation						
Property taxes		(1,200)	(1,344)	(1,505)	(1,686)	(1,888)
Heating		—	—	—	—	—
Utilities		—	—	—	—	—
Maintenance		(900)	(990)	(1,089)	(1,198)	(1,318)
Insurance		(400)	(440)	(484)	(532)	(586)
Other						
Total operating expenses		(2,500)	(2,774)	(3,078)	(3,416)	(3,792)
Net profit (loss) before interest and depreciation		(10,100)	(10,834)	(11,619)	(12,456)	(13,350)
Interest on debt		(9,511)	(9,441)	(9,371)	(9,371)	(9,231)
Depreciation		(589)	(1,393)	(2,248)	(3,085)	—
Total interest and depreciation		(10,100)	(10,834)	(11,619)	(12,456)	(9,231)

Taxable income (loss)		—	—	—	—	4,119)
Estimated income taxes		—	—	—	—	(2,060)
Net after-tax income (loss)		—	—	—	—	2,059
Add: Depreciation		589	1,393	2,248	3,085	—
Less: Capital outlays Cost of investment	(25,000)					
Expenses of acquisition						
Add: Sales proceeds net of expenses of sale						135,000
						(67,620)
Less: Debt repayment		(350)	(420)	(490)	(490)	(630)
Tax on gain and recapture						(13,658)
After-tax cash flow	(25,000)	239	973	1,758	2,595	55,151
Required rate of return	15%					
Present value factor (Table 3)	1.000	.870	.756	.658	.572	.497
Net present value $5,993	(25,000)	208	735	1,156	1,484	27,410

CHAPTER THIRTEEN

Investing in the Stock Market

As much as I want to help you make money in the stock market, you will probably understand why I cannot recommend any particular stock to you. By the time you read this, the investment climate can be considerably different from the way it was at the time this was written.

What I can do, however, is provide you with some practical guidelines to help you decide whether the purchase of a particular stock is consistent with your investment objectives. Everybody wants to double their money as quickly as possible. But, as you have already seen, the longer it takes for a profit to be made, the less valuable this profit is in today's dollars. Again, turn to Table 3 (see page 175). If you require a 20% rate of return on invested capital to make an investment palatable, a profit of $1 payable four years from now is only worth about 48¢ in today's money.

In this chapter, we will use an investment analysis form that is somewhat different from the one designed for use in real estate. The stock market form takes into account dividends and carrying charges instead of rental income and operating expenses. You will note, if you flip through this chapter quickly, that I have prepared all my sample investment analyses over three-year periods. Technically, you can buy a stock and hold it forever but, from a practical standpoint, I don't think it's too likely that you would contemplate holding any particular stock for a much longer term than three years.

If you have any interest in investment (and you must if you are reading this book) you don't need me to tell you that the stock market goes up and down. It doesn't seem possible that we will ever find a way to eliminate the business cycle and there is no point in buying a stock, watching it increase in value and then holding on to it long enough for your gain to be completely wiped out in the next downturn.

So, again, all I can do here is help you analyse a potential investment mathematically. If reasonable assumptions are made, can a particular investment help you attain your goals and objectives?

Receipt of Dividends

Before we can make any kind of analysis, we must understand the Canadian tax rules pertaining to dividends, carrying charges and capital gains. The rules here are somewhat different than the tax provisions in other countries.

Many stocks pay dividends to their shareholders and these dividends can provide a flow of income to be used on an after-tax basis either for personal living expenses or for additional investment capital.

The receipt of cash dividends from Canadian securities is treated quite differently for tax purposes than the receipt of interest. A dividend received by an individual is included in taxable income, subject to a calculation which "grosses up" the amount received, but also provides an offsetting dividend tax credit to reduce the tax payable. The "gross-up" is one-half of the cash dividend received.

Thus, for example, if you buy a stock that pays you a $100 dividend, you will include $150 in your income. Then, in arriving at your taxes payable, you will reduce your total tax by the amount of the gross-up. In other words, although your income is inflated by $50 for each $100 of dividends received, your total tax is reduced by the same $50. (Actually, the federal dividend tax credit is approximately three-quarters of the gross-up while a reduction in provincial income taxes payable provides the remaining credit for the balance.)

The dividend tax credit is provided for two reasons, one being that dividends are a distribution out of after-tax corporate earnings. If the system taxed the same dollar as income to both the corporation which earned it and the individual who ultimately received it, this would create double taxation. Second, the dividend tax credit provides a major incentive for Canadians to invest in their own corporations.

Figure 1 illustrates that taxpayers in all marginal brackets will retain more after tax from receipts of dividends than they would from equivalent receipts of interest.

Essentially, you must earn one-and-a-half times as much interest as dividends to wind up with the same after-tax dollars in your hands. This example shows you something that is, as already mentioned, uniquely Canadian. By comparison, in the United States, both interest and dividends are simply taxed in your top marginal bracket.

Figure 1
Comparative after-tax retention on Canadian dividends vs. interest

Individual's marginal tax bracket	40%	45%	50%
Alternative 1—$100 Canadian dividends			
Cash dividend	$100	$100	$100
1/2 gross-up	50	50	50
Taxable income	$150	$150	$150
Tax in marginal bracket	$ 60	$ 67	$ 75
Dividend tax credit (combined federal and provincial)	50	50	50
Net tax	$ 10	$ 17	$ 25
Net retention (cash dividend minus tax)	$ 90	$ 83	$ 75
Alternative 2—$100 Canadian interest			
Interest	$100	$100	$100
Tax in marginal bracket	40	45	50
Net retention	$ 60	$ 55	$ 50
Ratio of after-tax retention Dividends : Interest	3 : 2	3 : 2	3 : 2

From this example, you should now understand a very important point: for anyone with taxable income, a 10% dividend is equivalent to a 15% (before tax) interest yield, while a 6% dividend is equivalent to interest at 9%. In other words, a dividend yield on a Canadian security is certainly much more attractive than first meets the eye. I must stress, however, that this mathematical relationship is only valid where an individual is taxable in the first place. A dividend yield may not be that attractive to a senior citizen who has a few thousand dollars of savings and needs some income over and above government pensions.

Borrowing for Stock Market Investments

If you borrow to invest in the shares of Canadian public companies, you are always permitted to deduct your interest expense and other carrying charges, such as safekeeping fees, against other income. First you must apply as much of these expenses as you can to offset your grossed-up dividends. Even if the stocks which you buy do not presently bear dividends, your interest and other expenses are nevertheless tax-deductible. This is an extremely important factor in evaluating cash flows.

Perhaps the most important consideration of all, however, is the fact that carrying charges do not affect the availability of a dividend tax credit. It is therefore possible in Canada to obtain a tremendous advantage from the fact that *a dividend tax credit can offset carrying charges which are significantly higher than the actual dividends received.* Figure 2 shows the receipt of a cash dividend of $10,000 where an investor has incurred carrying charges on these and other investments of $15,000.

Figure 2
Effect of dividend tax credit on carrying charges

Assumptions:
• Cash dividend	$ 10,000
• Carrying charges	$ 15,000
Cash dividend	$ 10,000
Gross-up	5,000
Grossed-up dividend	15,000
Less: Carrying charges	(15,000)
Effect on taxable income	Nil
Excess of carrying charges over cash dividend	$ 5,000
Less: Tax savings from dividend tax credit	(5,000)
Negative cash flow	Nil

Because the dividend must be grossed-up by one-half, it can fully offset the amount of the carrying charges incurred in arriving at the individual's income. However, although none of the dividend is in fact taxable, the investor is still entitled to claim the dividend tax credit against the taxes on his other income. In terms of cash flow, the individual in this example will find that his tax savings make up for the fact that he has paid $5000 more in carrying charges than he has received in dividends.

Even if a stock does not pay a dividend, you should note that the carrying costs are always reduced substantially by tax savings. For example, an individual in a 50% bracket who borrows money at 14% is only incurring a cost of 7% after tax.

Capital Gains

Capital gains are not generally taxed until property is sold. At that time, one-half the gain is included in income.

Simple arithmetic can show you that an individual who borrows money at 14% for a stock market investment can come out ahead of the

Figure 3
It pays to borrow at 14% interest to buy Canadian securities— as long as the investment appreciates by at least 10% a year

Assumed capital growth before taxes	10.00%
Less: Assumed tax on capital gain	
One-half of gain taxed in 50% tax bracket	
(5.00% × 50%)	2.50
Net capital growth after taxes	7.50%
Carrying cost of investment	14.00%
Less: Tax saving in 50% tax bracket from interest write-off	7.00
Net cost to borrow	7.00%

game even if the investment appreciates in value by only 10% per annum. This is illustrated in Figure 3.

Let's be more realistic, though, and assess an example which calculates the *actual* return on invested capital if a stock is purchased for a medium-term holding period, such as three years. To do this, we may use an investment analysis form such as the one on page 97.

Assume that you have a little over $100,000 to invest and you buy 10,000 shares of a public company at $10 each, incurring, at the same time, $2000 in brokerage costs. The stock which you buy is expected to bear a 6% annual dividend. While this yield is not in itself particularly attractive, you further believe that the stock can be sold at the end of three years at $15 a share. This would represent a 50% increase in value over that three-year period. You are examining this potential investment and would be inclined to pursue it if you can earn a 20% net after-tax return on invested capital each year. Is this, in fact, feasible?

Now, take a few moments and examine the completed investment analysis form in Figure 4.

At the time of acquisition, the cash outlay is $102,000 including expenses of acquisition. Then, each year for a three-year period, a $6000 cash dividend is anticipated. For tax purposes, this dividend is grossed-up to $9000, resulting in taxes payable of $4500 before the dividend tax credit. The dividend tax credit is approximately equal to the gross-up and it results in a cash-flow saving. On the other hand, the dividend gross-up itself does not represent an inflow of funds. Thus, when the smoke clears, this investment produces a net after-tax cash flow of $4500 in the first two years for an investor in a 50% tax bracket. In the third year, we assume net proceeds of sale of $148,000 ($150,000

Figure 4
Investment analysis form to evaluate the net present value of a stock market investment

	Time of Acquisition	Year 1	Year 2	Year 3
Cash dividend		6,000	6,000	6,000
Gross-up		3,000	3,000	3,000
Taxable dividend		9,000	9,000	9,000
Less: Investment carrying charges				
—interest expense				
—other				
Taxable income (loss)		9,000	9,000	9,000
Estimated income taxes				
—(payable)		(4,500)	(4,500)	(4,500)
—recovered				
Net after-tax income (loss)		4,500	4,500	4,500
Less: Dividend gross-up		(3,000)	(3,000)	(3,000)
Add: Tax savings from dividend tax credit (equal to gross-up)		3,000	3,000	3,000
Less: Capital outlays				
—cash invested	(100,000)			
—expenses of acquisition	(2,000)			
Add: Proceeds from sale				150,000
Less: Expenses to sell				(2,000)
Debt repayment				
Tax on gain				(11,500)
After-tax cash flow	(102,000)	4,500	4,500	141,000
Required rate of return	20%			
Present value factor (Table 3)	1.000	.833	.694	.579
Net present value $(13,490)	(102,000)	3,748	3,123	81,639

minus $2000 in selling expenses). The capital gain and tax are computed in Figure 5.

Returning to the investment analysis form, we see that in year three the net after-tax cash flow is $141,000. Assuming that a rate of return of 20% is, however, required, the after-tax cash flow in year three is only worth roughly 58¢ on the dollar in today's money. You can see that the investment falls well short of the 20% target. In fact, the internal rate of return is actually around 14%, as illustrated in Figure 6.

Figure 5
Calculation of capital gain and taxes
on the disposition of a stock market investment

Net selling price	$148,000
Cost of investment including expenses of acquisition	102,000
Capital gain	$ 46,000
Taxable capital gain	$ 23,000
Tax payable by investor in 50% bracket	$ 11,500

Figure 6
Calculating the internal rate of return
on a stock market investment

Year	After-Tax Cash Flow	Present Value Factor at 14%	Present Value of Cash Flow
0	$(102,000)	1.000	$(102,000)
1	4,500	.877	3,946
2	4,500	.769	3,461
3	141,000	.675	95,175
			$ 582

Now let's make one fundamental change. Instead of investing $102,000, let's assume that you choose to invest $52,000 in cash and borrow $50,000 at 14% over a three-year period with no principal payments required (as long as the stock doesn't decline substantially in value). The investment analysis form in Figure 7 shows that realizing your required 20% rate of return is now possible. There are two reasons why this is true. First, the investment carrying charges of $7000 a year are tax-deductible, and second, you have a smaller initial cash outflow to recoup. In other words, if the investment performs in accordance with your objectives, you will benefit substantially from the use of *leverage*. The $50,000 pre-tax capital gain, instead of representing a 50% return on invested capital, now becomes a 100% return! Of course, it is deferred three years and, as such, the value of the profit is again only 58¢ on the dollar in today's money.

Preparing an analysis such as the one on page 99 is extremely important because it will help you decide whether it is to your advantage

Figure 7
Investment analysis form to evaluate the net present value of a stock market investment

	Time of Acquisition	Year 1	Year 2	Year 3
Cash dividend		6,000	6,000	6,000
Gross-up		3,000	3,000	3,000
Taxable dividend		9,000	9,000	9,000
Less: Investment carrying charges				
—interest expense		(7,000)	(7,000)	(7,000)
—other				
Taxable income (loss)		2,000	2,000	2,000
Estimated income taxes				
—(payable)		(1,000)	(1,000)	(1,000)
—recovered				
Net after-tax income (loss)		1,000	1,000	1,000
Less: Dividend gross-up		(3,000)	(3,000)	(3,000)
Add: Tax savings from dividend tax credit (equal to gross-up)		3,000	3,000	3,000
Less: Capital outlays				
—cash invested	(50,000)			
—expenses of acquisition	(2,000)			
Add: Proceeds from sale				150,000
Less: Expenses to sell				(2,000)
Debt repayment				(50,000)
Tax on gain				(11,500)
After-tax cash flow	(52,000)	1,000	1,000	87,500
Required rate of return	20%			
Present value factor (Table 3)	1.000	.833	.694	.579
Net present value $190	(52,000)	833	694	50,663

to borrow for investment purposes. In this case, although you are laying out $7000 in interest charges while receiving only $6000 in cash dividends, you are *ahead* by $1000 a year. This is, of course, hard to believe but it is nevertheless true. The $1000 interest outlay in excess of the dividend received is more than offset by tax savings from the dividend tax credit. (Of course, if your investment has been heavily financed by debt and it *declines* in value you've got problems.)

Stock Dividends

There is one further investment alternative and set of tax rules which is extremely important for you to understand before you can make any intelligent investment decisions. Specifically, there are many Canadian public companies which follow the procedure of paying *stock dividends* instead of cash dividends. A stock dividend is simply a payment in the form of additional shares. Let's modify the facts in the previous example a little bit. We'll assume that the original investment is, again, 10,000 shares at $10. Then, let's assume that the company pays a *6% stock dividend* each year for three years. As illustrated in the first half of Figure 8, you would then acquire an additional 1910 shares over that three-year period.

For Canadian tax purposes, a stock dividend paid by a public company does not trigger any immediate tax consequences, since it isn't treated as an ordinary dividend. Instead, the shares received have a zero tax cost and this will result in larger capital gains at the time the shares are sold. In this case, if 11,910 shares are sold at $15 each at the end of three years, the total proceeds becomes $178,650. The capital gain is

Figure 8
Calculation of capital gain and taxes on the disposition of a share investment on which stock dividends have been received

Original investment 10,000 shares @ $10 =	$100,000
Expenses of acquisition	$ 2,000
Stock dividends	
Year 1 6% × 10,000 shares = 600 shares	
Year 2 6% × 10,600 shares = 636 shares	
Year 3 6% × 11,236 shares = 674 shares	
Total shares—end of three years—11,910	
Selling price 11,910 × $15 =	$178,650
Less: Expenses of disposition	2,000
	176,650
Less: Cost of investment including expenses of acquisition	102,000
Capital gain	$ 74,650
Taxable capital gain (one-half)	$ 37,325
Tax payable (50%)	$ 18,663

Figure 9
Investment analysis form to evaluate the net present value of a stock market investment

	Time of Acquisition	Year 1	Year 2	Year 3
Cash dividend	—	—	—	—
Gross-up	—	—	—	—
Taxable dividend	—	—	—	—
Less: Investment carrying charges				
—interest expense		(7,000)	(7,000)	(7,000)
—other				
Taxable income (loss)		(7,000)	(7,000)	(7,000)
Estimated income taxes				
—(payable)				
—recovered		3,500	3,500	3,500
Net after-tax income (loss)		(3,500)	(3,500)	(3,500)
Less: Dividend gross-up				
Add: Tax saving from dividend tax credit (equal to gross-up)				
Less: Capital outlays				
—cash invested	(50,000)			
—expenses of acquisition	(2,000)			
Add: Proceeds from sale				178,650
Less: Expenses to sell				(2,000)
Debt repayment				(50,000)
Tax on gain				(18,663)
After-tax cash flow	(52,000)	(3,500)	(3,500)	104,487
Required rate of return	20%			
Present value factor (Table 3)	1.000	.833	.694	.579
Net present value $3,154	(52,000)	(2,915)	(2,429)	60,498

$74,650 and the tax payable is $18,663. The major advantage of receiving stock dividends is that instead of earning income taxable on an ongoing basis, the tax is deferred until the stock is sold.

If we look at the investment analysis form above, we can see that with a downpayment of $50,000 (plus a cash outlay to cover expenses of acquisition) the investment will yield a return better than 20%. Again, this is because the investment carrying charges are deductible on an ongoing basis while the stock dividend represents value on which the taxes are deferred.

Borrowing Money for Stock Market Investments

Borrowing money to invest in the stock market appears to make a lot of sense as long as your investments move in the right direction. The cost to borrow is basically only half for someone in a 50% tax bracket. In addition, if the stock which you choose to buy bears dividends, the dividend yield can defray a substantially larger percentage of interest expense. In other words, a 6% dividend yield will completely offset a 9% interest cost. If your actual interest cost is, say, 13%, you are then only out of pocket 4% before tax and 2% after (see Figure 10). The cost to carry your investments can therefore be negligible.

Figure 10
Borrowing at 13% to buy a stock paying a 6% dividend yield

Dividend yield	6.0%	
Less: Tax cost after gross-up and credit to investor in 50% tax bracket	1.5%	4.5%
Interest expense	13.0%	
Less: Tax savings from write-off	6.5%	(6.5)%
Net carrying cost of investment		(2.0)%

The Indexed Security Investment Plan (ISIP)

Before leaving the stock market, we should spend a few minutes on the subject of the Indexed Security Investment Plan (ISIP), which was unveiled by Finance Minister Lalonde as part of his April 19, 1983 federal Budget.

The ISIP program took effect on October 1, 1983. Many investment advisers feel that, over time, it will become the most effective way for many individuals to invest in publicly-traded Canadian common stocks.

The basic mechanics are straightforward. Say an investor buys $1000 of securities at the beginning of the year and these securities increase in value to $1100 by year end. If the securities were purchased in an ISIP and inflation were 6% over the year, the cost of these securities would be adjusted upwards to $1060 and the capital gain recognized for tax purposes would become $40 instead of the actual gain of $100.

Under the ISIP proposals, such an investor will be permitted to spread the tax on his net gain over several years. Even if he doesn't sell his investment, at the end of the first year he would have to take into account one-quarter of his real inflation-adjusted capital gain, or $10. Of course, only one-half of the $10 would be a taxable capital gain. The $30 balance of the real capital gain would then be deferred for tax purposes to later years. As long as the ISIP program is maintained, individuals would generally be required to report only one-quarter of their cumulative inflation-adjusted gains each year.

One-half of any plan administration fees will serve to reduce gains or increase losses. In the same way as the inflation adjustment in an ISIP would reduce a capital gain, it will increase the amount of a capital loss. There will be, however, no restriction on the amount of ISIP losses that can be deducted against income from other sources. Although a detailed discussion of the ISIP tax rules is beyond the scope of this book, it is worthwhile to examine how an investment return on such a program can be calculated.

To illustrate how an ISIP works, let's deal with a comparative illustration using the following assumptions:

1. You buy a stock for $10,000 at the start of year one

Figure 11
Stock investment using an indexed security investment plan

Year		0	1	2	3	4	5
$10,000 value end of year	(A)		$11,000	$12,100	$13,310	$14,641	$16,105
Indexed cost			10,600	11,342	12,223	13,245	14,410
Real gain			400	758	1,087	1,396	1,695
Reportable gain			100	189	272	349	1,695
Deferred gain	(B)		300	569	815	1,047	—
New indexed cost	(A – B)		10,700	11,531	12,495	13,594	—
Initial outlay		$(10,000)					
Taxes @ 25% on reportable gain			(25)	(47)	(68)	(87)	(424)
Proceeds of sale							16,105
Net cash inflow (outflow)		(10,000)	(25)	(47)	(68)	(87)	15,681
Required rate of return—7% P.V. factor		1.000	.935	.873	.816	.763	.713
Net present value $996		(10,000)	(23)	(41)	(55)	(66)	11,181

2. The stock value increases 10% yearly for five years
3. Inflation is 6% each year
4. You sell at the end of five years
5. You are in a 50% tax bracket
6. Your required rate of return on invested capital is 7% net after-tax
7. There are no administration fees

Over a five-year term, the return on your ISIP investment would be more than 7%, if your assumptions prove true. The net present value in Figure 11 is +$996.

By way of contrast, if we examine the normal capital gains provisions of an investment outside an ISIP (see Figure 12), the net present value, assuming a 7% required return, is only +$394. The higher net present value calculated in Figure 11 illustrates that the ISIP can be quite attractive.

However, the results could be quite different if the person administering the ISIP charges, say, $200 a year as an administration and reporting fee. Even after considering the fact that a portion of the fee would reduce taxes payable, the advantage of the ISIP can easily be dissipated. Whether in real life this will occur, only time will tell.

Figure 12
Stock investment outside an indexed security investment plan

Year	0	1	2	3	4	5
Initial outlay	$(10,000)					
Value end of year 5						$16,105
Reportable gain						6,105
Taxes @ 25% on reportable gain	_____					(1,526)
Net cash inflow (outflow)	(10,000)					14,579
Required rate of return—7% P.V. factor	1.000					.713
Net present value $394	(10,000)					10,394

CHAPTER FOURTEEN

Investing in Gold

Over the centuries, gold has been the universal medium of international financial exchange. This alone necessitates examining it as an investment. History has witnessed the rise and fall of many powerful civilizations. When all else of value lay in rubble, gold alone remained. To the present day, many people have credited their survival to having held substantial investments in gold. Gold is portable and can be bartered for food or, in fact, for one's life. Even in North America, the uncertain economic climate prompts most investment counsellors to suggest that every individual keep at least some investment capital in gold as a contingency.

At present it is very difficult to predict where the price of gold is headed. In fact, the price may not fluctuate to any great extent until there is some kind of panic internationally. For example, a large-scale war would almost certainly send the price of gold spiralling upwards. Also, if government deficits continue to increase and vast quantities of paper money are printed in order to pay outstanding bills, the potential hyperinflation could create a tremendous demand for this metal.

In this book, we will consider a mathematical approach towards gold as an investment. In one major respect, this precious metal differs from most real estate investments or from investing in the stock market. Specifically, the ownership of gold does not provide any income yield *during* the period in which it is held. It is only upon sale that a profit or loss is realized. If you buy gold today at a certain price and hold it for several years, remember the most important lesson which you have learned in this book—a profit due several years from now is worth only a fraction in today's money.

The Tax Consequences of Transactions in Gold

It is impossible to evaluate gold as an investment without understanding the tax implications, which are somewhat particular to Canada. Generally, profits from the disposition of gold, whether it is held in physical form (bullion or coins) or in certificates are subject to capital gains treatment. This is as a result of administrative discretion on the part of the Revenue authorities. Since gold has no capacity to pay interest or dividends and is held strictly as a speculation, whether short or long-term, any gain should theoretically be fully taxable. However, it has historically been the policy of Revenue Canada to accept capital gains treatment on these transactions.

You must nevertheless realize that *if you wish to benefit from capital gains treatment on your gold transactions, interest on money borrowed to make your investments is not deductible*. If you decide, on the other hand, to deduct interest expense, you must be prepared to pay taxes on your *full* profits.

An Approach to Investing in Gold

Most of the remainder of this chapter will be devoted to three specific case studies involving a hypothetical investment in gold. To start with, there are two broad possibilities: either you buy gold using your own money only, or the acquisition is financed, at least in part, with borrowed funds. If borrowed funds are used, there is another choice to be made. Either you claim an interest expense deduction for tax purposes on an ongoing basis, or you treat your interest expense as an adjustment to the tax cost of your investment. We will see, in reviewing these case studies, that the return on investment varies by at least several percentage points depending on whether:

- An investment in gold is made without borrowing money,
- Borrowed money is used and the interest is claimed as a tax deduction, or
- Borrowed money is used with the interest treated as part of the cost of the investment.

Background to a Hypothetical Case

Let's assume that you would like to invest $100,000 in the purchase of gold. If gold is presently trading at $500 an ounce, this means that you can afford to buy 200 ounces. Assume that you are looking at a medium-term holding period of, say, three years. Your criterion for successful investment performance is that you get a 15% net after-tax rate of return on invested capital.

Figure 1
Summary of a case study involving the purchase of gold

Buy Gold for $100,000
Assumption: Required rate of return is 15% for next three years
Net selling price required after three years (from Table 1)
$100,000 × 1.521 = $152,100

However, profit on sale is subject to tax.
If capital gain, tax is 25%
Therefore 75% of total profit = $52,100
Therefore, profit needed to return 15% net
$52,100 ÷ .75 = $69,466
Therefore, total selling price needed for a 15% net return
over three years
is $169,466 (approximately $170,000)

Even before we proceed with the investment analysis forms, we can calculate the selling price needed in order to attain a 15% return on investment over a three-year period. If we turn to Table 1, which deals with the compound value of $1 invested at various interest rates, and we look at page 155, we can see that to realize a 15% return annually over three years, a $100,000 investment must then be worth $100,000 × 1.521 or $152,100. In other words, $100,000 invested today at 15% would total $152,100 at the end of three years. Thus, on the surface, it would appear that if the price of gold rises from $500 to $760.50 an ounce, your 200-ounce investment will have met your objective of a 15% net increase in value.

However, what about income taxes? In order to achieve a 15% net after-tax rate of return, the growth of $52,100 must be an *after-tax* figure. If we assume that you are in a 50% tax bracket, the effective tax on a capital gain is 25%. Therefore to realize a 15% net after-tax growth, 75% of your total profit must equal $52,100. This would allow a 25% factor to cover your income tax liability. Thus, the *real* profit needed to return 15% *net* over three years is: $52,100 divided by .75, or $69,466. In other words, unless you could sell your gold at the end of three years for $169,466, your rate of return on invested capital would not be 15%. To round the numbers, you really need a selling price (based on 200 ounces) of $850 an ounce.

Now let's stop to think for a moment. In order to realize a 15% annual rate of return, the price of an ounce of gold (in this example) would have to increase by $350 over a three-year period. If this does not happen, even a relatively modest rate of return becomes inaccessible!

In Figure 3, you will see the first of three investment analysis forms. This one corresponds to the scenario with which we have just dealt. Specifically, it assumes a purchase of 200 ounces of gold at $500 per ounce, funded without borrowed money. Then, at the end of three years, a sale is projected for $170,000. The taxes on the $70,000 profit are $17,500 as shown in Figure 2.

Figure 2
Calculation of tax on capital gain on sale of gold

Selling price of gold	$170,000
Cost	100,000
Capital gain	$ 70,000
Taxable capital gain (1/2)	$ 35,000
Tax at 50%	$ 17,500

Figure 3
Investment analysis form to evaluate the net present value of an investment in gold

		Time of Acquisition	Year 1	Year 2	Year 3
Purchase price 200 oz. × $500	Total	$100,000			
Cash outlay		100,000			
Portion financed		—			
		$100,000			
Interest expense on financing					
Less: Income tax saving from deduction of interest (optional)					
Net after-tax loss					
Less:					
Capital outlay —cash invested		(100,000)			
—expenses of acquisition					
—interest capitalized					
Add: Proceeds from sale net of expenses to sell					170,000
Less: Debt repayment					—
Tax on profit					(17,500)
After-tax cash flow		(100,000)	—	—	152,500
Required rate of return		15%			
Present value factor (Table 3)		1.000	.870	.756	.658
Net present value $345		(100,000)	—	—	100,345

The net return at the end of three years is $152,500 and, using Table 3, the present value factor at 15% is .658 × $152,500, or $100,345. Thus, the net present value is $345, which means that the investment does provide a return slightly greater than 15%, if gold is worth $850 an ounce after three years.

Let's now look at a second alternative. Again, we will assume that you can buy 200 ounces of gold at $500, for a total investment of $100,000. This time, however, we will see what happens if you put down $50,000 of your own money and borrow the rest at 14% interest. Assume that you can arrange with your lending institution to pay interest only against the loan because the lending institution will hold your gold as collateral. In real life, this would not be an uncommon arrangement. The annual interest on your $50,000 debt at 14% is $7000.

Say that in this case you would like to claim the interest expense as a tax write-off. In exchange, you are prepared to pay full income taxes at regular tax rates on any gain from eventual sale. Now take a look at the investment analysis form shown as Figure 4.

Figure 4
Investment analysis form to evaluate the net present value of an investment in gold

		Time of Acquisition	Year 1	Year 2	Year 3
Purchase price 200 oz. × $500	Total	$100,000			
Cash outlay		50,000			
Portion financed		50,000			
		$100,000			
Interest expense on financing			(7,000)	(7,000)	(7,000)
Less: Income tax saving from deduction of interest (optional)			3,500	3,500	3,500
Net after-tax loss			(3,500)	(3,500)	(3,500)
Less:					
Capital outlay —cash invested		(50,000)			
—expenses of acquisition					
—interest capitalized					
Add: Proceeds from sale net of expenses to sell					170,000
Less: Debt repayment					(50,000)
Tax on profit					(35,000)
After-tax cash flow		(50,000)	(3,500)	(3,500)	81,500
Required rate of return		15%			
Present value factor (Table 3)		1.000	.870	.756	.658
Net present value $(2,064)		(50,000)	(3,045)	(2,646)	53,627

In our second investment analysis there is an initial cash outlay of $50,000. In each of the next two years, the only outlay is the interest expense, which after considering tax savings, produces a negative cash flow of $3500 a year. Of course, the present value of this outflow is only $5691 over the two-year period. Then, at the end of year three, we again assume that your investment can be sold for $170,000 and that your debt of $50,000 would then be repaid. However, as Figure 5 illustrates, your *full profit* of $70,000 on sale would be taxable and the government's share is $35,000.

Figure 5
Calculation of tax on profit from sale of gold
(no capital gains treatment)

Selling price of gold	$170,000
Cost	100,000
Profit from sale	$ 70,000
Tax at 50%	$ 35,000

The after-tax cash flow of year three ($81,500) has a present value of only $53,627, given a 15% discount factor. In the end, we see that the investment does *not* generate your required rate of return of 15%. In fact, the actual rate of return works out to be just over 13% (as shown in Figure 6).

Figure 6
Calculating the internal rate of return on an investment in gold

Year	Cash Flow	Present Value Factor at 13%	Present Value of Cash Flow
0	$(50,000)	1.000	$(50,000)
1	(3,500)	.885	(3,098)
2	(3,500)	.783	(2,740)
3	81,500	.693	56,479
			$ 641

In this case, by using borrowed money and deducting the interest, you would be sacrificing several percentage points in your potential return. This is because *the tax savings from the interest deduction over a short period of time is more than outweighed by the penalty of having to pay taxes at regular income tax rates on your eventual profit.*

Now let's look at a final alternative. You will still buy $100,000 worth of gold using $50,000 of borrowed money with the remainder coming from your own capital. In this case, however, we will assume that you do *not* try to deduct your interest expense. Instead, you add the interest to the tax cost of your gold to reduce your capital gain on eventual sale. Comparing the third investment analysis (Figure 7) to the one on page 109, you can see that, in years one and two, the cost of not deducting interest is somewhat higher. However, this is more than offset in the third year by the fact that your tax on your eventual profit, as calculated in Figure 8, is that much smaller.

Figure 7
Investment analysis form to evaluate the net present value of an investment in gold

		Time of Acquisition	Year 1	Year 2	Year 3
Purchase price 200 oz. × $500	Total	$100,000			
Cash outlay		50,000			
Portion financed		50,000			
		$100,000			
Interest expense on financing					
Less: Income tax saving from deduction of interest (optional)					
Net after-tax loss					
Less:					
Capital outlay —cash invested		(50,000)			
—expenses of acquisition					
—interest capitalized			(7,000)	(7,000)	(7,000)
Add: Proceeds from sale net of expenses to sell					170,000
Less: Debt repayment					(50,000)
Tax on profit					(12,250)
After-tax cash flow		(50,000)	(7,000)	(7,000)	100,750
Required rate of return		15%			
Present value factor (Table 3)		1.000	.870	.756	.658
Net present value $4,911		(50,000)	(6,090)	(5,292)	66,293

Figure 8
Calculation of tax on capital gain on sale of gold

Selling price of gold		$170,000
Cost		
Original cost	$100,000	
Interest capitalized	21,000	121,000
Capital gain		$ 49,000
Taxable capital gain (1/2)		$ 24,500
Tax at 50%		$ 12,250

In this particular case, the investment returns *more* than your required 15% rate of return.

Summary

As with any other type of investment, it is possible to quantify your goals and objectives. Do *you* think it is conceivable that the price of gold will increase from $500 an ounce to $850 an ounce over three years? Is an after-tax rate of return of 15% adequate for your purposes? On the other hand, is it more than *you* would really require? Should you use borrowed money to make such an investment? If so, should you attempt to deduct the interest expense? None of these questions can be answered without some mathematical analysis. And yet, as you can see, the procedure is certainly not difficult.

Finally, don't let the numbers scare you. In this chapter, we have chosen an investment of $100,000 because of the ease in dealing with nice round numbers. Remember that an investment in gold can be made by people at all income levels. At the time this is being written, a ¹/₁₀ oz. Krugerrand costs considerably less than $100. Of course, whether the price will eventually go up or down, and by how much, remains a matter for conjecture.

CHAPTER FIFTEEN

Investing in a Registered Retirement Savings Plan

In Chapter Two, I suggested that you think twice before making interest-bearing investments at modest rates solely for the sake of earning interest income—if you will be taxed in a high bracket. However, earning interest income even at relatively low rates can be profitable as long as it is tax-sheltered.

One of the best ways Canadians can earn tax-sheltered income is through a personal registered retirement savings plan (RRSP) program. This is probably the only interest-bearing investment that is safe to hold over an extended period of time. As you will see, an RRSP provides the opportunity to use untaxed dollars for your own investment portfolio, while also earning a tax-deferred investment yield.

Under the RRSP program, you are allowed to make tax-deductible contributions in a given taxation year or within sixty days following the end of that year. RRSP contributions can never exceed 20% of your "earned income"; moreover, the maximum annual amount is:

- $5500 where you are not a member of an employer-sponsored registered pension plan or deferred profit-sharing plan, or
- $3500 (minus your contributions to a registered pension program, if any).

Earned income is basically the sum of *net* receipts from employment, self-employment (business), pensions, rentals, and alimony. If you are not a member of an employer-sponsored pension or deferred profit-sharing program, the "magic" earned income required for full participation in an RRSP is $27,500. This is because 20% of $27,500 is $5500, which is the largest amount that ordinarily qualifies for an RRSP investment in any given year.

The RRSP program is a fairly straightforward investment. Each year that contributions are made, they are tax-deductible. As long as the amounts are invested in qualified investments such as term deposits or guaranteed income certificates, Canadian public company stocks and bonds, Canada Savings Bonds, or mortgages, the income earned within an RRSP compounds on a tax-deferred basis. After several years of ongoing contributions, the available capital starts to snowball and the build-up of capital continues until retirement. At that time, you can liquidate the assets in your plan and purchase an annuity that will provide you with a cash flow after your retirement. Although withdrawals from an RRSP are taxable, you will usually be in a lower tax bracket after retirement than previously.

The benefits of an RRSP are substantial, as we can confirm by simply taking a look at Table 2. Assuming a 10% yield, deposits of $1 a year made for ten years will amount to almost $16 at the end. After twenty years, you would have $57.28 and, after thirty years, $164.49.

For purposes of this chapter, we will assume that you can afford to contribute $2000 a year to your RRSP for various periods of time. Figure 1 illustrates how Table 2 can be used to calculate your total accumulation at various interest rates over these periods. For example, if you can earn an average of 10% on your money for thirty years, you will have $2000 × 164.49, or $328,988 at the end. Clearly, the higher the interest rate, the more significant the accumulation.

Figure 1
Value of an investment of $2000 each year into a registered retirement savings plan

Investment of $2000 a year for:	10%	12%	14%	16%
10 years	$31,875	$35,098	$ 38,674	$ 42,642
15 years	63,545	74,560	87,684	103,320
20 years	114,550	144,104	182,050	230,760
25 years	196,694	266,668	363,742	498,428
30 years	328,988	482,666	713,574	1,060,624
35 years	542,048	863,326	1,387,146	2,241,426

Table 2 provides you with calculations where deposits are made monthly, quarterly, semi-annually as well as annually. What if, instead of investing $2000 a year *once* a year, you were to invest $166.67 each month? Let's assume that you are, say, twenty-five years away from retirement. In Figure 2, you can see that putting aside money on a monthly basis produces a sizeable advantage. The difference is $24,449.

**Figure 2
Comparison of monthly investments vs. one annual
investment in an RRSP**

Investment of $166.67 per month at 10% for 25 years	$221,143
Investment of $2000 per year at 10% for 25 years	196,694
	$ 24,449

You can keep an RRSP open until you reach the age of seventy-one. After that time, you must start drawing funds out, generally in the form of an annuity. Annuities will be discussed later in this chapter.

I have provided detailed discussions of RRSP programs in several other books. Here, I will just caution you that interest on money borrowed to acquire an RRSP investment is not tax-deductible. On the other hand, you are permitted to split your contribution between a personal plan and a plan in the name of your spouse. The purpose of doing this would be to eventually receive *two* flows of annuity income and make use of the low tax brackets twice. I recommend that you read up on the RRSP rules, or discuss them with your own tax adviser, so that you can take maximum advantage of this program.

Should I Have an RRSP?

One of the most common questions serious investors ask is whether an RRSP is advisable, especially because of investment restrictions. Real estate is a non-qualified investment, as are precious metals such as gold and silver, and you can't invest to any great extent in foreign securities. Despite the limitations placed on an RRSP portfolio, I don't think you really have much choice—you *must* have an RRSP.

Let's examine the alternatives. Assume you are in a 40% income tax bracket and can save $2000 a year before income taxes. Assume the average yield you can earn on invested capital is 10%. You then have the choice between investing $2000 a year at 10% for, say, twenty-five years or having $1200 a year earning 6% for that same period of time. At the end of twenty-five years, assume that you completely deregister your RRSP investment in one lump-sum. Even if the tax cost at that point is 50% of the amount withdrawn, Figure 3 shows that you will still have made $32,509 more than you would without the RRSP. (The calculations to support this conclusion are also made using Table 2.)

So, in dealing with the question of whether or not an RRSP is attractive, simply ask yourself, what better choice is there?

Figure 3
Comparison of an investment in an RRSP to "outside" savings

RRSP investment of $2000 per year at 10% for 25 years	$196,694
Less: Income taxes on withdrawal at 50%	98,347
	98,347
Non-RRSP investment of $1200 per year at 6% for 25 years	65,838
Advantage of RRSP	$ 32,509

What Kind of Plan Should I Have?

RRSPs are administered by trust companies, banks and insurance companies. In addition, you are allowed to have a self-directed plan where you appoint trustees (or a trust company) and the trustees make whatever investments that you, as planholder, desire. Of course, your investments must fall within the acceptable tax guidelines discussed previously. Traditionally, people wait until the end of February to purchase their RRSP for the preceding year. Many millions of dollars are spent annually by companies trying to promote their own particular plans. To attempt to compare all the different alternative investments is a full-time job for a qualified investment counsellor. When it comes to selecting an RRSP, you can't even rely on past performance. Remember that the performance of a particular program is only a function of those people employed as fund managers.

You should, however, try to get the best return available. While a difference of 1% or 2% in the long run is not going to make or break the average middle-income or upper-income investor, the difference can still be very substantial over twenty-five years. Figure 4 uses Table 2 to show you the difference between a return of 10% and 11% on annual investments of $2000 over a twenty-five year period. The difference is $32,132.

Figure 4
Comparison of investments in an RRSP at different rates of return over twenty-five years

Investment of $2000 per year at 11% for 25 years	$228,826
Investment of $2000 per year at 10% for 25 years	196,694
	$ 32,132

You are permitted to move your money from one RRSP to another even if you change your trustees. Of course, you must always consider handing fees. If the increased return on investment is more than offset by additional handling costs, then it clearly won't be worthwhile to move your funds.

Cashing-In an RRSP

In Figure 3, we saw what happens when you invest in an RRSP for an extended period of time (twenty-five years) and then simply deregister the entire accumulation of $196,694 and pay taxes. This is not ordinarily what you would do. Instead, you would probably buy an annuity. This would provide you with a cash flow to subsidize your living costs after your retirement.

Until just a few years ago, there was only one way to cash-in an RRSP without paying immediate taxes. The Income Tax Act required that you use the RRSP funds to purchase a life annuity from an insurance company before you reached the age of seventy-one. The annuity benefits were then taxable as and when they were received. The only alternative was to make a lump-sum withdrawal from the RRSP and pay income tax on all amounts received at that time.

To safeguard against an early death, an individual was also permitted to modify the ordinary life annuity by adding a "guaranteed term" rider. A guaranteed term means that payments continue for at least that length of time even if the buyer dies before then. However, any time an individual lives beyond the guaranteed term, the payments only continue until the time of death. The guaranteed term permitted under an RRSP life annuity was, until recently, fifteen years. In the last couple of years, though, it has been extended to twenty years. In addition, you are also allowed to arrange a joint-and-last-survivor annuity program where RRSP payments continue until both husband and wife die. Even the joint-and-last-survivor option can now be structured to have a guaranteed term of up to twenty years.

Most people do not understand annuities, especially annuities beginning at age seventy-one. If you are seventy-one years old and you go to an insurance company with $200,000 in your RRSP, you would probably find that you could get approximately $30,000 a year if you do not opt for any guaranteed term. Of course, you would not ordinarily think that this is any bargain. If you are a male, you are probably conscious of the fact that your average life expectancy is only seventy-two years. So, how would you feel about receiving only one or two years' worth of annuity payments, or perhaps only $60,000 out of a $200,000 initial investment?

If you think this is a problem, you have fallen into the common trap. While it is true that the average life expectancy of a male would be approximately seventy-two years, *this is only true if that male person is younger than age forty.* Once you pass the age of forty, your life expectancy begins to increase.

It is now time to introduce the last of our tables, on page 00. This is the standard Canadian Mortality Table. If you look at this table closely, you can see that a seventy-year-old male has a life expectancy of another eleven years and that a female of the same age is projected to live another fourteen years. Thus, you would not be mistreated if you were offered $30,000 a year as an RRSP yield. In preparing calculations, the insurance company must budget for a payout of eleven to fourteen years, even without any guarantee.

Naturally, if you retire when you are sixty-five and begin to take an RRSP annuity at that age, you can expect to receive substantially less than if you wait until age seventy-one. Also, a woman will be offered a lower annual yield than a man, since she is expected to live longer.

Calculating Annuity Yields

In order to calculate annuity yields, we can use Table 5. This table provides us with periodic payments at the end of each period required to amortize a loan of $1 over a period of time. We have made use of Table 5 in Chapter Six in dealing with loans other than Canadian mortgages. In the previous application, we assumed that you are a borrower and you are paying back a loan with interest over a period of time. In an annuity situation the tables turn. In other words, *you* become the lender who deposits a sum of money with an insurance or trust company and then the insurance or trust company (i.e., the borrower) pays *you* back over a period of time, with interest.

Let's assume that you are dealing with an insurance company and you are seventy-one-years old. As I mentioned before, even without any guarantee, the insurance company must budget for a payout of eleven to fourteen years. Say you have $200,000 in your RRSP at that time and the going rate of interest is 10%. The insurance company will be prepared to pay you a monthly annuity for eleven to fourteen years in exchange for your $200,000 deposit. From Table 5, we can see that to amortize a loan of $1 at 10% interest over eleven years requires a monthly payment of

Figure 5
Calculating annuity yields

		Male	Female
Life expectancy at age 70 (from Table 13)		10.9	13.85
Assumed value of RRSP at age 70	(A)	$200,000	$200,000
Monthly annuity to yield 10% for		11 years	14 years
Factor (from Table 5)	(B)	.0125	.0111
(A) × (B)		$2500/mo.	$2220/mo.
Proof			
Present value of	(A)	$2500/mo.	$2220/mo.
for		11 years	14 years
at		10%	10%
Factor (from Table 8)	(B)	79.873	90.236
(A) × (B) =		$199,683	$200,324

$0.0125 and, over fourteen years, the factor is .0111. Thus, a $200,000 deposit can be amortized with monthly payments of $2500 a month over eleven years and $2220 a month over fourteen years. Therefore, a yield of $30,000 a year from age seventy is not the least bit unrealistic or unreasonable.

We can prove our numbers using Table 8. Table 8 gives us the present value of $1 per period payable at the end of each period. At 10% interest, the right to receive $2500 a month for eleven years is worth $199,683 ($2500 × 79.873). Of course, the difference between this amount and $200,000 is as a result of rounding. Similarly, the present value of the right to receive $2220 a month for fourteen years at 10% is $200,324 ($2220 × 90.236). Again, the $324 difference is due to rounding. Figure 5 illustrates these points in table form.

Evaluating Annuity Yields

By now you can appreciate why it is not possible to evaluate an annuity yield unless you have a clear understanding of the concept of life expectancy. In fact, in the next chapter you will see that a consideration of life expectancy is crucial when evaluating the cost of any life insurance policy.

Let's return to the situation where you have $200,000 in an RRSP and you would like to buy a life annuity. This time, suppose that you don't want to take a chance on dying prematurely and, instead, decide to opt

Figure 6
Monthly payments required to amortize a loan of $1 over various time periods (from Table 5)

Years	10%	11%	12%	13%	14%	15%
10	.0132	.0138	.0143	.0149	.0155	.0161
11	.0125	.0131	.0137	.0143	.0149	.0155
12	.0120	.0125	.0131	.0137	.0144	.0150
13	.0115	.0121	.0127	.0133	.0140	.0146
14	.0111	.0117	.0123	.0130	.0136	.0143
15	.0107	.0114	.0120	.0127	.0133	.0140
20	.0097	.0103	.0110	.0117	.0124	.0132

for a guaranteed term. Figure 6 is an extract from Table 5 which will enable you to determine the approximate monthly yield if you take a guaranteed term of ten to fifteen years. It also includes the factors for twenty years at different interest rates.

Now let's assume that a seventy-year-old man opts to convert a $200,000 RRSP accumulation into an annuity with a guaranteed term of fifteen years. Assume that he can get 10% on his money. His monthly income will then be $200,000 × .0107 or $2140. In other words, he would be sacrificing $360 a month in exchange for the guarantee.

Determining An Annuity Rate

Any time you wish to calculate the rate of return on an annuity, you need only know two things: the original amount invested and the anticipated length of time over which payments will be received. Then, by calculating your monthly return for each $1 of investment, you can determine the percentage yield from your tables.

Table 5 can be used to determine annuity yields when you know the initial deposit and the payments to be received on a monthly basis. For example, assume that at the age of seventy a man has $200,000 in an RRSP and he is told by another insurance company that they will give him $2970 per month for life with no guaranteed term. What is the rate of return? First, we have to examine the individual's life expectancy, which is eleven years. Then, if $200,000 provides $2970 a month, a $1 investment would provide 1/200,000 × $2970, or $0.01485 per month.

Now, turning to the extract from Table 5 in Figure 6, we can scan along the columns opposite an eleven-year payout and try to find the number that most closely approximates the factor we have just calculated. In this case, it is found under the column for a 14% return. In other words, if an insurance company were willing to provide $2970 per month for life with no guaranteed term in exchange for a lump-sum payment of $200,000 at age seventy, the yield is calculated to be approximately 14%. Of course, the actual yield may be greater or smaller depending on the age at death.

What if this same individual decided that he would rather have a life annuity with a twenty-year guaranteed term? Assume that, in these circumstances, the insurance company were willing to provide $2670 a month. In this case, the return for each dollar of original investment is 1/$200,000 × $2670, or $0.01335 per month.

If we now examine the numbers on the last line of our extract from Table 5 in Figure 6, we can see that the rate of return is slightly more than 15% over a twenty-year period. In the unlikely event that the individual survives beyond age ninety, the yield would be larger.

Summary

For most Canadians, the RRSP is the cornerstone to building a comfortable retirement. While the opportunity to set aside only a few thousand dollars a year may not seem to be attractive at the outset, the tax-deductibility of contributions along with the opportunity to compound interest without tax on an ongoing basis makes such a program extremely rewarding. This is especially true once you understand what is actually available at the end of the line.

CHAPTER SIXTEEN

Understanding Life Insurance Policies

How is this for a deal? Assume that you are thirty-five years old and a life insurance company offers you a $100,000 policy under the following terms. You pay $100 a month for ten years. At the end of ten years, you will have paid a total of $12,000 in premiums and this amount will then be refunded to you. In other words, *you get your money back*. Then, whenever you die (even if this happens before the ten years are up) the policy will pay $100,000 to your estate.

Sounds as if you are getting something for nothing. But is this really the case? As you will learn in the next few pages, it is impossible to properly evaluate a life insurance policy without a basic understanding of the math tables in this book.

Let's take a closer look at the "free" insurance offer. We will assume that an insurance company can earn 12% a year on its money. If you deposit $100 at *the beginning* of each month for ten years at 12% interest, Table 9 tells you that this will accumulate to $23,234. Then, when you are age forty-five, the insurance company could give you back your original capital investment of $12,000 and still retain $11,234.

Now it's time to look at Table 13—the standard Canadian Mortality Table. At age forty-five, a male can be expected to live an additional 28.77 years. So according to statistics, the insurance company will be allowed to keep $11,234 for twenty-eight years to earn 12% compounded annually—if this interest rate continues to hold. From Table 1, the future value of $11,234 invested at 12% is $11,234 × 23.884, or $268,313. Then, if you die at the end of twenty-eight years, the insurance company will be able to pay the death benefit of $100,000 and still retain $168,313 towards overhead and profit. In other words, as Figure 1 illustrates, you don't get anything for nothing.

Figure 1
Example of refundable premium insurance policy

Future value of $100 per month invested at the beginning
  of each month for 10 years at 12% (from Table 9)
    $100 × 232.339 = $ 23,233.90
Less: Original capital refunded after ten years
    $100 × 120 months   12,000.00
Funds retained by life insurance company $ 11,233.90

Future value of $11,234 invested to earn compound
  interest at 12% for a further 28 years (from Table 1)
    $11,234 × 23.884 = $268,313.00
Less: Life insurance proceeds paid at age 73   100,000.00
Net contribution to overhead and profits of insurance
  company $168,313.00

This is not to say that insurance companies should be condemned. First of all, the example I just gave you is purely hypothetical. Second, there is no guarantee that the insurance company will be able to earn an average of 12% net after-tax each year for the next thirty-eight years. Finally, what if *you* happen to die prematurely? The insurance company is taking the risk. All insurance companies are in business to make a profit. What you get in return if you take out a policy are two things:

1. Protection in the event of an *early* death, and
2. The security of knowing that you will have dollars available *when needed* to pay taxes or to provide income to your family.

If any of us was assured of living for many, many years, life insurance would probably not be necessary. Take a look at Table 4, which tells us how much must be invested at the end of each month to accumulate $1. Assume that you wish to have $100,000 at the end of thirty-eight years and you think that you can earn an average of 6% a year after tax. You need only invest $100,000 × .0006, or $60 a month.

Anyone who can guarantee himself a long life would be better off investing his money instead of paying insurance premiums. *Traditional life insurance policies are not an investment even though they are sometimes sold as such.* You will soon see that life insurance represents a *cost.* Again, its purpose is to provide protection as well as a source of cash when it is most needed.

Before tackling a mathematical approach to insurance policy evaluation, a little background is warranted. As a bare minimum, I think you should insure your life so that at the time of death there need be no forced sale of assets solely for the purpose of paying income taxes. For that reason, some kind of permanent insurance is necessary and term insurance will not usually be sufficient. Remember that a term policy will not help if it expires before your death. *Most term policies are not renewable beyond age seventy.* Keep in mind that you will probably live several years beyond your seventieth birthday, whether you are male or female. Take a good look at Table 13. It will tell you how much time you have left.

The tables in this book can help you determine the amount of insurance you will require to pay taxes, as long as you know how the law operates. Basically, the tax rules provide that, upon death, you are "deemed" or considered to have sold all your properties at fair market value. The exception is where you leave property to a spouse. In such a case, any increase in value will not ordinarily be taxed until your spouse dies.

From time to time, you should try to estimate the potential taxes owing as a result of death. You should project the future value of your investments and then compare these amounts with your costs. Then, you should apply combined federal and provincial marginal tax rates to your anticipated gains. To the extent that such a gain will be treated as a capital gain, only half will be taxable. In order to be fairly conservative, you should generally assume a tax rate of about 50%. You might note, however, that the tax burden produced by any deemed dispositions on death may be spread over ten years but each instalment bears interest and the instalment interest is not tax-deductible.

If you insure against your ultimate tax liability, one of the most important points to keep in mind is that no one will have to pay tax on your life insurance *benefits*. On the other hand, you *cannot* deduct the cost of your life insurance *premiums* from your income.

Insurance Programs Provide Income to Dependants

Many people rely totally on group life and pension programs instituted by their employers. This is a mistake, since the present level of such benefits will not generally provide adequately for either a middle-income or a highly paid key executive. In some cases, these shortcomings are created by government regulations, while others are caused by restrictions imposed by insurers themselves. For example, assume that an executive has annual earnings of $50,000. His company program limits his coverage to 2¹/₂ times earnings under its group life package. Let's assume that this executive now dies and his widow inherits $125,000 of tax-free insurance proceeds. Assume that the funds are then invested at 12% to yield $15,000 a year. Compare these (before tax) earnings to the deceased's annual income of $50,000. If the widow wishes to retain her capital intact, she must make a drastic change in her lifestyle. The thought of a 70% reduction in the level of family income is certainly not particularly attractive.

What about an employer-sponsored pension program? Take the example of an executive age fifty-five who anticipates retiring at age sixty-five after thirty-five years of service. (Actually, such a long period of service would be extremely rare in practice.) Again, assume a present income level of $50,000 a year and—assuming a 10% annual increase in pay—a final income of $118,000.

Traditionally, most pension plans are based on the average of the highest salaries earned over a five-year period. In this case, the average of the best five years would also be that of the last five years, or $98,000. Assume that the pension benefit is 2% for each year of service multiplied by the average of the best five years. This would provide an annual cash flow of 2% multiplied by thirty-five years multiplied by $98,000, or $68,000.

However, as of 1983, government regulations permit a maximum pension of only $60,000 a year. As a percentage of *final* earnings, this works out to only 51% in our case. If the retired individual decides to take his pension as an annuity guaranteed for fifteen years, the annual pension might be only approximately $54,000, or 46% of the final year's earnings. If taken as a joint-and-last-survivor annuity guaranteed for ten years (assuming a spouse who is five years younger) the pension is only $43,200 or 37% of final income. Then, if we assume that the taxpayer dies shortly after retirement, we can see that again the spouse is faced with the prospect of receiving an income that is only a fraction of what was previously received.

If you stop and think for a moment, a "standard" executive compensation program is not generally sufficient to meet your needs. Thus, the first role of the insurance you hold personally is to provide income to your surviving spouse and other dependants in the event that earned income from employment, business or a professional practice ceases.

A second use of life insurance is, as I described previously, to pay income taxes arising from deemed dispositions on death and on other income generated at that time. Also, insurance proceeds can be used to pay debts owing at the time of death and debts created by death itself (such as funeral costs, executors' fees and professional fees).

Insurance Provides Liquidity

In addition, one of the most important reasons for carrying life insurance is to provide liquidity to an estate so that assets yielding little or no current income can be retained. Your family home is one example. This is especially important if you have borrowed money to acquire these assets in the first place. Several times, this book has suggested that you consider borrowing money for investment purposes if you can finance your costs from surplus earnings from your job, business or profession. The actual amount that you decide to borrow depends largely on several facts, including the type of investment that you choose to acquire, the deductibility of interest and your own "comfort level".

The concept of borrowing money makes sense for many people—*but only as long as they are alive*. If your earnings cease, so does the cash flow needed to maintain debt. You never want to be in a position where assets must be sold at fire-sale prices just because your estate can no longer afford to carry them. As you know, all investment markets tend to be somewhat cyclical, and if your heirs must sell at a time where your particular investments are depressed, there can be a substantial penalty.

A general rule of thumb is that you should always carry sufficient insurance to *cover all debts owing at the time of death as well as debts created*. In other words, even if you don't adopt an aggressive investment philosophy, you should still insure your mortgage, car loans and any other personal debts. Then, additional insurance should be provided in order to maintain a flow of income so that your dependants do not have to suffer a reduction in their lifestyles. The amount of insurance required is not necessarily mind-boggling. For example, if you have a $50,000 mortgage against your house at 14% and there is insurance to cover that debt at the time of your death, technically your family could then afford to live on your take-home pay prior to death *minus* $587 a month (ignoring any inflation factor). The $587 represents the amount previously required to meet your monthly mortgage payments.

Other Uses for Insurance

One of the most underrated advantages of carrying life insurance is that it can facilitate distributions of an estate among family members. If, for example, you own a family farm or small business, you may wish to pass that on to one child rather than divide it equally among all your children. This is especially true where the one child is active in the farming or business operation. Leaving such an enterprise to be shared by all your children can create some serious inequities. Why should the one child who is active be forced to support inactive brothers and sisters? In addition, if the business can comfortably support one or two families, what happens when that business is then drained by the requirements of four or five families? In other words, it does not always make sense to give all your intended beneficiaries equal shares of each and every asset.

Does this mean that you must disinherit some of your children? Certainly not. The idea is to carry life insurance in sufficient amounts so that a family farm or business can pass to one child while the other children receive equivalent cash values from the insurance proceeds.

Life insurance can also be useful to meet obligations with respect to charitable bequests, or in special situations where you wish to provide for handicapped children or elderly parents. In addition, an insurance policy can help you achieve independence if you are contemplating a career change with an attendant loss of employer-benefit programs. If you own a part-interest in a private business, life insurance is almost mandatory to assist the surviving partners in buying out the estates of those who die first.

Borrowing Against Life Insurance Policies

As time goes on, some insurance policies develop "cash surrender values". A cash surrender value is the amount you would receive from the insurance company if you were to cancel the policy. In most cases, I would not recommend that you surrender your insurance—if for no other reason than the fact that the older you get, the more expensive it becomes to replace your coverage. In some cases, however, insurance companies will allow you to borrow against the cash surrender value at rates lower than those of other institutions. If you borrow for investment purposes, the interest is tax-deductible.

Unfortunately, the income tax rules surrounding life insurance policies are somewhat complex. Accordingly, I recommend that before you consider borrowing against any policy, you review the income tax implications with representatives of the insurance company that has issued the policy as well as with your own accountant.

Types of Life Insurance Products

Broadly speaking, there are two types of life insurance:

- term insurance, and
- permanent insurance

For individuals who maintain liquid estates and who require most of their protection in the early years, perhaps term insurance would be advisable. When it comes to a business situation, however, most advisers would recommend a more permanent type of coverage. This is because most term insurance policies expire when the holder reaches age seventy, whereas the average individual will probably not die until one or two years later. Term insurance therefore provides protection for your early needs while your children are young, but it is not adequate for long-range business planning and the preservation of property that is not liquid, such as real estate. When it comes to investment and estate planning, a good insurance agent is just as important a member of the team as your accountant or lawyer.

Generally, I recommend that in the decade between age twenty-five and thirty-five, while you are advancing in a career and at the same time beginning to raise a family, you should acquire term insurance to protect your family in the event of a premature death. Then, once you are more established, you should begin to transfer your coverage into more permanent-type policies. This is because the longer you wait, the more expensive permanent insurance becomes.

Characteristics of a Term Insurance Policy

As you would expect, term insurance tends to give the most protection for the least initial outlay. However, many term insurance policies do, in fact, expire by the time the individual reaches age seventy. Thus, the one major deficiency is lack of *permanent* coverage. Nevertheless, if you are considering a term insurance policy, there are several special considerations. First, there should be a guarantee that you can convert and renew it without providing evidence of your adequate health.

Generally, term insurance policies must be renewed annually or every few years and may be converted into whole-life insurance. You would want the right to obtain these benefits, especially if at some point your health should deteriorate and you would be unable to pass a medical examination. A guaranteed convertibility and renewability feature can easily be built into most term policies. You would also look for a provision which provides a waiver of premiums if you become disabled. This means that the policy would continue in force without your making any additional premium payments. Finally, you might also look for "double indemnity". This feature means that the policy would pay-off double if you die accidentally. This feature would be especially appealing if your lifestyle or job requires that you do a lot of travelling.

Permanent Insurance

There are many kinds of permanent insurance policies. Most common is the "whole-life" policy where payments continue until the time of death. As a variation, there is also the concept of "limited pay life" where your insurance premiums cease at a certain age (generally at the time of retirement). When I make recommendations for permanent insurance coverage to my clients, I generally suggest that the client not take any policy requiring insurance premiums to be paid after retirement. This is because, in many cases, one's cash flow tends to decrease once the "earned income years" are over. In addition to whole-life policies, permanent insurance also includes "endowment" policies and "single-premium" policies. Endowment policies have become somewhat unpopular in the last few years and single-premium policies have been rendered unattractive as a result of recent income tax changes.

An endowment policy provides a certain death benefit, or if one survives, the face amount is paid at age sixty five (or seventy). Proceeds from the surrender of the policy in excess of total premiums are fully taxable. This vehicle has not been popular since other savings plans can provide better yields.

Last-to-Die Policies

The "last-to-die" concept lends itself nicely to estate planning where the object is to pass assets intact to the next generation. Under Canadian law, a husband pays no tax on property he leaves to his wife and vice versa. It is therefore not necessary to pay taxes on death until both husband and wife die. (The sole exception is the Province of Quebec, the only jurisdiction which still levies succession duties at the provincial level.) A last-to-die policy can provide inexpensive insurance if one spouse is considerably younger than the other. It can also be useful if one spouse is not medically fit and the premiums to carry insurance on that person's life alone would otherwise be very high. As a variation on this theme, a last-to-die policy can be structured so that premium payments cease when the first spouse (or income earner) dies. The policy would still pay off at the time of the second death.

Evaluating Life Insurance Products

If you become conversant with the tables in this book, you will be able to evaluate any insurance product, no matter what type of policy it is and no matter which company is promoting it.

To illustrate what I mean, let's take the example of a forty-year-old man who is looking for insurance coverage of $100,000. Let's assume that his agent brings him three alternative policies. The first is a five-year renewable term-life program to age seventy. Under this type of policy, the premiums increase every five years. The second type of policy is a whole-life arrangement where premiums will have to be paid until the date of death. The premiums are however fixed each year, as is the death benefit. The third type is also a whole-life policy, but it involves higher premium payments and a death benefit which increases each year.

Figure 2
A present value approach to life insurance products
(numbers are for illustration only)

Male Age 40 Initial Coverage–$100,000 Years	5 Year Renewable Term to Age 70	Premium Cost	
		Whole Life Policy — Fixed Death Benefit	Whole Life Policy — Increasing Death Benefit
1– 5	$ 430	$ 1,160	$ 2,610
6–10	650	1,160	2,610
11–15	940	1,160	2,610
16–20	1,360	1,160	2,610
21–25	2,090	1,160	2,610
26–30	3,380	1,160	2,610
Death benefit at age 70 − 1 day	$100,000	$100,000	$278,000
Death benefit at age 70 + 1 day	0	100,000	278,000
Death benefit at age 73	0	100,000	341,000

Life expectancy from Table 13 is 33 years.
Assume a reasonable after-tax rate of return is 8% per annum and premiums are paid at the beginning of each year.

The first place to start is with life expectancy. In this case, for a male age forty, we must project payments for thirty-three years. Let's say that yearly premiums are paid at the beginning of each year and that a reasonable after-tax rate of return on investment capital is 8% a year. *Really, the rate of return you use doesn't make much difference as long as you are consistent and it is reasonable in relation to the prevailing interest rates.* The entire scenario is illustrated in Figure 2.

The first step in the analysis is to determine the present value of the premium costs. The present value of either whole-life policy is easily determined in a one-step calculation. From Table 12, the present value of thirty-three payments of $1 made at the beginning of each year assuming an 8% interest factor is $12.435. Thus, the present value of payments of $1160 and $2610 may be easily calculated.

On the other hand, calculating the present value of the term-insurance policy is much more difficult. Essentially, you must first determine the present value of five payments of $430. Table 12 again tells us that the factor at 8% interest for five years is 4.312 multiplied by the premium. Next you must determine the present value of five payments of $650 using the same factor (4.312) from Table 12. How-ever, you must *then* take the present value of the five payments of $650 ($2803) *back five years* using Table 3. Similarly, the present value of five payments of $940 must be brought back ten years and the present value of five payments of $1360 must be brought back fifteen years, and so on.

Figure 3
Calculation of the present value cost of term insurance

Annual Premiums	$ 430	$ 650	$ 940	$1,360	$2,090	$ 3,380
Present value of 5 annual payments factor (Table 12)	4.312	4.312	4.312	4.312	4.312	4.312
Present value end of year	0	5	10	15	20	25
Present value today	$1,854	$2,803	$4,053	$5,864	$9,012	$14,575
(Table 3) factor	1.000	.6806	.4632	.3152	.2145	.1460
Present value $11,546	$1,854	$1,907	$1,877	$1,848	$1,933	$ 2,127

In the final analysis, the total present value is, as illustrated in Figure 3, $11,546. Also, take a look at Figure 4, which is a time diagram showing exactly what is being done. In each case, you must first determine the present value of five payments and then bring that total figure back to today.

Figure 4
Calculation of the present value cost of term insurance

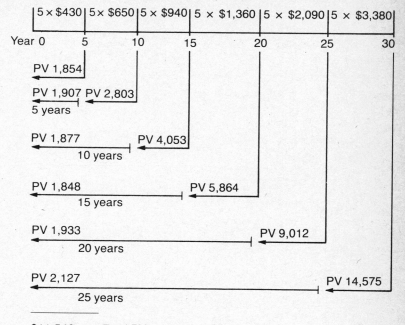

$11,546 Total PV

Once you have calculated the present value of the future premiums, the next step is to calculate the present value of the death benefit. This amount can be determined by using Table 3. Take a look at Figure 5.

The present value cost of the term insurance premiums is, as calculated, $11,546. Since the policy expires after thirty years, the present value of the death benefit, thirty-three years down the road, is clearly zero. In other words, if the insured person lives out his normal life expectancy, the net cost of his insurance becomes $11,546. Under the whole-life policy with the fixed benefit, the present value of thirty-three payments of $1160 is $14,424. On the other hand, the present value of the $100,000 death benefit at the end of thirty-three years is only $7890. The difference represents the net cost of insurance.

A comparison of this whole-life policy with the second one, which provides an increasing death benefit, is extremely interesting. On the one hand, the premiums paid are two-and-a-quarter times as high while

Figure 5
Calculating the cost of different insurance policies if death occurs at age seventy-three

If Death Occurs After 33 Years (Age 73)	5 Year Renewable Term Insurance to Age 70	Whole Life Policy Fixed Death Benefit	Whole Life Policy Increasing Death Benefit
Present value of insurance premiums as calculated	$11,546		
Present value of 33 payments made at the beginning of each year at 8% interest (Table 12)			
$1,160 × 12.435		$14,424	
$2,610 × 12.435			$32,455
Present value of death benefit payable at the end of 33 years assuming 8% interest			
Policy expires after 30 years	0		
$100,000 × .0789 (Table 3)		7,890	
$341,000 × .0789 (Table 3)			26,905
Net cost of insurance	$11,546	$ 6,534	$ 5,550

the death benefit at age seventy-three is 3.41 times as high. Nevertheless, when you apply present value techniques, the difference in cost is less than $1000. In other words, although the estate will wind up with $341,000 instead of $100,000, the deceased will have paid for the extra benefits.

Before leaving this example, however, there is one further possibility that is worth looking into. Let's assume that death occurs *one day* before the insured person's seventieth birthday. In other words, just less than thirty years after the policy is begun.

If this is the case, suddenly the term insurance policy is the one that has the smallest cost. Although the present value cost of the premiums hasn't changed, there is suddenly a death benefit of $100,000. In today's money, assuming an 8% interest factor, the present value of this benefit

Figure 6
Calculating the cost of different insurance policies if death occurs just before age seventy

If Death Occurs at Age 70 Minus 1 Day (just under 30 years)	5 Year Renewable Term Insurance to Age 70	Whole Life Policy Fixed Death Benefit	Whole Life Policy Increasing Death Benefit
Present value of insurance premiums as calculated	$11,546		
Present value of 30 payments made at the beginning of each year at 8% interest (Table 12)			
$1,160 × 12.158		$14,103	
$2,610 × 12.158			$31,732
Present value of death benefit payable at the end of 30 years assuming 8% interest			
$100,000 × .0994	9,940		
$100,000 × .0994		9,940	
$278,000 × .0994			27,633
Net cost of insurance	$ 1,606	$ 4,163	$ 4,099

is $9940 and the net cost of insurance becomes only $1606. Since the death benefit is brought three years closer under options two and three, the net cost of insurance is reduced as well. Again, the difference between the two whole-life alternatives is negligible.

In all cases, it becomes clear that life insurance is, as I mentioned previously, a *cost not an investment*.

On the other hand, before you rush out to cancel your insurance, you must understand that, if the results did not work out as shown, the insurance companies would all go bankrupt. Any business that pays out more than it takes in, goes out of business very quickly.

Why then, would anybody pay out more than what he hoped to receive? The answer is, protection. What happens if our hypothetical male age forty dies well before age seventy-three? He would then be paying smaller premiums for each year of decreased life span. Also, his estate would receive the insurance proceeds that much sooner.

On the other hand, if our forty-year-old male *outlives* his normal life expectancy, the cost of insurance becomes even more expensive. This is because he would be paying his premiums for more than thirty-three years and his estate would only receive the death benefit at a later time. The point, however, is that *insurance provides policyholders with protection.*

What if *you* are the one who dies prematurely? What happens if *your* dependents require income at an earlier time than they would if you were to live out your normal life expectancy?

How Much Insurance is Enough?

Realizing that insurance is a cost, you may decide to "buy term and invest the difference". Buying term insurance at a relatively cheap cost at an early age and investing the difference can be the best move that you will ever make—*if you are sure that you are going to die younger than most.* However, what happens if you outlive your policy? This too may not be a serious problem, if by that time, you have substantial liquid assets and if the needs of your dependants are more than adequately met from other sources. On the other hand, if you have invested heavily in illiquid investments and your family enjoys an expensive lifestyle, term insurance is probably not the answer.

Of course, one of the biggest problems is inflation. If you died today and your spouse inherited perhaps $300,000 of insurance, she could take these funds and invest conservatively to earn $30,000 a year before taxes. While your family might be able to live on this income today, what about five years from now, ten years from now or twenty years from now? Again, study Table 3. The present value of $1 due thirty years from now at 8% is only about 10¢.

On the other hand, if you were to carry double the insurance, your premium costs today would also be double. You must ask yourself whether it is worth depriving yourself and your family of disposable income today for the sake of insuring a future. How far you should go to obtain insurance coverage is a matter of personal choice. So sharpen your pencil and weigh the alternatives mathematically.

Summary

By using the present value analysis techniques illustrated in this chapter, it is not only possible to compare different types of policies issued by the same company but also to compare policies issued by different companies. One word of caution is, however, in order. If a policy is structured to provide a specific death benefit and premiums that are not subject to change, the analysis techniques described in this chapter will allow you to determine your cost with no great effort.

However, in many cases, insurance policy premiums and benefits are structured to be flexible. If, for example, interest rates jump drastically, it is possible that an insurance company will pass on the savings. This can be done in the form of either decreased premiums or increased death benefits, or in fact, a combination of the two. Usually, insurance companies, in making quotations, will specify the rate of return at which their calculations are made. In insurance jargon this is referred to as the "dividend" rate. Obviously, if one company projects a dividend rate of 12% while another company projects a rate of 17%, the second company's figures will appear much more attractive.

Don't try to compare apples and oranges. What you should do is ask the agent who presented you with the figures to have one insurance company recalculate its numbers using assumptions that are consistent with those made on the other projection. Then, if over the life of the policy, the actual results exceed the revised budget, you can only benefit. In other words, there won't be any unpleasant surprises.

Generally, insurance companies tend to be rather competitive. If, after applying present value analysis, you find that there are significant differences with respect to net costs, take an hour or so and sit down with your own independent financial advisers. They can help you determine whether your calculations are correct or whether, in fact, an error has been made.

CHAPTER 17

To Lease or Buy—That is the Question

Not only business owners but all of us in our personal financial planning often have a hard time deciding whether to buy things or lease them. Even with the aid of mathematical analysis, the decision is a tough one because it involves factors beyond dollars and cents.

For example, if you are considering a piece of equipment that is subject to quick obsolescence, you might be better off with a leasing rather than a purchase arrangement. This is because most leasing companies will allow you to "trade up". Within a business environment, leasing can also be beneficial since it doesn't tie up working capital or a line of credit. Assume, for instance, that a small business has a bank line of $75,000 and the owner requires a car which will be used for both business and pleasure. If the car that the owner wants costs $15,000, it would probably not be a good idea to tie up 20% of the line of credit in such a purchase. This is especially true since the car will depreciate over time.

On the other hand, consider the case of an individual who has just inherited $200,000. Suppose that he or she is very conservative and has most of his or her money tied up in term deposits yielding 11% interest. If this person is considering the alternatives of buying or leasing a $15,000 car, I would generally recommend a purchase. This is because the lease on that vehicle will reflect an interest rate significantly higher than 11%, and one would have to question whether it pays to earn 11% on one investment and pay out perhaps double to carry another.

A further factor to consider is maintenance. Again, my comments here are somewhat subjective, but many people feel that a company that leases equipment will tend to provide better service on these properties than if the customer buys. After all, the lessee does have the option of stopping his monthly payments (whether or not he is legally entitled to do so) if he is not satisfied with performance.

Then, of course, we must take income tax implications into account,

Figure 1
Extract from Canadian capital cost allowance regulations

Description of Property	First Year Depreciation	Subsequent Depreciation
Furniture and fixtures	10% of cost	20% of undepreciated* capital cost every year thereafter on a declining balance basis
Automobiles	15% of cost	30% of undepreciated* capital cost every year thereafter on a declining balance basis

*Undepreciated capital cost is cost minus the accumulated depreciation claimed previously.

especially in a business environment. Generally, lease payments are tax-deductible in the same way as office rent, provided any option to buy is reasonable in relation to the anticipated fair market value of the property at the end of the lease period. There is, however, a tax rule in Canada which states that if a lease option is exercised and the property is then sold, any gain made is not treated as a capital gain but is fully taxable. This will serve to reimburse the government in cases where the initial leasing write-offs were too generous. For example, say that I lease a $15,000 car for my business at $500 a month for three years. Then, there is an option to buy the vehicle for $2000. My business exercises the option and sells the car for $6000. The $4000 gain becomes ordinary income. This is because the business *previously* wrote off *all* of the $500 monthly payments as an expense for tax purposes.

If depreciable assets are bought for use in a business, interest on money borrowed to fund such purchases is tax-deductible. Then, the cost of the properties can be depreciated in accordance with the capital cost allowance rules. There are, at the time this is being written, thirty-seven different "classes" of property for Canadian income tax purposes, each with its own unique write-off rules and rates. Since this is not a book on taxes, Figure 1 only shows two of the more significant rates.

In a real life situation, before making any arithmetic analyses such as those which appear in the rest of this chapter, you would be well advised to contact your accountant, who can give you the tax information which is up-to-date and accurate in your circumstances.

Whenever you face a question of buying or leasing, it is important to start with as many hard facts as you possibly can and also try to ensure that your data is comparable. For example, if you are looking to buy property using borrowed funds, ask yourself what rate of interest will you have to pay. Second, don't try to compare the cost of buying a Volkswagen to the cost of leasing a Cadillac. Make sure that you are always talking about identical property, whether it is a car, a piece of computer equipment, a boat or whatever.

The Mathematics Behind Leasing Arrangements

To make calculations involving leasing arrangements, you must always keep in mind the fact that payments will be made at the *beginning* of each period and not at the end. Thus, to evaluate leases, you will have to rely on two of the tables which were introduced in Chapter Nine. The first is Table 11, which gives you the periodic payments at the beginning of each period required to amortize a loan of $1 over a period of time. This table will help you determine the effective interest rate of the lease.

The second is Table 12, which gives you the value today of a series of payments where the payments start immediately. This table will tell you the present value of your future lease payments.

Let's take a look at a simple example in which you try to determine whether to buy or lease a $15,000 car. We will first examine this question on the assumption that the car will be used for *personal purposes only*. In other words, tax write-offs will *not* be considered since they would have no relevance. (Later in the chapter, we'll see what happens if the vehicle will be used by someone in a 50% tax bracket who will be able to claim his entire costs for income tax purposes. A practical application would be the purchase or lease of a vehicle by a very profitable Canadian corporation.)

Assume you are deciding between the purchase or lease of a $15,000 car. If you buy the car, you can obtain a bank loan of $15,000 for a three-year period at 14% interest. Then, after three years, you figure that the car will be worth $6000. This last factor, which is often referred to by accountants as the "residual value", is extremely important. This is because you would always want to determine the real cost of ownership or leasing over a certain specific length of time. Ignoring present value concepts for the moment, what you are really looking at is the purchase of a $15,000 car which can then be sold for $6000 three years from now, giving you a *net cost* of $9000.

Suppose, however, that you are offered two alternatives to buying. You can lease an identical car for $400 a month for thirty-six months with an option to buy for $6000, or you can lease for $500 a month for that same thirty-six month period with an option to buy for only $2000.

Figure 2
Case study involving the purchase or lease of a car

Alternative A
Buy a $15,000 car with borrowed funds @ 14%
Pay for it over 3 years and then sell it for $6000
OR
Alternative B
Lease the same car at $400/month for 36 months
With an option to buy for $6000 at the end of this period
OR
Alternative C
Lease the same car at $500/month for 36 months
With an option to buy for $2000 at the end of this period

Before preparing any sophisticated evaluations, you can see that the option to buy for $6000 under the $400 a month lease really has no value. This is because, if you exercise your option and then sell the car for the same amount, the net cost or benefit at that point is zero. On the other hand, if you decide to pay the higher monthly lease payments of $500 a month and then exercise your option to buy for $2000, you will have a $4000 *profit* at the end of that three-year period. This is because I have assumed that the car could then be sold for $6000. The present value of that profit will *decrease* your cost under this second leasing option. The three alternatives are outlined in Figure 2 for your easy reference.

At this point, you should note that the operating costs will generally be the same whether you buy or lease. In cases where you lease property and maintenance is included in your monthly payment, you should attempt to subtract the maintenance costs from your figures and deal with the "raw" lease alone. Otherwise, you will not be in a position to compare "apples to apples".

Now let's proceed with our analysis. The first step is to determine the actual cost of ownership in today's dollars.

The cost to buy the car is, of course, $15,000. But this is before considering the trade-in value in three years. If we assume a 14% interest rate, the present value of $6000 due at the end of three years can be determined from Table 3: $6000 × .6750, or $4050. Thus, the actual cost of buying the car in today's dollars is, as calculated in Figure 3, $10,950.

Figure 3
Calculating the present value cost of buying a car

Present value of original cost	$15,000
Less: Present value of selling price in three years	
@ 14% ($6000 × .6750)	4,050
Net present value cost	$10,950

Under the second alternative, the same car can be leased for $400 a month with payments starting immediately for a thirty-six month period. From Table 12, we learn that the present value of $400 per month for thirty-six months (at the 14% rate it would cost you to borrow it) is: $400 × 29.600, or $11,840. Here, we don't have to be concerned with the present value of the option to buy. This is because the option to buy is for the same price as the anticipated selling price at the end of three years. In other words, if the car were bought for $6000 at that time, it could then be sold immediately for the same price. There would be no profit then, and, of course, the present value of a zero profit three years from now is zero.

The third alternative, however, is more interesting. In this case, the choice is to pay $500 a month for thirty-six months. The present value of this cash outflow can also be calculated (using a 14% rate) from Table 12 as $500 × 29.600. The cost here is $14,800 in today's dollars. On the other hand, at the end of three years there is a benefit. If you take this last option, you could buy the car for $2000 and sell it for $6000. In other words, there is a profit of $4000 three years down the road. If we assume the prevailing interest rate is still 14% (so that is what money is worth) and use Table 3, the present value of $4000 in three years is $4000 × .675, or $2700. The net cost under Alternative C is therefore $14,800 minus $2700 or $12,100. Thus, Alternative A ($10,950) is the cheapest, Alternative B ($11,840) comes second and Alternative C ($12,100) is third.

However, before making any final decisions, please keep in mind that the numbers used in these examples are purely hypothetical. Also, it would pay to reread the beginning of this chapter, since there are so many variables that should be taken into account in any specific situation. For example, do you really want to tie up a line of credit at your bank for the sake of only a few hundred dollars?

What is the Interest Rate?

Very often, you will find yourself in the position where you are given a quotation on a lease and you're curious as to what the interest rate is. Let's take the previous example and continue with it. You have just calculated that if you bought a particular car for $15,000 which would be worth $6000 at the end of three years, your present value cost is $10,950. What then is the interest cost built into a lease of $400 a month for thirty-six months with the same option to buy?

For all intents and purposes, what you would be doing is paying off a $10,950 cost over thirty-six months at $400 a month. The monthly factor is $400 divided by $10,950 = 0.0365. Now turn to Table 11. This table shows you the required payments beginning immediately which will amortize a loan of $1 over a period of time. Look through the table and try to find the monthly payment needed to discharge a loan of $1 over three years at various rates of interest. You will see that the factor (on page 249) for 19% is 0.0361 and, at 20%, the factor is 0.0366. Thus, for all intents and purposes, you can conclude that the interest rate built into the lease in my hypothetical example, is somewhere between 19% and 20%

Be very careful when you apply Table 11. Remember that *your lease payments don't usually amortize the full cost of the property which you are leasing*. There is usually a buy-out option at the end, and thus, what your lease payments are doing is amortizing *the price minus the present value of that future buy-out option*. In the previous case study, the $400 monthly payments amortized a cost of $10,950, not $15,000.

Taking Income Tax Implications Into Account

Now, let's see what happens if the person who will use the leased or purchased vehicle is in a position to treat the property as a business asset. If the car is leased, the monthly rent of $400 (using the figures in Alternative B) will be tax-deductible. If the car is purchased, capital cost allowance can be taken and the interest becomes deductible as well.

Before we can prepare an investment analysis form to cover this situation, we must first prepare a loan amortization schedule and a capital cost allowance schedule. These factors are important because, without them, we cannot determine after-tax cash flows under the purchase option.

From Table 5, we see that the monthly payments required to amortize a loan of $15,000 over three years at 14% are $15,000 × .0342, or $513 a month. The annual payments are therefore $513 × 12, or $6156. The table in Figure 4 shows the breakdown over the three-year period between interest and principal payments. You will note that at the end of the first year, 71.1% of the principal is still outstanding. Then, at the end of the second year, 37.9% of the original loan is still owing, while, at the end of the third year, the balance is zero.

Space does not permit me to include all conceivable math tables in this book. Table 8 in this book shows the balance outstanding each year on twenty-five-year Canadian mortgage loans but this table cannot be used for our purposes here. This is because we are dealing with a three-year loan only. If necessary, you could get the principal and interest breakdowns from your lending institution at the time you make your application for financing. Alternatively, if the loan is of short duration, you could take the interest evenly throughout the period or make a reasonable attempt to apportion it. The differences should not be that significant.

Figure 4
Periodic payments to amortize a loan of $15,000 over three years at 14%

Monthly Payments: $15,000 × .0342 (Table 5) = $513
Annual Payments: $513 × 12 = $6,156

Year	Loan Beginning of year	Loan End of Year		Principal	Interest
1	$15,000	.711 × $15,000 =	$10,665	$4,335	$1,821
2	10,665	.379 × 15,000 =	5,685	4,980	1,176
3	5,685	.000 × 15,000 =	0	5,685	471

Next, in Figure 5 we calculate the capital cost allowance for each year using the formula provided on page 139.

Figure 5
Calculation of capital cost allowance (tax depreciation) on an automobile

Original cost	$15,000	
CCA–Year 1	2,250	$15,000 × 15%
	12,750	
CCA–Year 2	3,825	$12,750 × 30%
	8,925	
CCA–Year 3	2,677	$8925 × 30%
	6,248	
Selling price	(6,000)	
Additional tax write-off in Year 3	$ 248	

You can see that, after normal capital cost allowances, there is still an undepreciated balance of $6248 at the end of the third year. If the car is then sold for $6000 and no other vehicle is purchased, the remaining $248 balance becomes a tax write-off. This is because the actual depreciation is a bit larger than the depreciation previously allowed for income tax purposes.

Now we are ready to tackle the investment analysis form in Figure 6.

Under the purchase option, the interest on the loan over a three-year period is a tax-deductible expenditure along with capital cost allowance. Thus, from a cash-flow standpoint, the tax saving represents a cash inflow. Notice then that the net after-tax cost of ownership is decreased by the capital cost allowance, which does not represent an outflow of funds. The cash out-flows are, however, increased by the principal

Figure 6
Investment analysis form to compare ownership vs. leasing

Option 1: Purchase	Year 1	Year 2	Year 3
Interest on loan to acquire property	(1,821)	(1,176)	(471)
Capital cost allowance	(2,250)	(3,825)	(2,925)
Deductible expenditures for tax purposes	(4,071)	(5,001)	(3,396)
Tax Savings in 50% bracket	2,035	2,501	1,698
Net after-tax cost	(2,036)	(2,500)	(1,698)
Less: Capital cost allowance	2,250	3,825	2,925
	214	1,325	1,227
Principal payments on debt	(4,335)	(4,980)	(5,685)
Selling price			6,000
Less: tax on recaptured depreciation			—
	(4,121)	(3,655)	1,542
Required rate of return 14%			
Present value factor (Table 3)	.877	.770	.675
Present value cost $(5,387)	(3,614)	(2,814)	1,041
Option 2: Lease			
Lease payments	(4,800)	(4,800)	(4,800)
Less: Tax savings thereon	2,400	2,400	2,400
Net after-tax cost	(2,400)	(2,400)	(2,400)
Option price			(6,000)
Selling price			6,000
			(2,400)
Required rate of return 14%			
Present value factor (Table 3)	.877	.770	.675
Present value cost $(5,573)	(2,105)	(1,848)	(1,620)

payments on the debt, in this case $15,000 over three years. At the end of the third year, there is one further in-flow, which is the proceeds from sale. In this example, there is no recaptured depreciation. If we assume that the prevailing interest rate is 14%, the present value of the two out-flows and the positive cash flow in year three represents a negative amount of $5387. This is the cost of ownership in today's dollars.

In the example on page 141, the cost of ownership was calculated at $10,950. Why the difference? This is because the last series of calculations takes into account the tax benefits from deducting interest and capital cost allowance. This reduces the cost of ownership by half.

Now, let's consider the lease. This involves a relatively straightforward set of calculations. The lease payments in all three years are tax-deductible, which means that the net cost becomes only half. Applying the same present value factors, we can see that the present value cost of leasing in this example is virtually identical to the cost of ownership ($5387 versus $5573). In other words, the tax advantages of leasing pretty well offset the results of the first analysis on pages 140 to 142, which showed that the net present cost of leasing was more expensive where there are no tax write-offs. This is why you must always prepare a detailed analysis before you can decide which alternative to choose.

Summary

Deciding whether to lease or buy is a difficult task. However, no matter how complex the arrangement might initially seem to be, if you keep your wits about you and go slowly, you can make an intelligent comparison. But you won't know until you try. Keep this book with you and use it before making *any* business or investment financing decision. You will find that the procedures which I have illustrated can be adapted to help you manage *your* money and make it grow.

TABLES

TABLE 1
The compound amount of $1

What is $1 invested today worth at some time in the future at various interest rates if interest is calculated at the end of each month, quarterly, semi-annually, or annually?

Applications
Chapter Two
- Compound interest calculations
- What will $1 invested today be worth at some time in the future?
- If you lend $1 to someone else at various interest rates, how much will he have to pay you as a single lump sum sometime in the future?
- By how much must an investment appreciate over a period of time to give you a required rate of return?
- What will the price of an item be after various time periods assuming different rates of inflation?
- How much can you expect to be earning if you are given percentage salary increases over various time periods?

Chapter Eleven
- What will a real estate property be worth in the future if it appreciates by a certain percentage each year?

The compound amount of $1

End of Year	5% Interest compounded				6% Interest compounded			
	Monthly	Quarterly	Semi-Annually	Annually	Monthly	Quarterly	Semi-Annually	Annually
1	1.051	1.051	1.051	1.050	1.062	1.061	1.061	1.060
2	1.105	1.104	1.104	1.103	1.127	1.126	1.126	1.124
3	1.161	1.161	1.160	1.158	1.197	1.196	1.194	1.191
4	1.221	1.220	1.218	1.216	1.270	1.269	1.267	1.262
5	1.283	1.282	1.280	1.276	1.349	1.347	1.344	1.338
6	1.349	1.347	1.345	1.340	1.432	1.430	1.426	1.419
7	1.418	1.416	1.413	1.407	1.520	1.517	1.513	1.504
8	1.491	1.488	1.485	1.477	1.614	1.610	1.605	1.594
9	1.567	1.564	1.560	1.551	1.714	1.709	1.702	1.689
10	1.647	1.644	1.639	1.629	1.819	1.814	1.806	1.791
11	1.731	1.727	1.722	1.710	1.932	1.925	1.916	1.898
12	1.820	1.815	1.809	1.796	2.051	2.043	2.033	2.012
13	1.913	1.908	1.900	1.886	2.177	2.169	2.157	2.133
14	2.011	2.005	1.996	1.980	2.312	2.302	2.288	2.261
15	2.114	2.107	2.098	2.079	2.454	2.443	2.427	2.397
16	2.222	2.215	2.204	2.183	2.605	2.593	2.575	2.540
17	2.336	2.327	2.315	2.292	2.766	2.752	2.732	2.693
18	2.455	2.446	2.433	2.407	2.937	2.921	2.898	2.854
19	2.581	2.571	2.556	2.527	3.118	3.100	3.075	3.026
20	2.713	2.701	2.685	2.653	3.310	3.291	3.262	3.207
21	2.851	2.839	2.821	2.786	3.514	3.493	3.461	3.400
22	2.997	2.984	2.964	2.925	3.731	3.707	3.671	3.604
23	3.151	3.136	3.114	3.072	3.961	3.934	3.895	3.820
24	3.312	3.296	3.271	3.225	4.206	4.176	4.132	4.049
25	3.481	3.463	3.437	3.386	4.465	4.432	4.384	4.292
26	3.659	3.640	3.611	3.556	4.740	4.704	4.651	4.549
27	3.847	3.825	3.794	3.733	5.033	4.993	4.934	4.822
28	4.043	4.020	3.986	3.920	5.343	5.299	5.235	5.112
29	4.250	4.225	4.188	4.116	5.673	5.624	5.553	5.418
30	4.468	4.440	4.400	4.322	6.023	5.969	5.892	5.743
31	4.696	4.666	4.623	4.538	6.394	6.336	6.250	6.088
32	4.937	4.904	4.857	4.765	6.788	6.724	6.631	6.453
33	5.189	5.154	5.102	5.003	7.207	7.137	7.035	6.841
34	5.455	5.417	5.361	5.253	7.652	7.575	7.463	7.251
35	5.734	5.693	5.632	5.516	8.124	8.040	7.918	7.686
36	6.027	5.983	5.917	5.792	8.625	8.533	8.400	8.147
37	6.335	6.287	6.217	6.081	9.157	9.057	8.912	8.636
38	6.660	6.608	6.532	6.385	9.721	9.613	9.454	9.154
39	7.000	6.944	6.862	6.705	10.321	10.202	10.030	9.704
40	7.358	7.298	7.210	7.040	10.957	10.828	10.641	10.286
41	7.735	7.670	7.575	7.392	11.633	11.493	11.289	10.903
42	8.131	8.061	7.958	7.762	12.351	12.198	11.976	11.557
43	8.547	8.471	8.361	8.150	13.113	12.947	12.706	12.250
44	8.984	8.903	8.784	8.557	13.921	13.741	13.480	12.985
45	9.443	9.356	9.229	8.985	14.780	14.584	14.300	13.765
46	9.927	9.833	9.696	9.434	15.692	15.479	15.171	14.590
47	10.435	10.334	10.187	9.906	16.659	16.429	16.095	15.466
48	10.968	10.860	10.703	10.401	17.687	17.437	17.076	16.394
49	11.530	11.414	11.244	10.921	18.778	18.507	18.115	17.378
50	12.119	11.995	11.814	11.467	19.936	19.643	19.219	18.420

The compound amount of $1

End of Year	7% Interest compounded				8% Interest compounded			
	Monthly	Quarterly	Semi-Annually	Annually	Monthly	Quarterly	Semi-Annually	Annually
1	1.072	1.072	1.071	1.070	1.083	1.082	1.082	1.080
2	1.150	1.149	1.148	1.145	1.173	1.172	1.170	1.166
3	1.233	1.231	1.229	1.225	1.270	1.268	1.265	1.260
4	1.322	1.320	1.317	1.311	1.376	1.373	1.369	1.360
5	1.418	1.415	1.411	1.403	1.490	1.486	1.480	1.469
6	1.520	1.516	1.511	1.501	1.614	1.608	1.601	1.587
7	1.630	1.625	1.619	1.606	1.747	1.741	1.732	1.714
8	1.748	1.742	1.734	1.718	1.892	1.885	1.873	1.851
9	1.874	1.867	1.857	1.838	2.050	2.040	2.026	1.999
10	2.010	2.002	1.990	1.967	2.220	2.208	2.191	2.159
11	2.155	2.145	2.132	2.105	2.404	2.390	2.370	2.332
12	2.311	2.300	2.283	2.252	2.603	2.587	2.563	2.518
13	2.478	2.465	2.446	2.410	2.819	2.800	2.772	2.720
14	2.657	2.642	2.620	2.579	3.053	3.031	2.999	2.937
15	2.849	2.832	2.807	2.759	3.307	3.281	3.243	3.172
16	3.055	3.035	3.007	2.952	3.581	3.551	3.508	3.426
17	3.276	3.253	3.221	3.159	3.879	3.844	3.794	3.700
18	3.513	3.487	3.450	3.380	4.201	4.161	4.104	3.996
19	3.766	3.738	3.696	3.617	4.549	4.504	4.439	4.316
20	4.039	4.006	3.959	3.870	4.927	4.875	4.801	4.661
21	4.331	4.294	4.241	4.141	5.336	5.277	5.193	5.034
22	4.644	4.603	4.543	4.430	5.779	5.712	5.617	5.437
23	4.979	4.934	4.867	4.741	6.258	6.183	6.075	5.871
24	5.339	5.288	5.214	5.072	6.778	6.693	6.571	6.341
25	5.725	5.668	5.585	5.427	7.340	7.245	7.107	6.848
26	6.139	6.075	5.983	5.807	7.949	7.842	7.687	7.396
27	6.583	6.512	6.409	6.214	8.609	8.488	8.314	7.988
28	7.059	6.980	6.865	6.649	9.324	9.188	8.992	8.627
29	7.569	7.482	7.354	7.114	10.098	9.945	9.726	9.317
30	8.116	8.019	7.878	7.612	10.936	10.765	10.520	10.063
31	8.703	8.595	8.439	8.145	11.843	11.653	11.378	10.868
32	9.332	9.213	9.040	8.715	12.826	12.613	12.306	11.737
33	10.007	9.875	9.684	9.325	13.891	13.653	13.311	12.676
34	10.730	10.585	10.374	9.978	15.044	14.778	14.397	13.690
35	11.506	11.345	11.113	10.677	16.293	15.996	15.572	14.785
36	12.338	12.161	11.904	11.424	17.645	17.315	16.842	15.968
37	13.230	13.034	12.752	12.224	19.109	18.742	18.217	17.246
38	14.186	13.971	13.660	13.079	20.695	20.287	19.703	18.625
39	15.212	14.975	14.633	13.995	22.413	21.960	21.311	20.115
40	16.311	16.051	15.676	14.974	24.273	23.770	23.050	21.725
41	17.491	17.205	16.792	16.023	26.288	25.729	24.931	23.462
42	18.755	18.441	17.988	17.144	28.470	27.850	26.965	25.339
43	20.111	19.766	19.269	18.344	30.833	30.146	29.165	27.367
44	21.565	21.186	20.642	19.628	33.392	32.631	31.545	29.556
45	23.123	22.709	22.112	21.002	36.164	35.321	34.119	31.920
46	24.795	24.341	23.687	22.473	39.165	38.232	36.903	34.474
47	26.588	26.090	25.374	24.046	42.416	41.384	39.915	37.232
48	28.510	27.965	27.182	25.729	45.936	44.795	43.172	40.211
49	30.570	29.974	29.118	27.530	49.749	48.488	46.695	43.427
50	32.780	32.128	31.191	29.457	53.878	52.485	50.505	46.902

The compound amount of $1

End of Year	9% Interest compounded				10% Interest compounded			
	Monthly	Quarterly	Semi-Annually	Annually	Monthly	Quarterly	Semi-Annually	Annually
1	1.094	1.093	1.092	1.090	1.105	1.104	1.103	1.100
2	1.196	1.195	1.193	1.188	1.220	1.218	1.216	1.210
3	1.309	1.306	1.302	1.295	1.348	1.345	1.340	1.331
4	1.431	1.428	1.422	1.412	1.489	1.485	1.477	1.464
5	1.566	1.561	1.553	1.539	1.645	1.639	1.629	1.611
6	1.713	1.706	1.696	1.677	1.818	1.809	1.796	1.772
7	1.873	1.865	1.852	1.828	2.008	1.996	1.980	1.949
8	2.049	2.038	2.022	1.993	2.218	2.204	2.183	2.144
9	2.241	2.228	2.208	2.172	2.450	2.433	2.407	2.358
10	2.451	2.435	2.412	2.367	2.707	2.685	2.653	2.594
11	2.681	2.662	2.634	2.580	2.991	2.964	2.925	2.853
12	2.933	2.910	2.876	2.813	3.304	3.271	3.225	3.138
13	3.208	3.180	3.141	3.066	3.650	3.611	3.556	3.452
14	3.509	3.477	3.430	3.342	4.032	3.986	3.920	3.797
15	3.838	3.800	3.745	3.642	4.454	4.400	4.322	4.177
16	4.198	4.154	4.090	3.970	4.920	4.857	4.765	4.595
17	4.592	4.541	4.466	4.328	5.436	5.361	5.253	5.054
18	5.023	4.963	4.877	4.717	6.005	5.917	5.792	5.560
19	5.494	5.425	5.326	5.142	6.633	6.532	6.385	6.116
20	6.009	5.930	5.816	5.604	7.328	7.210	7.040	6.727
21	6.573	6.482	6.352	6.109	8.095	7.958	7.762	7.400
22	7.189	7.086	6.936	6.659	8.943	8.784	8.557	8.140
23	7.864	7.745	7.574	7.258	9.880	9.696	9.434	8.954
24	8.602	8.466	8.271	7.911	10.914	10.703	10.401	9.850
25	9.408	9.254	9.033	8.623	12.057	11.814	11.467	10.835
26	10.291	10.115	9.864	9.399	13.319	13.040	12.643	11.918
27	11.256	11.057	10.772	10.245	14.714	14.394	13.939	13.110
28	12.312	12.086	11.763	11.167	16.255	15.888	15.367	14.421
29	13.467	13.211	12.845	12.172	17.957	17.538	16.943	15.863
30	14.731	14.441	14.027	13.268	19.837	19.358	18.679	17.449
31	16.112	15.785	15.318	14.462	21.915	21.368	20.594	19.194
32	17.624	17.255	16.728	15.763	24.209	23.586	22.705	21.114
33	19.277	18.861	18.267	17.182	26.744	26.035	25.032	23.225
34	21.085	20.616	19.948	18.728	29.545	28.737	27.598	25.548
35	23.063	22.535	21.784	20.414	32.639	31.721	30.426	28.102
36	25.227	24.633	23.789	22.251	36.056	35.014	33.545	30.913
37	27.593	26.926	25.978	24.254	39.832	38.648	36.984	34.004
38	30.182	29.432	28.369	26.437	44.003	42.661	40.774	37.404
39	33.013	32.172	30.979	28.816	48.611	47.089	44.954	41.145
40	36.110	35.167	33.830	31.409	53.701	51.978	49.561	45.259
41	39.497	38.440	36.943	34.236	59.324	57.374	54.641	49.785
42	43.202	42.018	40.343	37.318	65.536	63.330	60.242	54.764
43	47.255	45.929	44.056	40.676	72.398	69.904	66.417	60.240
44	51.688	50.205	48.110	44.337	79.979	77.161	73.225	66.264
45	56.537	54.878	52.537	48.327	88.354	85.172	80.730	72.890
46	61.840	59.986	57.372	52.677	97.606	94.014	89.005	80.180
47	67.641	65.570	62.651	57.418	107.827	103.774	98.128	88.197
48	73.986	71.673	68.417	62.585	119.118	114.547	108.186	97.017
49	80.927	78.345	74.713	68.218	131.591	126.438	119.276	106.719
50	88.518	85.637	81.589	74.358	145.370	139.564	131.501	117.391

The compound amount of $1

End of Year	11% Interest compounded				12% Interest compounded			
	Monthly	Quarterly	Semi-Annually	Annually	Monthly	Quarterly	Semi-Annually	Annually
1	1.116	1.115	1.113	1.110	1.127	1.126	1.124	1.120
2	1.245	1.242	1.239	1.232	1.270	1.267	1.262	1.254
3	1.389	1.385	1.379	1.368	1.431	1.426	1.419	1.405
4	1.550	1.544	1.535	1.518	1.612	1.605	1.594	1.574
5	1.729	1.720	1.708	1.685	1.817	1.806	1.791	1.762
6	1.929	1.918	1.901	1.870	2.047	2.033	2.012	1.974
7	2.152	2.137	2.116	2.076	2.307	2.288	2.261	2.211
8	2.401	2.382	2.355	2.305	2.599	2.575	2.540	2.476
9	2.679	2.655	2.621	2.558	2.929	2.898	2.854	2.773
10	2.989	2.960	2.918	2.839	3.300	3.262	3.207	3.106
11	3.335	3.299	3.248	3.152	3.719	3.671	3.604	3.479
12	3.721	3.677	3.615	3.498	4.191	4.132	4.049	3.896
13	4.152	4.099	4.023	3.883	4.722	4.651	4.549	4.363
14	4.632	4.569	4.478	4.310	5.321	5.235	5.112	4.887
15	5.168	5.092	4.984	4.785	5.996	5.892	5.743	5.474
16	5.766	5.676	5.547	5.311	6.756	6.631	6.453	6.130
17	6.433	6.327	6.174	5.895	7.613	7.463	7.251	6.866
18	7.178	7.052	6.872	6.544	8.579	8.400	8.147	7.690
19	8.008	7.860	7.649	7.263	9.667	9.454	9.154	8.613
20	8.935	8.761	8.513	8.062	10.893	10.641	10.286	9.646
21	9.969	9.765	9.476	8.949	12.274	11.976	11.557	10.804
22	11.123	10.884	10.546	9.934	13.831	13.480	12.985	12.100
23	12.410	12.132	11.739	11.026	15.585	15.171	14.590	13.552
24	13.846	13.522	13.065	12.239	17.561	17.076	16.394	15.179
25	15.448	15.072	14.542	13.585	19.788	19.219	18.420	17.000
26	17.236	16.800	16.186	15.080	22.298	21.631	20.697	19.040
27	19.230	18.726	18.015	16.739	25.126	24.346	23.255	21.325
28	21.455	20.872	20.051	18.580	28.313	27.401	26.129	23.884
29	23.938	23.264	22.317	20.624	31.903	30.840	29.359	26.750
30	26.708	25.931	24.840	22.892	35.950	34.711	32.988	29.960
31	29.799	28.903	27.647	25.410	40.509	39.068	37.065	33.555
32	33.247	32.216	30.772	28.206	45.647	43.971	41.646	37.582
33	37.094	35.909	34.250	31.308	51.436	49.490	46.794	42.092
34	41.387	40.025	38.121	34.752	57.959	55.701	52.577	47.143
35	46.176	44.612	42.430	38.575	65.310	62.692	59.076	52.800
36	51.519	49.726	47.226	42.818	73.592	70.560	66.378	59.136
37	57.481	55.426	52.563	47.528	82.926	79.416	74.582	66.232
38	64.133	61.779	58.504	52.756	93.443	89.384	83.800	74.180
39	71.554	68.860	65.117	58.559	105.294	100.602	94.158	83.081
40	79.834	76.753	72.476	65.001	118.648	113.229	105.796	93.051
41	89.073	85.550	80.668	72.151	133.695	127.440	118.872	104.217
42	99.380	95.356	89.786	80.088	150.651	143.435	133.565	116.723
43	110.880	106.286	99.934	88.897	169.757	161.437	150.074	130.730
44	123.711	118.468	111.229	98.676	191.287	181.699	168.623	146.418
45	138.027	132.047	123.800	109.530	215.547	204.503	189.465	163.988
46	153.999	147.183	137.793	121.579	242.884	230.170	212.882	183.666
47	171.820	164.053	153.367	134.952	273.687	259.059	239.195	205.706
48	191.703	182.857	170.701	149.797	308.398	291.573	268.759	230.391
49	213.887	203.816	189.995	166.275	347.510	328.168	301.978	258.038
50	238.637	227.178	211.469	184.565	391.583	369.356	339.302	289.002

The compound amount of $1

End of Year	13% Interest compounded				14% Interest compounded			
	Monthly	Quarterly	Semi-Annually	Annually	Monthly	Quarterly	Semi-Annually	Annually
1	1.138	1.136	1.134	1.130	1.149	1.148	1.145	1.140
2	1.295	1.292	1.286	1.277	1.321	1.317	1.311	1.300
3	1.474	1.468	1.459	1.443	1.518	1.511	1.501	1.482
4	1.677	1.668	1.655	1.630	1.745	1.734	1.718	1.689
5	1.909	1.896	1.877	1.842	2.006	1.990	1.967	1.925
6	2.172	2.155	2.129	2.082	2.305	2.283	2.252	2.195
7	2.472	2.449	2.415	2.353	2.649	2.620	2.579	2.502
8	2.813	2.783	2.739	2.658	3.045	3.007	2.952	2.853
9	3.202	3.163	3.107	3.004	3.500	3.450	3.380	3.252
10	3.644	3.594	3.524	3.395	4.022	3.959	3.870	3.707
11	4.147	4.085	3.997	3.836	4.623	4.543	4.430	4.226
12	4.719	4.642	4.533	4.335	5.314	5.214	5.072	4.818
13	5.370	5.276	5.141	4.898	6.107	5.983	5.807	5.492
14	6.112	5.996	5.832	5.535	7.019	6.865	6.649	6.261
15	6.955	6.814	6.614	6.254	8.068	7.878	7.612	7.138
16	7.915	7.744	7.502	7.067	9.272	9.040	8.715	8.137
17	9.008	8.801	8.509	7.986	10.657	10.374	9.978	9.276
18	10.251	10.002	9.651	9.024	12.249	11.904	11.424	10.575
19	11.666	11.367	10.947	10.197	14.078	13.660	13.079	12.056
20	13.277	12.918	12.416	11.523	16.180	15.676	14.974	13.743
21	15.109	14.681	14.083	13.021	18.597	17.988	17.144	15.668
22	17.195	16.685	15.973	14.714	21.374	20.642	19.628	17.861
23	19.568	18.962	18.117	16.627	24.566	23.687	22.473	20.362
24	22.270	21.550	20.549	18.788	28.235	27.182	25.729	23.212
25	25.343	24.491	23.307	21.231	32.451	31.191	29.457	26.462
26	28.842	27.833	26.435	23.991	37.298	35.793	33.725	30.167
27	32.823	31.632	29.983	27.109	42.868	41.073	38.612	34.390
28	37.353	35.949	34.008	30.633	49.270	47.132	44.207	39.204
29	42.509	40.855	38.572	34.616	56.628	54.085	50.613	44.693
30	48.377	46.431	43.750	39.116	65.085	62.064	57.946	50.950
31	55.055	52.768	49.622	44.201	74.805	71.220	66.343	58.083
32	62.654	59.969	56.283	49.947	85.976	81.727	75.956	66.215
33	71.302	68.153	63.837	56.440	98.816	93.783	86.962	75.485
34	81.144	77.455	72.406	63.777	113.573	107.619	99.563	86.053
35	92.345	88.025	82.124	72.069	130.534	123.495	113.989	98.100
36	105.092	100.039	93.148	81.437	150.029	141.713	130.506	111.834
37	119.598	113.692	105.650	92.024	172.434	162.619	149.417	127.491
38	136.106	129.208	119.831	103.987	198.186	186.609	171.067	145.340
39	154.893	146.842	135.916	117.506	227.783	214.138	195.855	165.687
40	176.273	166.882	154.159	132.782	261.801	245.729	224.234	188.884
41	200.605	189.657	174.851	150.043	300.899	281.979	256.726	215.327
42	228.295	215.541	198.320	169.549	345.836	323.578	293.926	245.473
43	259.807	244.957	224.940	191.590	397.484	371.313	336.515	279.839
44	295.668	278.388	255.132	216.497	456.845	426.090	385.276	319.017
45	336.480	316.381	289.377	244.641	525.071	488.948	441.103	363.679
46	382.925	359.560	328.219	276.445	603.486	561.079	505.019	414.594
47	435.782	408.631	372.274	312.383	693.612	643.852	578.196	472.637
48	495.934	464.399	422.243	352.992	797.197	738.834	661.977	538.807
49	564.389	527.779	478.918	398.881	916.252	847.830	757.897	614.239
50	642.293	599.808	543.201	450.736	1053.087	972.904	867.716	700.233

The compound amount of $1

End of Year	15% Interest compounded				16% Interest compounded			
	Monthly	Quarterly	Semi-Annually	Annually	Monthly	Quarterly	Semi-Annually	Annually
1	1.161	1.159	1.156	1.150	1.172	1.170	1.166	1.160
2	1.347	1.342	1.335	1.323	1.374	1.369	1.360	1.346
3	1.564	1.555	1.543	1.521	1.611	1.601	1.587	1.561
4	1.815	1.802	1.783	1.749	1.888	1.873	1.851	1.811
5	2.107	2.088	2.061	2.011	2.214	2.191	2.159	2.100
6	2.446	2.419	2.382	2.313	2.595	2.563	2.518	2.436
7	2.839	2.803	2.752	2.660	3.042	2.999	2.937	2.826
8	3.296	3.248	3.181	3.059	3.566	3.508	3.426	3.278
9	3.825	3.763	3.676	3.518	4.181	4.104	3.996	3.803
10	4.440	4.360	4.248	4.046	4.901	4.801	4.661	4.411
11	5.154	5.052	4.909	4.652	5.745	5.617	5.437	5.117
12	5.983	5.854	5.673	5.350	6.735	6.571	6.341	5.936
13	6.944	6.782	6.556	6.153	7.895	7.687	7.396	6.886
14	8.061	7.858	7.576	7.076	9.255	8.992	8.627	7.988
15	9.356	9.105	8.755	8.137	10.850	10.520	10.063	9.266
16	10.860	10.550	10.117	9.358	12.719	12.306	11.737	10.748
17	12.606	12.223	11.692	10.761	14.910	14.397	13.690	12.468
18	14.633	14.163	13.512	12.375	17.478	16.842	15.968	14.463
19	16.985	16.410	15.614	14.232	20.489	19.703	18.625	16.777
20	19.715	19.013	18.044	16.367	24.019	23.050	21.725	19.461
21	22.885	22.029	20.852	18.822	28.157	26.965	25.339	22.574
22	26.564	25.524	24.098	21.645	33.008	31.545	29.556	26.186
23	30.834	29.574	27.848	24.891	38.694	36.903	34.474	30.376
24	35.791	34.266	32.182	28.625	45.360	43.172	40.211	35.236
25	41.544	39.702	37.190	32.919	53.174	50.505	46.902	40.874
26	48.223	46.001	42.977	37.857	62.334	59.084	54.706	47.414
27	55.975	53.299	49.666	43.535	73.073	69.120	63.809	55.000
28	64.973	61.754	57.395	50.066	85.661	80.860	74.427	63.800
29	75.417	71.552	66.327	57.575	100.418	94.595	86.812	74.009
30	87.541	82.903	76.649	66.212	117.717	110.663	101.257	85.850
31	101.614	96.056	88.578	76.144	137.996	129.460	118.106	99.586
32	117.948	111.295	102.363	87.565	161.769	151.449	137.759	115.520
33	136.909	128.953	118.293	100.700	189.637	177.174	160.682	134.003
34	158.918	149.411	136.702	115.805	222.305	207.269	187.420	155.443
35	184.465	173.115	157.977	133.176	260.602	242.475	218.606	180.314
36	214.118	200.580	182.562	153.152	305.496	283.662	254.983	209.164
37	248.539	232.402	210.973	176.125	358.124	331.844	297.412	242.631
38	288.493	269.273	243.805	202.543	419.819	388.211	346.901	281.452
39	334.869	311.993	281.748	232.925	492.141	454.152	404.625	326.484
40	388.701	361.490	325.595	267.864	576.923	531.293	471.955	378.721
41	451.186	418.841	376.265	308.043	676.310	621.538	550.488	439.317
42	523.716	485.290	434.821	354.250	792.818	727.111	642.089	509.607
43	607.906	562.282	502.491	407.387	929.398	850.618	748.933	591.144
44	705.630	651.488	580.691	468.495	1089.506	995.102	873.555	685.727
45	819.063	754.847	671.061	538.769	1277.196	1164.129	1018.915	795.444
46	950.731	874.604	775.494	619.585	1497.220	1361.866	1188.463	922.715
47	1103.565	1013.360	896.181	712.522	1755.147	1593.191	1386.223	1070.349
48	1280.968	1174.130	1035.649	819.401	2057.508	1863.808	1616.890	1241.605
49	1486.890	1360.406	1196.822	942.311	2411.956	2180.392	1885.941	1440.262
50	1725.914	1576.235	1383.077	1083.657	2827.466	2550.750	2199.761	1670.704

The compound amount of $1

End of Year	17% Interest compounded				18% Interest compounded			
	Monthly	Quarterly	Semi-Annually	Annually	Monthly	Quarterly	Semi-Annually	Annually
1	1.184	1.181	1.177	1.170	1.196	1.193	1.188	1.180
2	1.402	1.395	1.386	1.369	1.430	1.422	1.412	1.392
3	1.659	1.648	1.631	1.602	1.709	1.696	1.677	1.643
4	1.964	1.946	1.921	1.874	2.043	2.022	1.993	1.939
5	2.326	2.299	2.261	2.192	2.443	2.412	2.367	2.288
6	2.753	2.715	2.662	2.565	2.921	2.876	2.813	2.700
7	3.260	3.207	3.133	3.001	3.493	3.430	3.342	3.185
8	3.859	3.788	3.689	3.511	4.176	4.090	3.970	3.759
9	4.569	4.474	4.342	4.108	4.993	4.877	4.717	4.435
10	5.409	5.285	5.112	4.807	5.969	5.816	5.604	5.234
11	6.404	6.242	6.018	5.624	7.137	6.936	6.659	6.176
12	7.581	7.373	7.085	6.580	8.533	8.271	7.911	7.288
13	8.975	8.709	8.340	7.699	10.202	9.864	9.399	8.599
14	10.626	10.286	9.818	9.007	12.198	11.763	11.167	10.147
15	12.580	12.150	11.558	10.539	14.584	14.027	13.268	11.974
16	14.893	14.351	13.607	12.330	17.437	16.728	15.763	14.129
17	17.632	16.950	16.018	14.426	20.848	19.948	18.728	16.672
18	20.874	20.021	18.857	16.879	24.927	23.789	22.251	19.673
19	24.713	23.647	22.199	19.748	29.803	28.369	26.437	23.214
20	29.258	27.931	26.133	23.106	35.633	33.830	31.409	27.393
21	34.638	32.991	30.764	27.034	42.603	40.343	37.318	32.324
22	41.008	38.967	36.217	31.629	50.937	48.110	44.337	38.142
23	48.548	46.025	42.635	37.006	60.901	57.372	52.677	45.008
24	57.476	54.363	50.191	43.297	72.815	68.417	62.585	53.109
25	68.046	64.211	59.086	50.658	87.059	81.589	74.358	62.669
26	80.559	75.842	69.558	59.270	104.089	97.296	88.344	73.949
27	95.373	89.581	81.885	69.345	124.451	116.027	104.962	87.260
28	112.911	105.808	96.397	81.134	148.796	138.364	124.705	102.967
29	133.674	124.975	113.481	94.927	177.903	165.002	148.162	121.501
30	158.256	147.614	133.593	111.065	212.704	196.768	176.031	143.371
31	187.358	174.354	157.269	129.946	254.313	234.650	209.143	169.177
32	221.811	205.938	185.141	152.036	304.061	279.824	248.483	199.629
33	262.600	243.243	217.953	177.883	363.540	333.695	295.222	235.563
34	310.891	287.306	256.580	208.123	434.656	397.938	350.753	277.964
35	368.061	339.351	302.052	243.503	519.682	474.549	416.730	327.997
36	435.744	400.823	355.583	284.899	621.341	565.908	495.117	387.037
37	515.874	473.432	418.601	333.332	742.887	674.856	588.249	456.703
38	610.739	559.193	492.788	389.998	888.209	804.778	698.898	538.910
39	723.049	660.490	580.122	456.298	1061.959	959.713	830.361	635.914
40	856.011	780.136	682.935	533.869	1269.698	1144.475	986.552	750.378
41	1013.425	921.456	803.968	624.626	1518.073	1364.808	1172.122	885.446
42	1199.785	1088.375	946.451	730.813	1815.036	1627.559	1392.598	1044.827
43	1420.416	1285.532	1114.185	855.051	2170.090	1940.895	1654.546	1232.896
44	1681.618	1518.404	1311.647	1000.410	2594.599	2314.553	1965.766	1454.817
45	1990.854	1793.459	1544.104	1170.479	3102.150	2760.147	2335.527	1716.684
46	2356.955	2118.340	1817.757	1369.461	3708.987	3291.527	2774.839	2025.687
47	2790.380	2502.073	2139.909	1602.269	4434.532	3925.207	3296.786	2390.311
48	3303.508	2955.318	2519.155	1874.655	5302.007	4680.883	3916.912	2820.567
49	3910.996	3490.667	2965.612	2193.346	6339.176	5582.040	4653.683	3328.269
50	4630.195	4122.994	3491.193	2566.215	7579.235	6656.686	5529.041	3927.357

The compound amount of $1

End of Year	19% Interest compounded				20% Interest compounded			
	Monthly	Quarterly	Semi-Annually	Annually	Monthly	Quarterly	Semi-Annually	Annually
1	1.207	1.204	1.199	1.190	1.219	1.216	1.210	1.200
2	1.458	1.450	1.438	1.416	1.487	1.477	1.464	1.440
3	1.760	1.745	1.724	1.685	1.813	1.796	1.772	1.728
4	2.126	2.101	2.067	2.005	2.211	2.183	2.144	2.074
5	2.567	2.530	2.478	2.386	2.696	2.653	2.594	2.488
6	3.099	3.046	2.971	2.840	3.287	3.225	3.138	2.986
7	3.742	3.667	3.563	3.379	4.009	3.920	3.797	3.583
8	4.518	4.415	4.272	4.021	4.888	4.765	4.595	4.300
9	5.455	5.316	5.122	4.785	5.961	5.792	5.560	5.160
10	6.587	6.400	6.142	5.695	7.268	7.040	6.727	6.192
11	7.954	7.705	7.364	6.777	8.863	8.557	8.140	7.430
12	9.604	9.277	8.830	8.064	10.807	10.401	9.850	8.916
13	11.596	11.169	10.587	9.596	13.178	12.643	11.918	10.699
14	14.001	13.447	12.694	11.420	16.069	15.367	14.421	12.839
15	16.906	16.190	15.220	13.590	19.595	18.679	17.449	15.407
16	20.413	19.492	18.250	16.172	23.894	22.705	21.114	18.488
17	24.648	23.468	21.882	19.244	29.136	27.598	25.548	22.186
18	29.761	28.255	26.237	22.901	35.528	33.545	30.913	26.623
19	35.935	34.018	31.458	27.252	43.323	40.774	37.404	31.948
20	43.390	40.956	37.719	32.429	52.828	49.561	45.259	38.338
21	52.391	49.310	45.227	38.591	64.417	60.242	54.764	46.005
22	63.260	59.368	54.228	45.923	78.550	73.225	66.264	55.206
23	76.383	71.478	65.020	54.649	95.783	89.005	80.180	66.247
24	92.229	86.057	77.961	65.032	116.797	108.186	97.017	79.497
25	111.362	103.610	93.477	77.388	142.421	131.501	117.391	95.396
26	134.464	124.744	112.082	92.092	173.667	159.841	142.043	114.475
27	162.359	150.188	134.389	109.589	211.769	194.287	171.872	137.371
28	196.041	180.822	161.135	130.411	258.229	236.157	207.965	164.845
29	236.710	217.705	193.205	155.189	314.882	287.051	251.638	197.814
30	285.815	262.110	231.658	184.675	383.964	348.912	304.482	237.376
31	345.108	315.573	277.764	219.764	468.202	424.105	368.423	284.852
32	416.701	379.941	333.046	261.519	570.922	515.502	445.792	341.822
33	503.146	457.438	399.330	311.207	696.177	626.596	539.408	410.186
34	607.524	550.742	478.807	370.337	848.912	761.631	652.683	492.224
35	733.556	663.078	574.101	440.701	1035.155	925.767	789.747	590.668
36	885.732	798.327	688.362	524.434	1262.259	1125.276	955.594	708.802
37	1069.478	961.162	825.363	624.076	1539.188	1367.780	1156.269	850.562
38	1291.343	1157.212	989.630	742.651	1876.872	1662.545	1399.085	1020.675
39	1559.233	1393.250	1186.592	883.754	2288.641	2020.834	1692.893	1224.810
40	1882.698	1677.433	1422.753	1051.668	2790.748	2456.336	2048.400	1469.772
41	2273.265	2019.581	1705.917	1251.484	3403.013	2985.692	2478.564	1763.726
42	2744.856	2431.517	2045.437	1489.266	4149.604	3629.128	2999.063	2116.471
43	3314.280	2927.477	2452.530	1772.227	5059.990	4411.227	3628.866	2539.765
44	4001.830	3524.598	2940.644	2108.950	6170.107	5361.874	4390.928	3047.718
45	4832.014	4243.515	3525.906	2509.651	7523.773	6517.392	5313.023	3657.262
46	5834.420	5109.070	4227.649	2986.484	9174.422	7921.931	6428.757	4388.714
47	7044.776	6151.173	5069.057	3553.916	11187.208	9629.156	7778.796	5266.457
48	8506.222	7405.836	6077.926	4229.160	13641.582	11704.299	9412.344	6319.749
49	10270.846	8916.414	7287.586	5032.701	16634.424	14226.649	11388.936	7583.698
50	12401.544	10735.106	8737.998	5988.914	20283.868	17292.581	13780.612	9100.438

The future value of an "ordinary annuity" assuming deposits are made monthly, quarterly, semi-annually or annually at various interest rates

Applications
Chapter Three
- How much will $1 invested at the end of each period amount to at some time in the future?

Chapter Fifteen
- Evaluating registered retirement savings plan yields.

The future value of $1 invested at the *end* of each period

End of Year	5% Interest compounded and Deposits made				6% Interest compounded and Deposits made			
	Monthly	Quarterly	Semi-Annually	Annually	Monthly	Quarterly	Semi-Annually	Annually
1	12.279	4.076	2.025	1.000	12.336	4.091	2.030	1.000
2	25.186	8.359	4.153	2.050	25.432	8.433	4.184	2.060
3	38.753	12.860	6.388	3.153	39.336	13.041	6.468	3.184
4	53.015	17.591	8.736	4.310	54.098	17.932	8.892	4.375
5	68.006	22.563	11.203	5.526	69.770	23.124	11.464	5.637
6	83.764	27.788	13.796	6.802	86.409	28.634	14.192	6.975
7	100.329	33.279	16.519	8.142	104.074	34.481	17.086	8.394
8	117.741	39.050	19.380	9.549	122.829	40.688	20.157	9.897
9	136.043	45.116	22.386	11.027	142.740	47.276	23.414	11.491
10	155.282	51.490	25.545	12.578	163.879	54.268	26.870	13.181
11	175.506	58.188	28.863	14.207	186.323	61.689	30.537	14.972
12	196.764	65.228	32.349	15.917	210.150	69.565	34.426	16.870
13	219.109	72.627	36.012	17.713	235.447	77.925	38.553	18.882
14	242.598	80.403	39.860	19.599	262.305	86.798	42.931	21.015
15	267.289	88.575	43.903	21.579	290.819	96.215	47.575	23.276
16	293.243	97.163	48.150	23.657	321.091	106.210	52.503	25.673
17	320.525	106.188	52.613	25.840	353.231	116.818	57.730	28.213
18	349.202	115.674	57.301	28.132	387.353	128.077	63.276	30.906
19	379.347	125.642	62.227	30.539	423.580	140.027	69.159	33.760
20	411.034	136.119	67.403	33.066	462.041	152.711	75.401	36.786
21	444.342	147.129	72.840	35.719	502.874	166.173	82.023	39.993
22	479.354	158.700	78.552	38.505	546.226	180.460	89.048	43.392
23	516.158	170.861	84.554	41.430	592.251	195.625	96.501	46.996
24	554.844	183.641	90.860	44.502	641.116	211.720	104.408	50.816
25	595.510	197.072	97.484	47.727	692.994	228.803	112.797	54.865
26	638.256	211.188	104.444	51.113	748.072	246.934	121.696	59.156
27	683.189	226.023	111.757	54.669	806.547	266.178	131.137	63.706
28	730.421	241.613	119.440	58.403	868.628	286.602	141.154	68.528
29	780.070	257.998	127.511	62.323	934.539	308.280	151.780	73.640
30	832.259	275.217	135.992	66.439	1004.515	331.288	163.053	79.058
31	887.117	293.314	144.901	70.761	1078.807	355.708	175.013	84.802
32	944.783	312.332	154.262	75.299	1157.681	381.627	187.702	90.890
33	1005.399	332.320	164.096	80.064	1241.420	409.135	201.163	97.343
34	1069.116	353.326	174.429	85.067	1330.323	438.332	215.444	104.184
35	1136.092	375.401	185.284	90.320	1424.710	469.321	230.594	111.435
36	1206.496	398.602	196.689	95.836	1524.919	502.211	246.667	119.121
37	1280.501	422.985	208.672	101.628	1631.308	537.119	263.719	127.268
38	1358.293	448.609	221.261	107.710	1744.259	574.170	281.810	135.904
39	1440.065	475.540	234.487	114.095	1864.177	613.494	301.002	145.058
40	1526.020	503.842	248.383	120.800	1991.491	655.231	321.363	154.762
41	1616.373	533.586	262.982	127.840	2126.657	699.529	342.964	165.048
42	1711.349	564.845	278.321	135.232	2270.160	746.545	365.881	175.951
43	1811.183	597.697	294.436	142.993	2422.514	796.447	390.193	187.508
44	1916.126	632.222	311.366	151.143	2584.265	849.411	415.985	199.758
45	2026.437	668.507	329.154	159.700	2755.993	905.625	443.349	212.744
46	2142.393	706.640	347.843	168.685	2938.312	965.288	472.379	226.508
47	2264.280	746.715	367.477	178.119	3131.876	1028.612	503.177	241.099
48	2392.404	788.833	388.106	188.025	3337.379	1095.822	535.850	256.565
49	2527.083	833.096	409.779	198.427	3555.557	1167.157	570.513	272.958
50	2668.652	879.614	432.549	209.348	3787.191	1242.869	607.288	290.336

The future value of $1 invested at the *end* of each period

End of Year	7% Interest compounded and Deposits made				8% Interest compounded and Deposits made			
	Monthly	Quarterly	Semi-Annually	Annually	Monthly	Quarterly	Semi-Annually	Annually
1	12.393	4.106	2.035	1.000	12.450	4.122	2.040	1.000
2	25.681	8.508	4.215	2.070	25.933	8.583	4.246	2.080
3	39.930	13.225	6.550	3.215	40.536	13.412	6.633	3.246
4	55.209	18.282	9.052	4.440	56.350	18.639	9.214	4.506
5	71.593	23.702	11.731	5.751	73.477	24.297	12.006	5.867
6	89.161	29.511	14.602	7.153	92.025	30.422	15.026	7.336
7	107.999	35.738	17.677	8.654	112.113	37.051	18.292	8.923
8	128.199	42.412	20.971	10.260	133.869	44.227	21.825	10.637
9	149.859	49.566	24.500	11.978	157.430	51.994	25.645	12.488
10	173.085	57.234	28.280	13.816	182.946	60.402	29.778	14.487
11	197.990	65.453	32.329	15.784	210.580	69.503	34.248	16.645
12	224.695	74.263	36.667	17.888	240.508	79.354	39.083	18.977
13	253.331	83.705	41.313	20.141	272.920	90.016	44.312	21.495
14	284.037	93.827	46.291	22.550	308.023	101.558	49.968	24.215
15	316.962	104.675	51.623	25.129	346.038	114.052	56.085	27.152
16	352.268	116.303	57.335	27.888	387.209	127.575	62.701	30.324
17	390.126	128.767	63.453	30.840	431.797	142.213	69.858	33.750
18	430.721	142.126	70.008	33.999	480.086	158.057	77.598	37.450
19	474.250	156.446	77.029	37.379	532.383	175.208	85.970	41.446
20	520.927	171.794	84.550	40.995	589.020	193.772	95.026	45.762
21	570.977	188.245	92.607	44.865	650.359	213.867	104.820	50.423
22	624.646	205.878	101.238	49.006	716.788	235.618	115.413	55.457
23	682.194	224.779	110.484	53.436	788.731	259.162	126.871	60.893
24	743.902	245.037	120.388	58.177	866.645	284.647	139.263	66.765
25	810.072	266.752	130.998	63.249	951.026	312.232	152.667	73.106
26	881.024	290.027	142.363	68.676	1042.411	342.092	167.165	79.954
27	957.106	314.974	154.538	74.484	1141.381	374.413	182.845	87.351
28	1038.688	341.714	167.580	80.698	1248.565	409.398	199.806	95.339
29	1126.168	370.375	181.551	87.347	1364.645	447.267	218.150	103.966
30	1219.971	401.096	196.517	94.461	1490.359	488.258	237.991	113.283
31	1320.555	434.025	212.549	102.073	1626.508	532.628	259.451	123.346
32	1428.411	469.320	229.723	110.218	1773.958	580.655	282.662	134.214
33	1544.064	507.151	248.120	118.933	1933.645	632.641	307.767	145.951
34	1668.077	547.700	267.827	128.259	2106.587	688.913	334.921	158.627
35	1801.055	591.164	288.938	138.237	2293.882	749.823	364.290	172.317
36	1943.646	637.750	311.552	148.913	2496.724	815.754	396.057	187.102
37	2096.544	687.685	335.778	160.337	2716.400	887.120	430.415	203.070
38	2260.496	741.207	361.729	172.561	2954.310	964.369	467.577	220.316
39	2436.300	798.576	389.528	185.640	3211.966	1047.986	507.771	238.941
40	2624.813	860.067	419.307	199.635	3491.008	1138.495	551.245	259.057
41	2826.954	925.977	451.207	214.610	3793.210	1236.466	598.267	280.781
42	3043.707	996.623	485.379	230.632	4120.494	1342.512	649.125	304.244
43	3276.130	1072.346	521.985	247.776	4474.943	1457.299	704.134	329.583
44	3525.354	1153.510	561.199	266.121	4858.811	1581.549	763.631	356.950
45	3792.595	1240.506	603.205	285.749	5274.540	1716.042	827.983	386.506
46	4079.154	1333.754	648.203	306.752	5724.774	1861.620	897.587	418.426
47	4386.429	1433.702	696.407	329.224	6212.377	2019.199	972.870	452.900
48	4715.917	1540.833	748.043	353.270	6740.452	2189.768	1054.296	490.132
49	5069.224	1655.662	803.358	378.999	7312.356	2374.397	1142.367	530.343
50	5448.071	1778.742	862.612	406.529	7931.727	2574.245	1237.624	573.770

The future value of $1 invested at the *end* of each period

End of Year	9% Interest compounded and Deposits made				10% Interest compounded and Deposits made			
	Monthly	Quarterly	Semi-Annually	Annually	Monthly	Quarterly	Semi-Annually	Annually
1	12.508	4.137	2.045	1.000	12.566	4.153	2.050	1.000
2	26.188	8.659	4.278	2.090	26.447	8.736	4.310	2.100
3	41.153	13.602	6.717	3.278	41.782	13.796	6.802	3.310
4	57.521	19.005	9.380	4.573	58.722	19.380	9.549	4.641
5	75.424	24.912	12.288	5.985	77.437	25.545	12.578	6.105
6	95.007	31.367	15.464	7.523	98.111	32.349	15.917	7.716
7	116.427	38.424	18.932	9.200	120.950	39.860	19.599	9.487
8	139.856	46.138	22.719	11.028	146.181	48.150	23.657	11.436
9	165.483	54.570	26.855	13.021	174.054	57.301	28.132	13.579
10	193.514	63.786	31.371	15.193	204.845	67.403	33.066	15.937
11	224.175	73.861	36.303	17.560	238.860	78.552	38.505	18.531
12	257.712	84.873	41.689	20.141	276.438	90.860	44.502	21.384
13	294.394	96.910	47.571	22.953	317.950	104.444	51.113	24.523
14	334.518	110.068	53.993	26.019	363.809	119.440	58.403	27.975
15	378.406	124.450	61.007	29.361	414.470	135.992	66.439	31.772
16	426.410	140.172	68.666	33.003	470.436	154.262	75.299	35.950
17	478.918	157.356	77.030	36.974	532.263	174.429	85.067	40.545
18	536.352	176.141	86.164	41.301	600.563	196.689	95.836	45.599
19	599.173	196.674	96.138	46.018	676.016	221.261	107.710	51.159
20	667.887	219.118	107.030	51.160	759.369	248.383	120.800	57.275
21	743.047	243.651	118.925	56.765	851.450	278.321	135.232	64.002
22	825.257	270.468	131.914	62.873	953.174	311.366	151.143	71.403
23	915.180	299.781	146.098	69.532	1065.549	347.843	168.685	79.543
24	1013.538	331.822	161.588	76.790	1189.692	388.106	188.025	88.497
25	1121.122	366.847	178.503	84.701	1326.833	432.549	209.348	98.347
26	1238.798	405.131	196.975	93.324	1478.336	481.605	232.856	109.182
27	1367.514	446.979	217.146	102.723	1645.702	535.755	258.774	121.100
28	1508.304	492.722	239.174	112.968	1830.595	595.525	287.348	134.210
29	1662.301	542.723	263.229	124.135	2034.847	661.501	318.851	148.631
30	1830.743	597.379	289.498	136.308	2260.488	734.326	353.584	164.494
31	2014.987	657.122	318.184	149.575	2509.756	814.711	391.876	181.943
32	2216.515	722.426	349.510	164.037	2785.126	903.441	434.093	201.138
33	2436.947	793.809	383.719	179.800	3089.331	1001.382	480.638	222.252
34	2678.057	871.836	421.075	196.982	3425.389	1109.491	531.953	245.477
35	2941.784	957.127	461.870	215.711	3796.638	1228.823	588.529	271.024
36	3230.252	1050.356	506.418	236.125	4206.761	1360.544	650.903	299.127
37	3545.779	1152.264	555.066	258.376	4659.830	1505.938	719.670	330.039
38	3890.905	1263.658	608.191	282.630	5160.340	1666.426	795.486	364.043
39	4268.407	1385.420	666.205	309.066	5713.261	1843.575	879.074	401.448
40	4681.320	1518.517	729.558	337.882	6324.080	2039.115	971.229	442.593
41	5132.968	1664.002	798.740	369.292	6998.859	2254.954	1072.830	487.852
42	5626.983	1823.030	874.289	403.528	7744.296	2493.199	1184.845	537.637
43	6167.341	1996.861	956.791	440.846	8567.791	2756.178	1308.341	592.401
44	6758.388	2186.872	1046.884	481.522	9477.516	3046.457	1444.496	652.641
45	7404.878	2394.571	1145.269	525.859	10482.502	3366.872	1594.607	718.905
46	8112.015	2621.602	1252.707	574.186	11592.722	3720.549	1760.105	791.795
47	8885.485	2869.767	1370.033	626.863	12819.197	4110.942	1942.565	871.975
48	9731.513	3141.031	1498.155	684.280	14174.100	4541.863	2143.728	960.172
49	10656.903	3437.546	1638.068	746.866	15670.879	5017.520	2365.510	1057.190
50	11669.102	3761.661	1790.856	815.084	17324.391	5542.556	2610.025	1163.909

The future value of $1 invested at the *end* of each period

End of Year	11% Interest compounded and Deposits made				12% Interest compounded and Deposits made			
	Monthly	Quarterly	Semi-Annually	Annually	Monthly	Quarterly	Semi-Annually	Annually
1	12.624	4.168	2.055	1.000	12.683	4.184	2.060	1.000
2	26.709	8.814	4.342	2.110	26.973	8.892	4.375	2.120
3	42.423	13.992	6.888	3.342	43.077	14.192	6.975	3.374
4	59.956	19.764	9.722	4.710	61.223	20.157	9.897	4.779
5	79.518	26.197	12.875	6.228	81.670	26.870	13.181	6.353
6	101.344	33.368	16.386	7.913	104.710	34.426	16.870	8.115
7	125.695	41.361	20.293	9.783	130.672	42.931	21.015	10.089
8	152.864	50.270	24.641	11.859	159.927	52.503	25.673	12.300
9	183.177	60.200	29.481	14.164	192.893	63.276	30.906	14.776
10	216.998	71.268	34.868	16.722	230.039	75.401	36.786	17.549
11	254.733	83.605	40.864	19.561	271.896	89.048	43.392	20.655
12	296.834	97.356	47.538	22.713	319.062	104.408	50.816	24.133
13	343.807	112.683	54.966	26.212	372.209	121.696	59.156	28.029
14	396.216	129.767	63.234	30.095	432.097	141.154	68.528	32.393
15	454.690	148.809	72.435	34.405	499.580	163.053	79.058	37.280
16	519.930	170.034	82.677	39.190	575.622	187.702	90.890	42.753
17	592.719	193.691	94.077	44.501	661.308	215.444	104.184	48.884
18	673.932	220.061	106.765	50.396	757.861	246.667	119.121	55.750
19	764.542	249.452	120.887	56.939	866.659	281.810	135.904	63.440
20	865.638	282.213	136.606	64.203	989.255	321.363	154.762	72.052
21	978.433	318.729	154.100	72.265	1127.400	365.881	175.951	81.699
22	1104.279	359.430	173.573	81.214	1283.065	415.985	199.758	92.503
23	1244.689	404.796	195.246	91.148	1458.473	472.379	226.508	104.603
24	1401.347	455.362	219.368	102.174	1656.126	535.850	256.565	118.155
25	1576.133	511.724	246.217	114.413	1878.847	607.288	290.336	133.334
26	1771.145	574.547	276.101	127.999	2129.814	687.691	328.281	150.334
27	1988.724	644.570	309.363	143.079	2412.610	778.186	370.917	169.374
28	2231.481	722.620	346.383	159.817	2731.272	880.039	418.822	190.699
29	2502.329	809.615	387.588	178.397	3090.348	994.675	472.649	214.583
30	2804.520	906.583	433.450	199.021	3494.964	1123.700	533.128	241.333
31	3141.679	1014.664	484.496	221.913	3950.896	1268.917	601.083	271.293
32	3517.855	1135.135	541.311	247.324	4464.651	1432.361	677.437	304.848
33	3937.561	1269.413	604.548	275.529	5043.562	1616.319	763.228	342.429
34	4405.834	1419.083	674.932	306.837	5695.895	1823.365	859.623	384.521
35	4928.296	1585.908	753.271	341.590	6430.959	2056.397	967.932	431.663
36	5511.217	1771.855	840.465	380.164	7259.249	2318.676	1089.629	484.463
37	6161.592	1979.115	937.513	422.982	8192.586	2613.874	1226.367	543.599
38	6887.229	2210.132	1045.531	470.511	9244.293	2946.122	1380.006	609.831
39	7696.835	2467.628	1165.757	523.267	10429.383	3320.070	1552.634	684.010
40	8600.127	2754.639	1299.571	581.826	11764.773	3740.952	1746.600	767.091
41	9607.948	3074.547	1448.510	646.827	13269.523	4214.658	1964.540	860.142
42	10732.392	3431.123	1614.283	718.978	14965.113	4747.818	2209.417	964.359
43	11986.956	3828.571	1798.793	799.065	16875.746	5347.895	2484.561	1081.083
44	13386.696	4271.575	2004.156	887.963	19028.696	6023.286	2793.712	1211.813
45	14948.413	4765.356	2232.731	986.639	21454.693	6783.445	3141.075	1358.230
46	16690.850	5315.735	2487.140	1096.169	24188.368	7639.011	3531.372	1522.218
47	18634.920	5929.200	2770.304	1217.747	27268.741	8601.958	3969.910	1705.884
48	20803.955	6612.980	3085.473	1352.700	30739.782	9685.763	4462.651	1911.590
49	23223.988	7375.136	3436.264	1502.497	34651.038	10905.595	5016.294	2141.981
50	25924.065	8224.651	3826.702	1668.771	39058.340	12278.527	5638.368	2400.018

162/ Table 2

The future value of $1 invested at the *end* of each period

End of Year	13% Interest compounded and Deposits made				14% Interest compounded and Deposits made			
	Monthly	Quarterly	Semi-Annually	Annually	Monthly	Quarterly	Semi-Annually	Annually
1	12.741	4.199	2.065	1.000	12.801	4.215	2.070	1.000
2	27.242	8.972	4.407	2.130	27.513	9.052	4.440	2.140
3	43.743	14.395	7.064	3.407	44.423	14.602	7.153	3.440
4	62.523	20.559	10.077	4.850	63.858	20.971	10.260	4.921
5	83.894	27.564	13.494	6.480	86.195	28.280	13.816	6.610
6	108.216	35.525	17.371	8.323	111.868	36.667	17.888	8.536
7	135.895	44.573	21.767	10.405	141.376	46.291	22.550	10.730
8	167.394	54.855	26.754	12.757	175.290	57.335	27.888	13.233
9	203.242	66.541	32.410	15.416	214.269	70.008	33.999	16.085
10	244.037	79.822	38.825	18.420	259.069	84.550	40.995	19.337
11	290.463	94.915	46.102	21.814	310.560	101.238	49.006	23.045
12	343.298	112.067	54.355	25.650	369.740	120.388	58.177	27.271
13	403.426	131.561	63.715	29.985	437.758	142.363	68.676	32.089
14	471.853	153.715	74.333	34.883	515.935	167.580	80.698	37.581
15	549.726	178.893	86.375	40.417	605.786	196.517	94.461	43.842
16	638.347	207.507	100.034	46.672	709.056	229.723	110.218	50.980
17	739.202	240.026	115.526	53.739	827.749	267.827	128.259	59.118
18	853.977	276.983	133.097	61.725	964.167	311.552	148.913	68.394
19	984.595	318.984	153.027	70.749	1120.959	361.729	172.561	78.969
20	1133.242	366.716	175.632	80.947	1301.166	419.307	199.635	91.025
21	1302.408	420.964	201.271	92.470	1508.286	485.379	230.632	104.768
22	1494.924	482.614	230.352	105.491	1746.337	561.199	266.121	120.436
23	1714.014	552.679	263.336	120.205	2019.939	648.203	306.752	138.297
24	1963.345	632.305	300.747	136.831	2334.401	748.043	353.270	158.659
25	2247.092	722.799	343.180	155.620	2695.826	862.612	406.529	181.871
26	2570.005	825.643	391.308	176.850	3111.227	994.082	467.505	208.333
27	2937.490	942.523	445.896	200.841	3588.665	1144.947	537.316	238.499
28	3355.701	1075.354	507.812	227.950	4137.404	1318.067	617.244	272.889
29	3831.638	1226.313	578.038	258.583	4768.093	1516.728	708.752	312.094
30	4373.270	1397.874	657.690	293.199	5492.971	1744.695	813.520	356.787
31	4989.665	1592.850	748.033	332.315	6326.103	2006.292	933.469	407.737
32	5691.142	1814.435	850.503	376.516	7283.657	2306.481	1070.799	465.820
33	6489.446	2066.261	966.727	426.463	8384.214	2650.956	1228.028	532.035
34	7397.941	2352.455	1098.551	482.903	9649.130	3046.247	1408.039	607.520
35	8431.839	2677.707	1248.069	546.681	11102.951	3499.854	1614.134	693.573
36	9608.448	3047.349	1417.656	618.749	12773.890	4020.378	1850.092	791.673
37	10947.468	3467.438	1610.006	700.187	14694.369	4617.691	2120.241	903.507
38	12471.315	3944.859	1828.174	792.211	16901.656	5303.121	2429.533	1030.998
39	14205.503	4487.437	2075.625	896.198	19438.585	6089.669	2783.643	1176.338
40	16179.066	5104.063	2356.291	1013.704	22354.383	6992.250	3189.063	1342.025
41	18425.044	5804.844	2674.629	1146.486	25705.633	8027.983	3653.228	1530.909
42	20981.040	6601.265	3035.696	1296.529	29557.365	9216.510	4184.651	1746.236
43	23889.846	7506.378	3445.227	1466.078	33984.323	10580.372	4793.076	1991.709
44	27200.162	8535.017	3909.728	1657.668	39072.411	12145.435	5489.663	2271.548
45	30967.409	9704.041	4436.576	1874.165	44920.365	13941.381	6287.185	2590.565
46	35254.659	11032.608	5034.141	2118.806	51641.665	16002.270	7200.269	2954.244
47	40133.689	12542.493	5711.913	2395.251	59366.736	18367.188	8245.658	3368.838
48	45686.183	14258.441	6480.660	2707.633	68245.486	21080.985	9442.523	3841.475
49	52005.102	16208.574	7352.591	3060.626	78450.206	24195.131	10812.815	4380.282
50	59196.236	18424.854	8341.558	3459.507	90178.920	27768.684	12381.662	4994.521

The future value of $1 invested at the *end* of each period

End of Year	15% Interest compounded and Deposits made				16% Interest compounded and Deposits made			
	Monthly	Quarterly	Semi-Annually	Annually	Monthly	Quarterly	Semi-Annually	Annually
1	12.860	4.231	2.075	1.000	12.920	4.246	2.080	1.000
2	27.788	9.133	4.473	2.150	28.066	9.214	4.506	2.160
3	45.116	14.812	7.244	3.473	45.822	15.026	7.336	3.506
4	65.228	21.393	10.446	4.993	66.636	21.825	10.637	5.066
5	88.575	29.017	14.147	6.742	91.036	29.778	14.487	6.877
6	115.674	37.852	18.424	8.754	119.639	39.083	18.977	8.977
7	147.129	48.088	23.366	11.067	153.169	49.968	24.215	11.414
8	183.641	59.947	29.077	13.727	192.476	62.701	30.324	14.240
9	226.023	73.689	35.677	16.786	238.554	77.598	37.450	17.519
10	275.217	89.610	43.305	20.304	292.571	95.026	45.762	21.321
11	332.320	108.057	52.119	24.349	355.892	115.413	55.457	25.733
12	398.602	129.431	62.305	29.002	430.122	139.263	66.765	30.850
13	475.540	154.197	74.076	34.352	517.140	167.165	79.954	36.786
14	564.845	182.891	87.679	40.505	619.149	199.806	95.339	43.672
15	668.507	216.137	103.399	47.580	738.730	237.991	113.283	51.660
16	788.833	254.658	121.566	55.717	878.912	282.662	134.214	60.925
17	928.501	299.290	142.560	65.075	1043.243	334.921	158.627	71.673
18	1090.623	351.003	166.820	75.836	1235.884	396.057	187.102	84.141
19	1278.805	410.921	194.857	88.212	1461.711	467.577	220.316	98.603
20	1497.239	480.344	227.257	102.444	1726.442	551.245	259.057	115.380
21	1750.788	560.782	264.698	118.810	2036.777	649.125	304.244	134.841
22	2045.095	653.980	307.967	137.632	2400.575	763.631	356.950	157.415
23	2386.714	761.965	357.969	159.276	2827.044	897.587	418.426	183.601
24	2783.249	887.082	415.753	184.168	3326.982	1054.296	490.132	213.978
25	3243.530	1032.049	482.530	212.793	3913.044	1237.624	573.770	249.214
26	3777.802	1200.014	559.699	245.712	4600.067	1452.091	671.326	290.088
27	4397.961	1394.628	648.877	283.569	5405.445	1702.988	785.114	337.502
28	5117.814	1620.117	751.933	327.104	6349.566	1996.501	917.837	392.503
29	5953.386	1881.380	871.028	377.170	7456.331	2339.871	1072.645	456.303
30	6923.280	2184.092	1008.657	434.745	8753.759	2741.564	1253.213	530.312
31	8049.088	2534.830	1167.704	500.957	10274.696	3211.489	1463.828	616.162
32	9355.876	2941.213	1351.503	577.100	12057.647	3761.234	1709.489	715.747
33	10872.736	3412.068	1563.905	664.666	14147.748	4404.358	1996.028	831.267
34	12633.438	3957.624	1809.363	765.365	16597.912	5156.723	2330.247	965.270
35	14677.180	4589.734	2093.020	881.170	19470.168	6036.882	2720.080	1120.713
36	17049.464	5322.128	2420.821	1014.346	22837.229	7066.545	3174.781	1301.027
37	19803.102	6170.716	2799.637	1167.498	26784.337	8271.105	3705.145	1510.191
38	22999.401	7153.934	3237.405	1343.622	31411.417	9680.269	4323.761	1752.822
39	26709.519	8293.139	3743.301	1546.165	36835.607	11328.792	5045.315	2034.273
40	31016.055	9613.079	4327.927	1779.090	43194.226	13257.331	5886.935	2360.757
41	36014.886	11142.429	5003.536	2046.954	50648.251	15513.449	6868.601	2739.478
42	41817.302	12914.411	5784.286	2354.997	59386.385	18152.787	8013.617	3178.795
43	48552.483	14967.518	6686.541	2709.246	69629.846	21240.440	9349.163	3688.402
44	56370.374	17346.352	7729.209	3116.633	81637.955	24852.557	10906.943	4279.546
45	65445.027	20102.588	8934.142	3585.128	95714.711	29078.223	12723.939	4965.274
46	75978.471	23296.103	10326.593	4123.898	112216.481	34021.654	14843.282	5760.718
47	88205.213	26996.270	11935.744	4743.482	131561.024	39804.770	17315.284	6683.433
48	102397.460	31283.470	13795.319	5456.005	154238.067	46570.197	20198.627	7753.782
49	118871.175	36250.836	15944.291	6275.405	180821.702	54484.790	23561.759	8995.387
50	137993.114	42006.277	18427.696	7217.716	211984.922	63743.745	27484.516	10435.649

The future value of $1 invested at the *end* of each period

End of Year	17% Interest compounded and Deposits made				18% Interest compounded and Deposits made			
	Monthly	Quarterly	Semi-Annually	Annually	Monthly	Quarterly	Semi-Annually	Annually
1	12.981	4.262	2.085	1.000	13.041	4.278	2.090	1.000
2	28.348	9.297	4.540	2.170	28.634	9.380	4.573	2.180
3	46.542	15.243	7.429	3.539	47.276	15.464	7.523	3.572
4	68.081	22.267	10.831	5.141	69.565	22.719	11.028	5.215
5	93.581	30.563	14.835	7.014	96.215	31.371	15.193	7.154
6	123.771	40.361	19.549	9.207	128.077	41.689	20.141	9.442
7	159.512	51.935	25.099	11.772	166.173	53.993	26.019	12.142
8	201.825	65.605	31.632	14.773	211.720	68.666	33.003	15.327
9	251.920	81.751	39.323	18.285	266.178	86.164	41.301	19.086
10	311.226	100.823	48.377	22.393	331.288	107.030	51.160	23.521
11	381.439	123.349	59.036	27.200	409.135	131.914	62.873	28.755
12	464.563	149.956	71.583	32.824	502.211	161.588	76.790	34.931
13	562.972	181.382	86.355	39.404	613.494	196.975	93.324	42.219
14	679.479	218.501	103.744	47.103	746.545	239.174	112.968	50.818
15	817.410	262.345	124.215	56.110	905.625	289.498	136.308	60.965
16	980.706	314.130	148.314	66.649	1095.822	349.510	164.037	72.939
17	1174.030	375.297	176.684	78.979	1323.226	421.075	196.982	87.068
18	1402.905	447.543	210.081	93.406	1595.115	506.418	236.125	103.740
19	1673.868	532.877	249.398	110.285	1920.189	608.191	282.630	123.414
20	1994.659	633.668	295.683	130.033	2308.854	729.558	337.882	146.628
21	2374.441	752.718	350.170	153.139	2773.549	874.289	403.528	174.021
22	2824.062	893.334	414.314	180.172	3329.147	1046.884	481.522	206.345
23	3356.364	1059.422	489.825	211.801	3993.430	1252.707	574.186	244.487
24	3986.552	1255.596	578.720	248.808	4787.659	1498.155	684.280	289.494
25	4732.626	1487.307	683.368	292.105	5737.253	1790.856	815.084	342.603
26	5615.898	1760.992	806.563	342.763	6872.606	2139.907	970.491	405.272
27	6661.595	2084.254	951.592	402.032	8230.053	2556.157	1155.130	479.221
28	7899.588	2466.074	1122.322	471.378	9853.042	3052.543	1374.500	566.481
29	9365.238	2917.060	1323.311	552.512	11793.518	3644.493	1635.134	669.447
30	11100.408	3449.742	1559.920	647.439	14113.585	4350.404	1944.792	790.948
31	13154.662	4078.917	1838.462	758.504	16887.500	5192.216	2312.698	934.319
32	15586.676	4822.067	2166.368	888.449	20204.044	6196.092	2749.806	1103.496
33	18465.917	5699.836	2552.387	1040.486	24169.363	7393.233	3269.134	1303.125
34	21874.628	6736.611	3006.819	1218.368	28910.371	8820.846	3886.149	1538.688
35	25910.171	7961.196	3541.788	1426.491	34578.806	10523.301	4619.223	1816.652
36	30687.818	9407.612	4171.566	1669.994	41356.090	12553.511	5490.189	2144.649
37	36344.034	11116.042	4912.957	1954.894	49459.133	14974.573	6524.984	2531.686
38	43040.382	13133.951	5785.741	2288.225	59147.280	17861.735	7754.423	2988.389
39	50968.133	15517.400	6813.204	2678.224	70730.604	21304.730	9215.120	3527.299
40	60353.732	18332.606	8022.759	3134.522	84579.836	25410.565	10950.574	4163.213
41	71465.264	21657.780	9446.677	3668.391	101138.230	30306.850	13012.467	4913.591
42	84620.116	25585.302	11122.950	4293.017	120935.747	36145.760	15462.202	5799.038
43	100194.036	30224.286	13096.299	5023.830	144606.018	43108.769	18372.732	6843.865
44	118631.871	35703.612	15419.376	5878.881	172906.624	51412.288	21830.733	8076.760
45	140460.272	42175.506	18154.160	6879.291	206743.343	61314.387	25939.184	9531.577
46	166302.734	49819.770	21373.616	8049.770	247199.139	73122.826	30820.435	11248.261
47	196897.412	58848.775	25163.640	9419.231	295568.824	87204.608	36619.849	13273.948
48	233118.198	69513.365	29625.351	11021.500	353400.498	103997.395	43510.132	15664.259
49	275999.687	82109.822	34877.789	12896.155	422545.099	124023.106	51696.478	18484.825
50	326766.727	96988.100	41061.090	15089.502	505215.639	147904.139	61422.675	21813.094

The future value of $1 invested at the *end* of each period

End of Year	19% Interest compounded and Deposits made				20% Interest compounded and Deposits made			
	Monthly	Quarterly	Semi-Annually	Annually	Monthly	Quarterly	Semi-Annually	Annually
1	13.102	4.294	2.095	1.000	13.163	4.310	2.100	1.000
2	28.922	9.464	4.607	2.190	29.215	9.549	4.641	2.200
3	48.025	15.689	7.619	3.606	48.788	15.917	7.716	3.640
4	71.089	23.183	11.230	5.291	72.655	23.657	11.436	5.368
5	98.939	32.206	15.560	7.297	101.758	33.066	15.937	7.442
6	132.566	43.069	20.752	9.683	137.247	44.502	21.384	9.930
7	173.170	56.148	26.977	12.523	180.521	58.403	27.975	12.916
8	222.196	71.894	34.442	15.902	233.289	75.299	35.950	16.499
9	281.393	90.853	43.391	19.923	297.634	95.836	45.599	20.799
10	352.870	113.678	54.122	24.709	376.095	120.800	57.275	25.959
11	439.176	141.160	66.989	30.404	471.771	151.143	71.403	32.150
12	543.385	174.246	82.416	37.180	588.436	188.025	88.497	39.581
13	669.213	214.082	100.914	45.244	730.698	232.856	109.182	48.497
14	821.145	262.042	123.094	54.841	904.170	287.348	134.210	59.196
15	1004.594	319.786	149.688	66.261	1115.700	353.584	164.494	72.035
16	1226.100	389.307	181.574	79.850	1373.638	434.093	201.138	87.442
17	1493.558	473.008	219.807	96.022	1688.165	531.953	245.477	105.931
18	1816.500	573.783	265.649	115.266	2071.697	650.903	299.127	128.117
19	2206.437	695.112	320.615	138.166	2539.373	795.486	364.043	154.740
20	2677.267	841.189	386.520	165.418	3109.652	971.229	442.593	186.688
21	3245.771	1017.061	465.542	197.847	3805.045	1184.845	537.637	225.026
22	3932.212	1228.807	560.292	236.438	4653.002	1444.496	652.641	271.031
23	4761.055	1483.742	673.899	282.362	5686.992	1760.105	791.795	326.237
24	5761.843	1790.677	810.116	337.010	6947.831	2143.728	960.172	392.484
25	6970.245	2160.218	973.445	402.042	8485.287	2610.025	1163.909	471.981
26	8429.332	2605.135	1169.280	479.431	10360.046	3176.812	1410.429	567.377
27	10191.107	3140.801	1404.091	571.522	12646.112	3865.745	1708.719	681.853
28	12318.365	3785.729	1685.635	681.112	15433.719	4703.147	2069.651	819.223
29	14886.924	4562.203	2023.213	811.523	18832.903	5721.015	2506.377	984.068
30	17988.334	5497.055	2427.978	966.712	22977.838	6958.240	3034.816	1181.882
31	21733.134	6622.591	2913.301	1151.387	28032.134	8462.094	3674.228	1419.258
32	26254.796	7977.703	3495.216	1371.151	34195.298	10290.038	4447.916	1704.109
33	31714.482	9609.220	4192.947	1632.670	41710.605	12511.916	5384.078	2045.931
34	38306.785	11573.519	5029.543	1943.877	50874.703	15212.622	6516.834	2456.118
35	46266.668	13938.478	6032.643	2314.214	62049.323	18495.347	7887.470	2948.341
36	55877.836	16785.821	7235.384	2754.914	75675.554	22485.521	9545.938	3539.009
37	67482.851	20213.941	8677.502	3279.348	92291.260	27335.601	11552.685	4247.811
38	81495.338	24341.299	10406.637	3903.424	112552.303	33230.904	13980.849	5098.373
39	98414.730	29310.518	12479.912	4646.075	137258.438	40396.681	16918.927	6119.048
40	118844.066	35293.317	14965.822	5529.829	167384.880	49106.729	20474.002	7343.858
41	143511.488	42496.434	17946.490	6581.496	204120.793	59693.846	24775.643	8813.629
42	173296.192	51168.780	21520.385	7832.981	248916.239	72562.553	29980.628	10577.355
43	209259.762	61610.035	25805.574	9322.247	303539.406	88204.547	36278.659	12693.826
44	252684.010	74181.007	30943.624	11094.474	370146.409	107217.488	43899.278	15233.592
45	305116.663	89316.096	37104.273	13203.424	451366.395	130327.837	53120.226	18281.310
46	368426.521	107538.308	44491.046	15713.075	550405.322	158418.610	64277.574	21938.572
47	444870.073	129477.328	53347.972	18699.559	671172.506	192563.121	77777.964	26327.286
48	537171.916	155891.278	63967.647	22253.475	818434.934	234065.987	94113.437	31593.744
49	648621.868	187692.916	76700.903	26482.636	998005.425	284512.981	113879.358	37913.492
50	783192.224	225981.174	91968.395	31515.336	1216972.082	345831.616	137796.123	45497.191

"Compound Discount Table for $1 Principal"

How much must be invested today to have $1 accumulated at some point in the future at various interest rates compounded monthly, quarterly, semi-annually or annually?

Applications
Chapter Four
- What is $1 due sometime in the future worth today?
- How much do I have to invest today to have $1 at the end of various time periods?
- How much can I borrow today so that I can repay my debt, principal plus interest, out of money which I have coming in at the end of a certain time period?
- What is the value of an insurance policy today where the benefits are payable sometime in the future, given a presumed rate for inflation?
- What is the present value of a future profit from the sale of a house or a stock market investment?

Chapters Eleven and Twelve
- Evaluating an investment in a home, vacation property or real estate using discounted cash flow.

Chapters Thirteen and Fourteen
- Evaluating an investment in the stock market or gold using discounted cash flow.

Chapter Sixteen
- Calculating the present value of an insurance policy death benefit.

The present value of $1
due at the *end* of various time periods

End of Year	5% Interest compounded				6% Interest compounded			
	Monthly	Quarterly	Semi-Annually	Annually	Monthly	Quarterly	Semi-Annually	Annually
1	0.9513	0.9515	0.9518	0.9524	0.9419	0.9422	0.9426	0.9434
2	0.9050	0.9054	0.9060	0.9070	0.8872	0.8877	0.8885	0.8900
3	0.8610	0.8615	0.8623	0.8638	0.8356	0.8364	0.8375	0.8396
4	0.8191	0.8197	0.8207	0.8227	0.7871	0.7880	0.7894	0.7921
5	0.7792	0.7800	0.7812	0.7835	0.7414	0.7425	0.7441	0.7473
6	0.7413	0.7422	0.7436	0.7462	0.6983	0.6995	0.7014	0.7050
7	0.7052	0.7062	0.7077	0.7107	0.6577	0.6591	0.6611	0.6651
8	0.6709	0.6720	0.6736	0.6768	0.6195	0.6210	0.6232	0.6274
9	0.6382	0.6394	0.6412	0.6446	0.5835	0.5851	0.5874	0.5919
10	0.6072	0.6084	0.6103	0.6139	0.5496	0.5513	0.5537	0.5584
11	0.5776	0.5789	0.5809	0.5847	0.5177	0.5194	0.5219	0.5268
12	0.5495	0.5509	0.5529	0.5568	0.4876	0.4894	0.4919	0.4970
13	0.5228	0.5242	0.5262	0.5303	0.4593	0.4611	0.4637	0.4688
14	0.4973	0.4987	0.5009	0.5051	0.4326	0.4344	0.4371	0.4423
15	0.4731	0.4746	0.4767	0.4810	0.4075	0.4093	0.4120	0.4173
16	0.4501	0.4516	0.4538	0.4581	0.3838	0.3856	0.3883	0.3936
17	0.4282	0.4297	0.4319	0.4363	0.3615	0.3633	0.3660	0.3714
18	0.4073	0.4088	0.4111	0.4155	0.3405	0.3423	0.3450	0.3503
19	0.3875	0.3890	0.3913	0.3957	0.3207	0.3225	0.3252	0.3305
20	0.3686	0.3702	0.3724	0.3769	0.3021	0.3039	0.3066	0.3118
21	0.3507	0.3522	0.3545	0.3589	0.2845	0.2863	0.2890	0.2942
22	0.3336	0.3351	0.3374	0.3418	0.2680	0.2698	0.2724	0.2775
23	0.3174	0.3189	0.3211	0.3256	0.2524	0.2542	0.2567	0.2618
24	0.3019	0.3034	0.3057	0.3101	0.2378	0.2395	0.2420	0.2470
25	0.2872	0.2887	0.2909	0.2953	0.2240	0.2256	0.2281	0.2330
26	0.2733	0.2747	0.2769	0.2812	0.2110	0.2126	0.2150	0.2198
27	0.2600	0.2614	0.2636	0.2678	0.1987	0.2003	0.2027	0.2074
28	0.2473	0.2487	0.2509	0.2551	0.1872	0.1887	0.1910	0.1956
29	0.2353	0.2367	0.2388	0.2429	0.1763	0.1778	0.1801	0.1846
30	0.2238	0.2252	0.2273	0.2314	0.1660	0.1675	0.1697	0.1741
31	0.2129	0.2143	0.2163	0.2204	0.1564	0.1578	0.1600	0.1643
32	0.2026	0.2039	0.2059	0.2099	0.1473	0.1487	0.1508	0.1550
33	0.1927	0.1940	0.1960	0.1999	0.1388	0.1401	0.1421	0.1462
34	0.1833	0.1846	0.1865	0.1904	0.1307	0.1320	0.1340	0.1379
35	0.1744	0.1757	0.1776	0.1813	0.1231	0.1244	0.1263	0.1301
36	0.1659	0.1672	0.1690	0.1727	0.1159	0.1172	0.1190	0.1227
37	0.1578	0.1591	0.1609	0.1644	0.1092	0.1104	0.1122	0.1158
38	0.1502	0.1513	0.1531	0.1566	0.1029	0.1040	0.1058	0.1092
39	0.1429	0.1440	0.1457	0.1491	0.0969	0.0980	0.0997	0.1031
40	0.1359	0.1370	0.1387	0.1420	0.0913	0.0923	0.0940	0.0972
41	0.1293	0.1304	0.1320	0.1353	0.0860	0.0870	0.0886	0.0917
42	0.1230	0.1241	0.1257	0.1288	0.0810	0.0820	0.0835	0.0865
43	0.1170	0.1180	0.1196	0.1227	0.0763	0.0772	0.0787	0.0816
44	0.1113	0.1123	0.1138	0.1169	0.0718	0.0728	0.0742	0.0770
45	0.1059	0.1069	0.1084	0.1113	0.0677	0.0686	0.0699	0.0727
46	0.1007	0.1017	0.1031	0.1060	0.0637	0.0646	0.0659	0.0685
47	0.0958	0.0968	0.0982	0.1009	0.0600	0.0609	0.0621	0.0647
48	0.0912	0.0921	0.0934	0.0961	0.0565	0.0573	0.0586	0.0610
49	0.0867	0.0876	0.0889	0.0916	0.0533	0.0540	0.0552	0.0575
50	0.0825	0.0834	0.0846	0.0872	0.0502	0.0509	0.0520	0.0543

The present value of $1
due at the *end* of various time periods

End of Year	9% Interest compounded				10% Interest compounded			
	Monthly	Quarterly	Semi-Annually	Annually	Monthly	Quarterly	Semi-Annually	Annually
1	0.9142	0.9148	0.9157	0.9174	0.9052	0.9060	0.9070	0.9091
2	0.8358	0.8369	0.8386	0.8417	0.8194	0.8207	0.8227	0.8264
3	0.7641	0.7657	0.7679	0.7722	0.7417	0.7436	0.7462	0.7513
4	0.6986	0.7005	0.7032	0.7084	0.6714	0.6736	0.6768	0.6830
5	0.6387	0.6408	0.6439	0.6499	0.6078	0.6103	0.6139	0.6209
6	0.5839	0.5862	0.5897	0.5963	0.5502	0.5529	0.5568	0.5645
7	0.5338	0.5363	0.5400	0.5470	0.4980	0.5009	0.5051	0.5132
8	0.4881	0.4907	0.4945	0.5019	0.4508	0.4538	0.4581	0.4665
9	0.4462	0.4489	0.4528	0.4604	0.4081	0.4111	0.4155	0.4241
10	0.4079	0.4106	0.4146	0.4224	0.3694	0.3724	0.3769	0.3855
11	0.3730	0.3757	0.3797	0.3875	0.3344	0.3374	0.3418	0.3505
12	0.3410	0.3437	0.3477	0.3555	0.3027	0.3057	0.3101	0.3186
13	0.3117	0.3144	0.3184	0.3262	0.2740	0.2769	0.2812	0.2897
14	0.2850	0.2876	0.2916	0.2992	0.2480	0.2509	0.2551	0.2633
15	0.2605	0.2631	0.2670	0.2745	0.2245	0.2273	0.2314	0.2394
16	0.2382	0.2407	0.2445	0.2519	0.2032	0.2059	0.2099	0.2176
17	0.2178	0.2202	0.2239	0.2311	0.1840	0.1865	0.1904	0.1978
18	0.1991	0.2015	0.2050	0.2120	0.1665	0.1690	0.1727	0.1799
19	0.1820	0.1843	0.1878	0.1945	0.1508	0.1531	0.1566	0.1635
20	0.1664	0.1686	0.1719	0.1784	0.1365	0.1387	0.1420	0.1486
21	0.1521	0.1543	0.1574	0.1637	0.1235	0.1257	0.1288	0.1351
22	0.1391	0.1411	0.1442	0.1502	0.1118	0.1138	0.1169	0.1228
23	0.1272	0.1291	0.1320	0.1378	0.1012	0.1031	0.1060	0.1117
24	0.1163	0.1181	0.1209	0.1264	0.0916	0.0934	0.0961	0.1015
25	0.1063	0.1081	0.1107	0.1160	0.0829	0.0846	0.0872	0.0923
26	0.0972	0.0989	0.1014	0.1064	0.0751	0.0767	0.0791	0.0839
27	0.0888	0.0904	0.0928	0.0976	0.0680	0.0695	0.0717	0.0763
28	0.0812	0.0827	0.0850	0.0895	0.0615	0.0629	0.0651	0.0693
29	0.0743	0.0757	0.0778	0.0822	0.0557	0.0570	0.0590	0.0630
30	0.0679	0.0692	0.0713	0.0754	0.0504	0.0517	0.0535	0.0573
31	0.0621	0.0634	0.0653	0.0691	0.0456	0.0468	0.0486	0.0521
32	0.0567	0.0580	0.0598	0.0634	0.0413	0.0424	0.0440	0.0474
33	0.0519	0.0530	0.0547	0.0582	0.0374	0.0384	0.0399	0.0431
34	0.0474	0.0485	0.0501	0.0534	0.0338	0.0348	0.0362	0.0391
35	0.0434	0.0444	0.0459	0.0490	0.0306	0.0315	0.0329	0.0356
36	0.0396	0.0406	0.0420	0.0449	0.0277	0.0286	0.0298	0.0323
37	0.0362	0.0371	0.0385	0.0412	0.0251	0.0259	0.0270	0.0294
38	0.0331	0.0340	0.0353	0.0378	0.0227	0.0234	0.0245	0.0267
39	0.0303	0.0311	0.0323	0.0347	0.0206	0.0212	0.0222	0.0243
40	0.0277	0.0284	0.0296	0.0318	0.0186	0.0192	0.0202	0.0221
41	0.0253	0.0260	0.0271	0.0292	0.0169	0.0174	0.0183	0.0201
42	0.0231	0.0238	0.0248	0.0268	0.0153	0.0158	0.0166	0.0183
43	0.0212	0.0218	0.0227	0.0246	0.0138	0.0143	0.0151	0.0166
44	0.0193	0.0199	0.0208	0.0226	0.0125	0.0130	0.0137	0.0151
45	0.0177	0.0182	0.0190	0.0207	0.0113	0.0117	0.0124	0.0137
46	0.0162	0.0167	0.0174	0.0190	0.0102	0.0106	0.0112	0.0125
47	0.0148	0.0153	0.0160	0.0174	0.0093	0.0096	0.0102	0.0113
48	0.0135	0.0140	0.0146	0.0160	0.0084	0.0087	0.0092	0.0103
49	0.0124	0.0128	0.0134	0.0147	0.0076	0.0079	0.0084	0.0094
50	0.0113	0.0117	0.0123	0.0134	0.0069	0.0072	0.0076	0.0085

The present value of $1
due at the *end* of various time periods

End of Year	13% Interest compounded				14% Interest compounded			
	Monthly	Quarterly	Semi-Annually	Annually	Monthly	Quarterly	Semi-Annually	Annually
1	0.8787	0.8799	0.8817	0.8850	0.8701	0.8714	0.8734	0.8772
2	0.7721	0.7742	0.7773	0.7831	0.7570	0.7594	0.7629	0.7695
3	0.6785	0.6813	0.6853	0.6931	0.6586	0.6618	0.6663	0.6750
4	0.5962	0.5995	0.6042	0.6133	0.5731	0.5767	0.5820	0.5921
5	0.5239	0.5275	0.5327	0.5428	0.4986	0.5026	0.5083	0.5194
6	0.4603	0.4641	0.4697	0.4803	0.4338	0.4380	0.4440	0.4556
7	0.4045	0.4084	0.4141	0.4251	0.3774	0.3817	0.3878	0.3996
8	0.3554	0.3594	0.3651	0.3762	0.3284	0.3326	0.3387	0.3506
9	0.3123	0.3162	0.3219	0.3329	0.2857	0.2898	0.2959	0.3075
10	0.2744	0.2782	0.2838	0.2946	0.2486	0.2526	0.2584	0.2697
11	0.2412	0.2448	0.2502	0.2607	0.2163	0.2201	0.2257	0.2366
12	0.2119	0.2154	0.2206	0.2307	0.1882	0.1918	0.1971	0.2076
13	0.1862	0.1895	0.1945	0.2042	0.1637	0.1671	0.1722	0.1821
14	0.1636	0.1668	0.1715	0.1807	0.1425	0.1457	0.1504	0.1597
15	0.1438	0.1468	0.1512	0.1599	0.1240	0.1269	0.1314	0.1401
16	0.1263	0.1291	0.1333	0.1415	0.1078	0.1106	0.1147	0.1229
17	0.1110	0.1136	0.1175	0.1252	0.0938	0.0964	0.1002	0.1078
18	0.0975	0.1000	0.1036	0.1108	0.0816	0.0840	0.0875	0.0946
19	0.0857	0.0880	0.0914	0.0981	0.0710	0.0732	0.0765	0.0829
20	0.0753	0.0774	0.0805	0.0868	0.0618	0.0638	0.0668	0.0728
21	0.0662	0.0681	0.0710	0.0768	0.0538	0.0556	0.0583	0.0638
22	0.0582	0.0599	0.0626	0.0680	0.0468	0.0484	0.0509	0.0560
23	0.0511	0.0527	0.0552	0.0601	0.0407	0.0422	0.0445	0.0491
24	0.0449	0.0464	0.0487	0.0532	0.0354	0.0368	0.0389	0.0431
25	0.0395	0.0408	0.0429	0.0471	0.0308	0.0321	0.0339	0.0378
26	0.0347	0.0359	0.0378	0.0417	0.0268	0.0279	0.0297	0.0331
27	0.0305	0.0316	0.0334	0.0369	0.0233	0.0243	0.0259	0.0291
28	0.0268	0.0278	0.0294	0.0326	0.0203	0.0212	0.0226	0.0255
29	0.0235	0.0245	0.0259	0.0289	0.0177	0.0185	0.0198	0.0224
30	0.0207	0.0215	0.0229	0.0256	0.0154	0.0161	0.0173	0.0196
31	0.0182	0.0190	0.0202	0.0226	0.0134	0.0140	0.0151	0.0172
32	0.0160	0.0167	0.0178	0.0200	0.0116	0.0122	0.0132	0.0151
33	0.0140	0.0147	0.0157	0.0177	0.0101	0.0107	0.0115	0.0132
34	0.0123	0.0129	0.0138	0.0157	0.0088	0.0093	0.0100	0.0116
35	0.0108	0.0114	0.0122	0.0139	0.0077	0.0081	0.0088	0.0102
36	0.0095	0.0100	0.0107	0.0123	0.0067	0.0071	0.0077	0.0089
37	0.0084	0.0088	0.0095	0.0109	0.0058	0.0061	0.0067	0.0078
38	0.0073	0.0077	0.0083	0.0096	0.0050	0.0054	0.0058	0.0069
39	0.0065	0.0068	0.0074	0.0085	0.0044	0.0047	0.0051	0.0060
40	0.0057	0.0060	0.0065	0.0075	0.0038	0.0041	0.0045	0.0053
41	0.0050	0.0053	0.0057	0.0067	0.0033	0.0035	0.0039	0.0046
42	0.0044	0.0046	0.0050	0.0059	0.0029	0.0031	0.0034	0.0041
43	0.0038	0.0041	0.0044	0.0052	0.0025	0.0027	0.0030	0.0036
44	0.0034	0.0036	0.0039	0.0046	0.0022	0.0023	0.0026	0.0031
45	0.0030	0.0032	0.0035	0.0041	0.0019	0.0020	0.0023	0.0027
46	0.0026	0.0028	0.0030	0.0036	0.0017	0.0018	0.0020	0.0024
47	0.0023	0.0024	0.0027	0.0032	0.0014	0.0016	0.0017	0.0021
48	0.0020	0.0022	0.0024	0.0028	0.0013	0.0014	0.0015	0.0019
49	0.0018	0.0019	0.0021	0.0025	0.0011	0.0012	0.0013	0.0016
50	0.0016	0.0017	0.0018	0.0022	0.0009	0.0010	0.0012	0.0014

The present value of $1
due at the *end* of various time periods

End of Year	15% Interest compounded				16% Interest compounded			
	Monthly	Quarterly	Semi-Annually	Annually	Monthly	Quarterly	Semi-Annually	Annually
1	0.8615	0.8631	0.8653	0.8696	0.8530	0.8548	0.8573	0.8621
2	0.7422	0.7449	0.7488	0.7561	0.7277	0.7307	0.7350	0.7432
3	0.6394	0.6429	0.6480	0.6575	0.6207	0.6246	0.6302	0.6407
4	0.5509	0.5549	0.5607	0.5718	0.5295	0.5339	0.5403	0.5523
5	0.4746	0.4789	0.4852	0.4972	0.4517	0.4564	0.4632	0.4761
6	0.4088	0.4133	0.4199	0.4323	0.3853	0.3901	0.3971	0.4104
7	0.3522	0.3567	0.3633	0.3759	0.3287	0.3335	0.3405	0.3538
8	0.3034	0.3079	0.3144	0.3269	0.2804	0.2851	0.2919	0.3050
9	0.2614	0.2657	0.2720	0.2843	0.2392	0.2437	0.2502	0.2630
10	0.2252	0.2293	0.2354	0.2472	0.2040	0.2083	0.2145	0.2267
11	0.1940	0.1979	0.2037	0.2149	0.1741	0.1780	0.1839	0.1954
12	0.1672	0.1708	0.1763	0.1869	0.1485	0.1522	0.1577	0.1685
13	0.1440	0.1474	0.1525	0.1625	0.1267	0.1301	0.1352	0.1452
14	0.1241	0.1273	0.1320	0.1413	0.1080	0.1112	0.1159	0.1252
15	0.1069	0.1098	0.1142	0.1229	0.0922	0.0951	0.0994	0.1079
16	0.0921	0.0948	0.0988	0.1069	0.0786	0.0813	0.0852	0.0930
17	0.0793	0.0818	0.0855	0.0929	0.0671	0.0695	0.0730	0.0802
18	0.0683	0.0706	0.0740	0.0808	0.0572	0.0594	0.0626	0.0691
19	0.0589	0.0609	0.0640	0.0703	0.0488	0.0508	0.0537	0.0596
20	0.0507	0.0526	0.0554	0.0611	0.0416	0.0434	0.0460	0.0514
21	0.0437	0.0454	0.0480	0.0531	0.0355	0.0371	0.0395	0.0443
22	0.0376	0.0392	0.0415	0.0462	0.0303	0.0317	0.0338	0.0382
23	0.0324	0.0338	0.0359	0.0402	0.0258	0.0271	0.0290	0.0329
24	0.0279	0.0292	0.0311	0.0349	0.0220	0.0232	0.0249	0.0284
25	0.0241	0.0252	0.0269	0.0304	0.0188	0.0198	0.0213	0.0245
26	0.0207	0.0217	0.0233	0.0264	0.0160	0.0169	0.0183	0.0211
27	0.0179	0.0188	0.0201	0.0230	0.0137	0.0145	0.0157	0.0182
28	0.0154	0.0162	0.0174	0.0200	0.0117	0.0124	0.0134	0.0157
29	0.0133	0.0140	0.0151	0.0174	0.0100	0.0106	0.0115	0.0135
30	0.0114	0.0121	0.0130	0.0151	0.0085	0.0090	0.0099	0.0116
31	0.0098	0.0104	0.0113	0.0131	0.0072	0.0077	0.0085	0.0100
32	0.0085	0.0090	0.0098	0.0114	0.0062	0.0066	0.0073	0.0087
33	0.0073	0.0078	0.0085	0.0099	0.0053	0.0056	0.0062	0.0075
34	0.0063	0.0067	0.0073	0.0086	0.0045	0.0048	0.0053	0.0064
35	0.0054	0.0058	0.0063	0.0075	0.0038	0.0041	0.0046	0.0055
36	0.0047	0.0050	0.0055	0.0065	0.0033	0.0035	0.0039	0.0048
37	0.0040	0.0043	0.0047	0.0057	0.0028	0.0030	0.0034	0.0041
38	0.0035	0.0037	0.0041	0.0049	0.0024	0.0026	0.0029	0.0036
39	0.0030	0.0032	0.0035	0.0043	0.0020	0.0022	0.0025	0.0031
40	0.0026	0.0028	0.0031	0.0037	0.0017	0.0019	0.0021	0.0026
41	0.0022	0.0024	0.0027	0.0032	0.0015	0.0016	0.0018	0.0023
42	0.0019	0.0021	0.0023	0.0028	0.0013	0.0014	0.0016	0.0020
43	0.0016	0.0018	0.0020	0.0025	0.0011	0.0012	0.0013	0.0017
44	0.0014	0.0015	0.0017	0.0021	0.0009	0.0010	0.0011	0.0015
45	0.0012	0.0013	0.0015	0.0019	0.0008	0.0009	0.0010	0.0013
46	0.0011	0.0011	0.0013	0.0016	0.0007	0.0007	0.0008	0.0011
47	0.0009	0.0010	0.0011	0.0014	0.0006	0.0006	0.0007	0.0009
48	0.0008	0.0009	0.0010	0.0012	0.0005	0.0005	0.0006	0.0008
49	0.0007	0.0007	0.0008	0.0011	0.0004	0.0005	0.0005	0.0007
50	0.0006	0.0006	0.0007	0.0009	0.0004	0.0004	0.0005	0.0006

The present value of $1
due at the *end* of various time periods

| End of Year | 17% Interest compounded | | | | 18% Interest compounded | | | |
	Monthly	Quarterly	Semi-Annually	Annually	Monthly	Quarterly	Semi-Annually	Annually
1	0.8447	0.8466	0.8495	0.8547	0.8364	0.8386	0.8417	0.8475
2	0.7135	0.7168	0.7216	0.7305	0.6995	0.7032	0.7084	0.7182
3	0.6026	0.6069	0.6129	0.6244	0.5851	0.5897	0.5963	0.6086
4	0.5090	0.5138	0.5207	0.5337	0.4894	0.4945	0.5019	0.5158
5	0.4300	0.4350	0.4423	0.4561	0.4093	0.4146	0.4224	0.4371
6	0.3632	0.3683	0.3757	0.3898	0.3423	0.3477	0.3555	0.3704
7	0.3068	0.3118	0.3191	0.3332	0.2863	0.2916	0.2992	0.3139
8	0.2591	0.2640	0.2711	0.2848	0.2395	0.2445	0.2519	0.2660
9	0.2189	0.2235	0.2303	0.2434	0.2003	0.2050	0.2120	0.2255
10	0.1849	0.1892	0.1956	0.2080	0.1675	0.1719	0.1784	0.1911
11	0.1562	0.1602	0.1662	0.1778	0.1401	0.1442	0.1502	0.1619
12	0.1319	0.1356	0.1412	0.1520	0.1172	0.1209	0.1264	0.1372
13	0.1114	0.1148	0.1199	0.1299	0.0980	0.1014	0.1064	0.1163
14	0.0941	0.0972	0.1019	0.1110	0.0820	0.0850	0.0895	0.0985
15	0.0795	0.0823	0.0865	0.0949	0.0686	0.0713	0.0754	0.0835
16	0.0671	0.0697	0.0735	0.0811	0.0573	0.0598	0.0634	0.0708
17	0.0567	0.0590	0.0624	0.0693	0.0480	0.0501	0.0534	0.0600
18	0.0479	0.0499	0.0530	0.0592	0.0401	0.0420	0.0449	0.0508
19	0.0405	0.0423	0.0450	0.0506	0.0336	0.0353	0.0378	0.0431
20	0.0342	0.0358	0.0383	0.0433	0.0281	0.0296	0.0318	0.0365
21	0.0289	0.0303	0.0325	0.0370	0.0235	0.0248	0.0268	0.0309
22	0.0244	0.0257	0.0276	0.0316	0.0196	0.0208	0.0226	0.0262
23	0.0206	0.0217	0.0235	0.0270	0.0164	0.0174	0.0190	0.0222
24	0.0174	0.0184	0.0199	0.0231	0.0137	0.0146	0.0160	0.0188
25	0.0147	0.0156	0.0169	0.0197	0.0115	0.0123	0.0134	0.0160
26	0.0124	0.0132	0.0144	0.0169	0.0096	0.0103	0.0113	0.0135
27	0.0105	0.0112	0.0122	0.0144	0.0080	0.0086	0.0095	0.0115
28	0.0089	0.0095	0.0104	0.0123	0.0067	0.0072	0.0080	0.0097
29	0.0075	0.0080	0.0088	0.0105	0.0056	0.0061	0.0067	0.0082
30	0.0063	0.0068	0.0075	0.0090	0.0047	0.0051	0.0057	0.0070
31	0.0053	0.0057	0.0064	0.0077	0.0039	0.0043	0.0048	0.0059
32	0.0045	0.0049	0.0054	0.0066	0.0033	0.0036	0.0040	0.0050
33	0.0038	0.0041	0.0046	0.0056	0.0028	0.0030	0.0034	0.0042
34	0.0032	0.0035	0.0039	0.0048	0.0023	0.0025	0.0029	0.0036
35	0.0027	0.0029	0.0033	0.0041	0.0019	0.0021	0.0024	0.0030
36	0.0023	0.0025	0.0028	0.0035	0.0016	0.0018	0.0020	0.0026
37	0.0019	0.0021	0.0024	0.0030	0.0013	0.0015	0.0017	0.0022
38	0.0016	0.0018	0.0020	0.0026	0.0011	0.0012	0.0014	0.0019
39	0.0014	0.0015	0.0017	0.0022	0.0009	0.0010	0.0012	0.0016
40	0.0012	0.0013	0.0015	0.0019	0.0008	0.0009	0.0010	0.0013
41	0.0010	0.0011	0.0012	0.0016	0.0007	0.0007	0.0009	0.0011
42	0.0008	0.0009	0.0011	0.0014	0.0006	0.0006	0.0007	0.0010
43	0.0007	0.0008	0.0009	0.0012	0.0005	0.0005	0.0006	0.0008
44	0.0006	0.0007	0.0008	0.0010	0.0004	0.0004	0.0005	0.0007
45	0.0005	0.0006	0.0006	0.0009	0.0003	0.0004	0.0004	0.0006
46	0.0004	0.0005	0.0006	0.0007	0.0003	0.0003	0.0004	0.0005
47	0.0004	0.0004	0.0005	0.0006	0.0002	0.0003	0.0003	0.0004
48	0.0003	0.0003	0.0004	0.0005	0.0002	0.0002	0.0003	0.0004
49	0.0003	0.0003	0.0003	0.0005	0.0002	0.0002	0.0002	0.0003
50	0.0002	0.0002	0.0003	0.0004	0.0001	0.0002	0.0002	0.0003

The present value of $1
due at the *end* of various time periods

End of Year	19% Interest compounded				20% Interest compounded			
	Monthly	Quarterly	Semi-Annually	Annually	Monthly	Quarterly	Semi-Annually	Annually
1	0.8282	0.8306	0.8340	0.8403	0.8201	0.8227	0.8264	0.8333
2	0.6859	0.6899	0.6956	0.7062	0.6725	0.6768	0.6830	0.6944
3	0.5681	0.5730	0.5801	0.5934	0.5515	0.5568	0.5645	0.5787
4	0.4705	0.4759	0.4838	0.4987	0.4523	0.4581	0.4665	0.4823
5	0.3896	0.3953	0.4035	0.4190	0.3709	0.3769	0.3855	0.4019
6	0.3227	0.3283	0.3365	0.3521	0.3042	0.3101	0.3186	0.3349
7	0.2672	0.2727	0.2807	0.2959	0.2495	0.2551	0.2633	0.2791
8	0.2213	0.2265	0.2341	0.2487	0.2046	0.2099	0.2176	0.2326
9	0.1833	0.1881	0.1952	0.2090	0.1678	0.1727	0.1799	0.1938
10	0.1518	0.1563	0.1628	0.1756	0.1376	0.1420	0.1486	0.1615
11	0.1257	0.1298	0.1358	0.1476	0.1128	0.1169	0.1228	0.1346
12	0.1041	0.1078	0.1133	0.1240	0.0925	0.0961	0.1015	0.1122
13	0.0862	0.0895	0.0945	0.1042	0.0759	0.0791	0.0839	0.0935
14	0.0714	0.0744	0.0788	0.0876	0.0622	0.0651	0.0693	0.0779
15	0.0592	0.0618	0.0657	0.0736	0.0510	0.0535	0.0573	0.0649
16	0.0490	0.0513	0.0548	0.0618	0.0419	0.0440	0.0474	0.0541
17	0.0406	0.0426	0.0457	0.0520	0.0343	0.0362	0.0391	0.0451
18	0.0336	0.0354	0.0381	0.0437	0.0281	0.0298	0.0323	0.0376
19	0.0278	0.0294	0.0318	0.0367	0.0231	0.0245	0.0267	0.0313
20	0.0230	0.0244	0.0265	0.0308	0.0189	0.0202	0.0221	0.0261
21	0.0191	0.0203	0.0221	0.0259	0.0155	0.0166	0.0183	0.0217
22	0.0158	0.0168	0.0184	0.0218	0.0127	0.0137	0.0151	0.0181
23	0.0131	0.0140	0.0154	0.0183	0.0104	0.0112	0.0125	0.0151
24	0.0108	0.0116	0.0128	0.0154	0.0086	0.0092	0.0103	0.0126
25	0.0090	0.0097	0.0107	0.0129	0.0070	0.0076	0.0085	0.0105
26	0.0074	0.0080	0.0089	0.0109	0.0058	0.0063	0.0070	0.0087
27	0.0062	0.0067	0.0074	0.0091	0.0047	0.0051	0.0058	0.0073
28	0.0051	0.0055	0.0062	0.0077	0.0039	0.0042	0.0048	0.0061
29	0.0042	0.0046	0.0052	0.0064	0.0032	0.0035	0.0040	0.0051
30	0.0035	0.0038	0.0043	0.0054	0.0026	0.0029	0.0033	0.0042
31	0.0029	0.0032	0.0036	0.0046	0.0021	0.0024	0.0027	0.0035
32	0.0024	0.0026	0.0030	0.0038	0.0018	0.0019	0.0022	0.0029
33	0.0020	0.0022	0.0025	0.0032	0.0014	0.0016	0.0019	0.0024
34	0.0016	0.0018	0.0021	0.0027	0.0012	0.0013	0.0015	0.0020
35	0.0014	0.0015	0.0017	0.0023	0.0010	0.0011	0.0013	0.0017
36	0.0011	0.0013	0.0015	0.0019	0.0008	0.0009	0.0010	0.0014
37	0.0009	0.0010	0.0012	0.0016	0.0006	0.0007	0.0009	0.0012
38	0.0008	0.0009	0.0010	0.0013	0.0005	0.0006	0.0007	0.0010
39	0.0006	0.0007	0.0008	0.0011	0.0004	0.0005	0.0006	0.0008
40	0.0005	0.0006	0.0007	0.0010	0.0004	0.0004	0.0005	0.0007
41	0.0004	0.0005	0.0006	0.0008	0.0003	0.0003	0.0004	0.0006
42	0.0004	0.0004	0.0005	0.0007	0.0002	0.0003	0.0003	0.0005
43	0.0003	0.0003	0.0004	0.0006	0.0002	0.0002	0.0003	0.0004
44	0.0002	0.0003	0.0003	0.0005	0.0002	0.0002	0.0002	0.0003
45	0.0002	0.0002	0.0003	0.0004	0.0001	0.0002	0.0002	0.0003
46	0.0002	0.0002	0.0002	0.0003	0.0001	0.0001	0.0002	0.0002
47	0.0001	0.0002	0.0002	0.0003	0.0001	0.0001	0.0001	0.0002
48	0.0001	0.0001	0.0002	0.0002	0.0001	0.0001	0.0001	0.0002
49	0.0001	0.0001	0.0001	0.0002	0.0001	0.0001	0.0001	0.0001
50	0.0001	0.0001	0.0001	0.0002	0.0000	0.0001	0.0001	0.0001

TABLE 4

How much must be invested at the *end* of each period to accumulate $1 by some future date, assuming deposits are made monthly, quarterly, semi-annually or annually at various interest rates?

Applications

Chapter Five

- Periodic deposits at the end of each period required to attain a certain savings level by the end of a given time period.
- How much must be deposited periodically in order to save a desired amount towards a child's college education?
- How much must you set aside on a periodic basis to become a millionaire by the time you retire?

How much must be invested at the *end* of each period to accumulate $1

End of Year	At 7% Interest compounded and Deposits made				At 8% Interest compounded and Deposits made			
	Monthly	Quarterly	Semi-Annually	Annually	Monthly	Quarterly	Semi-Annually	Annually
1	0.0807	0.2435	0.4914	1.0000	0.0803	0.2426	0.4902	1.0000
2	0.0389	0.1175	0.2373	0.4831	0.0386	0.1165	0.2355	0.4808
3	0.0250	0.0756	0.1527	0.3111	0.0247	0.0746	0.1508	0.3080
4	0.0181	0.0547	0.1105	0.2252	0.0177	0.0537	0.1085	0.2219
5	0.0140	0.0422	0.0852	0.1739	0.0136	0.0412	0.0833	0.1705
6	0.0112	0.0339	0.0685	0.1398	0.0109	0.0329	0.0666	0.1363
7	0.0093	0.0280	0.0566	0.1156	0.0089	0.0270	0.0547	0.1121
8	0.0078	0.0236	0.0477	0.0975	0.0075	0.0226	0.0458	0.0940
9	0.0067	0.0202	0.0408	0.0835	0.0064	0.0192	0.0390	0.0801
10	0.0058	0.0175	0.0354	0.0724	0.0055	0.0166	0.0336	0.0690
11	0.0051	0.0153	0.0309	0.0634	0.0047	0.0144	0.0292	0.0601
12	0.0045	0.0135	0.0273	0.0559	0.0042	0.0126	0.0256	0.0527
13	0.0039	0.0119	0.0242	0.0497	0.0037	0.0111	0.0226	0.0465
14	0.0035	0.0107	0.0216	0.0443	0.0032	0.0098	0.0200	0.0413
15	0.0032	0.0096	0.0194	0.0398	0.0029	0.0088	0.0178	0.0368
16	0.0028	0.0086	0.0174	0.0359	0.0026	0.0078	0.0159	0.0330
17	0.0026	0.0078	0.0158	0.0324	0.0023	0.0070	0.0143	0.0296
8	0.0023	0.0070	0.0143	0.0294	0.0021	0.0063	0.0129	0.0267
19	0.0021	0.0064	0.0130	0.0268	0.0019	0.0057	0.0116	0.0241
20	0.0019	0.0058	0.0118	0.0244	0.0017	0.0052	0.0105	0.0219
21	0.0018	0.0053	0.0108	0.0223	0.0015	0.0047	0.0095	0.0198
22	0.0016	0.0049	0.0099	0.0204	0.0014	0.0042	0.0087	0.0180
23	0.0015	0.0044	0.0091	0.0187	0.0013	0.0039	0.0079	0.0164
24	0.0013	0.0041	0.0083	0.0172	0.0012	0.0035	0.0072	0.0150
25	0.0012	0.0037	0.0076	0.0158	0.0011	0.0032	0.0066	0.0137
26	0.0011	0.0034	0.0070	0.0146	0.0010	0.0029	0.0060	0.0125
27	0.0010	0.0032	0.0065	0.0134	0.0009	0.0027	0.0055	0.0114
28	0.0010	0.0029	0.0060	0.0124	0.0008	0.0024	0.0050	0.0105
29	0.0009	0.0027	0.0055	0.0114	0.0007	0.0022	0.0046	0.0096
30	0.0008	0.0025	0.0051	0.0106	0.0007	0.0020	0.0042	0.0088
31	0.0008	0.0023	0.0047	0.0098	0.0006	0.0019	0.0039	0.0081
32	0.0007	0.0021	0.0044	0.0091	0.0006	0.0017	0.0035	0.0075
33	0.0006	0.0020	0.0040	0.0084	0.0005	0.0016	0.0032	0.0069
34	0.0006	0.0018	0.0037	0.0078	0.0005	0.0015	0.0030	0.0063
35	0.0006	0.0017	0.0035	0.0072	0.0004	0.0013	0.0027	0.0058
36	0.0005	0.0016	0.0032	0.0067	0.0004	0.0012	0.0025	0.0053
37	0.0005	0.0015	0.0030	0.0062	0.0004	0.0011	0.0023	0.0049
38	0.0004	0.0013	0.0028	0.0058	0.0003	0.0010	0.0021	0.0045
39	0.0004	0.0013	0.0026	0.0054	0.0003	0.0010	0.0020	0.0042
40	0.0004	0.0012	0.0024	0.0050	0.0003	0.0009	0.0018	0.0039
41	0.0004	0.0011	0.0022	0.0047	0.0003	0.0008	0.0017	0.0036
42	0.0003	0.0010	0.0021	0.0043	0.0002	0.0007	0.0015	0.0033
43	0.0003	0.0009	0.0019	0.0040	0.0002	0.0007	0.0014	0.0030
44	0.0003	0.0009	0.0018	0.0038	0.0002	0.0006	0.0013	0.0028
45	0.0003	0.0008	0.0017	0.0035	0.0002	0.0006	0.0012	0.0026
46	0.0002	0.0007	0.0015	0.0033	0.0002	0.0005	0.0011	0.0024
47	0.0002	0.0007	0.0014	0.0030	0.0002	0.0005	0.0010	0.0022
48	0.0002	0.0006	0.0013	0.0028	0.0001	0.0005	0.0009	0.0020
49	0.0002	0.0006	0.0012	0.0026	0.0001	0.0004	0.0009	0.0019
50	0.0002	0.0006	0.0012	0.0025	0.0001	0.0004	0.0008	0.0017

How much must be invested
at the *end* of each period
to accumulate $1

End of Year	At 9% Interest compounded and Deposits made				At 10% Interest compounded and Deposits made			
	Monthly	Quarterly	Semi-Annually	Annually	Monthly	Quarterly	Semi-Annually	Annually
1	0.0800	0.2417	0.4890	1.0000	0.0796	0.2408	0.4878	1.0000
2	0.0382	0.1155	0.2337	0.4785	0.0378	0.1145	0.2320	0.4762
3	0.0243	0.0735	0.1489	0.3051	0.0239	0.0725	0.1470	0.3021
4	0.0174	0.0526	0.1066	0.2187	0.0170	0.0516	0.1047	0.2155
5	0.0133	0.0401	0.0814	0.1671	0.0129	0.0391	0.0795	0.1638
6	0.0105	0.0319	0.0647	0.1329	0.0102	0.0309	0.0628	0.1296
7	0.0086	0.0260	0.0528	0.1087	0.0083	0.0251	0.0510	0.1054
8	0.0072	0.0217	0.0440	0.0907	0.0068	0.0208	0.0423	0.0874
9	0.0060	0.0183	0.0372	0.0768	0.0057	0.0175	0.0355	0.0736
10	0.0052	0.0157	0.0319	0.0658	0.0049	0.0148	0.0302	0.0627
11	0.0045	0.0135	0.0275	0.0569	0.0042	0.0127	0.0260	0.0540
12	0.0039	0.0118	0.0240	0.0497	0.0036	0.0110	0.0225	0.0468
13	0.0034	0.0103	0.0210	0.0436	0.0031	0.0096	0.0196	0.0408
14	0.0030	0.0091	0.0185	0.0384	0.0027	0.0084	0.0171	0.0357
15	0.0026	0.0080	0.0164	0.0341	0.0024	0.0074	0.0151	0.0315
16	0.0023	0.0071	0.0146	0.0303	0.0021	0.0065	0.0133	0.0278
17	0.0021	0.0064	0.0130	0.0270	0.0019	0.0057	0.0118	0.0247
18	0.0019	0.0057	0.0116	0.0242	0.0017	0.0051	0.0104	0.0219
19	0.0017	0.0051	0.0104	0.0217	0.0015	0.0045	0.0093	0.0195
20	0.0015	0.0046	0.0093	0.0195	0.0013	0.0040	0.0083	0.0175
21	0.0013	0.0041	0.0084	0.0176	0.0012	0.0036	0.0074	0.0156
22	0.0012	0.0037	0.0076	0.0159	0.0010	0.0032	0.0066	0.0140
23	0.0011	0.0033	0.0068	0.0144	0.0009	0.0029	0.0059	0.0126
24	0.0010	0.0030	0.0062	0.0130	0.0008	0.0026	0.0053	0.0113
25	0.0009	0.0027	0.0056	0.0118	0.0008	0.0023	0.0048	0.0102
26	0.0008	0.0025	0.0051	0.0107	0.0007	0.0021	0.0043	0.0092
27	0.0007	0.0022	0.0046	0.0097	0.0006	0.0019	0.0039	0.0083
28	0.0007	0.0020	0.0042	0.0089	0.0005	0.0017	0.0035	0.0075
29	0.0006	0.0018	0.0038	0.0081	0.0005	0.0015	0.0031	0.0067
30	0.0005	0.0017	0.0035	0.0073	0.0004	0.0014	0.0028	0.0061
31	0.0005	0.0015	0.0031	0.0067	0.0004	0.0012	0.0026	0.0055
32	0.0005	0.0014	0.0029	0.0061	0.0004	0.0011	0.0023	0.0050
33	0.0004	0.0013	0.0026	0.0056	0.0003	0.0010	0.0021	0.0045
34	0.0004	0.0011	0.0024	0.0051	0.0003	0.0009	0.0019	0.0041
35	0.0003	0.0010	0.0022	0.0046	0.0003	0.0008	0.0017	0.0037
36	0.0003	0.0010	0.0020	0.0042	0.0002	0.0007	0.0015	0.0033
37	0.0003	0.0009	0.0018	0.0039	0.0002	0.0007	0.0014	0.0030
38	0.0003	0.0008	0.0016	0.0035	0.0002	0.0006	0.0013	0.0027
39	0.0002	0.0007	0.0015	0.0032	0.0002	0.0005	0.0011	0.0025
40	0.0002	0.0007	0.0014	0.0030	0.0002	0.0005	0.0010	0.0023
41	0.0002	0.0006	0.0013	0.0027	0.0001	0.0004	0.0009	0.0020
42	0.0002	0.0005	0.0011	0.0025	0.0001	0.0004	0.0008	0.0019
43	0.0002	0.0005	0.0010	0.0023	0.0001	0.0004	0.0008	0.0017
44	0.0001	0.0005	0.0010	0.0021	0.0001	0.0003	0.0007	0.0015
45	0.0001	0.0004	0.0009	0.0019	0.0001	0.0003	0.0006	0.0014
46	0.0001	0.0004	0.0008	0.0017	0.0001	0.0003	0.0006	0.0013
47	0.0001	0.0003	0.0007	0.0016	0.0001	0.0002	0.0005	0.0011
48	0.0001	0.0003	0.0007	0.0015	0.0001	0.0002	0.0005	0.0010
49	0.0001	0.0003	0.0006	0.0013	0.0001	0.0002	0.0004	0.0009
50	0.0001	0.0003	0.0006	0.0012	0.0001	0.0002	0.0004	0.0009

How much must be invested
at the *end* of each period
to accumulate $1

End of Year	At 11% Interest compounded and Deposits made				At 12% Interest compounded and Deposits made			
	Monthly	Quarterly	Semi-Annually	Annually	Monthly	Quarterly	Semi-Annually	Annually
1	0.0792	0.2399	0.4866	1.0000	0.0788	0.2390	0.4854	1.0000
2	0.0374	0.1135	0.2303	0.4739	0.0371	0.1125	0.2286	0.4717
3	0.0236	0.0715	0.1452	0.2992	0.0232	0.0705	0.1434	0.2963
4	0.0167	0.0506	0.1029	0.2123	0.0163	0.0496	0.1010	0.2092
5	0.0126	0.0382	0.0777	0.1606	0.0122	0.0372	0.0759	0.1574
6	0.0099	0.0300	0.0610	0.1264	0.0096	0.0290	0.0593	0.1232
7	0.0080	0.0242	0.0493	0.1022	0.0077	0.0233	0.0476	0.0991
8	0.0065	0.0199	0.0406	0.0843	0.0063	0.0190	0.0390	0.0813
9	0.0055	0.0166	0.0339	0.0706	0.0052	0.0158	0.0324	0.0677
10	0.0046	0.0140	0.0287	0.0598	0.0043	0.0133	0.0272	0.0570
11	0.0039	0.0120	0.0245	0.0511	0.0037	0.0112	0.0230	0.0484
12	0.0034	0.0103	0.0210	0.0440	0.0031	0.0096	0.0197	0.0414
13	0.0029	0.0089	0.0182	0.0382	0.0027	0.0082	0.0169	0.0357
14	0.0025	0.0077	0.0158	0.0332	0.0023	0.0071	0.0146	0.0309
15	0.0022	0.0067	0.0138	0.0291	0.0020	0.0061	0.0126	0.0268
16	0.0019	0.0059	0.0121	0.0255	0.0017	0.0053	0.0110	0.0234
17	0.0017	0.0052	0.0106	0.0225	0.0015	0.0046	0.0096	0.0205
18	0.0015	0.0045	0.0094	0.0198	0.0013	0.0041	0.0084	0.0179
19	0.0013	0.0040	0.0083	0.0176	0.0012	0.0035	0.0074	0.0158
20	0.0012	0.0035	0.0073	0.0156	0.0010	0.0031	0.0065	0.0139
21	0.0010	0.0031	0.0065	0.0138	0.0009	0.0027	0.0057	0.0122
22	0.0009	0.0028	0.0058	0.0123	0.0008	0.0024	0.0050	0.0108
23	0.0008	0.0025	0.0051	0.0110	0.0007	0.0021	0.0044	0.0096
24	0.0007	0.0022	0.0046	0.0098	0.0006	0.0019	0.0039	0.0085
25	0.0006	0.0020	0.0041	0.0087	0.0005	0.0016	0.0034	0.0075
26	0.0006	0.0017	0.0036	0.0078	0.0005	0.0015	0.0030	0.0067
27	0.0005	0.0016	0.0032	0.0070	0.0004	0.0013	0.0027	0.0059
28	0.0004	0.0014	0.0029	0.0063	0.0004	0.0011	0.0024	0.0052
29	0.0004	0.0012	0.0026	0.0056	0.0003	0.0010	0.0021	0.0047
30	0.0004	0.0011	0.0023	0.0050	0.0003	0.0009	0.0019	0.0041
31	0.0003	0.0010	0.0021	0.0045	0.0003	0.0008	0.0017	0.0037
32	0.0003	0.0009	0.0018	0.0040	0.0002	0.0007	0.0015	0.0033
33	0.0003	0.0008	0.0017	0.0036	0.0002	0.0006	0.0013	0.0029
34	0.0002	0.0007	0.0015	0.0033	0.0002	0.0005	0.0012	0.0026
35	0.0002	0.0006	0.0013	0.0029	0.0002	0.0005	0.0010	0.0023
36	0.0002	0.0006	0.0012	0.0026	0.0001	0.0004	0.0009	0.0021
37	0.0002	0.0005	0.0011	0.0024	0.0001	0.0004	0.0008	0.0018
38	0.0001	0.0005	0.0010	0.0021	0.0001	0.0003	0.0007	0.0016
39	0.0001	0.0004	0.0009	0.0019	0.0001	0.0003	0.0006	0.0015
40	0.0001	0.0004	0.0008	0.0017	0.0001	0.0003	0.0006	0.0013
41	0.0001	0.0003	0.0007	0.0015	0.0001	0.0002	0.0005	0.0012
42	0.0001	0.0003	0.0006	0.0014	0.0001	0.0002	0.0005	0.0010
43	0.0001	0.0003	0.0006	0.0013	0.0001	0.0002	0.0004	0.0009
44	0.0001	0.0002	0.0005	0.0011	0.0001	0.0002	0.0004	0.0008
45	0.0001	0.0002	0.0004	0.0010	0.0000	0.0001	0.0003	0.0007
46	0.0001	0.0002	0.0004	0.0009	0.0000	0.0001	0.0003	0.0007
47	0.0001	0.0002	0.0004	0.0008	0.0000	0.0001	0.0003	0.0006
48	0.0000	0.0002	0.0003	0.0007	0.0000	0.0001	0.0002	0.0005
49	0.0000	0.0001	0.0003	0.0007	0.0000	0.0001	0.0002	0.0005
50	0.0000	0.0001	0.0003	0.0006	0.0000	0.0001	0.0002	0.0004

How much must be invested
at the *end* of each period
to accumulate $1

End of Year	At 13% Interest compounded and Deposits made				At 14% Interest compounded and Deposits made			
	Monthly	Quarterly	Semi-Annually	Annually	Monthly	Quarterly	Semi-Annually	Annually
1	0.0785	0.2381	0.4843	1.0000	0.0781	0.2373	0.4831	1.0000
2	0.0367	0.1115	0.2269	0.4695	0.0363	0.1105	0.2252	0.4673
3	0.0229	0.0695	0.1416	0.2935	0.0225	0.0685	0.1398	0.2907
4	0.0160	0.0486	0.0992	0.2062	0.0157	0.0477	0.0975	0.2032
5	0.0119	0.0363	0.0741	0.1543	0.0116	0.0354	0.0724	0.1513
6	0.0092	0.0281	0.0576	0.1202	0.0089	0.0273	0.0559	0.1172
7	0.0074	0.0224	0.0459	0.0961	0.0071	0.0216	0.0443	0.0932
8	0.0060	0.0182	0.0374	0.0784	0.0057	0.0174	0.0359	0.0756
9	0.0049	0.0150	0.0309	0.0649	0.0047	0.0143	0.0294	0.0622
10	0.0041	0.0125	0.0258	0.0543	0.0039	0.0118	0.0244	0.0517
11	0.0034	0.0105	0.0217	0.0458	0.0032	0.0099	0.0204	0.0434
12	0.0029	0.0089	0.0184	0.0390	0.0027	0.0083	0.0172	0.0367
13	0.0025	0.0076	0.0157	0.0334	0.0023	0.0070	0.0146	0.0312
14	0.0021	0.0065	0.0135	0.0287	0.0019	0.0060	0.0124	0.0266
15	0.0018	0.0056	0.0116	0.0247	0.0017	0.0051	0.0106	0.0228
16	0.0016	0.0048	0.0100	0.0214	0.0014	0.0044	0.0091	0.0196
17	0.0014	0.0042	0.0087	0.0186	0.0012	0.0037	0.0078	0.0169
18	0.0012	0.0036	0.0075	0.0162	0.0010	0.0032	0.0067	0.0146
19	0.0010	0.0031	0.0065	0.0141	0.0009	0.0028	0.0058	0.0127
20	0.0009	0.0027	0.0057	0.0124	0.0008	0.0024	0.0050	0.0110
21	0.0008	0.0024	0.0050	0.0108	0.0007	0.0021	0.0043	0.0095
22	0.0007	0.0021	0.0043	0.0095	0.0006	0.0018	0.0038	0.0083
23	0.0006	0.0018	0.0038	0.0083	0.0005	0.0015	0.0033	0.0072
24	0.0005	0.0016	0.0033	0.0073	0.0004	0.0013	0.0028	0.0063
25	0.0004	0.0014	0.0029	0.0064	0.0004	0.0012	0.0025	0.0055
26	0.0004	0.0012	0.0026	0.0057	0.0003	0.0010	0.0021	0.0048
27	0.0003	0.0011	0.0022	0.0050	0.0003	0.0009	0.0019	0.0042
28	0.0003	0.0009	0.0020	0.0044	0.0002	0.0008	0.0016	0.0037
29	0.0003	0.0008	0.0017	0.0039	0.0002	0.0007	0.0014	0.0032
30	0.0002	0.0007	0.0015	0.0034	0.0002	0.0006	0.0012	0.0028
31	0.0002	0.0006	0.0013	0.0030	0.0002	0.0005	0.0011	0.0025
32	0.0002	0.0006	0.0012	0.0027	0.0001	0.0004	0.0009	0.0021
33	0.0002	0.0005	0.0010	0.0023	0.0001	0.0004	0.0008	0.0019
34	0.0001	0.0004	0.0009	0.0021	0.0001	0.0003	0.0007	0.0016
35	0.0001	0.0004	0.0008	0.0018	0.0001	0.0003	0.0006	0.0014
36	0.0001	0.0003	0.0007	0.0016	0.0001	0.0002	0.0005	0.0013
37	0.0001	0.0003	0.0006	0.0014	0.0001	0.0002	0.0005	0.0011
38	0.0001	0.0003	0.0005	0.0013	0.0001	0.0002	0.0004	0.0010
39	0.0001	0.0002	0.0005	0.0011	0.0001	0.0002	0.0004	0.0009
40	0.0001	0.0002	0.0004	0.0010	0.0000	0.0001	0.0003	0.0007
41	0.0001	0.0002	0.0004	0.0009	0.0000	0.0001	0.0003	0.0007
42	0.0000	0.0002	0.0003	0.0008	0.0000	0.0001	0.0002	0.0006
43	0.0000	0.0001	0.0003	0.0007	0.0000	0.0001	0.0002	0.0005
44	0.0000	0.0001	0.0003	0.0006	0.0000	0.0001	0.0002	0.0004
45	0.0000	0.0001	0.0002	0.0005	0.0000	0.0001	0.0002	0.0004
46	0.0000	0.0001	0.0002	0.0005	0.0000	0.0001	0.0001	0.0003
47	0.0000	0.0001	0.0002	0.0004	0.0000	0.0001	0.0001	0.0003
48	0.0000	0.0001	0.0002	0.0004	0.0000	0.0000	0.0001	0.0003
49	0.0000	0.0001	0.0001	0.0003	0.0000	0.0000	0.0001	0.0002
50	0.0000	0.0001	0.0001	0.0003	0.0000	0.0000	0.0001	0.0002

How much must be invested
at the *end* of each period
to accumulate $1

End of Year	At 17% Interest compounded and Deposits made				At 18% Interest compounded and Deposits made			
	Monthly	Quarterly	Semi-Annually	Annually	Monthly	Quarterly	Semi-Annually	Annually
1	0.0770	0.2346	0.4796	1.0000	0.0767	0.2337	0.4785	1.0000
2	0.0353	0.1076	0.2203	0.4608	0.0349	0.1066	0.2187	0.4587
3	0.0215	0.0656	0.1346	0.2826	0.0212	0.0647	0.1329	0.2799
4	0.0147	0.0449	0.0923	0.1945	0.0144	0.0440	0.0907	0.1917
5	0.0107	0.0327	0.0674	0.1426	0.0104	0.0319	0.0658	0.1398
6	0.0081	0.0248	0.0512	0.1086	0.0078	0.0240	0.0497	0.1059
7	0.0063	0.0193	0.0398	0.0849	0.0060	0.0185	0.0384	0.0824
8	0.0050	0.0152	0.0316	0.0677	0.0047	0.0146	0.0303	0.0652
9	0.0040	0.0122	0.0254	0.0547	0.0038	0.0116	0.0242	0.0524
10	0.0032	0.0099	0.0207	0.0447	0.0030	0.0093	0.0195	0.0425
11	0.0026	0.0081	0.0169	0.0368	0.0024	0.0076	0.0159	0.0348
12	0.0022	0.0067	0.0140	0.0305	0.0020	0.0062	0.0130	0.0286
13	0.0018	0.0055	0.0116	0.0254	0.0016	0.0051	0.0107	0.0237
14	0.0015	0.0046	0.0096	0.0212	0.0013	0.0042	0.0089	0.0197
15	0.0012	0.0038	0.0081	0.0178	0.0011	0.0035	0.0073	0.0164
16	0.0010	0.0032	0.0067	0.0150	0.0009	0.0029	0.0061	0.0137
17	0.0009	0.0027	0.0057	0.0127	0.0008	0.0024	0.0051	0.0115
18	0.0007	0.0022	0.0048	0.0107	0.0006	0.0020	0.0042	0.0096
19	0.0006	0.0019	0.0040	0.0091	0.0005	0.0016	0.0035	0.0081
20	0.0005	0.0016	0.0034	0.0077	0.0004	0.0014	0.0030	0.0068
21	0.0004	0.0013	0.0029	0.0065	0.0004	0.0011	0.0025	0.0057
22	0.0004	0.0011	0.0024	0.0056	0.0003	0.0010	0.0021	0.0048
23	0.0003	0.0009	0.0020	0.0047	0.0003	0.0008	0.0017	0.0041
24	0.0003	0.0008	0.0017	0.0040	0.0002	0.0007	0.0015	0.0035
25	0.0002	0.0007	0.0015	0.0034	0.0002	0.0006	0.0012	0.0029
26	0.0002	0.0006	0.0012	0.0029	0.0001	0.0005	0.0010	0.0025
27	0.0002	0.0005	0.0011	0.0025	0.0001	0.0004	0.0009	0.0021
28	0.0001	0.0004	0.0009	0.0021	0.0001	0.0003	0.0007	0.0018
29	0.0001	0.0003	0.0008	0.0018	0.0001	0.0003	0.0006	0.0015
30	0.0001	0.0003	0.0006	0.0015	0.0001	0.0002	0.0005	0.0013
31	0.0001	0.0002	0.0005	0.0013	0.0001	0.0002	0.0004	0.0011
32	0.0001	0.0002	0.0005	0.0011	0.0000	0.0002	0.0004	0.0009
33	0.0001	0.0002	0.0004	0.0010	0.0000	0.0001	0.0003	0.0008
34	0.0000	0.0001	0.0003	0.0008	0.0000	0.0001	0.0003	0.0006
35	0.0000	0.0001	0.0003	0.0007	0.0000	0.0001	0.0002	0.0006
36	0.0000	0.0001	0.0002	0.0006	0.0000	0.0001	0.0002	0.0005
37	0.0000	0.0001	0.0002	0.0005	0.0000	0.0001	0.0002	0.0004
38	0.0000	0.0001	0.0002	0.0004	0.0000	0.0001	0.0001	0.0003
39	0.0000	0.0001	0.0001	0.0004	0.0000	0.0000	0.0001	0.0003
40	0.0000	0.0001	0.0001	0.0003	0.0000	0.0000	0.0001	0.0002
41	0.0000	0.0000	0.0001	0.0003	0.0000	0.0000	0.0001	0.0002
42	0.0000	0.0000	0.0001	0.0002	0.0000	0.0000	0.0001	0.0002
43	0.0000	0.0000	0.0001	0.0002	0.0000	0.0000	0.0001	0.0001
44	0.0000	0.0000	0.0001	0.0002	0.0000	0.0000	0.0000	0.0001
45	0.0000	0.0000	0.0001	0.0001	0.0000	0.0000	0.0000	0.0001
46	0.0000	0.0000	0.0000	0.0001	0.0000	0.0000	0.0000	0.0001
47	0.0000	0.0000	0.0000	0.0001	0.0000	0.0000	0.0000	0.0001
48	0.0000	0.0000	0.0000	0.0001	0.0000	0.0000	0.0000	0.0001
49	0.0000	0.0000	0.0000	0.0001	0.0000	0.0000	0.0000	0.0001
50	0.0000	0.0000	0.0000	0.0001	0.0000	0.0000	0.0000	0.0000

Table 4/ 183

How much must be invested
at the *end* of each period
to accumulate $1

End of Year	At 19% Interest compounded and Deposits made				At 20% Interest compounded and Deposits made			
	Monthly	Quarterly	Semi-Annually	Annually	Monthly	Quarterly	Semi-Annually	Annually
1	0.0763	0.2329	0.4773	1.0000	0.0760	0.2320	0.4762	1.0000
2	0.0346	0.1057	0.2171	0.4566	0.0342	0.1047	0.2155	0.4545
3	0.0208	0.0637	0.1313	0.2773	0.0205	0.0628	0.1296	0.2747
4	0.0141	0.0431	0.0890	0.1890	0.0138	0.0423	0.0874	0.1863
5	0.0101	0.0311	0.0643	0.1371	0.0098	0.0302	0.0627	0.1344
6	0.0075	0.0232	0.0482	0.1033	0.0073	0.0225	0.0468	0.1007
7	0.0058	0.0178	0.0371	0.0799	0.0055	0.0171	0.0357	0.0774
8	0.0045	0.0139	0.0290	0.0629	0.0043	0.0133	0.0278	0.0606
9	0.0036	0.0110	0.0230	0.0502	0.0034	0.0104	0.0219	0.0481
10	0.0028	0.0088	0.0185	0.0405	0.0027	0.0083	0.0175	0.0385
11	0.0023	0.0071	0.0149	0.0329	0.0021	0.0066	0.0140	0.0311
12	0.0018	0.0057	0.0121	0.0269	0.0017	0.0053	0.0113	0.0253
13	0.0015	0.0047	0.0099	0.0221	0.0014	0.0043	0.0092	0.0206
14	0.0012	0.0038	0.0081	0.0182	0.0011	0.0035	0.0075	0.0169
15	0.0010	0.0031	0.0067	0.0151	0.0009	0.0028	0.0061	0.0139
16	0.0008	0.0026	0.0055	0.0125	0.0007	0.0023	0.0050	0.0114
17	0.0007	0.0021	0.0045	0.0104	0.0006	0.0019	0.0041	0.0094
18	0.0006	0.0017	0.0038	0.0087	0.0005	0.0015	0.0033	0.0078
19	0.0005	0.0014	0.0031	0.0072	0.0004	0.0013	0.0027	0.0065
20	0.0004	0.0012	0.0026	0.0060	0.0003	0.0010	0.0023	0.0054
21	0.0003	0.0010	0.0021	0.0051	0.0003	0.0008	0.0019	0.0044
22	0.0003	0.0008	0.0018	0.0042	0.0002	0.0007	0.0015	0.0037
23	0.0002	0.0007	0.0015	0.0035	0.0002	0.0006	0.0013	0.0031
24	0.0002	0.0006	0.0012	0.0030	0.0001	0.0005	0.0010	0.0025
25	0.0001	0.0005	0.0010	0.0025	0.0001	0.0004	0.0009	0.0021
26	0.0001	0.0004	0.0009	0.0021	0.0001	0.0003	0.0007	0.0018
27	0.0001	0.0003	0.0007	0.0017	0.0001	0.0003	0.0006	0.0015
28	0.0001	0.0003	0.0006	0.0015	0.0001	0.0002	0.0005	0.0012
29	0.0001	0.0002	0.0005	0.0012	0.0001	0.0002	0.0004	0.0010
30	0.0001	0.0002	0.0004	0.0010	0.0000	0.0001	0.0003	0.0008
31	0.0000	0.0002	0.0003	0.0009	0.0000	0.0001	0.0003	0.0007
32	0.0000	0.0001	0.0003	0.0007	0.0000	0.0001	0.0002	0.0006
33	0.0000	0.0001	0.0002	0.0006	0.0000	0.0001	0.0002	0.0005
34	0.0000	0.0001	0.0002	0.0005	0.0000	0.0001	0.0002	0.0004
35	0.0000	0.0001	0.0002	0.0004	0.0000	0.0001	0.0001	0.0003
36	0.0000	0.0001	0.0001	0.0004	0.0000	0.0000	0.0001	0.0003
37	0.0000	0.0000	0.0001	0.0003	0.0000	0.0000	0.0001	0.0002
38	0.0000	0.0000	0.0001	0.0003	0.0000	0.0000	0.0001	0.0002
39	0.0000	0.0000	0.0001	0.0002	0.0000	0.0000	0.0001	0.0002
40	0.0000	0.0000	0.0001	0.0002	0.0000	0.0000	0.0000	0.0001
41	0.0000	0.0000	0.0001	0.0002	0.0000	0.0000	0.0000	0.0001
42	0.0000	0.0000	0.0000	0.0001	0.0000	0.0000	0.0000	0.0001
43	0.0000	0.0000	0.0000	0.0001	0.0000	0.0000	0.0000	0.0001
44	0.0000	0.0000	0.0000	0.0001	0.0000	0.0000	0.0000	0.0001
45	0.0000	0.0000	0.0000	0.0001	0.0000	0.0000	0.0000	0.0001
46	0.0000	0.0000	0.0000	0.0001	0.0000	0.0000	0.0000	0.0000
47	0.0000	0.0000	0.0000	0.0001	0.0000	0.0000	0.0000	0.0000
48	0.0000	0.0000	0.0000	0.0000	0.0000	0.0000	0.0000	0.0000
49	0.0000	0.0000	0.0000	0.0000	0.0000	0.0000	0.0000	0.0000
50	0.0000	0.0000	0.0000	0.0000	0.0000	0.0000	0.0000	0.0000

Applications

Chapter Six

- What are the instalment payments necessary to discharge a loan over a specific period of time?

Chapter Fifteen

- Calculating annuity yields.

Periodic payments at the *end* of each period required to amortize a loan of $1 over time

End of Year	At 7% Interest compounded and Payments made				At 8% Interest compounded and Payments made			
	Monthly	Quarterly	Semi-Annually	Annually	Monthly	Quarterly	Semi-Annually	Annually
1	0.0865	0.2610	0.5264	1.0700	0.0870	0.2626	0.5302	1.0800
2	0.0448	0.1350	0.2723	0.5531	0.0452	0.1365	0.2755	0.5608
3	0.0309	0.0931	0.1877	0.3811	0.0313	0.0946	0.1908	0.3880
4	0.0239	0.0722	0.1455	0.2952	0.0244	0.0737	0.1485	0.3019
5	0.0198	0.0597	0.1202	0.2439	0.0203	0.0612	0.1233	0.2505
6	0.0170	0.0514	0.1035	0.2098	0.0175	0.0529	0.1066	0.2163
7	0.0151	0.0455	0.0916	0.1856	0.0156	0.0470	0.0947	0.1921
8	0.0136	0.0411	0.0827	0.1675	0.0141	0.0426	0.0858	0.1740
9	0.0125	0.0377	0.0758	0.1535	0.0130	0.0392	0.0790	0.1601
10	0.0116	0.0350	0.0704	0.1424	0.0121	0.0366	0.0736	0.1490
11	0.0109	0.0328	0.0659	0.1334	0.0114	0.0344	0.0692	0.1401
12	0.0103	0.0310	0.0623	0.1259	0.0108	0.0326	0.0656	0.1327
13	0.0098	0.0294	0.0592	0.1197	0.0103	0.0311	0.0626	0.1265
14	0.0094	0.0282	0.0566	0.1143	0.0099	0.0298	0.0600	0.1213
15	0.0090	0.0271	0.0544	0.1098	0.0096	0.0288	0.0578	0.1168
16	0.0087	0.0261	0.0524	0.1059	0.0092	0.0278	0.0559	0.1130
17	0.0084	0.0253	0.0508	0.1024	0.0090	0.0270	0.0543	0.1096
18	0.0082	0.0245	0.0493	0.0994	0.0087	0.0263	0.0529	0.1067
19	0.0079	0.0239	0.0480	0.0968	0.0085	0.0257	0.0516	0.1041
20	0.0078	0.0233	0.0468	0.0944	0.0084	0.0252	0.0505	0.1019
21	0.0076	0.0228	0.0458	0.0923	0.0082	0.0247	0.0495	0.0998
22	0.0074	0.0224	0.0449	0.0904	0.0081	0.0242	0.0487	0.0980
23	0.0073	0.0219	0.0441	0.0887	0.0079	0.0239	0.0479	0.0964
24	0.0072	0.0216	0.0433	0.0872	0.0078	0.0235	0.0472	0.0950
25	0.0071	0.0212	0.0426	0.0858	0.0077	0.0232	0.0466	0.0937
26	0.0070	0.0209	0.0420	0.0846	0.0076	0.0229	0.0460	0.0925
27	0.0069	0.0207	0.0415	0.0834	0.0075	0.0227	0.0455	0.0914
28	0.0068	0.0204	0.0410	0.0824	0.0075	0.0224	0.0450	0.0905
29	0.0067	0.0202	0.0405	0.0814	0.0074	0.0222	0.0446	0.0896
30	0.0067	0.0200	0.0401	0.0806	0.0073	0.0220	0.0442	0.0888
31	0.0066	0.0198	0.0397	0.0798	0.0073	0.0219	0.0439	0.0881
32	0.0065	0.0196	0.0394	0.0791	0.0072	0.0217	0.0435	0.0875
33	0.0065	0.0195	0.0390	0.0784	0.0072	0.0216	0.0432	0.0869
34	0.0064	0.0193	0.0387	0.0778	0.0071	0.0215	0.0430	0.0863
35	0.0064	0.0192	0.0385	0.0772	0.0071	0.0213	0.0427	0.0858
36	0.0063	0.0191	0.0382	0.0767	0.0071	0.0212	0.0425	0.0853
37	0.0063	0.0190	0.0380	0.0762	0.0070	0.0211	0.0423	0.0849
38	0.0063	0.0188	0.0378	0.0758	0.0070	0.0210	0.0421	0.0845
39	0.0062	0.0188	0.0376	0.0754	0.0070	0.0210	0.0420	0.0842
40	0.0062	0.0187	0.0374	0.0750	0.0070	0.0209	0.0418	0.0839
41	0.0062	0.0186	0.0372	0.0747	0.0069	0.0208	0.0417	0.0836
42	0.0062	0.0185	0.0371	0.0743	0.0069	0.0207	0.0415	0.0833
43	0.0061	0.0184	0.0369	0.0740	0.0069	0.0207	0.0414	0.0830
44	0.0061	0.0184	0.0368	0.0738	0.0069	0.0206	0.0413	0.0828
45	0.0061	0.0183	0.0367	0.0735	0.0069	0.0206	0.0412	0.0826
46	0.0061	0.0182	0.0365	0.0733	0.0068	0.0205	0.0411	0.0824
47	0.0061	0.0182	0.0364	0.0730	0.0068	0.0205	0.0410	0.0822
48	0.0060	0.0181	0.0363	0.0728	0.0068	0.0205	0.0409	0.0820
49	0.0060	0.0181	0.0362	0.0726	0.0068	0.0204	0.0409	0.0819
50	0.0060	0.0181	0.0362	0.0725	0.0068	0.0204	0.0408	0.0817

Periodic payments at the *end* of each period required to amortize a loan of $1 over time

End of Year	At 11% Interest compounded and Payments made				At 12% Interest compounded and Payments made			
	Monthly	Quarterly	Semi-Annually	Annually	Monthly	Quarterly	Semi-Annually	Annually
1	0.0884	0.2674	0.5416	1.1100	0.0888	0.2690	0.5454	1.1200
2	0.0466	0.1410	0.2853	0.5839	0.0471	0.1425	0.2886	0.5917
3	0.0327	0.0990	0.2002	0.4092	0.0332	0.1005	0.2034	0.4163
4	0.0258	0.0781	0.1579	0.3223	0.0263	0.0796	0.1610	0.3292
5	0.0217	0.0657	0.1327	0.2706	0.0222	0.0672	0.1359	0.2774
6	0.0190	0.0575	0.1160	0.2364	0.0196	0.0590	0.1193	0.2432
7	0.0171	0.0517	0.1043	0.2122	0.0177	0.0533	0.1076	0.2191
8	0.0157	0.0474	0.0956	0.1943	0.0163	0.0490	0.0990	0.2013
9	0.0146	0.0441	0.0889	0.1806	0.0152	0.0458	0.0924	0.1877
10	0.0138	0.0415	0.0837	0.1698	0.0143	0.0433	0.0872	0.1770
11	0.0131	0.0395	0.0795	0.1611	0.0137	0.0412	0.0830	0.1684
12	0.0125	0.0378	0.0760	0.1540	0.0131	0.0396	0.0797	0.1614
13	0.0121	0.0364	0.0732	0.1482	0.0127	0.0382	0.0769	0.1557
14	0.0117	0.0352	0.0708	0.1432	0.0123	0.0371	0.0746	0.1509
15	0.0114	0.0342	0.0688	0.1391	0.0120	0.0361	0.0726	0.1468
16	0.0111	0.0334	0.0671	0.1355	0.0117	0.0353	0.0710	0.1434
17	0.0109	0.0327	0.0656	0.1325	0.0115	0.0346	0.0696	0.1405
18	0.0107	0.0320	0.0644	0.1298	0.0113	0.0341	0.0684	0.1379
19	0.0105	0.0315	0.0633	0.1276	0.0112	0.0335	0.0674	0.1358
20	0.0103	0.0310	0.0623	0.1256	0.0110	0.0331	0.0665	0.1339
21	0.0102	0.0306	0.0615	0.1238	0.0109	0.0327	0.0657	0.1322
22	0.0101	0.0303	0.0608	0.1223	0.0108	0.0324	0.0650	0.1308
23	0.0100	0.0300	0.0601	0.1210	0.0107	0.0321	0.0644	0.1296
24	0.0099	0.0297	0.0596	0.1198	0.0106	0.0319	0.0639	0.1285
25	0.0098	0.0295	0.0591	0.1187	0.0105	0.0316	0.0634	0.1275
26	0.0097	0.0292	0.0586	0.1178	0.0105	0.0315	0.0630	0.1267
27	0.0097	0.0291	0.0582	0.1170	0.0104	0.0313	0.0627	0.1259
28	0.0096	0.0289	0.0579	0.1163	0.0104	0.0311	0.0624	0.1252
29	0.0096	0.0287	0.0576	0.1156	0.0103	0.0310	0.0621	0.1247
30	0.0095	0.0286	0.0573	0.1150	0.0103	0.0309	0.0619	0.1241
31	0.0095	0.0285	0.0571	0.1145	0.0103	0.0308	0.0617	0.1237
32	0.0095	0.0284	0.0568	0.1140	0.0102	0.0307	0.0615	0.1233
33	0.0094	0.0283	0.0567	0.1136	0.0102	0.0306	0.0613	0.1229
34	0.0094	0.0282	0.0565	0.1133	0.0102	0.0305	0.0612	0.1226
35	0.0094	0.0281	0.0563	0.1129	0.0102	0.0305	0.0610	0.1223
36	0.0093	0.0281	0.0562	0.1126	0.0101	0.0304	0.0609	0.1221
37	0.0093	0.0280	0.0561	0.1124	0.0101	0.0304	0.0608	0.1218
38	0.0093	0.0280	0.0560	0.1121	0.0101	0.0303	0.0607	0.1216
39	0.0093	0.0279	0.0559	0.1119	0.0101	0.0303	0.0606	0.1215
40	0.0093	0.0279	0.0558	0.1117	0.0101	0.0303	0.0606	0.1213
41	0.0093	0.0278	0.0557	0.1115	0.0101	0.0302	0.0605	0.1212
42	0.0093	0.0278	0.0556	0.1114	0.0101	0.0302	0.0605	0.1210
43	0.0093	0.0278	0.0556	0.1113	0.0101	0.0302	0.0604	0.1209
44	0.0092	0.0277	0.0555	0.1111	0.0101	0.0302	0.0604	0.1208
45	0.0092	0.0277	0.0554	0.1110	0.0100	0.0301	0.0603	0.1207
46	0.0092	0.0277	0.0554	0.1109	0.0100	0.0301	0.0603	0.1207
47	0.0092	0.0277	0.0554	0.1108	0.0100	0.0301	0.0603	0.1206
48	0.0092	0.0277	0.0553	0.1107	0.0100	0.0301	0.0602	0.1205
49	0.0092	0.0276	0.0553	0.1107	0.0100	0.0301	0.0602	0.1205
50	0.0092	0.0276	0.0553	0.1106	0.0100	0.0301	0.0602	0.1204

Periodic payments at the *end* of each period required to amortize a loan of $1 over time

End of Year	At 13% Interest compounded and Payments made				At 14% Interest compounded and Payments made			
	Monthly	Quarterly	Semi-Annually	Annually	Monthly	Quarterly	Semi-Annually	Annually
1	0.0893	0.2706	0.5493	1.1300	0.0898	0.2723	0.5531	1.1400
2	0.0475	0.1440	0.2919	0.5995	0.0480	0.1455	0.2952	0.6073
3	0.0337	0.1020	0.2066	0.4235	0.0342	0.1035	0.2098	0.4307
4	0.0268	0.0811	0.1642	0.3362	0.0273	0.0827	0.1675	0.3432
5	0.0228	0.0688	0.1391	0.2843	0.0233	0.0704	0.1424	0.2913
6	0.0201	0.0606	0.1226	0.2502	0.0206	0.0623	0.1259	0.2572
7	0.0182	0.0549	0.1109	0.2261	0.0187	0.0566	0.1143	0.2332
8	0.0168	0.0507	0.1024	0.2084	0.0174	0.0524	0.1059	0.2156
9	0.0158	0.0475	0.0959	0.1949	0.0163	0.0493	0.0994	0.2022
10	0.0149	0.0450	0.0908	0.1843	0.0155	0.0468	0.0944	0.1917
11	0.0143	0.0430	0.0867	0.1758	0.0149	0.0449	0.0904	0.1834
12	0.0137	0.0414	0.0834	0.1690	0.0144	0.0433	0.0872	0.1767
13	0.0133	0.0401	0.0807	0.1634	0.0140	0.0420	0.0846	0.1712
14	0.0130	0.0390	0.0785	0.1587	0.0136	0.0410	0.0824	0.1666
15	0.0127	0.0381	0.0766	0.1547	0.0133	0.0401	0.0806	0.1628
16	0.0124	0.0373	0.0750	0.1514	0.0131	0.0394	0.0791	0.1596
17	0.0122	0.0367	0.0737	0.1486	0.0129	0.0387	0.0778	0.1569
18	0.0120	0.0361	0.0725	0.1462	0.0127	0.0382	0.0767	0.1546
19	0.0118	0.0356	0.0715	0.1441	0.0126	0.0378	0.0758	0.1527
20	0.0117	0.0352	0.0707	0.1424	0.0124	0.0374	0.0750	0.1510
21	0.0116	0.0349	0.0700	0.1408	0.0123	0.0371	0.0743	0.1495
22	0.0115	0.0346	0.0693	0.1395	0.0122	0.0368	0.0738	0.1483
23	0.0114	0.0343	0.0688	0.1383	0.0122	0.0365	0.0733	0.1472
24	0.0113	0.0341	0.0683	0.1373	0.0121	0.0363	0.0728	0.1463
25	0.0113	0.0339	0.0679	0.1364	0.0120	0.0362	0.0725	0.1455
26	0.0112	0.0337	0.0676	0.1357	0.0120	0.0360	0.0721	0.1448
27	0.0112	0.0336	0.0672	0.1350	0.0119	0.0359	0.0719	0.1442
28	0.0111	0.0334	0.0670	0.1344	0.0119	0.0358	0.0716	0.1437
29	0.0111	0.0333	0.0667	0.1339	0.0119	0.0357	0.0714	0.1432
30	0.0111	0.0332	0.0665	0.1334	0.0118	0.0356	0.0712	0.1428
31	0.0110	0.0331	0.0663	0.1330	0.0118	0.0355	0.0711	0.1425
32	0.0110	0.0331	0.0662	0.1327	0.0118	0.0354	0.0709	0.1421
33	0.0110	0.0330	0.0660	0.1323	0.0118	0.0354	0.0708	0.1419
34	0.0110	0.0329	0.0659	0.1321	0.0118	0.0353	0.0707	0.1416
35	0.0110	0.0329	0.0658	0.1318	0.0118	0.0353	0.0706	0.1414
36	0.0109	0.0328	0.0657	0.1316	0.0117	0.0352	0.0705	0.1413
37	0.0109	0.0328	0.0656	0.1314	0.0117	0.0352	0.0705	0.1411
38	0.0109	0.0328	0.0655	0.1313	0.0117	0.0352	0.0704	0.1410
39	0.0109	0.0327	0.0655	0.1311	0.0117	0.0352	0.0704	0.1409
40	0.0109	0.0327	0.0654	0.1310	0.0117	0.0351	0.0703	0.1407
41	0.0109	0.0327	0.0654	0.1309	0.0117	0.0351	0.0703	0.1407
42	0.0109	0.0327	0.0653	0.1308	0.0117	0.0351	0.0702	0.1406
43	0.0109	0.0326	0.0653	0.1307	0.0117	0.0351	0.0702	0.1405
44	0.0109	0.0326	0.0653	0.1306	0.0117	0.0351	0.0702	0.1404
45	0.0109	0.0326	0.0652	0.1305	0.0117	0.0351	0.0702	0.1404
46	0.0109	0.0326	0.0652	0.1305	0.0117	0.0351	0.0701	0.1403
47	0.0109	0.0326	0.0652	0.1304	0.0117	0.0351	0.0701	0.1403
48	0.0109	0.0326	0.0652	0.1304	0.0117	0.0350	0.0701	0.1403
49	0.0109	0.0326	0.0651	0.1303	0.0117	0.0350	0.0701	0.1402
50	0.0109	0.0326	0.0651	0.1303	0.0117	0.0350	0.0701	0.1402

Periodic payments at the *end* of each period required to amortize a loan of $1 over time

End of Year	At 17% Interest compounded and Payments made				At 18% Interest compounded and Payments made			
	Monthly	Quarterly	Semi-Annually	Annually	Monthly	Quarterly	Semi-Annually	Annually
1	0.0912	0.2771	0.5646	1.1700	0.0917	0.2787	0.5685	1.1800
2	0.0494	0.1501	0.3053	0.6308	0.0499	0.1516	0.3087	0.6387
3	0.0357	0.1081	0.2196	0.4526	0.0362	0.1097	0.2229	0.4599
4	0.0289	0.0874	0.1773	0.3645	0.0294	0.0890	0.1807	0.3717
5	0.0249	0.0752	0.1524	0.3126	0.0254	0.0769	0.1558	0.3198
6	0.0222	0.0673	0.1362	0.2786	0.0228	0.0690	0.1397	0.2859
7	0.0204	0.0618	0.1248	0.2549	0.0210	0.0635	0.1284	0.2624
8	0.0191	0.0577	0.1166	0.2377	0.0197	0.0596	0.1203	0.2452
9	0.0181	0.0547	0.1104	0.2247	0.0188	0.0566	0.1142	0.2324
10	0.0174	0.0524	0.1057	0.2147	0.0180	0.0543	0.1095	0.2225
11	0.0168	0.0506	0.1019	0.2068	0.0174	0.0526	0.1059	0.2148
12	0.0163	0.0492	0.0990	0.2005	0.0170	0.0512	0.1030	0.2086
13	0.0159	0.0480	0.0966	0.1954	0.0166	0.0501	0.1007	0.2037
14	0.0156	0.0471	0.0946	0.1912	0.0163	0.0492	0.0989	0.1997
15	0.0154	0.0463	0.0931	0.1878	0.0161	0.0485	0.0973	0.1964
16	0.0152	0.0457	0.0917	0.1850	0.0159	0.0479	0.0961	0.1937
17	0.0150	0.0452	0.0907	0.1827	0.0158	0.0474	0.0951	0.1915
18	0.0149	0.0447	0.0898	0.1807	0.0156	0.0470	0.0942	0.1896
19	0.0148	0.0444	0.0890	0.1791	0.0155	0.0466	0.0935	0.1881
20	0.0147	0.0441	0.0884	0.1777	0.0154	0.0464	0.0930	0.1868
21	0.0146	0.0438	0.0879	0.1765	0.0154	0.0461	0.0925	0.1857
22	0.0145	0.0436	0.0874	0.1756	0.0153	0.0460	0.0921	0.1848
23	0.0145	0.0434	0.0870	0.1747	0.0153	0.0458	0.0917	0.1841
24	0.0144	0.0433	0.0867	0.1740	0.0152	0.0457	0.0915	0.1835
25	0.0144	0.0432	0.0865	0.1734	0.0152	0.0456	0.0912	0.1829
26	0.0143	0.0431	0.0862	0.1729	0.0151	0.0455	0.0910	0.1825
27	0.0143	0.0430	0.0861	0.1725	0.0151	0.0454	0.0909	0.1821
28	0.0143	0.0429	0.0859	0.1721	0.0151	0.0453	0.0907	0.1818
29	0.0143	0.0428	0.0858	0.1718	0.0151	0.0453	0.0906	0.1815
30	0.0143	0.0428	0.0856	0.1715	0.0151	0.0452	0.0905	0.1813
31	0.0142	0.0427	0.0855	0.1713	0.0151	0.0452	0.0904	0.1811
32	0.0142	0.0427	0.0855	0.1711	0.0150	0.0452	0.0904	0.1809
33	0.0142	0.0427	0.0854	0.1710	0.0150	0.0451	0.0903	0.1808
34	0.0142	0.0426	0.0853	0.1708	0.0150	0.0451	0.0903	0.1806
35	0.0142	0.0426	0.0853	0.1707	0.0150	0.0451	0.0902	0.1806
36	0.0142	0.0426	0.0852	0.1706	0.0150	0.0451	0.0902	0.1805
37	0.0142	0.0426	0.0852	0.1705	0.0150	0.0451	0.0902	0.1804
38	0.0142	0.0426	0.0852	0.1704	0.0150	0.0451	0.0901	0.1803
39	0.0142	0.0426	0.0851	0.1704	0.0150	0.0450	0.0901	0.1803
40	0.0142	0.0426	0.0851	0.1703	0.0150	0.0450	0.0901	0.1802
41	0.0142	0.0425	0.0851	0.1703	0.0150	0.0450	0.0901	0.1802
42	0.0142	0.0425	0.0851	0.1702	0.0150	0.0450	0.0901	0.1802
43	0.0142	0.0425	0.0851	0.1702	0.0150	0.0450	0.0901	0.1801
44	0.0142	0.0425	0.0851	0.1702	0.0150	0.0450	0.0900	0.1801
45	0.0142	0.0425	0.0851	0.1701	0.0150	0.0450	0.0900	0.1801
46	0.0142	0.0425	0.0850	0.1701	0.0150	0.0450	0.0900	0.1801
47	0.0142	0.0425	0.0850	0.1701	0.0150	0.0450	0.0900	0.1801
48	0.0142	0.0425	0.0850	0.1701	0.0150	0.0450	0.0900	0.1801
49	0.0142	0.0425	0.0850	0.1701	0.0150	0.0450	0.0900	0.1801
50	0.0142	0.0425	0.0850	0.1701	0.0150	0.0450	0.0900	0.1800

Periodic payments at the *end* of each period required to amortize a loan of $1 over time

End of Year	At 21% Interest compounded and Payments made				At 22% Interest compounded and Payments made			
	Monthly	Quarterly	Semi-Annually	Annually	Monthly	Quarterly	Semi-Annually	Annually
1	0.0931	0.2837	0.5801	1.2100	0.0936	0.2853	0.5839	1.2200
2	0.0514	0.1563	0.3189	0.6625	0.0519	0.1579	0.3223	0.6705
3	0.0377	0.1144	0.2330	0.4822	0.0382	0.1160	0.2364	0.4897
4	0.0310	0.0939	0.1909	0.3936	0.0315	0.0956	0.1943	0.4010
5	0.0271	0.0820	0.1663	0.3418	0.0276	0.0837	0.1698	0.3492
6	0.0245	0.0742	0.1504	0.3082	0.0251	0.0760	0.1540	0.3158
7	0.0228	0.0690	0.1395	0.2851	0.0234	0.0708	0.1432	0.2928
8	0.0216	0.0652	0.1316	0.2684	0.0222	0.0671	0.1355	0.2763
9	0.0207	0.0624	0.1259	0.2561	0.0213	0.0644	0.1298	0.2641
10	0.0200	0.0603	0.1215	0.2467	0.0207	0.0623	0.1256	0.2549
11	0.0195	0.0587	0.1181	0.2394	0.0202	0.0608	0.1223	0.2478
12	0.0191	0.0574	0.1155	0.2337	0.0198	0.0596	0.1198	0.2423
13	0.0188	0.0564	0.1135	0.2292	0.0195	0.0586	0.1178	0.2379
14	0.0185	0.0557	0.1118	0.2256	0.0192	0.0579	0.1163	0.2345
15	0.0183	0.0551	0.1105	0.2228	0.0191	0.0573	0.1150	0.2317
16	0.0181	0.0546	0.1095	0.2204	0.0189	0.0568	0.1140	0.2295
17	0.0180	0.0542	0.1086	0.2186	0.0188	0.0565	0.1133	0.2278
18	0.0179	0.0539	0.1080	0.2170	0.0187	0.0562	0.1126	0.2263
19	0.0178	0.0536	0.1074	0.2158	0.0186	0.0560	0.1121	0.2251
20	0.0178	0.0534	0.1070	0.2147	0.0186	0.0558	0.1117	0.2242
21	0.0177	0.0532	0.1066	0.2139	0.0185	0.0556	0.1114	0.2234
22	0.0177	0.0531	0.1063	0.2132	0.0185	0.0555	0.1111	0.2228
23	0.0176	0.0530	0.1061	0.2127	0.0185	0.0554	0.1109	0.2223
24	0.0176	0.0529	0.1059	0.2122	0.0184	0.0553	0.1107	0.2219
25	0.0176	0.0528	0.1057	0.2118	0.0184	0.0553	0.1106	0.2215
26	0.0176	0.0528	0.1056	0.2115	0.0184	0.0552	0.1105	0.2213
27	0.0176	0.0527	0.1055	0.2112	0.0184	0.0552	0.1104	0.2210
28	0.0176	0.0527	0.1054	0.2110	0.0184	0.0551	0.1103	0.2208
29	0.0175	0.0526	0.1053	0.2108	0.0184	0.0551	0.1103	0.2207
30	0.0175	0.0526	0.1053	0.2107	0.0184	0.0551	0.1102	0.2206
31	0.0175	0.0526	0.1052	0.2106	0.0184	0.0551	0.1102	0.2205
32	0.0175	0.0526	0.1052	0.2105	0.0184	0.0551	0.1101	0.2204
33	0.0175	0.0526	0.1051	0.2104	0.0183	0.0550	0.1101	0.2203
34	0.0175	0.0525	0.1051	0.2103	0.0183	0.0550	0.1101	0.2203
35	0.0175	0.0525	0.1051	0.2103	0.0183	0.0550	0.1101	0.2202
36	0.0175	0.0525	0.1051	0.2102	0.0183	0.0550	0.1101	0.2202
37	0.0175	0.0525	0.1051	0.2102	0.0183	0.0550	0.1100	0.2201
38	0.0175	0.0525	0.1051	0.2102	0.0183	0.0550	0.1100	0.2201
39	0.0175	0.0525	0.1050	0.2101	0.0183	0.0550	0.1100	0.2201
40	0.0175	0.0525	0.1050	0.2101	0.0183	0.0550	0.1100	0.2201
41	0.0175	0.0525	0.1050	0.2101	0.0183	0.0550	0.1100	0.2201
42	0.0175	0.0525	0.1050	0.2101	0.0183	0.0550	0.1100	0.2201
43	0.0175	0.0525	0.1050	0.2101	0.0183	0.0550	0.1100	0.2200
44	0.0175	0.0525	0.1050	0.2100	0.0183	0.0550	0.1100	0.2200
45	0.0175	0.0525	0.1050	0.2100	0.0183	0.0550	0.1100	0.2200
46	0.0175	0.0525	0.1050	0.2100	0.0183	0.0550	0.1100	0.2200
47	0.0175	0.0525	0.1050	0.2100	0.0183	0.0550	0.1100	0.2200
48	0.0175	0.0525	0.1050	0.2100	0.0183	0.0550	0.1100	0.2200
49	0.0175	0.0525	0.1050	0.2100	0.0183	0.0550	0.1100	0.2200
50	0.0175	0.0525	0.1050	0.2100	0.0183	0.0550	0.1100	0.2200

TABLE 6
Monthly payments required to repay a Canadian mortgage loan of $1000 over various periods of time with interest compounded semi-annually

Applications
Chapter Seven
- Canadian mortgage loans.

Monthly payments required to repay a mortgage loan of $1000 over various periods of time with interest compounded semi-annually

End of Year	10.000	10.125	10.250	10.375	10.500	10.625	10.750	10.875
				% Interest				
1	87.822	87.878	87.933	87.989	88.045	88.101	88.156	88.212
2	46.052	46.107	46.162	46.218	46.273	46.328	46.384	46.439
3	32.172	32.229	32.285	32.341	32.398	32.454	32.510	32.567
4	25.266	25.323	25.381	25.438	25.496	25.554	25.612	25.669
5	21.148	21.207	21.266	21.325	21.384	21.443	21.502	21.562
6	18.424	18.484	18.545	18.605	18.666	18.727	18.788	18.848
7	16.497	16.559	16.621	16.683	16.745	16.807	16.869	16.932
8	15.067	15.131	15.194	15.258	15.321	15.385	15.449	15.513
9	13.969	14.034	14.099	14.164	14.229	14.295	14.360	14.426
10	13.103	13.170	13.236	13.303	13.369	13.436	13.503	13.570
11	12.406	12.473	12.541	12.609	12.677	12.746	12.814	12.883
12	11.834	11.903	11.973	12.042	12.112	12.181	12.251	12.321
13	11.360	11.430	11.501	11.572	11.643	11.714	11.785	11.857
14	10.961	11.033	11.105	11.177	11.249	11.322	11.395	11.468
15	10.623	10.696	10.769	10.843	10.916	10.990	11.064	11.139
16	10.333	10.408	10.483	10.557	10.632	10.708	10.783	10.859
17	10.084	10.160	10.236	10.312	10.388	10.465	10.542	10.619
18	9.869	9.946	10.023	10.100	10.178	10.255	10.333	10.411
19	9.681	9.759	9.837	9.916	9.994	10.073	10.153	10.232
20	9.517	9.596	9.675	9.755	9.835	9.915	9.995	10.076
21	9.372	9.453	9.533	9.614	9.695	9.776	9.857	9.939
22	9.245	9.327	9.408	9.490	9.572	9.654	9.737	9.819
23	9.133	9.215	9.298	9.381	9.464	9.547	9.630	9.714
24	9.033	9.117	9.200	9.284	9.368	9.452	9.537	9.621
25	8.945	9.029	9.114	9.198	9.283	9.368	9.454	9.539
26	8.866	8.951	9.037	9.122	9.208	9.294	9.380	9.467
27	8.796	8.882	8.968	9.055	9.141	9.228	9.315	9.403
28	8.733	8.820	8.907	8.994	9.082	9.170	9.257	9.346
29	8.677	8.765	8.852	8.940	9.029	9.117	9.206	9.295
30	8.627	8.715	8.804	8.892	8.981	9.071	9.160	9.250
31	8.582	8.671	8.760	8.849	8.939	9.029	9.119	9.209
32	8.541	8.631	8.721	8.811	8.901	8.992	9.082	9.173
33	8.505	8.595	8.686	8.776	8.867	8.958	9.050	9.141
34	8.472	8.563	8.654	8.745	8.837	8.929	9.021	9.113
35	8.442	8.534	8.626	8.718	8.810	8.902	8.994	9.087
36	8.416	8.508	8.600	8.693	8.785	8.878	8.971	9.064
37	8.392	8.484	8.577	8.670	8.763	8.857	8.950	9.044
38	8.370	8.463	8.556	8.650	8.743	8.837	8.931	9.025
39	8.351	8.444	8.538	8.632	8.726	8.820	8.914	9.009
40	8.333	8.427	8.521	8.615	8.710	8.804	8.899	8.994

Monthly payments required to repay a mortgage loan of $1000 over various periods of time with interest compounded semi-annually

End of Year	11.000	11.125	11.250	% Interest 11.375	11.500	11.625	11.750	11.875
1	88.268	88.324	88.379	88.435	88.491	88.546	88.602	88.658
2	46.495	46.550	46.606	46.661	46.716	46.772	46.827	46.883
3	32.623	32.680	32.736	32.793	32.850	32.906	32.963	33.020
4	25.727	25.785	25.843	25.901	25.959	26.017	26.075	26.134
5	21.621	21.680	21.740	21.800	21.859	21.919	21.979	22.039
6	18.909	18.970	19.032	19.093	19.154	19.215	19.277	19.338
7	16.994	17.057	17.120	17.183	17.246	17.309	17.372	17.435
8	15.577	15.641	15.706	15.770	15.835	15.899	15.964	16.029
9	14.491	14.557	14.623	14.689	14.755	14.822	14.888	14.955
10	13.637	13.705	13.772	13.840	13.908	13.976	14.044	14.112
11	12.951	13.020	13.089	13.159	13.228	13.298	13.367	13.437
12	12.392	12.462	12.533	12.603	12.674	12.745	12.817	12.888
13	11.928	12.000	12.072	12.145	12.217	12.289	12.362	12.435
14	11.541	11.614	11.687	11.761	11.835	11.909	11.983	12.058
15	11.213	11.288	11.363	11.438	11.513	11.589	11.664	11.740
16	10.935	11.011	11.087	11.163	11.240	11.317	11.394	11.471
17	10.696	10.773	10.851	10.928	11.006	11.084	11.163	11.241
18	10.490	10.568	10.647	10.726	10.805	10.885	10.964	11.044
19	10.312	10.391	10.471	10.552	10.632	10.713	10.793	10.874
20	10.156	10.237	10.319	10.400	10.481	10.563	10.645	10.727
21	10.021	10.103	10.185	10.268	10.350	10.433	10.516	10.600
22	9.902	9.985	10.069	10.152	10.236	10.320	10.404	10.488
23	9.798	9.882	9.967	10.051	10.136	10.221	10.306	10.391
24	9.706	9.791	9.877	9.962	10.048	10.134	10.220	10.306
25	9.625	9.711	9.798	9.884	9.971	10.057	10.144	10.232
26	9.554	9.641	9.728	9.815	9.902	9.990	10.078	10.166
27	9.490	9.578	9.666	9.754	9.842	9.931	10.019	10.108
28	9.434	9.522	9.611	9.700	9.789	9.878	9.968	10.057
29	9.384	9.473	9.563	9.652	9.742	9.832	9.922	10.012
30	9.339	9.429	9.519	9.610	9.700	9.791	9.882	9.973
31	9.300	9.390	9.481	9.572	9.663	9.755	9.846	9.938
32	9.264	9.356	9.447	9.539	9.630	9.722	9.814	9.907
33	9.233	9.325	9.417	9.509	9.601	9.694	9.786	9.879
34	9.205	9.297	9.390	9.482	9.575	9.668	9.761	9.855
35	9.180	9.273	9.366	9.459	9.552	9.646	9.739	9.833
36	9.157	9.251	9.344	9.438	9.532	9.626	9.720	9.814
37	9.137	9.231	9.325	9.419	9.513	9.608	9.702	9.797
38	9.119	9.214	9.308	9.402	9.497	9.592	9.687	9.782
39	9.103	9.198	9.293	9.388	9.483	9.578	9.673	9.768
40	9.089	9.184	9.279	9.374	9.470	9.565	9.661	9.756

Monthly payments required to repay a mortgage loan of $1000 over various periods of time with interest compounded semi-annually

End of Year	12.000	12.125	12.250	12.375	12.500	12.625	12.750	12.875
				% Interest				
1	88.713	88.769	88.825	88.880	88.936	88.992	89.047	89.103
2	46.938	46.994	47.049	47.105	47.161	47.216	47.272	47.327
3	33.076	33.133	33.190	33.247	33.303	33.360	33.417	33.474
4	26.192	26.250	26.309	26.367	26.425	26.484	26.542	26.601
5	22.098	22.158	22.218	22.279	22.339	22.399	22.459	22.520
6	19.400	19.462	19.523	19.585	19.647	19.709	19.771	19.834
7	17.498	17.562	17.625	17.689	17.753	17.816	17.880	17.944
8	16.094	16.159	16.225	16.290	16.355	16.421	16.487	16.552
9	15.021	15.088	15.155	15.222	15.290	15.357	15.424	15.492
10	14.180	14.249	14.317	14.386	14.455	14.524	14.593	14.663
11	13.507	13.577	13.647	13.718	13.788	13.859	13.930	14.001
12	12.960	13.031	13.103	13.175	13.247	13.320	13.392	13.465
13	12.508	12.581	12.655	12.728	12.802	12.876	12.950	13.024
14	12.132	12.207	12.282	12.357	12.432	12.508	12.583	12.659
15	11.816	11.892	11.969	12.045	12.122	12.199	12.276	12.353
16	11.548	11.626	11.704	11.782	11.860	11.938	12.016	12.095
17	11.320	11.399	11.478	11.557	11.637	11.716	11.796	11.876
18	11.124	11.204	11.285	11.365	11.446	11.527	11.608	11.689
19	10.956	11.037	11.119	11.200	11.282	11.364	11.447	11.529
20	10.810	10.892	10.975	11.058	11.141	11.224	11.308	11.391
21	10.683	10.767	10.851	10.935	11.019	11.103	11.188	11.273
22	10.573	10.658	10.743	10.828	10.913	10.998	11.084	11.170
23	10.477	10.563	10.648	10.735	10.821	10.907	10.994	11.081
24	10.393	10.479	10.566	10.653	10.740	10.828	10.915	11.003
25	10.319	10.407	10.494	10.582	10.670	10.758	10.847	10.935
26	10.254	10.343	10.431	10.520	10.609	10.698	10.787	10.876
27	10.197	10.286	10.376	10.465	10.555	10.645	10.735	10.825
28	10.147	10.237	10.327	10.417	10.508	10.598	10.689	10.780
29	10.103	10.194	10.284	10.375	10.466	10.557	10.649	10.740
30	10.064	10.155	10.247	10.338	10.430	10.522	10.614	10.706
31	10.029	10.121	10.213	10.305	10.398	10.490	10.583	10.675
32	9.999	10.091	10.184	10.277	10.369	10.462	10.555	10.649
33	9.972	10.065	10.158	10.251	10.345	10.438	10.532	10.625
34	9.948	10.041	10.135	10.229	10.323	10.417	10.511	10.605
35	9.927	10.021	10.115	10.209	10.303	10.398	10.492	10.587
36	9.908	10.002	10.097	10.191	10.286	10.381	10.476	10.571
37	9.891	9.986	10.081	10.176	10.271	10.366	10.461	10.557
38	9.877	9.972	10.067	10.162	10.258	10.353	10.449	10.544
39	9.864	9.959	10.055	10.150	10.246	10.342	10.437	10.533
40	9.852	9.948	10.044	10.139	10.235	10.331	10.428	10.524

Monthly payments required to repay a mortgage loan of $1000 over various periods of time with interest compounded semi-annually

End of Year	13.000	13.125	13.250	% Interest 13.375	13.500	13.625	13.750	13.875
1	89.158	89.214	89.270	89.325	89.381	89.436	89.492	89.547
2	47.383	47.438	47.494	47.550	47.605	47.661	47.717	47.772
3	33.531	33.588	33.645	33.702	33.759	33.816	33.873	33.931
4	26.660	26.718	26.777	26.836	26.895	26.954	27.012	27.071
5	22.580	22.641	22.701	22.762	22.822	22.883	22.944	23.005
6	19.896	19.958	20.021	20.083	20.146	20.208	20.271	20.334
7	18.008	18.073	18.137	18.201	18.266	18.330	18.395	18.459
8	16.618	16.684	16.750	16.817	16.883	16.949	17.016	17.083
9	15.560	15.627	15.695	15.763	15.831	15.900	15.968	16.037
10	14.732	14.802	14.871	14.941	15.011	15.081	15.151	15.222
11	14.072	14.143	14.215	14.286	14.358	14.430	14.502	14.574
12	13.537	13.610	13.683	13.757	13.830	13.904	13.977	14.051
13	13.099	13.173	13.248	13.323	13.398	13.473	13.548	13.624
14	12.735	12.811	12.887	12.964	13.040	13.117	13.194	13.271
15	12.430	12.508	12.586	12.664	12.742	12.820	12.898	12.977
16	12.174	12.253	12.332	12.411	12.491	12.570	12.650	12.730
17	11.956	12.036	12.117	12.198	12.278	12.359	12.441	12.522
18	11.771	11.852	11.934	12.016	12.098	12.180	12.263	12.345
19	11.612	11.695	11.778	11.861	11.944	12.028	12.111	12.195
20	11.475	11.559	11.643	11.728	11.812	11.897	11.982	12.067
21	11.358	11.443	11.528	11.613	11.699	11.785	11.870	11.957
22	11.256	11.342	11.428	11.515	11.601	11.688	11.775	11.862
23	11.167	11.255	11.342	11.429	11.517	11.604	11.692	11.780
24	11.091	11.179	11.267	11.355	11.444	11.532	11.621	11.710
25	11.024	11.113	11.202	11.291	11.380	11.470	11.559	11.649
26	10.966	11.056	11.145	11.235	11.325	11.415	11.506	11.596
27	10.915	11.005	11.096	11.187	11.277	11.368	11.459	11.551
28	10.871	10.962	11.053	11.144	11.236	11.327	11.419	11.511
29	10.832	10.924	11.015	11.107	11.199	11.292	11.384	11.476
30	10.798	10.890	10.983	11.075	11.168	11.261	11.353	11.446
31	10.768	10.861	10.954	11.047	11.140	11.233	11.327	11.420
32	10.742	10.835	10.929	11.022	11.116	11.210	11.304	11.398
33	10.719	10.813	10.907	11.001	11.095	11.189	11.283	11.378
34	10.699	10.793	10.887	10.982	11.076	11.171	11.266	11.361
35	10.681	10.776	10.871	10.965	11.060	11.155	11.250	11.345
36	10.666	10.761	10.856	10.951	11.046	11.142	11.237	11.332
37	10.652	10.747	10.843	10.938	11.034	11.129	11.225	11.321
38	10.640	10.736	10.831	10.927	11.023	11.119	11.215	11.311
39	10.629	10.725	10.821	10.917	11.014	11.110	11.206	11.302
40	10.620	10.716	10.813	10.909	11.005	11.102	11.198	11.295

Monthly payments required to repay a mortgage loan of $1000 over various periods of time with interest compounded semi-annually

End of Year	14.000	14.125	14.250	% Interest 14.375	14.500	14.625	14.750	14.875
1	89.603	89.658	89.714	89.769	89.825	89.880	89.936	89.991
2	47.828	47.884	47.939	47.995	48.051	48.107	48.162	48.218
3	33.988	34.045	34.102	34.159	34.217	34.274	34.331	34.389
4	27.130	27.189	27.249	27.308	27.367	27.426	27.485	27.545
5	23.066	23.127	23.188	23.249	23.310	23.371	23.432	23.494
6	20.397	20.460	20.523	20.586	20.649	20.712	20.775	20.839
7	18.524	18.589	18.654	18.719	18.784	18.850	18.915	18.981
8	17.149	17.216	17.283	17.350	17.417	17.485	17.552	17.619
9	16.105	16.174	16.243	16.312	16.381	16.450	16.519	16.589
10	15.292	15.363	15.433	15.504	15.575	15.646	15.717	15.789
11	14.646	14.718	14.791	14.864	14.936	15.009	15.082	15.155
12	14.125	14.199	14.273	14.348	14.422	14.497	14.571	14.646
13	13.699	13.775	13.851	13.927	14.003	14.079	14.156	14.232
14	13.348	13.425	13.503	13.580	13.658	13.736	13.814	13.892
15	13.055	13.134	13.213	13.292	13.372	13.451	13.530	13.610
16	12.810	12.890	12.971	13.051	13.132	13.213	13.294	13.375
17	12.603	12.685	12.767	12.849	12.931	13.013	13.095	13.178
18	12.428	12.511	12.594	12.677	12.761	12.844	12.928	13.012
19	12.279	12.363	12.447	12.532	12.616	12.701	12.786	12.871
20	12.152	12.237	12.322	12.408	12.494	12.580	12.665	12.752
21	12.043	12.129	12.215	12.302	12.389	12.476	12.563	12.650
22	11.949	12.036	12.124	12.211	12.299	12.387	12.475	12.563
23	11.868	11.957	12.045	12.134	12.222	12.311	12.400	12.489
24	11.799	11.888	11.977	12.067	12.156	12.246	12.335	12.425
25	11.739	11.829	11.919	12.009	12.099	12.190	12.280	12.371
26	11.687	11.777	11.868	11.959	12.050	12.141	12.233	12.324
27	11.642	11.733	11.825	11.916	12.008	12.100	12.192	12.283
28	11.603	11.695	11.787	11.879	11.971	12.064	12.156	12.249
29	11.569	11.661	11.754	11.847	11.940	12.033	12.126	12.219
30	11.539	11.633	11.726	11.819	11.912	12.006	12.099	12.193
31	11.514	11.607	11.701	11.795	11.889	11.983	12.077	12.171
32	11.492	11.586	11.680	11.774	11.868	11.963	12.057	12.151
33	11.472	11.567	11.661	11.756	11.851	11.945	12.040	12.135
34	11.455	11.550	11.645	11.740	11.835	11.930	12.025	12.121
35	11.441	11.536	11.631	11.726	11.822	11.917	12.013	12.108
36	11.428	11.523	11.619	11.715	11.810	11.906	12.002	12.097
37	11.417	11.512	11.608	11.704	11.800	11.896	11.992	12.088
38	11.407	11.503	11.599	11.695	11.791	11.888	11.984	12.080
39	11.398	11.495	11.591	11.687	11.784	11.880	11.977	12.073
40	11.391	11.488	11.584	11.681	11.777	11.874	11.970	12.067

Monthly payments required to repay a mortgage loan of $1000 over various periods of time with interest compounded semi-annually

End of Year	% Interest							
	15.000	15.125	15.250	15.375	15.500	15.625	15.750	15.875
1	90.047	90.102	90.158	90.213	90.269	90.324	90.380	90.435
2	48.274	48.330	48.385	48.441	48.497	48.553	48.609	48.665
3	34.446	34.504	34.561	34.619	34.676	34.734	34.791	34.849
4	27.604	27.663	27.723	27.782	27.842	27.901	27.961	28.021
5	23.555	23.617	23.678	23.740	23.801	23.863	23.925	23.987
6	20.902	20.966	21.029	21.093	21.157	21.221	21.285	21.349
7	19.046	19.112	19.177	19.243	19.309	19.375	19.441	19.507
8	17.687	17.755	17.822	17.890	17.958	18.026	18.094	18.163
9	16.658	16.728	16.798	16.867	16.937	17.007	17.078	17.148
10	15.860	15.932	16.003	16.075	16.147	16.219	16.291	16.363
11	15.229	15.302	15.376	15.449	15.523	15.597	15.671	15.745
12	14.721	14.797	14.872	14.947	15.023	15.099	15.174	15.250
13	14.309	14.386	14.463	14.540	14.617	14.695	14.772	14.850
14	13.970	14.049	14.128	14.206	14.285	14.364	14.443	14.523
15	13.690	13.770	13.850	13.930	14.011	14.091	14.172	14.253
16	13.456	13.538	13.619	13.701	13.783	13.865	13.947	14.029
17	13.261	13.343	13.426	13.509	13.593	13.676	13.759	13.843
18	13.096	13.180	13.264	13.348	13.433	13.517	13.602	13.687
19	12.956	13.041	13.127	13.212	13.298	13.384	13.470	13.556
20	12.838	12.924	13.011	13.097	13.184	13.271	13.358	13.445
21	12.737	12.825	12.912	13.000	13.088	13.175	13.263	13.352
22	12.651	12.740	12.828	12.917	13.006	13.094	13.183	13.272
23	12.578	12.667	12.757	12.846	12.936	13.025	13.115	13.205
24	12.515	12.605	12.696	12.786	12.876	12.967	13.057	13.148
25	12.461	12.552	12.643	12.734	12.825	12.917	13.008	13.099
26	12.415	12.507	12.598	12.690	12.782	12.874	12.966	13.058
27	12.376	12.468	12.560	12.652	12.745	12.837	12.930	13.022
28	12.341	12.434	12.527	12.620	12.713	12.806	12.899	12.992
29	12.312	12.405	12.499	12.592	12.685	12.779	12.873	12.966
30	12.287	12.380	12.474	12.568	12.662	12.756	12.850	12.944
31	12.265	12.359	12.453	12.548	12.642	12.736	12.831	12.925
32	12.246	12.341	12.435	12.530	12.625	12.719	12.814	12.909
33	12.230	12.325	12.420	12.515	12.610	12.705	12.800	12.895
34	12.216	12.311	12.406	12.502	12.597	12.692	12.788	12.883
35	12.204	12.299	12.395	12.490	12.586	12.682	12.777	12.873
36	12.193	12.289	12.385	12.481	12.577	12.672	12.768	12.864
37	12.184	12.280	12.376	12.472	12.568	12.665	12.761	12.857
38	12.176	12.273	12.369	12.465	12.561	12.658	12.754	12.850
39	12.170	12.266	12.363	12.459	12.555	12.652	12.748	12.845
40	12.164	12.260	12.357	12.454	12.550	12.647	12.744	12.840

Monthly payments required to repay a mortgage loan of $1000 over various periods of time with interest compounded semi-annually

End of Year	16.000	16.125	16.250	16.375	16.500	16.625	16.750	16.875
				% Interest				
1	90.490	90.546	90.601	90.656	90.712	90.767	90.823	90.878
2	48.720	48.776	48.832	48.888	48.944	49.000	49.056	49.112
3	34.906	34.964	35.022	35.079	35.137	35.195	35.253	35.311
4	28.080	28.140	28.200	28.260	28.320	28.380	28.440	28.500
5	24.049	24.111	24.173	24.235	24.297	24.359	24.421	24.483
6	21.413	21.477	21.541	21.605	21.670	21.734	21.799	21.863
7	19.573	19.640	19.706	19.773	19.839	19.906	19.973	20.039
8	18.231	18.299	18.368	18.436	18.505	18.574	18.643	18.712
9	17.218	17.289	17.359	17.430	17.501	17.572	17.643	17.714
10	16.436	16.508	16.581	16.653	16.726	16.799	16.872	16.945
11	15.819	15.894	15.968	16.043	16.117	16.192	16.267	16.342
12	15.326	15.403	15.479	15.555	15.632	15.709	15.785	15.862
13	14.928	15.006	15.084	15.162	15.240	15.319	15.397	15.476
14	14.602	14.682	14.761	14.841	14.921	15.001	15.081	15.162
15	14.334	14.415	14.496	14.578	14.659	14.741	14.822	14.904
16	14.112	14.194	14.277	14.360	14.443	14.526	14.609	14.692
17	13.927	14.011	14.095	14.179	14.263	14.347	14.432	14.516
18	13.772	13.857	13.942	14.028	14.113	14.199	14.284	14.370
19	13.642	13.728	13.815	13.901	13.988	14.074	14.161	14.248
20	13.532	13.620	13.707	13.795	13.882	13.970	14.058	14.146
21	13.440	13.528	13.617	13.705	13.794	13.883	13.971	14.060
22	13.362	13.451	13.540	13.630	13.719	13.809	13.899	13.988
23	13.295	13.385	13.475	13.566	13.656	13.746	13.837	13.928
24	13.239	13.330	13.420	13.512	13.603	13.694	13.785	13.876
25	13.191	13.282	13.374	13.466	13.557	13.649	13.741	13.833
26	13.150	13.242	13.334	13.427	13.519	13.611	13.704	13.797
27	13.115	13.208	13.301	13.393	13.486	13.579	13.672	13.766
28	13.085	13.179	13.272	13.365	13.459	13.552	13.646	13.739
29	13.060	13.154	13.247	13.341	13.435	13.529	13.623	13.717
30	13.038	13.132	13.227	13.321	13.415	13.510	13.604	13.698
31	13.020	13.114	13.209	13.303	13.398	13.493	13.588	13.682
32	13.004	13.099	13.194	13.289	13.384	13.479	13.574	13.669
33	12.990	13.086	13.181	13.276	13.371	13.467	13.562	13.657
34	12.979	13.074	13.170	13.265	13.361	13.456	13.552	13.647
35	12.969	13.065	13.160	13.256	13.352	13.448	13.543	13.639
36	12.960	13.056	13.152	13.248	13.344	13.440	13.536	13.632
37	12.953	13.049	13.145	13.241	13.338	13.434	13.530	13.626
38	12.947	13.043	13.139	13.236	13.332	13.428	13.525	13.621
39	12.941	13.038	13.134	13.231	13.327	13.424	13.520	13.617
40	12.937	13.033	13.130	13.227	13.323	13.420	13.516	13.613

Monthly payments required to repay a mortgage loan of $1000 over various periods of time with interest compounded semi-annually

End of Year	17.000	17.125	17.250	% Interest 17.375	17.500	17.625	17.750	17.875
1	90.933	90.989	91.044	91.099	91.155	91.210	91.265	91.320
2	49.168	49.224	49.279	49.335	49.391	49.447	49.503	49.559
3	35.368	35.426	35.484	35.542	35.600	35.658	35.716	35.774
4	28.560	28.620	28.680	28.740	28.800	28.861	28.921	28.981
5	24.546	24.608	24.671	24.733	24.796	24.858	24.921	24.984
6	21.928	21.993	22.057	22.122	22.187	22.252	22.317	22.382
7	20.106	20.173	20.240	20.307	20.375	20.442	20.509	20.577
8	18.781	18.850	18.919	18.989	19.058	19.128	19.197	19.267
9	17.785	17.856	17.928	17.999	18.071	18.143	18.215	18.286
10	17.019	17.092	17.165	17.239	17.313	17.387	17.460	17.534
11	16.418	16.493	16.568	16.644	16.719	16.795	16.871	16.947
12	15.939	16.017	16.094	16.171	16.249	16.326	16.404	16.482
13	15.555	15.633	15.712	15.792	15.871	15.950	16.030	16.109
14	15.242	15.322	15.403	15.484	15.565	15.646	15.727	15.808
15	14.986	15.068	15.150	15.233	15.315	15.398	15.480	15.563
16	14.775	14.859	14.943	15.026	15.110	15.194	15.278	15.362
17	14.601	14.686	14.771	14.856	14.941	15.026	15.112	15.197
18	14.456	14.542	14.628	14.715	14.801	14.887	14.974	15.061
19	14.335	14.422	14.510	14.597	14.685	14.772	14.860	14.947
20	14.234	14.322	14.411	14.499	14.588	14.676	14.765	14.853
21	14.149	14.239	14.328	14.417	14.507	14.596	14.686	14.775
22	14.078	14.168	14.258	14.348	14.439	14.529	14.619	14.710
23	14.018	14.109	14.200	14.291	14.382	14.473	14.564	14.655
24	13.968	14.059	14.151	14.242	14.334	14.426	14.518	14.610
25	13.925	14.017	14.110	14.202	14.294	14.386	14.479	14.571
26	13.889	13.982	14.075	14.167	14.260	14.353	14.446	14.539
27	13.859	13.952	14.045	14.139	14.232	14.325	14.419	14.512
28	13.833	13.927	14.020	14.114	14.208	14.302	14.396	14.490
29	13.811	13.905	13.999	14.094	14.188	14.282	14.376	14.471
30	13.793	13.887	13.982	14.076	14.171	14.265	14.360	14.455
31	13.777	13.872	13.967	14.062	14.156	14.251	14.346	14.441
32	13.764	13.859	13.954	14.049	14.144	14.240	14.335	14.430
33	13.753	13.848	13.943	14.039	14.134	14.230	14.325	14.420
34	13.743	13.839	13.934	14.030	14.126	14.221	14.317	14.412
35	13.735	13.831	13.927	14.022	14.118	14.214	14.310	14.406
36	13.728	13.824	13.920	14.016	14.112	14.208	14.304	14.400
37	13.722	13.818	13.915	14.011	14.107	14.203	14.299	14.395
38	13.717	13.814	13.910	14.006	14.102	14.199	14.295	14.391
39	13.713	13.810	13.906	14.002	14.099	14.195	14.291	14.388
40	13.710	13.806	13.903	13.999	14.096	14.192	14.288	14.385

Monthly payments required to repay a mortgage loan of $1000 over various periods of time with interest compounded semi-annually

End of Year	19.000	19.125	19.250	% Interest 19.375	19.500	19.625	19.750	19.875
1	91.818	91.873	91.928	91.983	92.038	92.093	92.149	92.204
2	50.064	50.120	50.176	50.232	50.288	50.344	50.400	50.457
3	36.297	36.356	36.414	36.472	36.531	36.589	36.648	36.706
4	29.526	29.587	29.648	29.709	29.769	29.830	29.891	29.952
5	25.551	25.614	25.677	25.741	25.804	25.868	25.931	25.995
6	22.971	23.037	23.103	23.169	23.235	23.301	23.367	23.433
7	21.187	21.256	21.324	21.392	21.461	21.529	21.598	21.667
8	19.899	19.969	20.040	20.111	20.182	20.253	20.324	20.395
9	18.938	19.011	19.084	19.157	19.230	19.303	19.376	19.450
10	18.205	18.280	18.355	18.430	18.505	18.581	18.656	18.732
11	17.636	17.713	17.790	17.867	17.944	18.022	18.099	18.177
12	17.187	17.266	17.345	17.424	17.503	17.583	17.662	17.742
13	16.830	16.911	16.992	17.073	17.154	17.235	17.316	17.397
14	16.544	16.626	16.709	16.791	16.874	16.956	17.039	17.122
15	16.312	16.396	16.480	16.564	16.648	16.732	16.817	16.901
16	16.124	16.209	16.295	16.380	16.465	16.551	16.636	16.722
17	15.971	16.057	16.143	16.230	16.317	16.403	16.490	16.577
18	15.845	15.932	16.020	16.107	16.195	16.283	16.371	16.459
19	15.741	15.830	15.918	16.007	16.096	16.185	16.274	16.363
20	15.656	15.745	15.835	15.924	16.014	16.104	16.194	16.284
21	15.585	15.676	15.766	15.857	15.947	16.038	16.128	16.219
22	15.527	15.618	15.709	15.800	15.892	15.983	16.074	16.166
23	15.479	15.571	15.662	15.754	15.846	15.938	16.030	16.122
24	15.439	15.531	15.623	15.716	15.808	15.901	15.993	16.086
25	15.406	15.498	15.591	15.684	15.777	15.870	15.963	16.056
26	15.378	15.471	15.565	15.658	15.751	15.845	15.938	16.032
27	15.355	15.449	15.543	15.636	15.730	15.824	15.918	16.012
28	15.336	15.430	15.524	15.618	15.712	15.807	15.901	15.995
29	15.320	15.414	15.509	15.603	15.698	15.792	15.887	15.981
30	15.307	15.402	15.496	15.591	15.686	15.780	15.875	15.970
31	15.296	15.391	15.486	15.581	15.676	15.771	15.866	15.961
32	15.287	15.382	15.477	15.572	15.667	15.762	15.858	15.953
33	15.279	15.374	15.470	15.565	15.660	15.756	15.851	15.946
34	15.273	15.368	15.464	15.559	15.655	15.750	15.846	15.941
35	15.267	15.363	15.459	15.554	15.650	15.745	15.841	15.937
36	15.263	15.359	15.454	15.550	15.646	15.742	15.837	15.933
37	15.259	15.355	15.451	15.547	15.643	15.738	15.834	15.930
38	15.256	15.352	15.448	15.544	15.640	15.736	15.832	15.928
39	15.254	15.350	15.446	15.542	15.638	15.734	15.830	15.925
40	15.251	15.348	15.444	15.540	15.636	15.732	15.828	15.924

Monthly payments required to repay a mortgage loan of $1000 over various periods of time with interest compounded semi-annually

End of Year	20.000	20.125	20.250	% Interest 20.375	20.500	20.625	20.750	20.875
1	92.259	92.314	92.369	92.424	92.479	92.534	92.590	92.645
2	50.513	50.569	50.625	50.681	50.737	50.794	50.850	50.906
3	36.764	36.823	36.881	36.940	36.999	37.057	37.116	37.174
4	30.013	30.074	30.135	30.197	30.258	30.319	30.380	30.442
5	26.059	26.122	26.186	26.250	26.314	26.378	26.442	26.506
6	23.500	23.566	23.632	23.699	23.765	23.832	23.898	23.965
7	21.736	21.804	21.873	21.942	22.011	22.080	22.150	22.219
8	20.466	20.537	20.608	20.680	20.751	20.823	20.895	20.966
9	19.523	19.597	19.671	19.744	19.818	19.892	19.966	20.040
10	18.807	18.883	18.959	19.035	19.111	19.187	19.263	19.340
11	18.254	18.332	18.410	18.488	18.566	18.644	18.722	18.801
12	17.821	17.901	17.981	18.060	18.140	18.220	18.301	18.381
13	17.478	17.560	17.641	17.723	17.805	17.886	17.968	18.050
14	17.205	17.288	17.371	17.454	17.538	17.621	17.704	17.788
15	16.985	17.070	17.154	17.239	17.324	17.409	17.494	17.579
16	16.808	16.894	16.980	17.066	17.152	17.238	17.324	17.410
17	16.664	16.751	16.838	16.926	17.013	17.100	17.188	17.275
18	16.547	16.635	16.724	16.812	16.900	16.989	17.077	17.166
19	16.452	16.541	16.630	16.719	16.809	16.898	16.987	17.077
20	16.374	16.464	16.554	16.644	16.734	16.824	16.914	17.005
21	16.310	16.400	16.491	16.582	16.673	16.764	16.855	16.946
22	16.257	16.349	16.440	16.532	16.623	16.715	16.807	16.898
23	16.214	16.306	16.398	16.490	16.583	16.675	16.767	16.859
24	16.179	16.271	16.364	16.457	16.549	16.642	16.735	16.828
25	16.149	16.243	16.336	16.429	16.522	16.615	16.708	16.802
26	16.125	16.219	16.312	16.406	16.500	16.593	16.687	16.780
27	16.106	16.199	16.293	16.387	16.481	16.575	16.669	16.763
28	16.089	16.183	16.278	16.372	16.466	16.560	16.655	16.749
29	16.076	16.170	16.265	16.359	16.454	16.548	16.643	16.737
30	16.065	16.159	16.254	16.349	16.443	16.538	16.633	16.728
31	16.055	16.150	16.245	16.340	16.435	16.530	16.625	16.720
32	16.048	16.143	16.238	16.333	16.428	16.523	16.618	16.713
33	16.042	16.137	16.232	16.327	16.423	16.518	16.613	16.708
34	16.036	16.132	16.227	16.323	16.418	16.513	16.609	16.704
35	16.032	16.128	16.223	16.319	16.414	16.510	16.605	16.700
36	16.029	16.124	16.220	16.315	16.411	16.506	16.602	16.697
37	16.026	16.121	16.217	16.313	16.408	16.504	16.599	16.695
38	16.023	16.119	16.215	16.311	16.406	16.502	16.597	16.693
39	16.021	16.117	16.213	16.309	16.404	16.500	16.596	16.691
40	16.020	16.116	16.211	16.307	16.403	16.499	16.594	16.690

TABLE 7
Balance outstanding on a Canadian mortgage loan of $1000 for 25 years at various rates of interest with interest compounded semi-annually

Applications
Chapter Seven
- Canadian mortgage loans.

Balance outstanding on a mortgage loan of $1000 for 25 years at various rates of interest compounded semi-annually

End of Year	10.00%	10.25%	10.50%	10.75%	11.00%	11.25%	11.50%	11.75%
1	990	991	991	991	992	992	992	993
2	979	980	981	982	982	983	984	984
3	968	969	970	971	972	973	974	975
4	954	956	958	959	961	962	963	965
5	940	942	944	946	948	950	951	953
6	924	926	929	931	933	936	938	940
7	906	909	912	915	918	920	923	925
8	887	890	894	897	900	903	906	909
9	866	869	873	877	880	884	887	890
10	842	846	850	854	858	862	866	870
11	816	821	825	830	834	838	842	847
12	787	792	797	802	807	812	816	821
13	756	761	766	772	777	782	787	792
14	721	727	732	738	743	749	754	759
15	683	689	694	700	706	711	717	722
16	640	646	652	658	664	670	676	681
17	594	600	606	612	618	624	630	635
18	542	548	554	560	566	572	578	584
19	485	491	497	503	509	515	521	526
20	423	429	434	440	445	451	456	462
21	354	359	364	369	374	379	384	389
22	278	282	287	291	295	299	304	308
23	194	197	201	204	207	210	213	217
24	102	104	105	107	109	111	113	114
25	0	0	0	0	0	0	0	0

Balance outstanding on a mortgage loan of $1000 for 25 years at various rates of interest compounded semi-annually

End of Year	12.00%	12.25%	12.50%	12.75%	13.00%	13.25%	13.50%	13.75%
1	993	993	993	994	994	994	994	995
2	985	986	986	987	987	988	988	989
3	976	977	978	979	979	980	981	982
4	966	967	968	970	971	972	973	974
5	955	956	958	959	961	962	963	965
6	942	944	946	948	949	951	953	954
7	928	930	932	934	937	939	941	943
8	912	914	917	920	922	924	927	929
9	894	897	900	903	906	908	911	914
10	873	877	880	884	887	890	893	896
11	851	854	858	862	866	869	873	876
12	825	829	833	838	842	846	849	853
13	796	801	805	810	814	819	823	827
14	764	769	774	779	783	788	793	797
15	728	733	738	743	748	753	758	763
16	687	692	698	703	709	714	719	724
17	641	647	652	658	663	669	674	679
18	590	595	601	607	612	618	623	628
19	532	538	543	549	554	560	565	570
20	467	472	478	483	488	493	499	504
21	394	399	404	409	414	418	423	428
22	312	316	320	325	329	333	337	341
23	220	223	226	229	233	236	239	242
24	116	118	120	122	124	125	127	129
25	0	0	0	0	0	0	0	0

Balance outstanding on a mortgage loan of $1000 for 25 years at various rates of interest compounded semi-annually

End of Year	14.00%	14.25%	14.50%	14.75%	15.00%	15.25%	15.50%	15.75%
1	995	995	995	996	996	996	996	996
2	989	990	990	990	991	991	991	992
3	982	983	984	984	985	986	986	987
4	975	976	977	978	978	979	980	981
5	966	967	968	970	971	972	973	974
6	956	958	959	960	962	963	964	966
7	945	946	948	950	952	953	955	956
8	931	934	936	938	940	942	944	945
9	916	919	921	924	926	928	931	933
10	899	902	905	908	910	913	915	918
11	879	883	886	889	892	895	898	901
12	857	861	864	868	871	874	877	881
13	831	835	839	843	846	850	854	857
14	801	806	810	814	818	822	826	830
15	768	772	777	781	786	790	794	798
16	729	734	739	743	748	753	757	762
17	685	690	695	700	705	709	714	719
18	634	639	644	649	654	659	664	669
19	576	581	586	591	596	601	606	611
20	509	514	519	524	529	534	539	544
21	433	437	442	447	451	456	461	465
22	345	350	354	358	362	366	370	374
23	245	249	252	255	258	261	264	268
24	131	133	135	137	138	140	142	144
25	0	0	0	0	0	0	0	0

Balance outstanding on a mortgage loan of $1000 for 25 years at various rates of interest compounded semi-annually

End of Year	16.00%	16.25%	16.50%	16.75%	17.00%	17.25%	17.50%	17.75%
1	996	997	997	997	997	997	997	997
2	992	992	993	993	993	994	994	994
3	987	988	988	989	989	990	990	990
4	981	982	983	984	984	985	985	986
5	975	976	977	977	978	979	980	981
6	967	968	969	970	971	972	973	974
7	958	959	961	962	963	965	966	967
8	947	949	951	952	954	955	957	958
9	935	937	939	941	942	944	946	948
10	920	923	925	927	929	931	933	935
11	903	906	909	911	914	916	918	921
12	884	887	890	892	895	898	901	903
13	861	864	867	870	874	877	880	883
14	834	838	841	845	848	852	855	858
15	803	807	811	814	818	822	826	829
16	766	770	775	779	783	787	791	795
17	724	728	733	737	741	746	750	754
18	674	679	683	688	693	697	702	706
19	616	621	626	630	635	640	644	649
20	549	553	558	563	567	572	576	581
21	470	474	479	483	488	492	496	501
22	378	382	386	390	394	398	402	405
23	271	274	277	280	283	286	289	292
24	146	148	149	151	153	155	157	159
25	0	0	0	0	0	0	0	0

Balance outstanding on a mortgage loan of $1000 for 25 years at various rates of interest compounded semi-annually

End of Year	18.00%	18.25%	18.50%	18.75%	19.00%	19.25%	19.50%	19.75%
1	997	998	998	998	998	998	998	998
2	994	995	995	995	995	995	996	996
3	991	991	991	992	992	992	993	993
4	986	987	988	988	988	989	989	990
5	981	982	983	983	984	985	985	986
6	975	976	977	978	979	979	980	981
7	968	969	970	971	972	973	974	975
8	960	961	962	963	965	966	967	968
9	949	951	952	954	955	957	958	960
10	937	939	941	943	944	946	948	949
11	923	925	927	929	931	933	935	937
12	906	908	911	913	915	918	920	922
13	886	888	891	894	896	899	901	904
14	861	865	868	871	874	876	879	882
15	833	836	840	843	846	849	853	856
16	799	803	806	810	813	817	820	824
17	758	762	766	770	774	778	782	785
18	710	715	719	723	727	731	735	739
19	653	658	662	666	671	675	679	683
20	585	590	594	599	603	607	611	616
21	505	509	513	518	522	526	530	534
22	409	413	417	421	424	428	432	436
23	296	299	302	305	308	311	314	317
24	160	162	164	166	168	170	171	173
25	0	0	0	0	0	0	0	0

Balance outstanding on a mortgage loan of $1000 for 25 years at various rates of interest compounded semi-annually

End of Year	20.00%	20.25%	20.50%	20.75%	21.00%	21.25%	21.50%	21.75%
1	998	998	998	998	998	999	999	999
2	996	996	996	996	997	997	997	997
3	993	994	994	994	994	995	995	995
4	990	991	991	991	992	992	992	993
5	986	987	987	988	988	989	989	990
6	982	982	983	984	984	985	985	986
7	976	977	978	978	979	980	981	981
8	969	970	971	972	973	974	975	976
9	961	962	963	964	966	967	968	969
10	951	952	954	955	956	958	959	960
11	939	940	942	944	945	947	948	950
12	924	926	928	930	932	934	935	937
13	906	909	911	913	915	917	919	921
14	885	887	890	892	895	897	900	902
15	859	862	865	867	870	873	876	878
16	827	830	834	837	840	843	846	849
17	789	793	796	800	803	806	810	813
18	743	747	751	754	758	762	765	769
19	687	691	695	699	703	707	711	714
20	620	624	628	632	636	640	644	648
21	538	542	546	550	554	558	562	565
22	439	443	447	450	454	457	461	464
23	320	323	326	329	332	334	337	340
24	175	177	179	180	182	184	186	188
25	0	0	0	0	0	0	0	0

Balance outstanding on a mortgage loan of $1000 for 25 years at various rates of interest compounded semi-annually

End of Year	22.00%	22.25%	22.50%	22.75%	23.00%	23.25%	23.50%	23.75%
1	999	999	999	999	999	999	999	999
2	997	997	997	998	998	998	998	998
3	995	995	996	996	996	996	996	996
4	993	993	993	994	994	994	994	995
5	990	990	991	991	991	992	992	992
6	986	987	987	988	988	989	989	990
7	982	983	983	984	984	985	985	986
8	977	977	978	979	980	980	981	982
9	970	971	972	973	974	974	975	976
10	962	963	964	965	966	967	968	969
11	951	953	954	955	957	958	959	960
12	939	940	942	944	945	947	948	949
13	923	925	927	929	931	932	934	936
14	904	906	909	911	913	915	917	919
15	881	883	886	888	890	893	895	897
16	852	855	857	860	863	865	868	871
17	816	819	822	825	828	831	834	837
18	772	776	779	782	786	789	792	795
19	718	722	725	729	732	736	739	743
20	651	655	659	663	666	670	673	677
21	569	573	577	580	584	588	591	595
22	468	471	475	478	482	485	488	492
23	343	346	349	352	355	357	360	363
24	189	191	193	195	196	198	200	202
25	0	0	0	0	0	0	0	0

What is $1 payable at the end of each period worth today at various interest rates?

How much must be invested today in order for one to be able to draw $1 at the end of each period for a given number of periods?

Applications
Chapter Six
• What is the value today of the right to receive periodic payments at the end of various time periods?

Chapter Eight
• How much can one afford to borrow given the ability to make specific monthly payments?

Chapter Fifteen
• Proving annuity yields.

The present value of a $1 annuity at the *end* of each period

End of Year	At 5% Interest compounded and Payments or Withdrawals made				At 6% Interest compounded and Payments or Withdrawals made			
	Monthly	Quarterly	Semi-Annually	Annually	Monthly	Quarterly	Semi-Annually	Annually
1	11.681	3.878	1.927	0.952	11.619	3.854	1.913	0.943
2	22.794	7.568	3.762	1.859	22.563	7.486	3.717	1.833
3	33.366	11.079	5.508	2.723	32.871	10.908	5.417	2.673
4	43.423	14.420	7.170	3.546	42.580	14.131	7.020	3.465
5	52.991	17.599	8.752	4.329	51.726	17.169	8.530	4.212
6	62.093	20.624	10.258	5.076	60.340	20.030	9.954	4.917
7	70.752	23.503	11.691	5.786	68.453	22.727	11.296	5.582
8	78.989	26.241	13.055	6.463	76.095	25.267	12.561	6.210
9	86.826	28.847	14.353	7.108	83.293	27.661	13.754	6.802
10	94.281	31.327	15.589	7.722	90.073	29.916	14.877	7.360
11	101.374	33.686	16.765	8.306	96.460	32.041	15.937	7.887
12	108.121	35.931	17.885	8.863	102.475	34.043	16.936	8.384
13	114.540	38.068	18.951	9.394	108.140	35.929	17.877	8.853
14	120.646	40.100	19.965	9.899	113.477	37.706	18.764	9.295
15	126.455	42.035	20.930	10.380	118.504	39.380	19.600	9.712
16	131.982	43.875	21.849	10.838	123.238	40.958	20.389	10.106
17	137.239	45.626	22.724	11.274	127.697	42.444	21.132	10.477
18	142.241	47.292	23.556	11.690	131.898	43.845	21.832	10.828
19	146.999	48.878	24.349	12.085	135.854	45.164	22.492	11.158
20	151.525	50.387	25.103	12.462	139.581	46.407	23.115	11.470
21	155.832	51.822	25.821	12.821	143.091	47.579	23.701	11.764
22	159.928	53.188	26.504	13.163	146.397	48.682	24.254	12.042
23	163.825	54.488	27.154	13.489	149.511	49.722	24.775	12.303
24	167.533	55.725	27.773	13.799	152.444	50.702	25.267	12.550
25	171.060	56.901	28.362	14.094	155.207	51.625	25.730	12.783
26	174.415	58.021	28.923	14.375	157.809	52.494	26.166	13.003
27	177.608	59.087	29.457	14.643	160.260	53.314	26.578	13.211
28	180.644	60.100	29.965	14.898	162.569	54.086	26.965	13.406
29	183.533	61.065	30.448	15.141	164.743	54.813	27.331	13.591
30	186.282	61.983	30.909	15.372	166.792	55.498	27.676	13.765
31	188.896	62.856	31.347	15.593	168.721	56.144	28.000	13.929
32	191.383	63.687	31.764	15.803	170.538	56.753	28.306	14.084
33	193.750	64.478	32.161	16.003	172.250	57.326	28.595	14.230
34	196.001	65.231	32.538	16.193	173.862	57.866	28.867	14.368
35	198.142	65.946	32.898	16.374	175.380	58.375	29.123	14.498
36	200.180	66.628	33.240	16.547	176.811	58.854	29.365	14.621
37	202.118	67.276	33.566	16.711	178.158	59.306	29.593	14.737
38	203.962	67.893	33.876	16.868	179.427	59.731	29.808	14.846
39	205.716	68.480	34.171	17.017	180.622	60.132	30.010	14.949
40	207.384	69.038	34.452	17.159	181.748	60.510	30.201	15.046
41	208.972	69.570	34.719	17.294	182.808	60.866	30.381	15.138
42	210.482	70.075	34.974	17.423	183.807	61.201	30.550	15.225
43	211.919	70.556	35.216	17.546	184.747	61.517	30.710	15.306
44	213.285	71.014	35.446	17.663	185.634	61.815	30.860	15.383
45	214.586	71.450	35.666	17.774	186.468	62.096	31.002	15.456
46	215.823	71.864	35.875	17.880	187.254	62.360	31.136	15.524
47	216.999	72.259	36.073	17.981	187.995	62.609	31.262	15.589
48	218.119	72.634	36.263	18.077	188.692	62.843	31.381	15.650
49	219.184	72.991	36.443	18.169	189.349	63.064	31.493	15.708
50	220.197	73.331	36.614	18.256	189.968	63.273	31.599	15.762

The present value of a $1 annuity at the *end* of each period

End of Year	At 7% Interest compounded and Payments or Withdrawals made				At 8% Interest compounded and Payments or Withdrawals made			
	Monthly	Quarterly	Semi-Annually	Annually	Monthly	Quarterly	Semi-Annually	Annually
1	11.557	3.831	1.900	0.935	11.496	3.808	1.886	0.926
2	22.335	7.405	3.673	1.808	22.111	7.325	3.630	1.783
3	32.386	10.740	5.329	2.624	31.912	10.575	5.242	2.577
4	41.760	13.850	6.874	3.387	40.962	13.578	6.733	3.312
5	50.502	16.753	8.317	4.100	49.318	16.351	8.111	3.993
6	58.654	19.461	9.663	4.767	57.035	18.914	9.385	4.623
7	66.257	21.987	10.921	5.389	64.159	21.281	10.563	5.206
8	73.348	24.344	12.094	5.971	70.738	23.468	11.652	5.747
9	79.960	26.543	13.190	6.515	76.812	25.489	12.659	6.247
10	86.126	28.594	14.212	7.024	82.421	27.355	13.590	6.710
11	91.877	30.508	15.167	7.499	87.601	29.080	14.451	7.139
12	97.240	32.294	16.058	7.943	92.383	30.673	15.247	7.536
13	102.242	33.960	16.890	8.358	96.798	32.145	15.983	7.904
14	106.906	35.514	17.667	8.745	100.876	33.505	16.663	8.244
15	111.256	36.964	18.392	9.108	104.641	34.761	17.292	8.559
16	115.313	38.317	19.069	9.447	108.117	35.921	17.874	8.851
17	119.096	39.579	19.701	9.763	111.327	36.994	18.411	9.122
18	122.624	40.756	20.290	10.059	114.291	37.984	18.908	9.372
19	125.914	41.855	20.841	10.336	117.027	38.899	19.368	9.604
20	128.983	42.880	21.355	10.594	119.554	39.745	19.793	9.818
21	131.844	43.836	21.835	10.836	121.888	40.526	20.186	10.017
22	134.513	44.728	22.283	11.061	124.042	41.247	20.549	10.201
23	137.001	45.561	22.701	11.272	126.031	41.914	20.885	10.371
24	139.322	46.337	23.091	11.469	127.868	42.529	21.195	10.529
25	141.487	47.061	23.456	11.654	129.565	43.098	21.482	10.675
26	143.505	47.737	23.796	11.826	131.131	43.624	21.748	10.810
27	145.388	48.368	24.113	11.987	132.577	44.110	21.993	10.935
28	147.144	48.956	24.410	12.137	133.912	44.558	22.220	11.051
29	148.781	49.505	24.686	12.278	135.145	44.973	22.430	11.158
30	150.308	50.017	24.945	12.409	136.283	45.355	22.623	11.258
31	151.731	50.495	25.186	12.532	137.335	45.709	22.803	11.350
32	153.059	50.941	25.411	12.647	138.305	46.036	22.969	11.435
33	154.298	51.356	25.621	12.754	139.202	46.338	23.122	11.514
34	155.453	51.744	25.817	12.854	140.029	46.617	23.264	11.587
35	156.530	52.106	26.000	12.948	140.793	46.874	23.395	11.655
36	157.534	52.444	26.171	13.035	141.499	47.112	23.516	11.717
37	158.471	52.759	26.331	13.117	142.150	47.332	23.628	11.775
38	159.344	53.053	26.480	13.193	142.752	47.535	23.731	11.829
39	160.159	53.327	26.619	13.265	143.307	47.723	23.827	11.879
40	160.919	53.583	26.749	13.332	143.820	47.896	23.915	11.925
41	161.627	53.821	26.870	13.394	144.294	48.057	23.997	11.967
42	162.288	54.044	26.983	13.452	144.731	48.205	24.073	12.007
43	162.904	54.252	27.089	13.507	145.135	48.341	24.143	12.043
44	163.479	54.446	27.187	13.558	145.508	48.468	24.207	12.077
45	164.015	54.627	27.279	13.606	145.852	48.584	24.267	12.108
46	164.515	54.795	27.365	13.650	146.170	48.692	24.323	12.137
47	164.981	54.953	27.445	13.692	146.464	48.792	24.374	12.164
48	165.416	55.099	27.520	13.730	146.735	48.884	24.421	12.189
49	165.821	55.236	27.590	13.767	146.985	48.969	24.465	12.212
50	166.199	55.364	27.655	13.801	147.216	49.047	24.505	12.233

The present value of a $1 annuity at the *end* of each period

End of Year	At 9% Interest compounded and Payments or Withdrawals made				At 10% Interest compounded and Payments or Withdrawals made			
	Monthly	Quarterly	Semi-Annually	Annually	Monthly	Quarterly	Semi-Annually	Annually
1	11.435	3.785	1.873	0.917	11.375	3.762	1.859	0.909
2	21.889	7.247	3.588	1.759	21.671	7.170	3.546	1.736
3	31.447	10.415	5.158	2.531	30.991	10.258	5.076	2.487
4	40.185	13.313	6.596	3.240	39.428	13.055	6.463	3.170
5	48.173	15.964	7.913	3.890	47.065	15.589	7.722	3.791
6	55.477	18.389	9.119	4.486	53.979	17.885	8.863	4.355
7	62.154	20.608	10.223	5.033	60.237	19.965	9.899	4.868
8	68.258	22.638	11.234	5.535	65.901	21.849	10.838	5.335
9	73.839	24.495	12.160	5.995	71.029	23.556	11.690	5.759
10	78.942	26.194	13.008	6.418	75.671	25.103	12.462	6.145
11	83.606	27.748	13.784	6.805	79.873	26.504	13.163	6.495
12	87.871	29.170	14.495	7.161	83.677	27.773	13.799	6.814
13	91.770	30.470	15.147	7.487	87.120	28.923	14.375	7.103
14	95.335	31.660	15.743	7.786	90.236	29.965	14.898	7.367
15	98.593	32.749	16.289	8.061	93.057	30.909	15.372	7.606
16	101.573	33.745	16.789	8.313	95.611	31.764	15.803	7.824
17	104.297	34.656	17.247	8.544	97.923	32.538	16.193	8.022
18	106.787	35.490	17.666	8.756	100.016	33.240	16.547	8.201
19	109.064	36.252	18.050	8.950	101.910	33.876	16.868	8.365
20	111.145	36.950	18.402	9.129	103.625	34.452	17.159	8.514
21	113.048	37.588	18.724	9.292	105.177	34.974	17.423	8.649
22	114.788	38.172	19.018	9.442	106.582	35.446	17.663	8.772
23	116.378	38.706	19.288	9.580	107.854	35.875	17.880	8.883
24	117.832	39.195	19.536	9.707	109.005	36.263	18.077	8.985
25	119.162	39.642	19.762	9.823	110.047	36.614	18.256	9.077
26	120.377	40.051	19.969	9.929	110.991	36.933	18.418	9.161
27	121.488	40.425	20.159	10.027	111.845	37.221	18.565	9.237
28	122.504	40.767	20.333	10.116	112.618	37.482	18.699	9.307
29	123.433	41.080	20.492	10.198	113.317	37.719	18.820	9.370
30	124.282	41.367	20.638	10.274	113.951	37.934	18.929	9.427
31	125.058	41.629	20.772	10.343	114.524	38.128	19.029	9.479
32	125.768	41.869	20.894	10.406	115.043	38.304	19.119	9.526
33	126.417	42.088	21.006	10.464	115.513	38.464	19.201	9.569
34	127.010	42.289	21.108	10.518	115.938	38.608	19.275	9.609
35	127.552	42.472	21.202	10.567	116.323	38.739	19.343	9.644
36	128.048	42.640	21.288	10.612	116.672	38.858	19.404	9.677
37	128.501	42.794	21.367	10.653	116.987	38.965	19.459	9.706
38	128.916	42.934	21.439	10.691	117.273	39.062	19.509	9.733
39	129.295	43.063	21.505	10.726	117.531	39.151	19.555	9.757
40	129.641	43.181	21.565	10.757	117.765	39.230	19.596	9.779
41	129.958	43.288	21.621	10.787	117.977	39.303	19.634	9.799
42	130.247	43.387	21.671	10.813	118.169	39.368	19.668	9.817
43	130.512	43.477	21.718	10.838	118.343	39.428	19.699	9.834
44	130.754	43.559	21.760	10.861	118.500	39.482	19.727	9.849
45	130.975	43.635	21.799	10.881	118.642	39.530	19.752	9.863
46	131.177	43.704	21.835	10.900	118.771	39.575	19.775	9.875
47	131.362	43.767	21.868	10.918	118.887	39.615	19.796	9.887
48	131.531	43.824	21.897	10.934	118.993	39.651	19.815	9.897
49	131.686	43.877	21.925	10.948	119.088	39.684	19.832	9.906
50	131.827	43.925	21.950	10.962	119.175	39.713	19.848	9.915

The present value of a $1 annuity at the *end* of each period

End of Year	At 13% Interest compounded and Payments or Withdrawals made				At 14% Interest compounded and Payments or Withdrawals made			
	Monthly	Quarterly	Semi-Annually	Annually	Monthly	Quarterly	Semi-Annually	Annually
1	11.196	3.695	1.821	0.885	11.137	3.673	1.808	0.877
2	21.034	6.946	3.426	1.668	20.828	6.874	3.387	1.647
3	29.679	9.807	4.841	2.361	29.259	9.663	4.767	2.322
4	37.275	12.324	6.089	2.974	36.595	12.094	5.971	2.914
5	43.950	14.539	7.189	3.517	42.977	14.212	7.024	3.433
6	49.815	16.488	8.159	3.998	48.530	16.058	7.943	3.889
7	54.969	18.203	9.014	4.423	53.362	17.667	8.745	4.288
8	59.498	19.712	9.768	4.799	57.566	19.069	9.447	4.639
9	63.478	21.040	10.432	5.132	61.223	20.290	10.059	4.946
10	66.974	22.208	11.019	5.426	64.405	21.355	10.594	5.216
11	70.047	23.236	11.535	5.687	67.174	22.283	11.061	5.453
12	72.747	24.141	11.991	5.918	69.583	23.091	11.469	5.660
13	75.120	24.937	12.392	6.122	71.679	23.796	11.826	5.842
14	77.204	25.637	12.746	6.302	73.503	24.410	12.137	6.002
15	79.036	26.254	13.059	6.462	75.090	24.945	12.409	6.142
16	80.646	26.796	13.334	6.604	76.470	25.411	12.647	6.265
17	82.060	27.273	13.577	6.729	77.671	25.817	12.854	6.373
18	83.303	27.693	13.791	6.840	78.716	26.171	13.035	6.467
19	84.395	28.062	13.979	6.938	79.626	26.480	13.193	6.550
20	85.355	28.387	14.146	7.025	80.417	26.749	13.332	6.623
21	86.198	28.673	14.292	7.102	81.105	26.983	13.452	6.687
22	86.939	28.925	14.421	7.170	81.704	27.187	13.558	6.743
23	87.591	29.147	14.535	7.230	82.225	27.365	13.650	6.792
24	88.163	29.341	14.636	7.283	82.679	27.520	13.730	6.835
25	88.665	29.513	14.725	7.330	83.073	27.655	13.801	6.873
26	89.107	29.664	14.803	7.372	83.416	27.773	13.862	6.906
27	89.495	29.797	14.872	7.409	83.715	27.876	13.916	6.935
28	89.836	29.913	14.932	7.441	83.975	27.965	13.963	6.961
29	90.136	30.016	14.986	7.470	84.201	28.043	14.003	6.983
30	90.400	30.107	15.033	7.496	84.397	28.111	14.039	7.003
31	90.631	30.186	15.075	7.518	84.568	28.170	14.070	7.020
32	90.834	30.256	15.111	7.538	84.717	28.222	14.098	7.035
33	91.013	30.318	15.144	7.556	84.847	28.267	14.121	7.048
34	91.170	30.372	15.172	7.572	84.960	28.306	14.142	7.060
35	91.308	30.420	15.197	7.586	85.058	28.340	14.160	7.070
36	91.429	30.462	15.219	7.598	85.143	28.370	14.176	7.079
37	91.536	30.499	15.239	7.609	85.217	28.396	14.190	7.087
38	91.629	30.531	15.256	7.618	85.282	28.418	14.202	7.094
39	91.712	30.560	15.271	7.627	85.338	28.438	14.213	7.100
40	91.784	30.585	15.285	7.634	85.387	28.455	14.222	7.105
41	91.848	30.607	15.297	7.641	85.429	28.470	14.230	7.110
42	91.903	30.626	15.307	7.647	85.466	28.483	14.237	7.114
43	91.952	30.644	15.316	7.652	85.499	28.494	14.243	7.117
44	91.995	30.659	15.324	7.657	85.527	28.504	14.249	7.120
45	92.033	30.672	15.331	7.661	85.551	28.513	14.253	7.123
46	92.067	30.684	15.338	7.664	85.572	28.521	14.257	7.126
47	92.096	30.694	15.343	7.668	85.591	28.527	14.261	7.128
48	92.122	30.703	15.348	7.671	85.607	28.533	14.264	7.130
49	92.144	30.711	15.352	7.673	85.621	28.538	14.267	7.131
50	92.164	30.718	15.356	7.675	85.633	28.542	14.269	7.133

The present value of a $1 annuity at the *end* of each period

End of Year	At 17% Interest compounded and Payments or Withdrawals made				At 18% Interest compounded and Payments or Withdrawals made			
	Monthly	Quarterly	Semi-Annually	Annually	Monthly	Quarterly	Semi-Annually	Annually
1	10.964	3.609	1.771	0.855	10.908	3.588	1.759	0.847
2	20.226	6.664	3.276	1.585	20.030	6.596	3.240	1.566
3	28.048	9.250	4.554	2.210	27.661	9.119	4.486	2.174
4	34.656	11.440	5.639	2.743	34.043	11.234	5.535	2.690
5	40.237	13.294	6.561	3.199	39.380	13.008	6.418	3.127
6	44.952	14.864	7.345	3.589	43.845	14.495	7.161	3.498
7	48.934	16.193	8.010	3.922	47.579	15.743	7.786	3.812
8	52.297	17.318	8.575	4.207	50.702	16.789	8.313	4.078
9	55.138	18.271	9.055	4.451	53.314	17.666	8.756	4.303
10	57.538	19.077	9.463	4.659	55.498	18.402	9.129	4.494
11	59.565	19.760	9.810	4.836	57.326	19.018	9.442	4.656
12	61.277	20.338	10.104	4.988	58.854	19.536	9.707	4.793
13	62.724	20.828	10.354	5.118	60.132	19.969	9.929	4.910
14	63.945	21.242	10.566	5.229	61.201	20.333	10.116	5.008
15	64.977	21.593	10.747	5.324	62.096	20.638	10.274	5.092
16	65.849	21.890	10.900	5.405	62.843	20.894	10.406	5.162
17	66.585	22.141	11.030	5.475	63.469	21.108	10.518	5.222
18	67.207	22.354	11.141	5.534	63.992	21.288	10.612	5.273
19	67.732	22.534	11.235	5.584	64.430	21.439	10.691	5.316
20	68.176	22.687	11.315	5.628	64.796	21.565	10.757	5.353
21	68.550	22.816	11.382	5.665	65.102	21.671	10.813	5.384
22	68.867	22.926	11.440	5.696	65.358	21.760	10.861	5.410
23	69.134	23.018	11.489	5.723	65.572	21.835	10.900	5.432
24	69.360	23.097	11.530	5.746	65.751	21.897	10.934	5.451
25	69.551	23.163	11.566	5.766	65.901	21.950	10.962	5.467
26	69.712	23.219	11.596	5.783	66.026	21.994	10.985	5.480
27	69.848	23.267	11.621	5.798	66.131	22.031	11.005	5.492
28	69.963	23.307	11.643	5.810	66.219	22.062	11.022	5.502
29	70.060	23.341	11.661	5.820	66.292	22.088	11.036	5.510
30	70.142	23.370	11.677	5.829	66.353	22.109	11.048	5.517
31	70.211	23.394	11.690	5.837	66.405	22.128	11.058	5.523
32	70.270	23.415	11.701	5.844	66.447	22.143	11.066	5.528
33	70.319	23.433	11.711	5.849	66.483	22.156	11.073	5.532
34	70.361	23.448	11.719	5.854	66.513	22.166	11.079	5.536
35	70.396	23.460	11.726	5.858	66.538	22.175	11.084	5.539
36	70.426	23.471	11.732	5.862	66.559	22.183	11.089	5.541
37	70.451	23.480	11.737	5.865	66.577	22.189	11.092	5.543
38	70.473	23.487	11.741	5.867	66.592	22.195	11.095	5.545
39	70.491	23.494	11.744	5.869	66.604	22.199	11.098	5.547
40	70.506	23.499	11.747	5.871	66.614	22.203	11.100	5.548
41	70.519	23.504	11.750	5.873	66.623	22.206	11.102	5.549
42	70.529	23.508	11.752	5.874	66.630	22.209	11.103	5.550
43	70.539	23.511	11.754	5.875	66.636	22.211	11.104	5.551
44	70.546	23.514	11.756	5.876	66.641	22.213	11.105	5.552
45	70.553	23.516	11.757	5.877	66.645	22.214	11.106	5.552
46	70.558	23.518	11.758	5.878	66.649	22.215	11.107	5.553
47	70.563	23.520	11.759	5.879	66.652	22.217	11.108	5.553
48	70.567	23.521	11.760	5.879	66.654	22.217	11.108	5.554
49	70.570	23.523	11.761	5.880	66.656	22.218	11.109	5.554
50	70.573	23.524	11.761	5.880	66.658	22.219	11.109	5.554

The present value of a $1 annuity at the *end* of each period

End of Year	At 19% Interest compounded and Payments or Withdrawals made				At 20% Interest compounded and Payments or Withdrawals made			
	Monthly	Quarterly	Semi-Annually	Annually	Monthly	Quarterly	Semi-Annually	Annually
1	10.851	3.567	1.747	0.840	10.795	3.546	1.736	0.833
2	19.838	6.529	3.204	1.547	19.648	6.463	3.170	1.528
3	27.281	8.990	4.420	2.140	26.908	8.863	4.355	2.106
4	33.445	11.033	5.433	2.639	32.862	10.838	5.335	2.589
5	38.550	12.731	6.279	3.058	37.745	12.462	6.145	2.991
6	42.778	14.141	6.984	3.410	41.749	13.799	6.814	3.326
7	46.279	15.312	7.572	3.706	45.032	14.898	7.367	3.605
8	49.179	16.284	8.062	3.954	47.725	15.803	7.824	3.837
9	51.581	17.092	8.471	4.163	49.934	16.547	8.201	4.031
10	53.570	17.763	8.812	4.339	51.745	17.159	8.514	4.192
11	55.217	18.320	9.097	4.486	53.230	17.663	8.772	4.327
12	56.581	18.783	9.334	4.611	54.448	18.077	8.985	4.439
13	57.711	19.168	9.532	4.715	55.447	18.418	9.161	4.533
14	58.647	19.487	9.697	4.802	56.266	18.699	9.307	4.611
15	59.422	19.752	9.835	4.876	56.938	18.929	9.427	4.675
16	60.064	19.973	9.950	4.938	57.489	19.119	9.526	4.730
17	60.596	20.156	10.045	4.990	57.941	19.275	9.609	4.775
18	61.036	20.308	10.125	5.033	58.311	19.404	9.677	4.812
19	61.400	20.434	10.192	5.070	58.615	19.509	9.733	4.843
20	61.702	20.539	10.247	5.101	58.864	19.596	9.779	4.870
21	61.952	20.626	10.294	5.127	59.069	19.668	9.817	4.891
22	62.160	20.698	10.332	5.149	59.236	19.727	9.849	4.909
23	62.331	20.758	10.364	5.167	59.374	19.775	9.875	4.925
24	62.473	20.808	10.391	5.182	59.486	19.815	9.897	4.937
25	62.591	20.849	10.414	5.195	59.579	19.848	9.915	4.948
26	62.688	20.884	10.432	5.206	59.655	19.875	9.930	4.956
27	62.769	20.912	10.448	5.215	59.717	19.897	9.942	4.964
28	62.836	20.936	10.461	5.223	59.768	19.915	9.952	4.970
29	62.891	20.956	10.472	5.229	59.809	19.930	9.960	4.975
30	62.937	20.972	10.481	5.235	59.844	19.943	9.967	4.979
31	62.975	20.986	10.488	5.239	59.872	19.953	9.973	4.982
32	63.006	20.997	10.495	5.243	59.895	19.961	9.978	4.985
33	63.032	21.007	10.500	5.246	59.914	19.968	9.981	4.988
34	63.054	21.014	10.504	5.249	59.929	19.974	9.985	4.990
35	63.072	21.021	10.508	5.251	59.942	19.978	9.987	4.992
36	63.087	21.026	10.511	5.253	59.952	19.982	9.990	4.993
37	63.099	21.031	10.514	5.255	59.961	19.985	9.991	4.994
38	63.109	21.034	10.516	5.256	59.968	19.988	9.993	4.995
39	63.117	21.038	10.517	5.257	59.974	19.990	9.994	4.996
40	63.124	21.040	10.519	5.258	59.979	19.992	9.995	4.997
41	63.130	21.042	10.520	5.259	59.982	19.993	9.996	4.997
42	63.135	21.044	10.521	5.260	59.986	19.994	9.997	4.998
43	63.139	21.045	10.522	5.260	59.988	19.995	9.997	4.998
44	63.142	21.047	10.523	5.261	59.990	19.996	9.998	4.998
45	63.145	21.048	10.523	5.261	59.992	19.997	9.998	4.999
46	63.147	21.049	10.524	5.261	59.993	19.997	9.998	4.999
47	63.149	21.049	10.524	5.262	59.995	19.998	9.999	4.999
48	63.150	21.050	10.525	5.262	59.996	19.998	9.999	4.999
49	63.152	21.050	10.525	5.262	59.996	19.999	9.999	4.999
50	63.153	21.051	10.525	5.262	59.997	19.999	9.999	4.999

The future value of "an annuity due" assuming deposits are made monthly, quarterly, semi-annually or annually at various interest rates

Applications
Chapter Nine
- How much will $1 invested at the beginning of each period amount to at some time in the future?

Chapter Sixteen
- The future value of a series of life insurance premiums.

The future value of $1
invested at the *beginning* of each period

End of Year	5% Interest compounded and Deposits made				6% Interest compounded and Deposits made			
	Monthly	Quarterly	Semi-Annually	Annually	Monthly	Quarterly	Semi-Annually	Annually
1	12.330	4.127	2.076	1.050	12.397	4.152	2.091	1.060
2	25.291	8.463	4.256	2.153	25.559	8.559	4.309	2.184
3	38.915	13.021	6.547	3.310	39.533	13.237	6.662	3.375
4	53.236	17.811	8.955	4.526	54.368	18.201	9.159	4.637
5	68.289	22.845	11.483	5.802	70.119	23.471	11.808	5.975
6	84.113	28.135	14.140	7.142	86.841	29.063	14.618	7.394
7	100.747	33.695	16.932	8.549	104.594	34.999	17.599	8.897
8	118.231	39.539	19.865	10.027	123.443	41.299	20.762	10.491
9	136.610	45.679	22.946	11.578	143.454	47.985	24.117	12.181
10	155.929	52.133	26.183	13.207	164.699	55.082	27.676	13.972
11	176.237	58.916	29.584	14.917	187.254	62.614	31.453	15.870
12	197.584	66.044	33.158	16.713	211.201	70.609	35.459	17.882
13	220.022	73.535	36.912	18.599	236.625	79.094	39.710	20.015
14	243.609	81.408	40.856	20.579	263.616	88.100	44.219	22.276
15	268.403	89.682	45.000	22.657	292.273	97.658	49.003	24.673
16	294.465	98.377	49.354	24.840	322.697	107.803	54.078	27.213
17	321.860	107.516	53.928	27.132	354.997	118.570	59.462	29.906
18	350.657	117.120	58.734	29.539	389.290	129.998	65.174	32.760
19	380.927	127.213	63.783	32.066	425.698	142.128	71.234	35.786
20	412.746	137.820	69.088	34.719	464.351	155.002	77.663	38.993
21	446.193	148.968	74.661	37.505	505.388	168.665	84.484	42.392
22	481.351	160.684	80.516	40.430	548.957	183.167	91.720	45.996
23	518.308	172.997	86.668	43.502	595.213	198.559	99.397	49.816
24	557.156	185.937	93.131	46.727	644.321	214.896	107.541	53.865
25	597.991	199.536	99.921	50.113	696.459	232.235	116.181	58.156
26	640.915	213.828	107.056	53.669	751.812	250.638	125.347	62.706
27	686.036	228.848	114.551	57.403	810.580	270.170	135.072	67.528
28	733.465	244.633	122.426	61.323	872.972	290.901	145.388	72.640
29	783.320	261.223	130.699	65.439	939.212	312.904	156.333	78.058
30	835.726	278.657	139.391	69.761	1009.538	336.258	167.945	83.802
31	890.814	296.980	148.524	74.299	1084.201	361.044	180.264	89.890
32	948.719	316.236	158.118	79.064	1163.469	387.351	193.333	96.343
33	1009.588	336.474	168.199	84.067	1247.627	415.272	207.198	103.184
34	1073.570	357.742	178.789	89.320	1336.975	444.907	221.907	110.435
35	1140.826	380.094	189.916	94.836	1431.834	476.361	237.512	118.121
36	1211.523	403.585	201.606	100.628	1532.543	509.744	254.067	126.268
37	1285.837	428.272	213.888	106.710	1639.465	545.176	271.631	134.904
38	1363.953	454.217	226.792	113.095	1752.980	582.782	290.264	144.058
39	1446.065	481.484	240.349	119.800	1873.498	622.696	310.032	153.762
40	1532.379	510.140	254.592	126.840	2001.448	665.059	331.004	164.048
41	1623.108	540.256	269.557	134.232	2137.290	710.022	353.253	174.951
42	1718.479	571.906	285.279	141.993	2281.511	757.744	376.857	186.508
43	1818.730	605.168	301.796	150.143	2434.627	808.394	401.898	198.758
44	1924.110	640.125	319.150	158.700	2597.187	862.152	428.465	211.744
45	2034.881	676.863	337.383	167.685	2769.773	919.209	456.649	225.508
46	2151.319	715.473	356.539	177.119	2953.003	979.767	486.550	240.099
47	2273.715	756.049	376.664	187.025	3147.535	1044.041	518.272	255.565
48	2402.372	798.693	397.808	197.427	3354.066	1112.260	551.926	271.958
49	2537.612	843.509	420.023	208.348	3573.334	1184.664	587.629	289.336
50	2679.771	890.609	443.362	219.815	3806.127	1261.512	625.506	307.756

The future value of $1
invested at the *beginning* of each period

End of Year	7% Interest compounded and Deposits made				8% Interest compounded and Deposits made			
	Monthly	Quarterly	Semi-Annually	Annually	Monthly	Quarterly	Semi-Annually	Annually
1	12.465	4.178	2.106	1.070	12.533	4.204	2.122	1.080
2	25.831	8.656	4.362	2.215	26.106	8.755	4.416	2.246
3	40.163	13.457	6.779	3.440	40.806	13.680	6.898	3.506
4	55.531	18.602	9.368	4.751	56.726	19.012	9.583	4.867
5	72.011	24.116	12.142	6.153	73.967	24.783	12.486	6.336
6	89.681	30.027	15.113	7.654	92.639	31.030	15.627	7.923
7	108.629	36.363	18.296	9.260	112.861	37.792	19.024	9.637
8	128.947	43.154	21.705	10.978	134.761	45.112	22.698	11.488
9	150.733	50.434	25.357	12.816	158.479	53.034	26.671	13.487
10	174.094	58.236	29.269	14.784	184.166	61.610	30.969	15.645
11	199.145	66.599	33.460	16.888	211.984	70.893	35.618	17.977
12	226.006	75.562	37.950	19.141	242.112	80.941	40.646	20.495
13	254.809	85.170	42.759	21.550	274.740	91.817	46.084	23.215
14	285.694	95.469	47.911	24.129	310.076	103.589	51.966	26.152
15	318.811	106.507	53.429	26.888	348.345	116.333	58.328	29.324
16	354.323	118.339	59.341	29.840	389.791	130.126	65.210	32.750
17	392.402	131.020	65.674	32.999	434.676	145.057	72.652	36.450
18	433.234	144.613	72.458	36.379	483.287	161.218	80.702	40.446
19	477.017	159.183	79.725	39.995	535.932	178.712	89.409	44.762
20	523.965	174.800	87.510	43.865	592.947	197.647	98.827	49.423
21	574.308	191.539	95.849	48.006	654.694	218.144	109.012	54.457
22	628.289	209.481	104.782	52.436	721.567	240.330	120.029	59.893
23	686.173	228.712	114.351	57.177	793.989	264.345	131.945	65.765
24	748.242	249.326	124.602	62.249	872.423	290.340	144.834	72.106
25	814.797	271.420	135.583	67.676	957.367	318.477	158.774	78.954
26	886.164	295.102	147.346	73.484	1049.360	348.934	173.851	86.351
27	962.689	320.486	159.947	79.698	1148.990	381.901	190.159	94.339
28	1044.747	347.694	173.445	86.347	1256.888	417.586	207.798	102.966
29	1132.737	376.857	187.905	93.461	1373.742	456.213	226.876	112.283
30	1227.087	408.115	203.395	101.073	1500.295	498.023	247.510	122.346
31	1328.259	441.620	219.988	109.218	1637.352	543.280	269.829	133.214
32	1436.743	477.533	237.763	117.933	1785.784	592.268	293.968	144.951
33	1553.071	516.026	256.804	127.259	1946.536	645.294	320.078	157.627
34	1677.807	557.285	277.201	137.237	2120.631	702.691	348.318	171.317
35	1811.561	601.509	299.051	147.913	2309.175	764.820	378.862	186.102
36	1954.984	648.911	322.457	159.337	2513.368	832.070	411.899	202.070
37	2108.774	699.719	347.530	171.561	2734.510	904.863	447.631	219.316
38	2273.683	754.179	374.389	184.640	2974.005	983.657	486.280	237.941
39	2450.512	812.551	403.161	198.635	3233.379	1068.946	528.082	258.057
40	2640.125	875.118	433.983	213.610	3514.281	1161.265	573.295	279.781
41	2843.445	942.182	466.999	229.632	3818.498	1261.195	622.197	303.244
42	3061.462	1014.064	502.367	246.776	4147.964	1369.362	675.090	328.583
43	3295.240	1091.112	540.255	265.121	4504.776	1486.445	732.299	355.950
44	3545.919	1173.696	580.841	284.749	4891.203	1613.180	794.176	385.506
45	3814.718	1262.215	624.317	305.752	5309.703	1750.362	861.103	417.426
46	4102.949	1357.094	670.890	328.224	5762.939	1898.853	933.490	451.900
47	4412.017	1458.792	720.781	352.270	6253.793	2059.583	1011.785	489.132
48	4743.427	1567.797	774.225	377.999	6785.388	2233.563	1096.468	529.343
49	5098.794	1684.636	831.475	405.529	7361.105	2421.885	1188.061	572.770
50	5479.851	1809.870	892.803	434.986	7984.606	2625.730	1287.129	619.672

The future value of $1
invested at the *beginning* of each period

End of Year	9% Interest compounded and Deposits made				10% Interest compounded and Deposits made			
	Monthly	Quarterly	Semi-Annually	Annually	Monthly	Quarterly	Semi-Annually	Annually
1	12.601	4.230	2.137	1.090	12.670	4.256	2.153	1.100
2	26.385	8.854	4.471	2.278	26.667	8.955	4.526	2.310
3	41.461	13.908	7.019	3.573	42.130	14.140	7.142	3.641
4	57.952	19.433	9.802	4.985	59.212	19.865	10.027	5.105
5	75.990	25.472	12.841	6.523	78.082	26.183	13.207	6.716
6	95.720	32.073	16.160	8.200	98.929	33.158	16.713	8.487
7	117.300	39.289	19.784	10.028	121.958	40.856	20.579	10.436
8	140.905	47.176	23.742	12.021	147.399	49.354	24.840	12.579
9	166.724	55.797	28.064	14.193	175.504	58.734	29.539	14.937
10	194.966	65.221	32.783	16.560	206.552	69.088	34.719	17.531
11	225.856	75.523	37.937	19.141	240.851	80.516	40.430	20.384
12	259.644	86.783	43.565	21.953	278.742	93.131	46.727	23.523
13	296.602	99.091	49.711	25.019	320.600	107.056	53.669	26.975
14	337.027	112.544	56.423	28.361	366.841	122.426	61.323	30.772
15	381.244	127.251	63.752	32.003	417.924	139.391	69.761	34.950
16	429.609	143.326	71.756	35.974	474.357	158.118	79.064	39.545
17	482.510	160.897	80.497	40.301	536.698	178.789	89.320	44.599
18	540.374	180.104	90.041	45.018	605.568	201.606	100.628	50.159
19	603.667	201.099	100.464	50.160	681.649	226.792	113.095	56.275
20	672.896	224.048	111.847	55.765	765.697	254.592	126.840	63.002
21	748.620	249.133	124.276	61.873	858.546	285.279	141.993	70.403
22	831.447	276.553	137.850	68.532	961.117	319.150	158.700	78.543
23	922.044	306.526	152.673	75.790	1074.429	356.539	177.119	87.497
24	1021.139	339.288	168.859	83.701	1199.606	397.808	197.427	97.347
25	1129.530	375.101	186.536	92.324	1337.890	443.362	219.815	108.182
26	1248.089	414.246	205.839	101.723	1490.655	493.645	244.499	120.100
27	1377.770	457.036	226.918	111.968	1659.417	549.149	271.713	133.210
28	1519.616	503.808	249.937	123.135	1845.849	610.414	301.716	147.631
29	1674.768	554.935	275.075	135.308	2051.804	678.039	334.794	163.494
30	1844.474	610.820	302.525	148.575	2279.325	752.684	371.263	180.943
31	2030.100	671.907	332.502	163.037	2530.671	835.079	411.470	200.138
32	2233.139	738.681	365.238	178.800	2808.335	926.027	455.798	221.252
33	2455.224	811.670	400.986	195.982	3115.075	1026.417	504.670	244.477
34	2698.142	891.453	440.024	214.711	3453.934	1137.229	558.551	270.024
35	2963.848	978.662	482.654	235.125	3828.277	1259.544	617.955	298.127
36	3254.479	1073.989	529.207	257.376	4241.818	1394.557	683.448	329.039
37	3572.373	1178.190	580.044	281.630	4698.662	1543.586	755.654	363.043
38	3920.087	1292.090	635.560	308.066	5203.343	1708.087	835.261	400.448
39	4300.420	1416.592	696.184	336.882	5760.871	1889.665	923.027	441.593
40	4716.430	1552.683	762.388	368.292	6376.780	2090.093	1019.790	486.852
41	5171.465	1701.442	834.684	402.528	7057.183	2311.327	1126.471	536.637
42	5669.186	1864.048	913.632	439.846	7808.832	2555.529	1244.087	591.401
43	6213.596	2041.790	999.846	480.522	8639.189	2825.083	1373.758	651.641
44	6809.075	2236.077	1093.994	524.859	9556.496	3122.619	1516.721	717.905
45	7460.415	2448.448	1196.806	573.186	10569.856	3451.043	1674.338	790.795
46	8172.855	2680.588	1309.079	625.863	11689.328	3813.562	1848.110	870.975
47	8952.126	2934.336	1431.684	683.280	12926.024	4213.716	2039.694	959.172
48	9804.499	3211.704	1565.572	745.866	14292.218	4655.410	2250.915	1056.190
49	10736.830	3514.891	1711.781	814.084	15801.470	5142.958	2483.786	1162.909
50	11756.620	3846.298	1871.444	888.441	17468.761	5681.120	2740.526	1280.299

The future value of $1
invested at the *beginning* of each period

End of Year	11% Interest compounded and Deposits made				12% Interest compounded and Deposits made			
	Monthly	Quarterly	Semi-Annually	Annually	Monthly	Quarterly	Semi-Annually	Annually
1	12.740	4.283	2.168	1.110	12.809	4.309	2.184	1.120
2	26.953	9.056	4.581	2.342	27.243	9.159	4.637	2.374
3	42.812	14.377	7.267	3.710	43.508	14.618	7.394	3.779
4	60.506	20.307	10.256	5.228	61.835	20.762	10.491	5.353
5	80.247	26.918	13.583	6.913	82.486	27.676	13.972	7.115
6	102.273	34.286	17.287	8.783	105.757	35.459	17.882	9.089
7	126.847	42.498	21.409	10.859	131.979	44.219	22.276	11.300
8	154.265	51.652	25.996	13.164	161.527	54.078	27.213	13.776
9	184.856	61.855	31.103	15.722	194.822	65.174	32.760	16.549
10	218.987	73.228	36.786	18.561	232.339	77.663	38.993	19.655
11	257.068	85.904	43.112	21.713	274.615	91.720	45.996	23.133
12	299.555	100.033	50.153	25.212	322.252	107.541	53.865	27.029
13	346.959	115.782	57.989	29.095	375.931	125.347	62.706	31.393
14	399.848	133.336	66.711	33.405	436.418	145.388	72.640	36.280
15	458.858	152.901	76.419	38.190	504.576	167.945	83.802	41.753
16	524.696	174.710	87.225	43.501	581.378	193.333	96.343	47.884
17	598.152	199.018	99.251	49.396	667.921	221.907	110.435	54.750
18	680.109	226.112	112.637	55.939	765.439	254.067	126.268	62.440
19	771.551	256.312	127.536	63.203	875.325	290.264	144.058	71.052
20	873.573	289.974	144.119	71.265	999.148	331.004	164.048	80.699
21	987.402	327.494	162.576	80.214	1138.674	376.857	186.508	91.503
22	1114.402	369.314	183.119	90.148	1295.896	428.465	211.744	103.603
23	1256.099	415.928	205.984	101.174	1473.057	486.550	240.099	117.155
24	1414.193	467.885	231.434	113.413	1672.687	551.926	271.958	132.334
25	1590.581	525.797	259.759	126.999	1897.635	625.506	307.756	149.334
26	1787.381	590.347	291.287	142.079	2151.112	708.322	347.978	168.374
27	2006.954	662.296	326.377	158.817	2436.736	801.532	393.172	189.699
28	2251.936	742.492	365.434	177.397	2758.585	906.440	443.952	213.583
29	2525.267	831.880	408.906	198.021	3121.252	1024.516	501.008	240.333
30	2830.228	931.514	457.290	220.913	3529.914	1157.411	565.116	270.293
31	3170.478	1042.568	511.143	246.324	3990.405	1306.985	637.148	303.848
32	3550.102	1166.351	571.083	274.529	4509.297	1475.332	718.083	341.429
33	3973.655	1304.322	637.798	305.837	5093.998	1664.808	809.022	383.521
34	4446.221	1458.108	712.053	340.590	5752.854	1878.066	911.200	430.663
35	4973.472	1629.520	794.701	379.164	6495.269	2118.089	1026.008	483.463
36	5561.736	1820.581	886.690	421.982	7331.841	2388.237	1155.006	542.599
37	6218.074	2033.541	989.076	469.511	8274.511	2692.290	1299.949	608.831
38	6950.362	2270.910	1103.035	522.267	9336.736	3034.506	1462.806	683.010
39	7767.389	2535.488	1229.873	580.826	10533.677	3419.672	1645.792	766.091
40	8678.962	2830.391	1371.048	645.827	11882.420	3853.180	1851.396	859.142
41	9696.021	3159.097	1528.179	717.978	13402.218	4341.097	2082.412	963.359
42	10830.772	3525.479	1703.069	798.065	15114.764	4890.253	2341.982	1080.083
43	12096.836	3933.857	1897.726	886.963	17044.504	5508.332	2633.634	1210.813
44	13509.408	4389.043	2114.385	985.639	19218.983	6203.985	2961.335	1357.230
45	15085.440	4896.403	2355.531	1095.169	21669.240	6986.949	3329.540	1521.218
46	16843.850	5461.918	2623.933	1216.747	24430.251	7868.181	3743.254	1704.884
47	18805.740	6092.253	2922.671	1351.700	27541.428	8860.017	4208.104	1910.590
48	20994.658	6794.837	3255.174	1501.497	31047.180	9976.336	4730.410	2140.981
49	23436.875	7577.952	3625.258	1667.771	34997.549	11232.763	5317.272	2399.018
50	26161.702	8450.829	4037.171	1852.336	39448.923	12646.883	5976.670	2688.020

The future value of $1
invested at the *beginning* of each period

End of Year	13% Interest compounded and Deposits made				14% Interest compounded and Deposits made			
	Monthly	Quarterly	Semi-Annually	Annually	Monthly	Quarterly	Semi-Annually	Annually
1	12.879	4.336	2.199	1.130	12.950	4.362	2.215	1.140
2	27.537	9.263	4.694	2.407	27.834	9.368	4.751	2.440
3	44.217	14.863	7.523	3.850	44.941	15.113	7.654	3.921
4	63.200	21.227	10.732	5.480	64.603	21.705	10.978	5.610
5	84.803	28.460	14.372	7.323	87.201	29.269	14.784	7.536
6	109.388	36.680	18.500	9.405	113.174	37.950	19.141	9.730
7	137.367	46.022	23.182	11.757	143.025	47.911	24.129	12.233
8	169.208	56.638	28.493	14.416	177.335	59.341	29.840	15.085
9	205.443	68.704	34.517	17.420	216.769	72.458	36.379	18.337
10	246.681	82.416	41.349	20.814	262.091	87.510	43.865	22.045
11	293.610	97.999	49.098	24.650	314.183	104.782	52.436	26.271
12	347.017	115.710	57.888	28.985	374.054	124.602	62.249	31.089
13	407.796	135.837	67.857	33.883	442.865	147.346	73.484	36.581
14	476.965	158.711	79.164	39.417	521.954	173.445	86.347	42.842
15	555.681	184.707	91.989	45.672	612.854	203.395	101.073	49.980
16	645.263	214.251	106.536	52.739	717.329	237.763	117.933	58.118
17	747.210	247.827	123.035	60.725	837.406	277.201	137.237	67.394
18	863.228	285.985	141.748	69.749	975.416	322.457	159.337	77.969
19	995.261	329.351	162.974	79.947	1134.037	374.389	184.640	90.025
20	1145.519	378.635	187.048	91.470	1316.346	433.983	213.610	103.768
21	1316.517	434.645	214.354	104.491	1525.882	502.367	246.776	119.436
22	1511.119	498.299	245.325	119.205	1766.711	580.841	284.749	137.297
23	1732.582	570.641	280.453	135.831	2043.505	670.890	328.224	157.659
24	1984.614	652.855	320.295	154.620	2361.636	774.225	377.999	180.871
25	2271.435	746.290	365.486	175.850	2727.278	892.803	434.986	207.333
26	2597.846	852.477	416.743	199.841	3147.525	1028.875	500.230	237.499
27	2969.313	973.155	474.880	226.950	3630.533	1185.020	574.929	271.889
28	3392.054	1110.303	540.819	257.580	4185.674	1364.200	660.451	311.094
29	3873.147	1266.168	615.610	292.199	4823.721	1569.813	758.365	355.787
30	4420.647	1443.305	700.440	331.315	5557.056	1805.759	870.467	406.737
31	5043.719	1644.617	796.655	375.516	6399.908	2076.513	998.812	464.820
32	5752.796	1873.404	905.786	425.463	7368.633	2387.208	1145.755	531.035
33	6559.748	2133.414	1029.564	481.903	8482.030	2743.739	1313.990	606.520
34	7478.086	2428.909	1169.956	545.681	9761.703	3152.866	1506.602	692.573
35	8523.184	2764.733	1329.193	617.749	11232.486	3622.349	1727.124	790.673
36	9712.540	3146.388	1509.803	699.187	12922.918	4161.091	1979.599	902.507
37	11066.065	3580.130	1714.656	791.211	14865.803	4779.310	2268.657	1029.998
38	12606.421	4073.067	1947.005	895.198	17098.842	5488.731	2599.601	1175.338
39	14359.396	4633.279	2210.541	1012.704	19665.368	6302.807	2978.498	1341.025
40	16354.339	5269.945	2509.450	1145.486	22615.184	7236.979	3412.297	1529.909
41	18624.648	5993.502	2848.480	1295.529	26005.532	8308.962	3908.954	1745.236
42	21208.334	6815.806	3233.016	1465.078	29902.201	9539.087	4477.576	1990.709
43	24148.653	7750.336	3669.167	1656.668	34380.807	10950.685	5128.592	2270.548
44	27494.831	8812.406	4163.860	1873.165	39528.256	12570.525	5873.940	2589.565
45	31302.890	10019.423	4724.954	2117.806	45444.436	14429.329	6727.288	2953.244
46	35636.585	11391.168	5361.360	2394.251	52244.151	16562.349	7704.287	3367.838
47	40568.470	12950.124	6083.188	2706.633	60059.348	19010.039	8822.854	3840.475
48	46181.117	14721.840	6901.903	3059.626	69041.683	21818.820	10103.500	4379.282
49	52568.490	16735.353	7830.510	3458.507	79365.458	25041.960	11569.712	4993.521
50	59837.529	19023.661	8883.759	3909.243	91231.007	28740.588	13248.378	5693.754

The future value of $1
invested at the *beginning* of each period

End of Year	15% Interest compounded and Deposits made				16% Interest compounded and Deposits made			
	Monthly	Quarterly	Semi-Annually	Annually	Monthly	Quarterly	Semi-Annually	Annually
1	13.021	4.389	2.231	1.150	13.093	4.416	2.246	1.160
2	28.135	9.475	4.808	2.473	28.441	9.583	4.867	2.506
3	45.679	15.368	7.787	3.993	46.433	15.627	7.923	4.066
4	66.044	22.195	11.230	5.742	67.524	22.698	11.488	5.877
5	89.682	30.106	15.208	7.754	92.249	30.969	15.645	7.977
6	117.120	39.271	19.806	10.067	121.234	40.646	20.495	10.414
7	148.968	49.891	25.118	12.727	155.211	51.966	26.152	13.240
8	185.937	62.195	31.258	15.786	195.042	65.210	32.750	16.519
9	228.848	76.452	38.353	19.304	241.735	80.702	40.446	20.321
10	278.657	92.970	46.553	23.349	296.472	98.827	49.423	24.733
11	336.474	112.110	56.028	28.002	360.637	120.029	59.893	29.850
12	403.585	134.285	66.978	33.352	435.857	144.834	72.106	35.786
13	481.484	159.979	79.632	39.505	524.035	173.851	86.351	42.672
14	571.906	189.749	94.255	46.580	627.404	207.798	102.966	50.660
15	676.863	224.242	111.154	54.717	748.580	247.510	122.346	59.925
16	798.693	264.207	130.683	64.075	890.631	293.968	144.951	70.673
17	940.108	310.513	153.252	74.836	1057.153	348.318	171.317	83.141
18	1104.255	364.166	179.332	87.212	1252.363	411.899	202.070	97.603
19	1294.790	426.330	209.471	101.444	1481.201	486.280	237.941	114.380
20	1515.955	498.357	244.301	117.810	1749.461	573.295	279.781	133.841
21	1772.673	581.811	284.551	136.632	2063.934	675.090	328.583	156.415
22	2070.659	678.505	331.065	158.276	2432.583	794.176	385.506	182.601
23	2416.548	790.539	384.817	183.168	2864.738	933.490	451.900	212.978
24	2818.040	920.348	446.935	211.793	3371.342	1096.468	529.343	248.214
25	3284.074	1070.751	518.720	244.712	3965.218	1287.129	619.672	289.088
26	3825.025	1245.015	601.676	282.569	4661.402	1510.175	725.032	336.502
27	4452.936	1446.927	697.543	326.104	5477.518	1771.107	847.923	391.503
28	5181.786	1680.871	808.328	376.170	6434.227	2076.361	991.264	455.303
29	6027.803	1951.932	936.355	433.745	7555.748	2433.465	1158.457	529.312
30	7009.821	2265.996	1084.306	499.957	8870.476	2851.227	1353.470	615.162
31	8149.702	2629.886	1255.281	576.100	10411.692	3339.948	1580.934	714.747
32	9472.825	3051.508	1452.865	663.666	12218.415	3911.683	1846.248	830.267
33	11008.645	3540.020	1681.198	764.365	14336.384	4580.532	2155.710	964.270
34	12791.356	4106.035	1945.065	880.170	16819.217	5362.991	2516.667	1119.713
35	14860.645	4761.849	2249.997	1013.346	19729.770	6278.358	2937.686	1300.027
36	17262.582	5521.708	2602.383	1166.498	23141.726	7349.207	3428.764	1509.191
37	20050.641	6402.118	3009.609	1342.622	27141.462	8601.949	4001.557	1751.822
38	23286.893	7422.206	3480.210	1545.165	31830.235	10067.480	4669.662	2033.273
39	27043.388	8604.132	4024.049	1778.090	37326.748	11781.944	5448.940	2359.757
40	31403.755	9973.570	4652.522	2045.954	43770.149	13787.624	6357.890	2738.478
41	36465.072	11560.270	5378.801	2353.997	51323.561	16133.986	7418.090	3177.795
42	42340.018	13398.701	6218.108	2708.246	60178.204	18878.899	8654.706	3687.402
43	49159.389	15528.800	7188.032	3115.633	70558.244	22090.057	10097.096	4278.546
44	57075.004	17996.840	8308.900	3584.128	82726.461	25846.659	11779.499	4964.274
45	66263.089	20856.435	9604.203	4122.898	96990.907	30241.352	13741.854	5759.718
46	76928.202	24169.707	11101.088	4742.482	113712.701	35382.520	16030.745	6682.433
47	89307.779	28008.630	12830.925	5455.005	133315.171	41396.961	18700.507	7752.782
48	103677.429	32456.600	14829.968	6274.405	156294.575	48433.005	21814.518	8994.387
49	120357.065	37610.243	17140.113	7216.716	183232.658	56664.182	25446.700	10434.649
50	139718.028	43581.513	19809.773	8300.374	214811.387	66293.495	29683.277	12105.353

The future value of $1 invested at the *beginning* of each period

End of Year	17% Interest compounded and Deposits made				18% Interest compounded and Deposits made			
	Monthly	Quarterly	Semi-Annually	Annually	Monthly	Quarterly	Semi-Annually	Annually
1	13.164	4.443	2.262	1.170	13.237	4.471	2.278	1.180
2	28.750	9.692	4.925	2.539	29.063	9.802	4.985	2.572
3	47.201	15.891	8.060	4.141	47.985	16.160	8.200	4.215
4	69.046	23.213	11.751	6.014	70.609	23.742	12.021	6.154
5	94.907	31.861	16.096	8.207	97.658	32.783	16.560	8.442
6	125.524	42.076	21.211	10.772	129.998	43.565	21.953	11.142
7	161.771	54.142	27.232	13.773	168.665	56.423	28.361	14.327
8	204.684	68.393	34.321	17.285	214.896	71.756	35.974	18.086
9	255.488	85.226	42.665	21.393	270.170	90.041	45.018	22.521
10	315.635	105.108	52.489	26.200	336.258	111.847	55.765	27.755
11	386.842	128.591	64.054	31.824	415.272	137.850	68.532	33.931
12	471.144	156.329	77.668	38.404	509.744	168.859	83.701	41.219
13	570.948	189.091	93.695	46.103	622.696	205.839	101.723	49.818
14	689.105	227.788	112.562	55.110	757.744	249.937	123.135	59.965
15	828.990	273.494	134.773	65.649	919.209	302.525	148.575	71.939
16	994.599	327.481	160.920	77.979	1112.260	365.238	178.800	86.068
17	1190.662	391.247	191.702	92.406	1343.075	440.024	214.711	102.740
18	1422.779	466.564	227.938	109.285	1619.041	529.207	257.376	122.414
19	1697.581	555.524	270.597	129.033	1948.992	635.560	308.066	145.628
20	2022.917	660.599	320.816	152.139	2343.487	762.388	368.292	173.021
21	2408.079	784.709	379.934	179.172	2815.153	913.632	439.846	205.345
22	2864.069	931.301	449.530	210.801	3379.085	1093.994	524.859	243.487
23	3403.912	1104.447	531.461	247.808	4053.332	1309.079	625.863	288.494
24	4043.028	1308.959	627.911	291.105	4859.474	1565.572	745.866	341.603
25	4799.672	1550.518	741.455	341.763	5823.312	1871.444	888.441	404.272
26	5695.456	1835.834	875.121	401.032	6975.695	2236.203	1057.835	478.221
27	6755.968	2172.835	1032.477	470.378	8353.504	2671.184	1259.092	565.481
28	8011.499	2570.882	1217.720	551.512	10000.838	3189.908	1498.205	668.447
29	9497.912	3041.035	1435.792	646.439	11970.421	3808.495	1782.296	789.948
30	11257.664	3596.356	1692.513	757.504	14325.289	4546.172	2119.823	933.319
31	13341.020	4252.271	1994.731	887.449	17140.813	5425.865	2520.840	1102.496
32	15807.487	5027.005	2350.509	1039.486	20507.104	6474.916	2997.288	1302.125
33	18727.518	5942.079	2769.340	1217.368	24531.903	7725.929	3563.357	1537.688
34	22184.518	7022.917	3262.399	1425.491	29344.026	9217.784	4235.902	1815.652
35	26277.232	8299.547	3842.840	1668.994	35097.488	10996.850	5034.953	2143.649
36	31122.562	9807.435	4526.149	1953.894	41976.431	13118.419	5984.306	2530.686
37	36858.908	11588.474	5330.558	2287.225	50201.020	15648.429	7112.232	2987.389
38	43650.121	13692.144	6277.529	2677.224	60034.489	18665.514	8452.321	3526.299
39	51690.182	16176.890	7392.326	3133.522	71791.563	22263.443	10044.481	4162.213
40	61208.743	19111.742	8704.693	3667.391	85848.534	26554.040	11936.126	4912.591
41	72477.689	22578.236	10249.645	4292.017	102655.304	31670.658	14183.589	5798.038
42	85818.901	26672.677	12068.400	5022.830	122749.784	37772.319	16853.800	6842.865
43	101613.452	31508.818	14209.485	5877.881	146775.109	45048.664	20026.278	8075.760
44	120312.489	37221.016	16730.023	6878.291	175500.224	53725.840	23795.499	9530.577
45	142450.125	43967.965	19697.264	8048.770	209844.493	64073.535	28273.711	11247.261
46	168658.690	51937.110	23190.373	9418.231	250907.126	76413.353	33594.274	13272.948
47	199686.792	61349.848	27302.550	11020.500	300002.356	91128.815	39915.635	15663.259
48	236420.706	72467.683	32143.506	12895.155	358701.506	108677.278	47426.044	18483.825
49	279909.682	85599.489	37842.401	15088.502	428883.275	129604.146	56349.161	21812.094
50	331395.922	101110.094	44551.283	17654.717	512793.874	154559.826	66950.716	25739.451

The future value of $1
invested at the *beginning* of each period

End of Year	19% Interest compounded and Deposits made				20% Interest compounded and Deposits made			
	Monthly	Quarterly	Semi-Annually	Annually	Monthly	Quarterly	Semi-Annually	Annually
1	13.310	4.498	2.294	1.190	13.383	4.526	2.310	1.200
2	29.380	9.914	5.045	2.606	29.702	10.027	5.105	2.640
3	48.785	16.434	8.343	4.291	49.601	16.713	8.487	4.368
4	72.215	24.284	12.297	6.297	73.866	24.840	12.579	6.442
5	100.506	33.735	17.039	8.683	103.454	34.719	17.531	8.930
6	134.665	45.115	22.724	11.523	139.534	46.727	23.523	11.916
7	175.911	58.815	29.540	14.902	183.529	61.323	30.772	15.499
8	225.714	75.309	37.714	18.923	237.177	79.064	39.545	19.799
9	285.848	95.168	47.513	23.709	302.594	100.628	50.159	24.959
10	358.457	119.078	59.264	29.404	382.364	126.840	63.002	31.150
11	446.129	147.865	73.353	36.180	479.634	158.700	78.543	38.581
12	551.989	182.523	90.246	44.244	598.244	197.427	97.347	47.497
13	679.809	224.251	110.501	53.841	742.876	244.499	120.100	58.196
14	834.146	274.489	134.788	65.261	919.239	301.716	147.631	71.035
15	1020.500	334.975	163.908	78.850	1134.295	371.263	180.943	86.442
16	1245.514	407.799	198.824	95.022	1396.532	455.798	221.252	104.931
17	1517.206	495.476	240.688	114.266	1716.301	558.551	270.024	127.117
18	1845.262	601.037	290.886	137.166	2106.226	683.448	329.039	153.740
19	2241.373	728.130	351.073	164.418	2581.696	835.261	400.448	185.688
20	2719.657	881.145	423.239	196.847	3161.479	1019.790	486.852	224.026
21	3297.163	1065.372	509.769	235.438	3868.463	1244.087	591.401	270.031
22	3994.472	1287.175	613.519	281.362	4730.552	1516.721	717.905	325.237
23	4836.439	1554.220	737.919	336.010	5781.775	1848.110	870.975	391.484
24	5853.072	1875.734	887.077	401.042	7063.628	2250.915	1056.190	470.981
25	7080.608	2262.828	1065.922	478.431	8626.708	2740.526	1280.299	566.377
26	8562.796	2728.878	1280.361	570.522	10532.714	3335.653	1551.472	680.853
27	10352.467	3289.989	1537.479	680.112	12856.880	4059.032	1879.591	818.223
28	12513.406	3965.551	1845.770	810.523	15690.948	4938.305	2276.616	983.068
29	15122.634	4778.907	2215.418	965.712	19146.785	6007.066	2757.015	1180.882
30	18273.149	5758.165	2658.636	1150.387	23360.802	7306.152	3338.298	1418.258
31	22077.241	6937.164	3190.065	1370.151	28499.336	8885.199	4041.651	1703.109
32	26670.497	8356.644	3827.262	1631.670	34765.219	10804.540	4892.707	2044.931
33	32216.628	10065.658	4591.277	1942.877	42405.781	13137.512	5922.486	2455.118
34	38913.309	12123.261	5507.349	2313.214	51722.615	15973.253	7168.518	2947.341
35	46999.223	14600.556	6605.744	2753.914	63083.478	19420.115	8676.217	3538.009
36	56762.569	17583.148	7922.746	3278.348	76936.814	23609.797	10500.532	4246.811
37	68551.330	21174.103	9501.864	3902.424	93829.448	28702.381	12707.954	5097.373
38	82785.681	25497.510	11395.267	4645.075	114428.175	34892.449	15378.934	6118.048
39	99972.963	30702.768	13665.504	5528.829	139546.079	42416.515	18610.820	7342.858
40	120725.763	36969.749	16387.575	6580.496	170174.628	51562.065	22521.402	8812.629
41	145783.753	44515.014	19651.406	7831.981	207522.807	62678.538	27253.207	10576.355
42	176040.048	53599.297	23564.821	9321.247	253064.843	76190.681	32978.690	12692.826
43	212573.041	64536.512	28257.104	11093.474	308598.396	92614.774	39906.525	15232.592
44	256684.840	77704.605	33883.268	13202.424	376315.516	112578.362	48289.206	18280.310
45	309947.676	93558.610	40629.179	15712.075	458889.169	136844.229	58432.249	21937.572
46	374259.941	112646.378	48717.696	18698.559	559578.744	166339.541	70705.331	26326.286
47	451913.849	135627.501	58416.029	22252.475	682358.714	202191.277	85555.760	31592.744
48	545677.138	163296.114	70044.573	26481.636	832075.516	245769.287	103524.780	37912.492
49	658891.714	196608.329	83987.489	31514.336	1014638.849	298738.630	125267.294	45496.191
50	795592.767	236715.280	100705.393	37503.250	1237254.950	363123.197	151575.736	54596.629

Applications
Chapter Nine
• Periodic payments at the beginning of each period required to attain a certain savings level by the end of a given time period.

How much must be invested at the *beginning* of each period to accumulate $1

End of Year	At 5% Interest compounded and Deposits made				At 6% Interest compounded and Deposits made			
	Monthly	Quarterly	Semi-Annually	Annually	Monthly	Quarterly	Semi-Annually	Annually
1	0.0811	0.2423	0.4818	0.9524	0.0807	0.2408	0.4783	0.9434
2	0.0395	0.1182	0.2349	0.4646	0.0391	0.1168	0.2321	0.4580
3	0.0257	0.0768	0.1527	0.3021	0.0253	0.0755	0.1501	0.2963
4	0.0188	0.0561	0.1117	0.2210	0.0184	0.0549	0.1092	0.2157
5	0.0146	0.0438	0.0871	0.1724	0.0143	0.0426	0.0847	0.1674
6	0.0119	0.0355	0.0707	0.1400	0.0115	0.0344	0.0684	0.1352
7	0.0099	0.0297	0.0591	0.1170	0.0096	0.0286	0.0568	0.1124
8	0.0085	0.0253	0.0503	0.0997	0.0081	0.0242	0.0482	0.0953
9	0.0073	0.0219	0.0436	0.0864	0.0070	0.0208	0.0415	0.0821
10	0.0064	0.0192	0.0382	0.0757	0.0061	0.0182	0.0361	0.0716
11	0.0057	0.0170	0.0338	0.0670	0.0053	0.0160	0.0318	0.0630
12	0.0051	0.0151	0.0302	0.0598	0.0047	0.0142	0.0282	0.0559
13	0.0045	0.0136	0.0271	0.0538	0.0042	0.0126	0.0252	0.0500
14	0.0041	0.0123	0.0245	0.0486	0.0038	0.0114	0.0226	0.0449
15	0.0037	0.0112	0.0222	0.0441	0.0034	0.0102	0.0204	0.0405
16	0.0034	0.0102	0.0203	0.0403	0.0031	0.0093	0.0185	0.0367
17	0.0031	0.0093	0.0185	0.0369	0.0028	0.0084	0.0168	0.0334
18	0.0029	0.0085	0.0170	0.0339	0.0026	0.0077	0.0153	0.0305
19	0.0026	0.0079	0.0157	0.0312	0.0023	0.0070	0.0140	0.0279
20	0.0024	0.0073	0.0145	0.0288	0.0022	0.0065	0.0129	0.0256
21	0.0022	0.0067	0.0134	0.0267	0.0020	0.0059	0.0118	0.0236
22	0.0021	0.0062	0.0124	0.0247	0.0018	0.0055	0.0109	0.0217
23	0.0019	0.0058	0.0115	0.0230	0.0017	0.0050	0.0101	0.0201
24	0.0018	0.0054	0.0107	0.0214	0.0016	0.0047	0.0093	0.0186
25	0.0017	0.0050	0.0100	0.0200	0.0014	0.0043	0.0086	0.0172
26	0.0016	0.0047	0.0093	0.0186	0.0013	0.0040	0.0080	0.0159
27	0.0015	0.0044	0.0087	0.0174	0.0012	0.0037	0.0074	0.0148
28	0.0014	0.0041	0.0082	0.0163	0.0011	0.0034	0.0069	0.0138
29	0.0013	0.0038	0.0077	0.0153	0.0011	0.0032	0.0064	0.0128
30	0.0012	0.0036	0.0072	0.0143	0.0010	0.0030	0.0060	0.0119
31	0.0011	0.0034	0.0067	0.0135	0.0009	0.0028	0.0055	0.0111
32	0.0011	0.0032	0.0063	0.0126	0.0009	0.0026	0.0052	0.0104
33	0.0010	0.0030	0.0059	0.0119	0.0008	0.0024	0.0048	0.0097
34	0.0009	0.0028	0.0056	0.0112	0.0007	0.0022	0.0045	0.0091
35	0.0009	0.0026	0.0053	0.0105	0.0007	0.0021	0.0042	0.0085
36	0.0008	0.0025	0.0050	0.0099	0.0007	0.0020	0.0039	0.0079
37	0.0008	0.0023	0.0047	0.0094	0.0006	0.0018	0.0037	0.0074
38	0.0007	0.0022	0.0044	0.0088	0.0006	0.0017	0.0034	0.0069
39	0.0007	0.0021	0.0042	0.0083	0.0005	0.0016	0.0032	0.0065
40	0.0007	0.0020	0.0039	0.0079	0.0005	0.0015	0.0030	0.0061
41	0.0006	0.0019	0.0037	0.0074	0.0005	0.0014	0.0028	0.0057
42	0.0006	0.0017	0.0035	0.0070	0.0004	0.0013	0.0027	0.0054
43	0.0005	0.0017	0.0033	0.0067	0.0004	0.0012	0.0025	0.0050
44	0.0005	0.0016	0.0031	0.0063	0.0004	0.0012	0.0023	0.0047
45	0.0005	0.0015	0.0030	0.0060	0.0004	0.0011	0.0022	0.0044
46	0.0005	0.0014	0.0028	0.0056	0.0003	0.0010	0.0021	0.0042
47	0.0004	0.0013	0.0027	0.0053	0.0003	0.0010	0.0019	0.0039
48	0.0004	0.0013	0.0025	0.0051	0.0003	0.0009	0.0018	0.0037
49	0.0004	0.0012	0.0024	0.0048	0.0003	0.0008	0.0017	0.0035
50	0.0004	0.0011	0.0023	0.0045	0.0003	0.0008	0.0016	0.0032

How much must be invested at the *beginning* of each period to accumulate $1

End of Year	At 7% Interest compounded and Deposits made				At 8% Interest compounded and Deposits made			
	Monthly	Quarterly	Semi-Annually	Annually	Monthly	Quarterly	Semi-Annually	Annually
1	0.0802	0.2393	0.4748	0.9346	0.0798	0.2379	0.4713	0.9259
2	0.0387	0.1155	0.2292	0.4515	0.0383	0.1142	0.2264	0.4452
3	0.0249	0.0743	0.1475	0.2907	0.0245	0.0731	0.1450	0.2852
4	0.0180	0.0538	0.1067	0.2105	0.0176	0.0526	0.1044	0.2055
5	0.0139	0.0415	0.0824	0.1625	0.0135	0.0403	0.0801	0.1578
6	0.0112	0.0333	0.0662	0.1307	0.0108	0.0322	0.0640	0.1262
7	0.0092	0.0275	0.0547	0.1080	0.0089	0.0265	0.0526	0.1038
8	0.0078	0.0232	0.0461	0.0911	0.0074	0.0222	0.0441	0.0871
9	0.0066	0.0198	0.0394	0.0780	0.0063	0.0189	0.0375	0.0741
10	0.0057	0.0172	0.0342	0.0676	0.0054	0.0162	0.0323	0.0639
11	0.0050	0.0150	0.0299	0.0592	0.0047	0.0141	0.0281	0.0556
12	0.0044	0.0132	0.0264	0.0522	0.0041	0.0124	0.0246	0.0488
13	0.0039	0.0117	0.0234	0.0464	0.0036	0.0109	0.0217	0.0431
14	0.0035	0.0105	0.0209	0.0414	0.0032	0.0097	0.0192	0.0382
15	0.0031	0.0094	0.0187	0.0372	0.0029	0.0086	0.0171	0.0341
16	0.0028	0.0085	0.0169	0.0335	0.0026	0.0077	0.0153	0.0305
17	0.0025	0.0076	0.0152	0.0303	0.0023	0.0069	0.0138	0.0274
18	0.0023	0.0069	0.0138	0.0275	0.0021	0.0062	0.0124	0.0247
19	0.0021	0.0063	0.0125	0.0250	0.0019	0.0056	0.0112	0.0223
20	0.0019	0.0057	0.0114	0.0228	0.0017	0.0051	0.0101	0.0202
21	0.0017	0.0052	0.0104	0.0208	0.0015	0.0046	0.0092	0.0184
22	0.0016	0.0048	0.0095	0.0191	0.0014	0.0042	0.0083	0.0167
23	0.0015	0.0044	0.0087	0.0175	0.0013	0.0038	0.0076	0.0152
24	0.0013	0.0040	0.0080	0.0161	0.0011	0.0034	0.0069	0.0139
25	0.0012	0.0037	0.0074	0.0148	0.0010	0.0031	0.0063	0.0127
26	0.0011	0.0034	0.0068	0.0136	0.0010	0.0029	0.0058	0.0116
27	0.0010	0.0031	0.0063	0.0125	0.0009	0.0026	0.0053	0.0106
28	0.0010	0.0029	0.0058	0.0116	0.0008	0.0024	0.0048	0.0097
29	0.0009	0.0027	0.0053	0.0107	0.0007	0.0022	0.0044	0.0089
30	0.0008	0.0025	0.0049	0.0099	0.0007	0.0020	0.0040	0.0082
31	0.0008	0.0023	0.0045	0.0092	0.0006	0.0018	0.0037	0.0075
32	0.0007	0.0021	0.0042	0.0085	0.0006	0.0017	0.0034	0.0069
33	0.0006	0.0019	0.0039	0.0079	0.0005	0.0015	0.0031	0.0063
34	0.0006	0.0018	0.0036	0.0073	0.0005	0.0014	0.0029	0.0058
35	0.0006	0.0017	0.0033	0.0068	0.0004	0.0013	0.0026	0.0054
36	0.0005	0.0015	0.0031	0.0063	0.0004	0.0012	0.0024	0.0049
37	0.0005	0.0014	0.0029	0.0058	0.0004	0.0011	0.0022	0.0046
38	0.0004	0.0013	0.0027	0.0054	0.0003	0.0010	0.0021	0.0042
39	0.0004	0.0012	0.0025	0.0050	0.0003	0.0009	0.0019	0.0039
40	0.0004	0.0011	0.0023	0.0047	0.0003	0.0009	0.0017	0.0036
41	0.0004	0.0011	0.0021	0.0044	0.0003	0.0008	0.0016	0.0033
42	0.0003	0.0010	0.0020	0.0041	0.0002	0.0007	0.0015	0.0030
43	0.0003	0.0009	0.0019	0.0038	0.0002	0.0007	0.0014	0.0028
44	0.0003	0.0009	0.0017	0.0035	0.0002	0.0006	0.0013	0.0026
45	0.0003	0.0008	0.0016	0.0033	0.0002	0.0006	0.0012	0.0024
46	0.0002	0.0007	0.0015	0.0030	0.0002	0.0005	0.0011	0.0022
47	0.0002	0.0007	0.0014	0.0028	0.0002	0.0005	0.0010	0.0020
48	0.0002	0.0006	0.0013	0.0026	0.0001	0.0004	0.0009	0.0019
49	0.0002	0.0006	0.0012	0.0025	0.0001	0.0004	0.0008	0.0017
50	0.0002	0.0006	0.0011	0.0023	0.0001	0.0004	0.0008	0.0016

How much must be invested at the *beginning* of each period to accumulate $1

End of Year	At 11% Interest compounded and Deposits made				At 12% Interest compounded and Deposits made			
	Monthly	Quarterly	Semi-Annually	Annually	Monthly	Quarterly	Semi-Annually	Annually
1	0.0785	0.2335	0.4612	0.9009	0.0781	0.2321	0.4580	0.8929
2	0.0371	0.1104	0.2183	0.4270	0.0367	0.1092	0.2157	0.4212
3	0.0234	0.0696	0.1376	0.2696	0.0230	0.0684	0.1352	0.2646
4	0.0165	0.0492	0.0975	0.1913	0.0162	0.0482	0.0953	0.1868
5	0.0125	0.0372	0.0736	0.1447	0.0121	0.0361	0.0716	0.1405
6	0.0098	0.0292	0.0578	0.1139	0.0095	0.0282	0.0559	0.1100
7	0.0079	0.0235	0.0467	0.0921	0.0076	0.0226	0.0449	0.0885
8	0.0065	0.0194	0.0385	0.0760	0.0062	0.0185	0.0367	0.0726
9	0.0054	0.0162	0.0322	0.0636	0.0051	0.0153	0.0305	0.0604
10	0.0046	0.0137	0.0272	0.0539	0.0043	0.0129	0.0256	0.0509
11	0.0039	0.0116	0.0232	0.0461	0.0036	0.0109	0.0217	0.0432
12	0.0033	0.0100	0.0199	0.0397	0.0031	0.0093	0.0186	0.0370
13	0.0029	0.0086	0.0172	0.0344	0.0027	0.0080	0.0159	0.0319
14	0.0025	0.0075	0.0150	0.0299	0.0023	0.0069	0.0138	0.0276
15	0.0022	0.0065	0.0131	0.0262	0.0020	0.0060	0.0119	0.0240
16	0.0019	0.0057	0.0115	0.0230	0.0017	0.0052	0.0104	0.0209
17	0.0017	0.0050	0.0101	0.0202	0.0015	0.0045	0.0091	0.0183
18	0.0015	0.0044	0.0089	0.0179	0.0013	0.0039	0.0079	0.0160
19	0.0013	0.0039	0.0078	0.0158	0.0011	0.0034	0.0069	0.0141
20	0.0011	0.0034	0.0069	0.0140	0.0010	0.0030	0.0061	0.0124
21	0.0010	0.0031	0.0062	0.0125	0.0009	0.0027	0.0054	0.0109
22	0.0009	0.0027	0.0055	0.0111	0.0008	0.0023	0.0047	0.0097
23	0.0008	0.0024	0.0049	0.0099	0.0007	0.0021	0.0042	0.0085
24	0.0007	0.0021	0.0043	0.0088	0.0006	0.0018	0.0037	0.0076
25	0.0006	0.0019	0.0038	0.0079	0.0005	0.0016	0.0032	0.0067
26	0.0006	0.0017	0.0034	0.0070	0.0005	0.0014	0.0029	0.0059
27	0.0005	0.0015	0.0031	0.0063	0.0004	0.0012	0.0025	0.0053
28	0.0004	0.0013	0.0027	0.0056	0.0004	0.0011	0.0023	0.0047
29	0.0004	0.0012	0.0024	0.0050	0.0003	0.0010	0.0020	0.0042
30	0.0004	0.0011	0.0022	0.0045	0.0003	0.0009	0.0018	0.0037
31	0.0003	0.0010	0.0020	0.0041	0.0003	0.0008	0.0016	0.0033
32	0.0003	0.0009	0.0018	0.0036	0.0002	0.0007	0.0014	0.0029
33	0.0003	0.0008	0.0016	0.0033	0.0002	0.0006	0.0012	0.0026
34	0.0002	0.0007	0.0014	0.0029	0.0002	0.0005	0.0011	0.0023
35	0.0002	0.0006	0.0013	0.0026	0.0002	0.0005	0.0010	0.0021
36	0.0002	0.0005	0.0011	0.0024	0.0001	0.0004	0.0009	0.0018
37	0.0002	0.0005	0.0010	0.0021	0.0001	0.0004	0.0008	0.0016
38	0.0001	0.0004	0.0009	0.0019	0.0001	0.0003	0.0007	0.0015
39	0.0001	0.0004	0.0008	0.0017	0.0001	0.0003	0.0006	0.0013
40	0.0001	0.0004	0.0007	0.0015	0.0001	0.0003	0.0005	0.0012
41	0.0001	0.0003	0.0007	0.0014	0.0001	0.0002	0.0005	0.0010
42	0.0001	0.0003	0.0006	0.0013	0.0001	0.0002	0.0004	0.0009
43	0.0001	0.0003	0.0005	0.0011	0.0001	0.0002	0.0004	0.0008
44	0.0001	0.0002	0.0005	0.0010	0.0001	0.0002	0.0003	0.0007
45	0.0001	0.0002	0.0004	0.0009	0.0000	0.0001	0.0003	0.0007
46	0.0001	0.0002	0.0004	0.0008	0.0000	0.0001	0.0003	0.0006
47	0.0001	0.0002	0.0003	0.0007	0.0000	0.0001	0.0002	0.0005
48	0.0000	0.0001	0.0003	0.0007	0.0000	0.0001	0.0002	0.0005
49	0.0000	0.0001	0.0003	0.0006	0.0000	0.0001	0.0002	0.0004
50	0.0000	0.0001	0.0002	0.0005	0.0000	0.0001	0.0002	0.0004

How much must be invested at the *beginning* of each period to accumulate $1

End of Year	At 15% Interest compounded and Deposits made				At 16% Interest compounded and Deposits made			
	Monthly	Quarterly	Semi-Annually	Annually	Monthly	Quarterly	Semi-Annually	Annually
1	0.0768	0.2278	0.4483	0.8696	0.0764	0.2264	0.4452	0.8621
2	0.0355	0.1055	0.2080	0.4044	0.0352	0.1044	0.2055	0.3991
3	0.0219	0.0651	0.1284	0.2504	0.0215	0.0640	0.1262	0.2459
4	0.0151	0.0451	0.0890	0.1741	0.0148	0.0441	0.0871	0.1702
5	0.0112	0.0332	0.0658	0.1290	0.0108	0.0323	0.0639	0.1254
6	0.0085	0.0255	0.0505	0.0993	0.0082	0.0246	0.0488	0.0960
7	0.0067	0.0200	0.0398	0.0786	0.0064	0.0192	0.0382	0.0755
8	0.0054	0.0161	0.0320	0.0633	0.0051	0.0153	0.0305	0.0605
9	0.0044	0.0131	0.0261	0.0518	0.0041	0.0124	0.0247	0.0492
10	0.0036	0.0108	0.0215	0.0428	0.0034	0.0101	0.0202	0.0404
11	0.0030	0.0089	0.0178	0.0357	0.0028	0.0083	0.0167	0.0335
12	0.0025	0.0074	0.0149	0.0300	0.0023	0.0069	0.0139	0.0279
13	0.0021	0.0063	0.0126	0.0253	0.0019	0.0058	0.0116	0.0234
14	0.0017	0.0053	0.0106	0.0215	0.0016	0.0048	0.0097	0.0197
15	0.0015	0.0045	0.0090	0.0183	0.0013	0.0040	0.0082	0.0167
16	0.0013	0.0038	0.0077	0.0156	0.0011	0.0034	0.0069	0.0141
17	0.0011	0.0032	0.0065	0.0134	0.0009	0.0029	0.0058	0.0120
18	0.0009	0.0027	0.0056	0.0115	0.0008	0.0024	0.0049	0.0102
19	0.0008	0.0023	0.0048	0.0099	0.0007	0.0021	0.0042	0.0087
20	0.0007	0.0020	0.0041	0.0085	0.0006	0.0017	0.0036	0.0075
21	0.0006	0.0017	0.0035	0.0073	0.0005	0.0015	0.0030	0.0064
22	0.0005	0.0015	0.0030	0.0063	0.0004	0.0013	0.0026	0.0055
23	0.0004	0.0013	0.0026	0.0055	0.0003	0.0011	0.0022	0.0047
24	0.0004	0.0011	0.0022	0.0047	0.0003	0.0009	0.0019	0.0040
25	0.0003	0.0009	0.0019	0.0041	0.0003	0.0008	0.0016	0.0035
26	0.0003	0.0008	0.0017	0.0035	0.0002	0.0007	0.0014	0.0030
27	0.0002	0.0007	0.0014	0.0031	0.0002	0.0006	0.0012	0.0026
28	0.0002	0.0006	0.0012	0.0027	0.0002	0.0005	0.0010	0.0022
29	0.0002	0.0005	0.0011	0.0023	0.0001	0.0004	0.0009	0.0019
30	0.0001	0.0004	0.0009	0.0020	0.0001	0.0004	0.0007	0.0016
31	0.0001	0.0004	0.0008	0.0017	0.0001	0.0003	0.0006	0.0014
32	0.0001	0.0003	0.0007	0.0015	0.0001	0.0003	0.0005	0.0012
33	0.0001	0.0003	0.0006	0.0013	0.0001	0.0002	0.0005	0.0010
34	0.0001	0.0002	0.0005	0.0011	0.0001	0.0002	0.0004	0.0009
35	0.0001	0.0002	0.0004	0.0010	0.0001	0.0002	0.0003	0.0008
36	0.0001	0.0002	0.0004	0.0009	0.0000	0.0001	0.0003	0.0007
37	0.0000	0.0002	0.0003	0.0007	0.0000	0.0001	0.0002	0.0006
38	0.0000	0.0001	0.0003	0.0006	0.0000	0.0001	0.0002	0.0005
39	0.0000	0.0001	0.0002	0.0006	0.0000	0.0001	0.0002	0.0004
40	0.0000	0.0001	0.0002	0.0005	0.0000	0.0001	0.0002	0.0004
41	0.0000	0.0001	0.0002	0.0004	0.0000	0.0001	0.0001	0.0003
42	0.0000	0.0001	0.0002	0.0004	0.0000	0.0001	0.0001	0.0003
43	0.0000	0.0001	0.0001	0.0003	0.0000	0.0000	0.0001	0.0002
44	0.0000	0.0001	0.0001	0.0003	0.0000	0.0000	0.0001	0.0002
45	0.0000	0.0000	0.0001	0.0002	0.0000	0.0000	0.0001	0.0002
46	0.0000	0.0000	0.0001	0.0002	0.0000	0.0000	0.0001	0.0001
47	0.0000	0.0000	0.0001	0.0002	0.0000	0.0000	0.0001	0.0001
48	0.0000	0.0000	0.0001	0.0002	0.0000	0.0000	0.0000	0.0001
49	0.0000	0.0000	0.0001	0.0001	0.0000	0.0000	0.0000	0.0001
50	0.0000	0.0000	0.0001	0.0001	0.0000	0.0000	0.0000	0.0001

How much must be invested at the *beginning* of each period to accumulate $1

End of Year	At 19% Interest compounded and Deposits made				At 20% Interest compounded and Deposits made			
	Monthly	Quarterly	Semi-Annually	Annually	Monthly	Quarterly	Semi-Annually	Annually
1	0.0751	0.2223	0.4359	0.8403	0.0747	0.2210	0.4329	0.8333
2	0.0340	0.1009	0.1982	0.3837	0.0337	0.0997	0.1959	0.3788
3	0.0205	0.0608	0.1199	0.2330	0.0202	0.0598	0.1178	0.2289
4	0.0138	0.0412	0.0813	0.1588	0.0135	0.0403	0.0795	0.1552
5	0.0099	0.0296	0.0587	0.1152	0.0097	0.0288	0.0570	0.1120
6	0.0074	0.0222	0.0440	0.0868	0.0072	0.0214	0.0425	0.0839
7	0.0057	0.0170	0.0339	0.0671	0.0054	0.0163	0.0325	0.0645
8	0.0044	0.0133	0.0265	0.0528	0.0042	0.0126	0.0253	0.0505
9	0.0035	0.0105	0.0210	0.0422	0.0033	0.0099	0.0199	0.0401
10	0.0028	0.0084	0.0169	0.0340	0.0026	0.0079	0.0159	0.0321
11	0.0022	0.0068	0.0136	0.0276	0.0021	0.0063	0.0127	0.0259
12	0.0018	0.0055	0.0111	0.0226	0.0017	0.0051	0.0103	0.0211
13	0.0015	0.0045	0.0090	0.0186	0.0013	0.0041	0.0083	0.0172
14	0.0012	0.0036	0.0074	0.0153	0.0011	0.0033	0.0068	0.0141
15	0.0010	0.0030	0.0061	0.0127	0.0009	0.0027	0.0055	0.0116
16	0.0008	0.0025	0.0050	0.0105	0.0007	0.0022	0.0045	0.0095
17	0.0007	0.0020	0.0042	0.0088	0.0006	0.0018	0.0037	0.0079
18	0.0005	0.0017	0.0034	0.0073	0.0005	0.0015	0.0030	0.0065
19	0.0004	0.0014	0.0028	0.0061	0.0004	0.0012	0.0025	0.0054
20	0.0004	0.0011	0.0024	0.0051	0.0003	0.0010	0.0021	0.0045
21	0.0003	0.0009	0.0020	0.0042	0.0003	0.0008	0.0017	0.0037
22	0.0003	0.0008	0.0016	0.0036	0.0002	0.0007	0.0014	0.0031
23	0.0002	0.0006	0.0014	0.0030	0.0002	0.0005	0.0011	0.0026
24	0.0002	0.0005	0.0011	0.0025	0.0001	0.0004	0.0009	0.0021
25	0.0001	0.0004	0.0009	0.0021	0.0001	0.0004	0.0008	0.0018
26	0.0001	0.0004	0.0008	0.0018	0.0001	0.0003	0.0006	0.0015
27	0.0001	0.0003	0.0007	0.0015	0.0001	0.0002	0.0005	0.0012
28	0.0001	0.0003	0.0005	0.0012	0.0001	0.0002	0.0004	0.0010
29	0.0001	0.0002	0.0005	0.0010	0.0001	0.0002	0.0004	0.0008
30	0.0001	0.0002	0.0004	0.0009	0.0000	0.0001	0.0003	0.0007
31	0.0000	0.0001	0.0003	0.0007	0.0000	0.0001	0.0002	0.0006
32	0.0000	0.0001	0.0003	0.0006	0.0000	0.0001	0.0002	0.0005
33	0.0000	0.0001	0.0002	0.0005	0.0000	0.0001	0.0002	0.0004
34	0.0000	0.0001	0.0002	0.0004	0.0000	0.0001	0.0001	0.0003
35	0.0000	0.0001	0.0002	0.0004	0.0000	0.0001	0.0001	0.0003
36	0.0000	0.0001	0.0001	0.0003	0.0000	0.0000	0.0001	0.0002
37	0.0000	0.0000	0.0001	0.0003	0.0000	0.0000	0.0001	0.0002
38	0.0000	0.0000	0.0001	0.0002	0.0000	0.0000	0.0001	0.0002
39	0.0000	0.0000	0.0001	0.0002	0.0000	0.0000	0.0001	0.0001
40	0.0000	0.0000	0.0001	0.0002	0.0000	0.0000	0.0000	0.0001
41	0.0000	0.0000	0.0001	0.0001	0.0000	0.0000	0.0000	0.0001
42	0.0000	0.0000	0.0000	0.0001	0.0000	0.0000	0.0000	0.0001
43	0.0000	0.0000	0.0000	0.0001	0.0000	0.0000	0.0000	0.0001
44	0.0000	0.0000	0.0000	0.0001	0.0000	0.0000	0.0000	0.0001
45	0.0000	0.0000	0.0000	0.0001	0.0000	0.0000	0.0000	0.0000
46	0.0000	0.0000	0.0000	0.0001	0.0000	0.0000	0.0000	0.0000
47	0.0000	0.0000	0.0000	0.0000	0.0000	0.0000	0.0000	0.0000
48	0.0000	0.0000	0.0000	0.0000	0.0000	0.0000	0.0000	0.0000
49	0.0000	0.0000	0.0000	0.0000	0.0000	0.0000	0.0000	0.0000
50	0.0000	0.0000	0.0000	0.0000	0.0000	0.0000	0.0000	0.0000

Applications
Chapters Nine and Seventeen
- What are the instalment (lease) payments necessary to recover the cost of an investment over a specific period of time along with a desired return on investment?

Periodic payments at the *beginning* of each period required to amortize a loan of $1 over time

End of Year	At 9% Interest compounded and Payments made				At 10% Interest compounded and Payments made			
	Monthly	Quarterly	Semi-Annually	Annually	Monthly	Quarterly	Semi-Annually	Annually
1	0.0868	0.2584	0.5110	1.0000	0.0872	0.2593	0.5122	1.0000
2	0.0453	0.1349	0.2667	0.5215	0.0458	0.1361	0.2686	0.5238
3	0.0316	0.0939	0.1855	0.3624	0.0320	0.0951	0.1876	0.3656
4	0.0247	0.0735	0.1451	0.2832	0.0252	0.0747	0.1474	0.2868
5	0.0206	0.0613	0.1209	0.2359	0.0211	0.0626	0.1233	0.2398
6	0.0179	0.0532	0.1049	0.2045	0.0184	0.0545	0.1075	0.2087
7	0.0160	0.0475	0.0936	0.1823	0.0165	0.0489	0.0962	0.1867
8	0.0145	0.0432	0.0852	0.1658	0.0150	0.0447	0.0879	0.1704
9	0.0134	0.0399	0.0787	0.1530	0.0140	0.0414	0.0815	0.1579
10	0.0126	0.0373	0.0736	0.1430	0.0131	0.0389	0.0764	0.1480
11	0.0119	0.0352	0.0694	0.1348	0.0124	0.0368	0.0724	0.1400
12	0.0113	0.0335	0.0660	0.1281	0.0119	0.0351	0.0690	0.1334
13	0.0108	0.0321	0.0632	0.1225	0.0114	0.0337	0.0663	0.1280
14	0.0104	0.0309	0.0608	0.1178	0.0110	0.0326	0.0639	0.1234
15	0.0101	0.0299	0.0587	0.1138	0.0107	0.0316	0.0620	0.1195
16	0.0098	0.0290	0.0570	0.1104	0.0104	0.0307	0.0603	0.1162
17	0.0095	0.0282	0.0555	0.1074	0.0101	0.0300	0.0588	0.1133
18	0.0093	0.0276	0.0542	0.1048	0.0099	0.0294	0.0576	0.1108
19	0.0091	0.0270	0.0530	0.1025	0.0097	0.0288	0.0565	0.1087
20	0.0089	0.0265	0.0520	0.1005	0.0096	0.0283	0.0555	0.1068
21	0.0088	0.0260	0.0511	0.0987	0.0094	0.0279	0.0547	0.1051
22	0.0086	0.0256	0.0503	0.0972	0.0093	0.0275	0.0539	0.1036
23	0.0085	0.0253	0.0496	0.0958	0.0092	0.0272	0.0533	0.1023
24	0.0084	0.0250	0.0490	0.0945	0.0091	0.0269	0.0527	0.1012
25	0.0083	0.0247	0.0484	0.0934	0.0090	0.0266	0.0522	0.1002
26	0.0082	0.0244	0.0479	0.0924	0.0089	0.0264	0.0517	0.0992
27	0.0082	0.0242	0.0475	0.0915	0.0089	0.0262	0.0513	0.0984
28	0.0081	0.0240	0.0471	0.0907	0.0088	0.0260	0.0509	0.0977
29	0.0080	0.0238	0.0467	0.0900	0.0088	0.0259	0.0506	0.0970
30	0.0080	0.0236	0.0464	0.0893	0.0087	0.0257	0.0503	0.0964
31	0.0079	0.0235	0.0461	0.0887	0.0087	0.0256	0.0500	0.0959
32	0.0079	0.0234	0.0458	0.0882	0.0086	0.0255	0.0498	0.0954
33	0.0079	0.0232	0.0456	0.0877	0.0086	0.0254	0.0496	0.0950
34	0.0078	0.0231	0.0453	0.0872	0.0086	0.0253	0.0494	0.0946
35	0.0078	0.0230	0.0451	0.0868	0.0085	0.0252	0.0492	0.0943
36	0.0078	0.0229	0.0450	0.0865	0.0085	0.0251	0.0491	0.0939
37	0.0077	0.0229	0.0448	0.0861	0.0085	0.0250	0.0489	0.0937
38	0.0077	0.0228	0.0446	0.0858	0.0085	0.0250	0.0488	0.0934
39	0.0077	0.0227	0.0445	0.0855	0.0084	0.0249	0.0487	0.0932
40	0.0077	0.0226	0.0444	0.0853	0.0084	0.0249	0.0486	0.0930
41	0.0076	0.0226	0.0443	0.0851	0.0084	0.0248	0.0485	0.0928
42	0.0076	0.0225	0.0442	0.0848	0.0084	0.0248	0.0484	0.0926
43	0.0076	0.0225	0.0441	0.0846	0.0084	0.0247	0.0483	0.0924
44	0.0076	0.0225	0.0440	0.0845	0.0084	0.0247	0.0483	0.0923
45	0.0076	0.0224	0.0439	0.0843	0.0084	0.0247	0.0482	0.0922
46	0.0076	0.0224	0.0438	0.0842	0.0084	0.0247	0.0482	0.0921
47	0.0076	0.0223	0.0438	0.0840	0.0083	0.0246	0.0481	0.0920
48	0.0075	0.0223	0.0437	0.0839	0.0083	0.0246	0.0481	0.0919
49	0.0075	0.0223	0.0436	0.0838	0.0083	0.0246	0.0480	0.0918
50	0.0075	0.0223	0.0436	0.0837	0.0083	0.0246	0.0480	0.0917

Periodic payments at the *beginning* of each period required to amortize a loan of $1 over time

End of Year	At 11% Interest compounded and Payments made				At 12% Interest compounded and Payments made			
	Monthly	Quarterly	Semi-Annually	Annually	Monthly	Quarterly	Semi-Annually	Annually
1	0.0876	0.2603	0.5134	1.0000	0.0880	0.2612	0.5146	1.0000
2	0.0462	0.1372	0.2704	0.5261	0.0466	0.1383	0.2723	0.5283
3	0.0324	0.0963	0.1897	0.3687	0.0329	0.0975	0.1919	0.3717
4	0.0256	0.0760	0.1496	0.2904	0.0261	0.0773	0.1519	0.2940
5	0.0215	0.0639	0.1258	0.2438	0.0220	0.0653	0.1282	0.2477
6	0.0189	0.0559	0.1100	0.2130	0.0194	0.0573	0.1125	0.2172
7	0.0170	0.0503	0.0988	0.1912	0.0175	0.0517	0.1015	0.1956
8	0.0156	0.0461	0.0906	0.1751	0.0161	0.0476	0.0934	0.1797
9	0.0145	0.0429	0.0843	0.1627	0.0150	0.0445	0.0871	0.1676
10	0.0136	0.0404	0.0793	0.1530	0.0142	0.0420	0.0822	0.1580
11	0.0130	0.0384	0.0753	0.1452	0.0135	0.0400	0.0783	0.1504
12	0.0124	0.0368	0.0721	0.1388	0.0130	0.0384	0.0752	0.1441
13	0.0120	0.0354	0.0694	0.1335	0.0126	0.0371	0.0726	0.1390
14	0.0116	0.0343	0.0671	0.1290	0.0122	0.0360	0.0704	0.1347
15	0.0113	0.0333	0.0652	0.1253	0.0119	0.0351	0.0685	0.1311
16	0.0110	0.0325	0.0636	0.1221	0.0116	0.0343	0.0670	0.1280
17	0.0108	0.0318	0.0622	0.1193	0.0114	0.0336	0.0657	0.1254
18	0.0106	0.0312	0.0610	0.1170	0.0112	0.0331	0.0645	0.1232
19	0.0104	0.0307	0.0600	0.1149	0.0110	0.0326	0.0635	0.1212
20	0.0102	0.0302	0.0591	0.1131	0.0109	0.0321	0.0627	0.1195
21	0.0101	0.0298	0.0583	0.1116	0.0108	0.0318	0.0620	0.1181
22	0.0100	0.0295	0.0576	0.1102	0.0107	0.0315	0.0613	0.1168
23	0.0099	0.0292	0.0570	0.1090	0.0106	0.0312	0.0608	0.1157
24	0.0098	0.0289	0.0565	0.1079	0.0105	0.0309	0.0603	0.1147
25	0.0097	0.0287	0.0560	0.1070	0.0104	0.0307	0.0599	0.1138
26	0.0096	0.0285	0.0556	0.1061	0.0104	0.0305	0.0595	0.1131
27	0.0096	0.0283	0.0552	0.1054	0.0103	0.0304	0.0591	0.1124
28	0.0095	0.0281	0.0549	0.1047	0.0103	0.0302	0.0589	0.1118
29	0.0095	0.0280	0.0546	0.1041	0.0102	0.0301	0.0586	0.1113
30	0.0094	0.0278	0.0543	0.1036	0.0102	0.0300	0.0584	0.1108
31	0.0094	0.0277	0.0541	0.1032	0.0102	0.0299	0.0582	0.1104
32	0.0094	0.0276	0.0539	0.1027	0.0101	0.0298	0.0580	0.1101
33	0.0093	0.0275	0.0537	0.1024	0.0101	0.0297	0.0578	0.1098
34	0.0093	0.0274	0.0535	0.1020	0.0101	0.0297	0.0577	0.1095
35	0.0093	0.0274	0.0534	0.1017	0.0101	0.0296	0.0576	0.1092
36	0.0093	0.0273	0.0533	0.1015	0.0100	0.0295	0.0575	0.1090
37	0.0092	0.0273	0.0531	0.1012	0.0100	0.0295	0.0574	0.1088
38	0.0092	0.0272	0.0530	0.1010	0.0100	0.0295	0.0573	0.1086
39	0.0092	0.0272	0.0529	0.1008	0.0100	0.0294	0.0572	0.1084
40	0.0092	0.0271	0.0529	0.1006	0.0100	0.0294	0.0571	0.1083
41	0.0092	0.0271	0.0528	0.1005	0.0100	0.0294	0.0571	0.1082
42	0.0092	0.0270	0.0527	0.1004	0.0100	0.0293	0.0570	0.1081
43	0.0092	0.0270	0.0527	0.1002	0.0100	0.0293	0.0570	0.1080
44	0.0092	0.0270	0.0526	0.1001	0.0100	0.0293	0.0569	0.1079
45	0.0091	0.0270	0.0526	0.1000	0.0099	0.0293	0.0569	0.1078
46	0.0091	0.0269	0.0525	0.0999	0.0099	0.0293	0.0569	0.1077
47	0.0091	0.0269	0.0525	0.0998	0.0099	0.0292	0.0568	0.1077
48	0.0091	0.0269	0.0524	0.0998	0.0099	0.0292	0.0568	0.1076
49	0.0091	0.0269	0.0524	0.0997	0.0099	0.0292	0.0568	0.1076
50	0.0091	0.0269	0.0524	0.0996	0.0099	0.0292	0.0568	0.1075

Periodic payments at the *beginning* of each period required to amortize a loan of $1 over time

End of Year	At 17% Interest compounded and Payments made				At 18% Interest compounded and Payments made			
	Monthly	Quarterly	Semi-Annually	Annually	Monthly	Quarterly	Semi-Annually	Annually
1	0.0899	0.2658	0.5204	1.0000	0.0903	0.2667	0.5215	1.0000
2	0.0488	0.1439	0.2814	0.5392	0.0492	0.1451	0.2832	0.5413
3	0.0352	0.1037	0.2024	0.3868	0.0356	0.1049	0.2045	0.3898
4	0.0285	0.0838	0.1634	0.3116	0.0289	0.0852	0.1658	0.3150
5	0.0245	0.0722	0.1405	0.2671	0.0250	0.0736	0.1430	0.2710
6	0.0219	0.0645	0.1255	0.2381	0.0225	0.0660	0.1281	0.2423
7	0.0202	0.0592	0.1151	0.2179	0.0207	0.0608	0.1178	0.2223
8	0.0189	0.0554	0.1075	0.2032	0.0194	0.0570	0.1104	0.2078
9	0.0179	0.0525	0.1018	0.1920	0.0185	0.0542	0.1048	0.1969
10	0.0171	0.0503	0.0974	0.1835	0.0178	0.0520	0.1005	0.1886
11	0.0166	0.0485	0.0940	0.1767	0.0172	0.0503	0.0972	0.1820
12	0.0161	0.0472	0.0912	0.1713	0.0167	0.0490	0.0945	0.1768
13	0.0157	0.0461	0.0890	0.1670	0.0164	0.0479	0.0924	0.1726
14	0.0154	0.0452	0.0872	0.1634	0.0161	0.0471	0.0907	0.1692
15	0.0152	0.0444	0.0858	0.1605	0.0159	0.0464	0.0893	0.1664
16	0.0150	0.0438	0.0846	0.1581	0.0157	0.0458	0.0882	0.1642
17	0.0148	0.0433	0.0836	0.1561	0.0155	0.0453	0.0872	0.1623
18	0.0147	0.0429	0.0827	0.1544	0.0154	0.0450	0.0865	0.1607
19	0.0146	0.0426	0.0820	0.1530	0.0153	0.0446	0.0858	0.1594
20	0.0145	0.0423	0.0815	0.1519	0.0152	0.0444	0.0853	0.1583
21	0.0144	0.0420	0.0810	0.1509	0.0151	0.0442	0.0848	0.1574
22	0.0143	0.0418	0.0806	0.1500	0.0151	0.0440	0.0845	0.1566
23	0.0143	0.0417	0.0802	0.1493	0.0150	0.0438	0.0842	0.1560
24	0.0142	0.0415	0.0799	0.1487	0.0150	0.0437	0.0839	0.1555
25	0.0142	0.0414	0.0797	0.1482	0.0150	0.0436	0.0837	0.1550
26	0.0141	0.0413	0.0795	0.1478	0.0149	0.0435	0.0835	0.1546
27	0.0141	0.0412	0.0793	0.1474	0.0149	0.0434	0.0834	0.1543
28	0.0141	0.0412	0.0792	0.1471	0.0149	0.0434	0.0832	0.1540
29	0.0141	0.0411	0.0790	0.1468	0.0149	0.0433	0.0831	0.1538
30	0.0141	0.0410	0.0789	0.1466	0.0148	0.0433	0.0830	0.1536
31	0.0140	0.0410	0.0788	0.1464	0.0148	0.0432	0.0830	0.1534
32	0.0140	0.0410	0.0788	0.1463	0.0148	0.0432	0.0829	0.1533
33	0.0140	0.0409	0.0787	0.1461	0.0148	0.0432	0.0828	0.1532
34	0.0140	0.0409	0.0786	0.1460	0.0148	0.0432	0.0828	0.1531
35	0.0140	0.0409	0.0786	0.1459	0.0148	0.0432	0.0828	0.1530
36	0.0140	0.0409	0.0786	0.1458	0.0148	0.0431	0.0827	0.1529
37	0.0140	0.0409	0.0785	0.1457	0.0148	0.0431	0.0827	0.1529
38	0.0140	0.0408	0.0785	0.1457	0.0148	0.0431	0.0827	0.1528
39	0.0140	0.0408	0.0785	0.1456	0.0148	0.0431	0.0827	0.1528
40	0.0140	0.0408	0.0785	0.1456	0.0148	0.0431	0.0827	0.1527
41	0.0140	0.0408	0.0784	0.1455	0.0148	0.0431	0.0826	0.1527
42	0.0140	0.0408	0.0784	0.1455	0.0148	0.0431	0.0826	0.1527
43	0.0140	0.0408	0.0784	0.1455	0.0148	0.0431	0.0826	0.1527
44	0.0140	0.0408	0.0784	0.1454	0.0148	0.0431	0.0826	0.1526
45	0.0140	0.0408	0.0784	0.1454	0.0148	0.0431	0.0826	0.1526
46	0.0140	0.0408	0.0784	0.1454	0.0148	0.0431	0.0826	0.1526
47	0.0140	0.0408	0.0784	0.1454	0.0148	0.0431	0.0826	0.1526
48	0.0140	0.0408	0.0784	0.1454	0.0148	0.0431	0.0826	0.1526
49	0.0140	0.0408	0.0784	0.1454	0.0148	0.0431	0.0826	0.1526
50	0.0140	0.0408	0.0784	0.1454	0.0148	0.0431	0.0826	0.1526

Periodic payments at the *beginning* of each period required to amortize a loan of $1 over time

End of Year	At 21% Interest compounded and Payments made				At 22% Interest compounded and Payments made			
	Monthly	Quarterly	Semi-Annually	Annually	Monthly	Quarterly	Semi-Annually	Annually
1	0.0915	0.2695	0.5249	1.0000	0.0919	0.2704	0.5261	1.0000
2	0.0505	0.1485	0.2886	0.5475	0.0509	0.1496	0.2904	0.5495
3	0.0370	0.1087	0.2108	0.3985	0.0375	0.1100	0.2130	0.4014
4	0.0304	0.0892	0.1727	0.3253	0.0309	0.0906	0.1751	0.3287
5	0.0266	0.0779	0.1505	0.2825	0.0271	0.0793	0.1530	0.2862
6	0.0241	0.0705	0.1361	0.2547	0.0247	0.0721	0.1388	0.2588
7	0.0224	0.0655	0.1262	0.2356	0.0230	0.0671	0.1290	0.2400
8	0.0212	0.0619	0.1191	0.2218	0.0218	0.0636	0.1221	0.2265
9	0.0203	0.0593	0.1139	0.2116	0.0209	0.0610	0.1170	0.2165
10	0.0196	0.0573	0.1099	0.2039	0.0203	0.0591	0.1131	0.2089
11	0.0191	0.0557	0.1069	0.1979	0.0198	0.0576	0.1102	0.2031
12	0.0187	0.0546	0.1045	0.1932	0.0194	0.0565	0.1079	0.1986
13	0.0184	0.0536	0.1027	0.1894	0.0191	0.0556	0.1061	0.1950
14	0.0182	0.0529	0.1012	0.1865	0.0189	0.0549	0.1047	0.1922
15	0.0180	0.0523	0.1000	0.1841	0.0187	0.0543	0.1036	0.1899
16	0.0178	0.0518	0.0991	0.1822	0.0186	0.0539	0.1027	0.1881
17	0.0177	0.0515	0.0983	0.1806	0.0185	0.0535	0.1020	0.1867
18	0.0176	0.0512	0.0977	0.1794	0.0184	0.0533	0.1015	0.1855
19	0.0175	0.0509	0.0972	0.1783	0.0183	0.0530	0.1010	0.1845
20	0.0175	0.0507	0.0968	0.1775	0.0182	0.0529	0.1006	0.1838
21	0.0174	0.0506	0.0965	0.1768	0.0182	0.0527	0.1004	0.1831
22	0.0174	0.0504	0.0962	0.1762	0.0182	0.0526	0.1001	0.1826
23	0.0173	0.0503	0.0960	0.1757	0.0181	0.0525	0.0999	0.1822
24	0.0173	0.0503	0.0958	0.1754	0.0181	0.0524	0.0998	0.1819
25	0.0173	0.0502	0.0957	0.1750	0.0181	0.0524	0.0996	0.1816
26	0.0173	0.0501	0.0956	0.1748	0.0181	0.0523	0.0995	0.1814
27	0.0173	0.0501	0.0955	0.1746	0.0181	0.0523	0.0995	0.1812
28	0.0172	0.0500	0.0954	0.1744	0.0180	0.0523	0.0994	0.1810
29	0.0172	0.0500	0.0953	0.1742	0.0180	0.0522	0.0993	0.1809
30	0.0172	0.0500	0.0953	0.1741	0.0180	0.0522	0.0993	0.1808
31	0.0172	0.0500	0.0952	0.1740	0.0180	0.0522	0.0993	0.1807
32	0.0172	0.0500	0.0952	0.1739	0.0180	0.0522	0.0992	0.1806
33	0.0172	0.0499	0.0952	0.1739	0.0180	0.0522	0.0992	0.1806
34	0.0172	0.0499	0.0951	0.1738	0.0180	0.0522	0.0992	0.1805
35	0.0172	0.0499	0.0951	0.1738	0.0180	0.0522	0.0992	0.1805
36	0.0172	0.0499	0.0951	0.1737	0.0180	0.0522	0.0992	0.1805
37	0.0172	0.0499	0.0951	0.1737	0.0180	0.0522	0.0991	0.1804
38	0.0172	0.0499	0.0951	0.1737	0.0180	0.0521	0.0991	0.1804
39	0.0172	0.0499	0.0951	0.1737	0.0180	0.0521	0.0991	0.1804
40	0.0172	0.0499	0.0951	0.1736	0.0180	0.0521	0.0991	0.1804
41	0.0172	0.0499	0.0950	0.1736	0.0180	0.0521	0.0991	0.1804
42	0.0172	0.0499	0.0950	0.1736	0.0180	0.0521	0.0991	0.1804
43	0.0172	0.0499	0.0950	0.1736	0.0180	0.0521	0.0991	0.1804
44	0.0172	0.0499	0.0950	0.1736	0.0180	0.0521	0.0991	0.1804
45	0.0172	0.0499	0.0950	0.1736	0.0180	0.0521	0.0991	0.1804
46	0.0172	0.0499	0.0950	0.1736	0.0180	0.0521	0.0991	0.1803
47	0.0172	0.0499	0.0950	0.1736	0.0180	0.0521	0.0991	0.1803
48	0.0172	0.0499	0.0950	0.1736	0.0180	0.0521	0.0991	0.1803
49	0.0172	0.0499	0.0950	0.1736	0.0180	0.0521	0.0991	0.1803
50	0.0172	0.0499	0.0950	0.1736	0.0180	0.0521	0.0991	0.1803

What is $1 payable at the beginning of each period worth today at various interest rates?

How much must be invested today to be able to draw $1 at the beginning of each period for a given number of periods?

Applications
Chapter Nine
- What is the value today of the right to receive periodic payments at the beginning of various time periods?

Chapter Sixteen
- What is the present value of a series of insurance premiums?

Chapter Seventeen
- What is the present value of a series of lease payments?

The present value of a $1 annuity due at the *beginning* of each period

End of Year	At 5% Interest compounded				At 6% Interest compounded			
	Monthly	Quarterly	Semi-Annually	Annually	Monthly	Quarterly	Semi-Annually	Annually
1	11.730	3.927	1.976	1.000	11.677	3.912	1.971	1.000
2	22.889	7.663	3.856	1.952	22.676	7.598	3.829	1.943
3	33.505	11.218	5.646	2.859	33.035	11.071	5.580	2.833
4	43.604	14.601	7.349	3.723	42.793	14.343	7.230	3.673
5	53.212	17.819	8.971	4.546	51.984	17.426	8.786	4.465
6	62.351	20.882	10.514	5.329	60.641	20.331	10.253	5.212
7	71.047	23.796	11.983	6.076	68.795	23.068	11.635	5.917
8	79.319	26.569	13.381	6.786	76.476	25.646	12.938	6.582
9	87.188	29.208	14.712	7.463	83.710	28.076	14.166	7.210
10	94.674	31.719	15.979	8.108	90.524	30.365	15.324	7.802
11	101.796	34.107	17.185	8.722	96.942	32.521	16.415	8.360
12	108.571	36.381	18.332	9.306	102.987	34.553	17.444	8.887
13	115.017	38.544	19.424	9.863	108.681	36.468	18.413	9.384
14	121.149	40.602	20.464	10.394	114.044	38.271	19.327	9.853
15	126.982	42.560	21.454	10.899	119.096	39.971	20.188	10.295
16	132.532	44.423	22.395	11.380	123.854	41.572	21.000	10.712
17	137.811	46.197	23.292	11.838	128.336	43.081	21.766	11.106
18	142.833	47.884	24.145	12.274	132.557	44.502	22.487	11.477
19	147.611	49.489	24.957	12.690	136.534	45.842	23.167	11.828
20	152.157	51.016	25.730	13.085	140.279	47.103	23.808	12.158
21	156.481	52.470	26.466	13.462	143.806	48.292	24.412	12.470
22	160.595	53.853	27.166	13.821	147.129	49.412	24.982	12.764
23	164.508	55.169	27.833	14.163	150.259	50.468	25.519	13.042
24	168.231	56.421	28.467	14.489	153.206	51.462	26.025	13.303
25	171.773	57.613	29.071	14.799	155.983	52.399	26.502	13.550
26	175.142	58.746	29.646	15.094	158.598	53.282	26.951	13.783
27	178.348	59.825	30.193	15.375	161.061	54.113	27.375	14.003
28	181.397	60.852	30.714	15.643	163.382	54.897	27.774	14.211
29	184.298	61.828	31.210	15.898	165.567	55.635	28.151	14.406
30	187.058	62.758	31.681	16.141	167.626	56.331	28.506	14.591
31	189.683	63.642	32.130	16.372	169.564	56.986	28.840	14.765
32	192.181	64.483	32.558	16.593	171.391	57.604	29.156	14.929
33	194.557	65.284	32.965	16.803	173.111	58.186	29.453	15.084
34	196.817	66.046	33.352	17.003	174.731	58.734	29.733	15.230
35	198.968	66.771	33.720	17.193	176.257	59.250	29.997	15.368
36	201.014	67.461	34.071	17.374	177.695	59.737	30.246	15.498
37	202.960	68.117	34.405	17.547	179.048	60.195	30.481	15.621
38	204.811	68.741	34.723	17.711	180.324	60.627	30.702	15.737
39	206.573	69.336	35.025	17.868	181.525	61.034	30.910	15.846
40	208.248	69.901	35.313	18.017	182.656	61.418	31.107	15.949
41	209.842	70.439	35.587	18.159	183.722	61.779	31.292	16.046
42	211.359	70.951	35.848	18.294	184.726	62.119	31.467	16.138
43	212.802	71.438	36.096	18.423	185.671	62.440	31.631	16.225
44	214.174	71.902	36.333	18.546	186.562	62.742	31.786	16.306
45	215.480	72.343	36.557	18.663	187.401	63.027	31.932	16.383
46	216.722	72.762	36.771	18.774	188.191	63.295	32.070	16.456
47	217.904	73.162	36.975	18.880	188.935	63.548	32.200	16.524
48	219.028	73.542	37.169	18.981	189.636	63.786	32.323	16.589
49	220.097	73.903	37.354	19.077	190.296	64.010	32.438	16.650
50	221.114	74.247	37.529	19.169	190.918	64.222	32.547	16.708

The present value of a $1 annuity due at the *beginning* of each period

End of Year	At 9% Interest compounded				At 10% Interest compounded			
	Monthly	Quarterly	Semi-Annually	Annually	Monthly	Quarterly	Semi-Annually	Annually
1	11.521	3.870	1.957	1.000	11.469	3.856	1.952	1.000
2	22.053	7.410	3.749	1.917	21.851	7.349	3.723	1.909
3	31.683	10.649	5.390	2.759	31.249	10.514	5.329	2.736
4	40.486	13.612	6.893	3.531	39.757	13.381	6.786	3.487
5	48.535	16.323	8.269	4.240	47.458	15.979	8.108	4.170
6	55.893	18.803	9.529	4.890	54.428	18.332	9.306	4.791
7	62.620	21.072	10.683	5.486	60.739	20.464	10.394	5.355
8	68.770	23.147	11.740	6.033	66.451	22.395	11.380	5.868
9	74.393	25.046	12.707	6.535	71.621	24.145	12.274	6.335
10	79.534	26.783	13.593	6.995	76.302	25.730	13.085	6.759
11	84.233	28.372	14.405	7.418	80.539	27.166	13.821	7.145
12	88.530	29.826	15.148	7.805	84.374	28.467	14.489	7.495
13	92.458	31.156	15.828	8.161	87.846	29.646	15.094	7.814
14	96.050	32.373	16.451	8.487	90.988	30.714	15.643	8.103
15	99.333	33.486	17.022	8.786	93.833	31.681	16.141	8.367
16	102.335	34.504	17.544	9.061	96.408	32.558	16.593	8.606
17	105.079	35.436	18.023	9.313	98.739	33.352	17.003	8.824
18	107.588	36.288	18.461	9.544	100.849	34.071	17.374	9.022
19	109.882	37.068	18.862	9.756	102.759	34.723	17.711	9.201
20	111.979	37.781	19.230	9.950	104.488	35.313	18.017	9.365
21	113.896	38.434	19.566	10.129	106.053	35.848	18.294	9.514
22	115.648	39.031	19.874	10.292	107.470	36.333	18.546	9.649
23	117.251	39.577	20.156	10.442	108.753	36.771	18.774	9.772
24	118.716	40.077	20.415	10.580	109.913	37.169	18.981	9.883
25	120.055	40.534	20.651	10.707	110.964	37.529	19.169	9.985
26	121.280	40.952	20.868	10.823	111.916	37.856	19.339	10.077
27	122.399	41.334	21.066	10.929	112.777	38.152	19.493	10.161
28	123.423	41.684	21.248	11.027	113.556	38.419	19.633	10.237
29	124.359	42.005	21.414	11.116	114.262	38.662	19.761	10.307
30	125.214	42.298	21.567	11.198	114.900	38.882	19.876	10.370
31	125.996	42.566	21.706	11.274	115.479	39.081	19.980	10.427
32	126.711	42.811	21.834	11.343	116.002	39.262	20.075	10.479
33	127.365	43.035	21.951	11.406	116.476	39.425	20.161	10.526
34	127.962	43.240	22.058	11.464	116.905	39.573	20.239	10.569
35	128.509	43.428	22.156	11.518	117.293	39.707	20.310	10.609
36	129.008	43.600	22.246	11.567	117.644	39.829	20.374	10.644
37	129.465	43.757	22.328	11.612	117.962	39.939	20.432	10.677
38	129.883	43.900	22.404	11.653	118.250	40.039	20.485	10.706
39	130.264	44.032	22.473	11.691	118.511	40.129	20.533	10.733
40	130.613	44.152	22.536	11.726	118.747	40.211	20.576	10.757
41	130.932	44.262	22.594	11.757	118.960	40.285	20.616	10.779
42	131.224	44.363	22.647	11.787	119.154	40.353	20.651	10.799
43	131.491	44.455	22.695	11.813	119.329	40.413	20.684	10.817
44	131.734	44.539	22.740	11.838	119.487	40.469	20.713	10.834
45	131.957	44.616	22.780	11.861	119.631	40.519	20.740	10.849
46	132.161	44.687	22.817	11.881	119.760	40.564	20.764	10.863
47	132.347	44.751	22.852	11.900	119.878	40.605	20.786	10.875
48	132.518	44.810	22.883	11.918	119.984	40.642	20.806	10.887
49	132.673	44.864	22.911	11.934	120.080	40.676	20.824	10.897
50	132.816	44.914	22.938	11.948	120.168	40.706	20.840	10.906

The present value of a $1 annuity
due at the *beginning* of each period

End of Year	At 11% Interest compounded				At 12% Interest compounded			
	Monthly	Quarterly	Semi-Annually	Annually	Monthly	Quarterly	Semi-Annually	Annually
1	11.418	3.842	1.948	1.000	11.368	3.829	1.943	1.000
2	21.652	7.289	3.698	1.901	21.456	7.230	3.673	1.893
3	30.825	10.382	5.270	2.713	30.409	10.253	5.212	2.690
4	39.046	13.157	6.683	3.444	38.354	12.938	6.582	3.402
5	46.415	15.646	7.952	4.102	45.405	15.324	7.802	4.037
6	53.019	17.879	9.093	4.696	51.662	17.444	8.887	4.605
7	58.938	19.883	10.117	5.231	57.215	19.327	9.853	5.111
8	64.244	21.681	11.038	5.712	62.143	21.000	10.712	5.564
9	68.999	23.293	11.865	6.146	66.516	22.487	11.477	5.968
10	73.261	24.740	12.608	6.537	70.398	23.808	12.158	6.328
11	77.081	26.038	13.275	6.889	73.842	24.982	12.764	6.650
12	80.504	27.203	13.875	7.207	76.899	26.025	13.303	6.938
13	83.573	28.248	14.414	7.492	79.611	26.951	13.783	7.194
14	86.323	29.185	14.898	7.750	82.018	27.774	14.211	7.424
15	88.788	30.026	15.333	7.982	84.155	28.506	14.591	7.628
16	90.998	30.781	15.724	8.191	86.051	29.156	14.929	7.811
17	92.978	31.458	16.075	8.379	87.733	29.733	15.230	7.974
18	94.753	32.065	16.391	8.549	89.227	30.246	15.498	8.120
19	96.344	32.610	16.674	8.702	90.552	30.702	15.737	8.250
20	97.770	33.099	16.929	8.839	91.728	31.107	15.949	8.366
21	99.048	33.537	17.157	8.963	92.771	31.467	16.138	8.469
22	100.193	33.931	17.363	9.075	93.697	31.786	16.306	8.562
23	101.220	34.284	17.548	9.176	94.519	32.070	16.456	8.645
24	102.140	34.601	17.714	9.266	95.249	32.323	16.589	8.718
25	102.964	34.885	17.863	9.348	95.896	32.547	16.708	8.784
26	103.703	35.140	17.997	9.422	96.470	32.746	16.813	8.843
27	104.366	35.368	18.117	9.488	96.980	32.923	16.907	8.896
28	104.960	35.574	18.225	9.548	97.433	33.080	16.991	8.943
29	105.492	35.758	18.322	9.602	97.834	33.220	17.065	8.984
30	105.969	35.923	18.410	9.650	98.191	33.344	17.131	9.022
31	106.396	36.071	18.488	9.694	98.507	33.455	17.190	9.055
32	106.780	36.204	18.558	9.733	98.787	33.553	17.242	9.085
33	107.123	36.323	18.622	9.769	99.036	33.640	17.289	9.112
34	107.431	36.430	18.679	9.801	99.257	33.717	17.331	9.135
35	107.707	36.526	18.730	9.829	99.454	33.786	17.368	9.157
36	107.954	36.612	18.776	9.855	99.628	33.847	17.401	9.176
37	108.176	36.690	18.817	9.879	99.782	33.901	17.430	9.192
38	108.374	36.759	18.854	9.900	99.919	33.949	17.456	9.208
39	108.552	36.821	18.887	9.919	100.041	33.992	17.479	9.221
40	108.712	36.877	18.917	9.936	100.149	34.030	17.500	9.233
41	108.855	36.927	18.944	9.951	100.245	34.064	17.518	9.244
42	108.983	36.972	18.968	9.965	100.330	34.094	17.534	9.253
43	109.098	37.012	18.990	9.977	100.405	34.121	17.549	9.262
44	109.201	37.048	19.009	9.989	100.472	34.144	17.562	9.270
45	109.293	37.081	19.027	9.999	100.531	34.165	17.573	9.276
46	109.376	37.110	19.043	10.008	100.584	34.184	17.584	9.283
47	109.450	37.136	19.057	10.016	100.631	34.201	17.593	9.288
48	109.517	37.159	19.069	10.024	100.673	34.216	17.601	9.293
49	109.576	37.180	19.081	10.030	100.709	34.229	17.608	9.297
50	109.630	37.199	19.091	10.036	100.742	34.240	17.615	9.301

The present value of a $1 annuity
due at the *beginning* of each period

End of Year	At 13% Interest compounded				At 14% Interest compounded			
	Monthly	Quarterly	Semi-Annually	Annually	Monthly	Quarterly	Semi-Annually	Annually
1	11.317	3.815	1.939	1.000	11.267	3.802	1.935	1.000
2	21.262	7.172	3.648	1.885	21.071	7.115	3.624	1.877
3	30.000	10.126	5.156	2.668	29.600	10.002	5.100	2.647
4	37.679	12.725	6.485	3.361	37.021	12.517	6.389	3.322
5	44.426	15.012	7.656	3.974	43.478	14.710	7.515	3.914
6	50.355	17.024	8.689	4.517	49.096	16.620	8.499	4.433
7	55.565	18.795	9.600	4.998	53.984	18.285	9.358	4.889
8	60.143	20.353	10.403	5.423	58.237	19.736	10.108	5.288
9	64.165	21.724	11.111	5.799	61.937	21.001	10.763	5.639
10	67.700	22.930	11.735	6.132	65.157	22.102	11.336	5.946
11	70.806	23.992	12.285	6.426	67.958	23.063	11.836	6.216
12	73.535	24.926	12.770	6.687	70.395	23.899	12.272	6.453
13	75.933	25.747	13.198	6.918	72.516	24.629	12.654	6.660
14	78.041	26.471	13.575	7.122	74.360	25.264	12.987	6.842
15	79.892	27.107	13.907	7.302	75.966	25.818	13.278	7.002
16	81.520	27.667	14.201	7.462	77.362	26.300	13.532	7.142
17	82.949	28.159	14.459	7.604	78.578	26.721	13.754	7.265
18	84.206	28.593	14.687	7.729	79.635	27.087	13.948	7.373
19	85.310	28.974	14.888	7.840	80.555	27.407	14.117	7.467
20	86.280	29.310	15.065	7.938	81.355	27.685	14.265	7.550
21	87.132	29.605	15.221	8.025	82.051	27.928	14.394	7.623
22	87.881	29.865	15.359	8.102	82.657	28.139	14.507	7.687
23	88.539	30.094	15.480	8.170	83.184	28.323	14.606	7.743
24	89.118	30.295	15.587	8.230	83.643	28.484	14.692	7.792
25	89.626	30.472	15.682	8.283	84.042	28.623	14.767	7.835
26	90.073	30.628	15.765	8.330	84.389	28.745	14.832	7.873
27	90.465	30.765	15.838	8.372	84.691	28.851	14.890	7.906
28	90.810	30.886	15.903	8.409	84.954	28.944	14.940	7.935
29	91.113	30.992	15.960	8.441	85.183	29.025	14.984	7.961
30	91.379	31.085	16.010	8.470	85.382	29.095	15.022	7.983
31	91.613	31.167	16.054	8.496	85.555	29.156	15.055	8.003
32	91.818	31.239	16.094	8.518	85.706	29.210	15.084	8.020
33	91.999	31.303	16.128	8.538	85.837	29.256	15.110	8.035
34	92.158	31.359	16.158	8.556	85.951	29.297	15.132	8.048
35	92.297	31.408	16.185	8.572	86.050	29.332	15.152	8.060
36	92.420	31.452	16.209	8.586	86.136	29.363	15.169	8.070
37	92.528	31.490	16.230	8.598	86.211	29.390	15.183	8.079
38	92.622	31.523	16.248	8.609	86.277	29.413	15.196	8.087
39	92.705	31.553	16.264	8.618	86.334	29.433	15.208	8.094
40	92.778	31.579	16.278	8.627	86.383	29.451	15.218	8.100
41	92.843	31.602	16.291	8.634	86.426	29.467	15.226	8.105
42	92.899	31.622	16.302	8.641	86.464	29.480	15.234	8.110
43	92.949	31.640	16.312	8.647	86.496	29.492	15.240	8.114
44	92.992	31.655	16.320	8.652	86.524	29.502	15.246	8.117
45	93.030	31.669	16.328	8.657	86.549	29.511	15.251	8.120
46	93.064	31.681	16.335	8.661	86.571	29.519	15.255	8.123
47	93.094	31.691	16.341	8.664	86.589	29.525	15.259	8.126
48	93.120	31.701	16.346	8.668	86.606	29.531	15.263	8.128
49	93.142	31.709	16.350	8.671	86.620	29.537	15.266	8.130
50	93.162	31.716	16.354	8.673	86.632	29.541	15.268	8.131

The present value of a $1 annuity due at the *beginning* of each period

End of Year	At 15% Interest compounded				At 16% Interest compounded			
	Monthly	Quarterly	Semi-Annually	Annually	Monthly	Quarterly	Semi-Annually	Annually
1	11.218	3.788	1.930	1.000	11.169	3.775	1.926	1.000
2	20.882	7.058	3.601	1.870	20.696	7.002	3.577	1.862
3	29.208	9.880	5.046	2.626	28.823	9.760	4.993	2.605
4	36.381	12.315	6.297	3.283	35.756	12.118	6.206	3.246
5	42.560	14.417	7.379	3.855	41.670	14.134	7.247	3.798
6	47.884	16.232	8.315	4.352	46.715	15.857	8.139	4.274
7	52.470	17.797	9.126	4.784	51.019	17.330	8.904	4.685
8	56.421	19.149	9.827	5.160	54.690	18.588	9.559	5.039
9	59.825	20.315	10.434	5.487	57.821	19.665	10.122	5.344
10	62.758	21.322	10.959	5.772	60.493	20.584	10.604	5.607
11	65.284	22.190	11.413	6.019	62.772	21.371	11.017	5.833
12	67.461	22.940	11.807	6.234	64.716	22.043	11.371	6.029
13	69.336	23.587	12.147	6.421	66.374	22.617	11.675	6.197
14	70.951	24.146	12.441	6.583	67.789	23.109	11.935	6.342
15	72.343	24.628	12.696	6.724	68.995	23.528	12.158	6.468
16	73.542	25.044	12.917	6.847	70.025	23.887	12.350	6.575
17	74.575	25.403	13.107	6.954	70.903	24.194	12.514	6.668
18	75.464	25.713	13.273	7.047	71.652	24.456	12.655	6.749
19	76.231	25.981	13.415	7.128	72.291	24.680	12.775	6.818
20	76.892	26.212	13.539	7.198	72.836	24.872	12.879	6.877
21	77.461	26.411	13.646	7.259	73.301	25.036	12.967	6.929
22	77.951	26.583	13.739	7.312	73.698	25.176	13.043	6.973
23	78.373	26.731	13.819	7.359	74.036	25.295	13.108	7.011
24	78.737	26.859	13.888	7.399	74.325	25.398	13.164	7.044
25	79.050	26.970	13.948	7.434	74.571	25.485	13.212	7.073
26	79.320	27.065	14.000	7.464	74.781	25.560	13.253	7.097
27	79.553	27.148	14.045	7.491	74.960	25.624	13.288	7.118
28	79.753	27.219	14.084	7.514	75.113	25.678	13.319	7.136
29	79.926	27.280	14.117	7.534	75.243	25.725	13.344	7.152
30	80.075	27.333	14.146	7.551	75.354	25.765	13.367	7.166
31	80.203	27.379	14.172	7.566	75.449	25.799	13.386	7.177
32	80.313	27.418	14.193	7.579	75.530	25.828	13.402	7.187
33	80.408	27.452	14.212	7.591	75.599	25.853	13.416	7.196
34	80.490	27.481	14.228	7.600	75.658	25.875	13.428	7.203
35	80.561	27.507	14.243	7.609	75.708	25.893	13.438	7.210
36	80.622	27.529	14.255	7.617	75.751	25.908	13.447	7.215
37	80.674	27.548	14.265	7.623	75.788	25.922	13.455	7.220
38	80.719	27.564	14.275	7.629	75.819	25.933	13.461	7.224
39	80.758	27.578	14.282	7.634	75.846	25.943	13.467	7.228
40	80.792	27.590	14.289	7.638	75.868	25.951	13.471	7.231
41	80.820	27.601	14.295	7.642	75.888	25.958	13.475	7.233
42	80.845	27.610	14.300	7.645	75.904	25.964	13.479	7.236
43	80.867	27.617	14.305	7.648	75.918	25.969	13.482	7.238
44	80.885	27.624	14.309	7.650	75.930	25.974	13.485	7.239
45	80.901	27.630	14.312	7.652	75.940	25.978	13.487	7.241
46	80.915	27.635	14.315	7.654	75.949	25.981	13.489	7.242
47	80.927	27.639	14.317	7.656	75.957	25.984	13.490	7.243
48	80.937	27.643	14.319	7.657	75.963	25.986	13.492	7.244
49	80.946	27.646	14.321	7.659	75.968	25.988	13.493	7.245
50	80.953	27.649	14.323	7.660	75.973	25.990	13.494	7.246

Table 12/ 257

The present value of a $1 annuity due at the *beginning* of each period

End of Year	At 17% Interest compounded				At 18% Interest compounded			
	Monthly	Quarterly	Semi-Annually	Annually	Monthly	Quarterly	Semi-Annually	Annually
1	11.120	3.762	1.922	1.000	11.071	3.749	1.917	1.000
2	20.512	6.947	3.554	1.855	20.331	6.893	3.531	1.847
3	28.446	9.644	4.941	2.585	28.076	9.529	4.890	2.566
4	35.147	11.927	6.119	3.210	34.553	11.740	6.033	3.174
5	40.807	13.859	7.119	3.743	39.971	13.593	6.995	3.690
6	45.588	15.496	7.969	4.199	44.502	15.148	7.805	4.127
7	49.627	16.881	8.691	4.589	48.292	16.451	8.487	4.498
8	53.038	18.054	9.304	4.922	51.462	17.544	9.061	4.812
9	55.920	19.047	9.825	5.207	54.113	18.461	9.544	5.078
10	58.353	19.888	10.268	5.451	56.331	19.230	9.950	5.303
11	60.409	20.600	10.644	5.659	58.186	19.874	10.292	5.494
12	62.145	21.203	10.963	5.836	59.737	20.415	10.580	5.656
13	63.612	21.713	11.234	5.988	61.034	20.868	10.823	5.793
14	64.851	22.145	11.465	6.118	62.119	21.248	11.027	5.910
15	65.898	22.510	11.660	6.229	63.027	21.567	11.198	6.008
16	66.782	22.820	11.827	6.324	63.786	21.834	11.343	6.092
17	67.528	23.082	11.968	6.405	64.421	22.058	11.464	6.162
18	68.159	23.304	12.088	6.475	64.952	22.246	11.567	6.222
19	68.691	23.492	12.190	6.534	65.396	22.404	11.653	6.273
20	69.141	23.651	12.276	6.584	65.768	22.536	11.726	6.316
21	69.521	23.786	12.350	6.628	66.078	22.647	11.787	6.353
22	69.843	23.900	12.412	6.665	66.338	22.740	11.838	6.384
23	70.114	23.996	12.465	6.696	66.556	22.817	11.881	6.410
24	70.343	24.078	12.510	6.723	66.737	22.883	11.918	6.432
25	70.536	24.147	12.549	6.746	66.889	22.938	11.948	6.451
26	70.700	24.206	12.581	6.766	67.017	22.984	11.974	6.467
27	70.838	24.256	12.609	6.783	67.123	23.022	11.996	6.480
28	70.954	24.298	12.632	6.798	67.212	23.054	12.014	6.492
29	71.053	24.333	12.652	6.810	67.286	23.081	12.029	6.502
30	71.136	24.363	12.669	6.820	67.349	23.104	12.042	6.510
31	71.206	24.389	12.684	6.829	67.401	23.123	12.053	6.517
32	71.265	24.410	12.696	6.837	67.444	23.139	12.062	6.523
33	71.316	24.429	12.706	6.844	67.481	23.153	12.070	6.528
34	71.358	24.444	12.715	6.849	67.511	23.164	12.077	6.532
35	71.394	24.457	12.722	6.854	67.536	23.173	12.082	6.536
36	71.424	24.468	12.729	6.858	67.558	23.181	12.087	6.539
37	71.449	24.478	12.734	6.862	67.576	23.188	12.091	6.541
38	71.471	24.486	12.739	6.865	67.590	23.193	12.094	6.543
39	71.489	24.492	12.743	6.867	67.603	23.198	12.097	6.545
40	71.505	24.498	12.746	6.869	67.613	23.202	12.099	6.547
41	71.518	24.503	12.749	6.871	67.622	23.205	12.101	6.548
42	71.529	24.507	12.751	6.873	67.629	23.208	12.102	6.549
43	71.538	24.510	12.753	6.874	67.635	23.210	12.104	6.550
44	71.546	24.513	12.755	6.875	67.641	23.212	12.105	6.551
45	71.552	24.516	12.756	6.876	67.645	23.214	12.106	6.552
46	71.558	24.518	12.758	6.877	67.648	23.215	12.107	6.552
47	71.563	24.520	12.759	6.878	67.651	23.216	12.107	6.553
48	71.567	24.521	12.760	6.879	67.654	23.217	12.108	6.553
49	71.570	24.522	12.760	6.879	67.656	23.218	12.109	6.554
50	71.573	24.523	12.761	6.880	67.658	23.219	12.109	6.554

The present value of a $1 annuity
due at the *beginning* of each period

End of Year	At 19% Interest compounded				At 20% Interest compounded			
	Monthly	Quarterly	Semi-Annually	Annually	Monthly	Quarterly	Semi-Annually	Annually
1	11.023	3.736	1.913	1.000	10.975	3.723	1.909	1.000
2	20.152	6.839	3.509	1.840	19.975	6.786	3.487	1.833
3	27.713	9.417	4.840	2.547	27.357	9.306	4.791	2.528
4	33.974	11.557	5.950	3.140	33.410	11.380	5.868	3.106
5	39.160	13.335	6.875	3.639	38.374	13.085	6.759	3.589
6	43.455	14.812	7.647	4.058	42.445	14.489	7.495	3.991
7	47.012	16.039	8.291	4.410	45.783	15.643	8.103	4.326
8	49.958	17.058	8.828	4.706	48.521	16.593	8.606	4.605
9	52.397	17.904	9.276	4.954	50.766	17.374	9.022	4.837
10	54.418	18.607	9.650	5.163	52.607	18.017	9.365	5.031
11	56.091	19.191	9.961	5.339	54.117	18.546	9.649	5.192
12	57.477	19.675	10.221	5.486	55.356	18.981	9.883	5.327
13	58.625	20.078	10.438	5.611	56.371	19.339	10.077	5.439
14	59.576	20.413	10.618	5.715	57.204	19.633	10.237	5.533
15	60.363	20.691	10.769	5.802	57.887	19.876	10.370	5.611
16	61.015	20.921	10.895	5.876	58.447	20.075	10.479	5.675
17	61.555	21.113	11.000	5.938	58.906	20.239	10.569	5.730
18	62.002	21.272	11.087	5.990	59.283	20.374	10.644	5.775
19	62.373	21.404	11.160	6.033	59.592	20.485	10.706	5.812
20	62.679	21.514	11.221	6.070	59.845	20.576	10.757	5.843
21	62.933	21.605	11.271	6.101	60.053	20.651	10.799	5.870
22	63.144	21.681	11.314	6.127	60.223	20.713	10.834	5.891
23	63.318	21.744	11.349	6.149	60.363	20.764	10.863	5.909
24	63.462	21.796	11.378	6.167	60.478	20.806	10.887	5.925
25	63.582	21.840	11.403	6.182	60.572	20.840	10.906	5.937
26	63.681	21.876	11.423	6.195	60.649	20.869	10.923	5.948
27	63.763	21.906	11.441	6.206	60.712	20.892	10.936	5.956
28	63.831	21.931	11.455	6.215	60.764	20.911	10.947	5.964
29	63.887	21.951	11.467	6.223	60.806	20.927	10.956	5.970
30	63.933	21.968	11.477	6.229	60.841	20.940	10.964	5.975
31	63.972	21.983	11.485	6.235	60.870	20.950	10.970	5.979
32	64.004	21.995	11.492	6.239	60.893	20.959	10.975	5.982
33	64.030	22.004	11.497	6.243	60.912	20.966	10.980	5.985
34	64.052	22.013	11.502	6.246	60.928	20.972	10.983	5.988
35	64.070	22.019	11.506	6.249	60.941	20.977	10.986	5.990
36	64.085	22.025	11.510	6.251	60.952	20.981	10.988	5.992
37	64.098	22.030	11.512	6.253	60.960	20.985	10.990	5.993
38	64.108	22.034	11.515	6.255	60.967	20.987	10.992	5.994
39	64.117	22.037	11.517	6.256	60.973	20.990	10.994	5.995
40	64.124	22.039	11.518	6.257	60.978	20.991	10.995	5.996
41	64.130	22.042	11.520	6.258	60.982	20.993	10.996	5.997
42	64.135	22.044	11.521	6.259	60.985	20.994	10.996	5.997
43	64.139	22.045	11.522	6.260	60.988	20.995	10.997	5.998
44	64.142	22.046	11.522	6.260	60.990	20.996	10.997	5.998
45	64.145	22.047	11.523	6.261	60.992	20.997	10.998	5.998
46	64.147	22.048	11.524	6.261	60.993	20.997	10.998	5.999
47	64.149	22.049	11.524	6.261	60.995	20.998	10.999	5.999
48	64.150	22.050	11.524	6.262	60.996	20.998	10.999	5.999
49	64.152	22.050	11.525	6.262	60.996	20.999	10.999	5.999
50	64.153	22.051	11.525	6.262	60.997	20.999	10.999	5.999

Table 13
Evaluating annuity yields

Mortality Table
Male and female life tables, Canada 1970–1972
expectation of life in years

Age	Male	Female	Age	Male	Female
10	61.17	67.91	50	24.52	29.86
11	60.19	66.93	51	23.71	28.98
12	59.22	65.95	52	22.91	28.11
13	58.24	64.97	53	22.11	27.24
14	57.28	63.99	54	21.34	26.38
15	56.33	63.02	55	20.57	25.53
16	55.39	62.05	56	19.82	24.68
17	54.46	61.08	57	19.08	23.85
18	53.53	60.11	58	18.35	23.02
19	52.62	59.15	59	17.64	22.20
20	51.71	58.18	60	16.95	21.39
21	50.80	57.21	61	16.27	20.58
22	49.89	56.25	62	15.61	19.79
23	48.98	55.28	63	14.96	19.01
24	48.07	54.31	64	14.33	18.25
25	47.16	53.34	65	13.72	17.47
26	46.23	52.37	66	13.12	16.72
27	45.30	51.40	67	12.54	15.98
28	44.37	50.44	68	11.98	15.26
29	43.44	49.47	69	11.43	14.55
30	42.50	48.51	70	10.90	13.85
31	41.56	47.54	71	10.38	13.17
32	40.63	46.58	72	9.88	12.51
33	39.69	45.62	73	9.39	11.86
34	38.76	44.67	74	8.92	11.24
35	37.83	43.71	75	8.47	10.63
36	36.90	42.76	76	8.02	10.03
37	35.97	41.81	77	7.60	9.46
38	35.05	40.87	78	7.19	8.91
39	34.13	39.92	79	6.79	8.38
40	33.22	38.99	80	6.41	7.88
41	32.32	38.05	81	6.05	7.39
42	31.42	37.13	82	5.70	6.93
43	30.53	36.20	83	5.36	6.48
44	29.65	35.28	84	5.04	6.06
45	28.77	34.37	85	4.74	5.67
46	27.90	33.45			
47	27.04	32.55			
48	26.19	31.65			
49	25.35	30.75			